RRSPs & RRIFs For Dummies, 2nd Edition

Cheat Sheet

Make the Most of Mutual Funds

- **Practise spotting and avoiding the losers.** Picking mutual fund winners is difficult because past performance is no guarantee of future returns. Losers can be identified by long-term continuous losses and (usually) high management expense ratios.

- **Diversify fund management style.** Two mutual funds with the same investment style provide no real diversification. Examine the top ten holdings in a fund to determine its style: Financial versus resources? Growth versus value? Small-cap versus large-cap? Strive for a mix.

- **Examine your financial adviser's mutual fund proposals very carefully, if he/she works on commission.** Ask about no-load funds, which pay no commission but often out-perform those that do.

- **Avoid having too many funds.** Most RRSPs require no more than six funds for acceptable diversification. Fewer funds are easier to track and understand.

- **Watch for high MER charges.** When choosing among several qualifying mutual funds — those that meet your needs — favour those with lower Management Expense Ratios (MERs). They take less of your money off the top, leaving more in your RRSP.

Build Your RRSP Over Time

- **Learn the basic risk/reward rule.** Risk and reward move in lockstep, and a comfortable increase in your risk level can generate a substantial gain in rewards. Determine your personal risk level, gather all the data you can, obtain professional advice, then make your decision.

- **Apply basic rules of diversification.** Mix your RRSP investment between bonds (for security) and equity-based mutual funds (for long-term growth). Then diversify within each group — choose different bond maturity dates and select various (no more than six) equity funds, each with different objectives. Mix value funds (steady, big, blue-chip companies) with growth funds (technology companies, often Internet-based).

- **Maintain the foreign content of your RRSP to at least 30 percent of book value.** That's Canada Customs and Revenue Agency's limit, but there are ways to exceed it legally.

- **Consider a spousal RRSP.** If you earn substantially more income than your spouse, and are likely to build a much larger retirement fund than him or her, a spousal RRSP will balance assets and growth. Having equal retirement incomes, as opposed to one high and one low income, reduces income-tax levels.

- **Set a target for your retirement needs.** Don't underestimate the income you will need to pursue an active, rewarding retirement.

...For Dummies: *Bestselling Book Series for Beginners*

RRSPs & RRIFs For Dummies, 2nd Edition

Cheat Sheet

Cashing In

- ✔ **Bypass annuities as a source of retirement income.** You must collapse your RRSP by age 69 by converting to a Registered Retirement Income Fund (RRIF), purchasing an annuity, or withdrawing assets as a lump sum. RRIFs offer more flexibility and potentially more income than annuities do. Consider delaying the purchase of an annuity until you approach age 80.

- ✔ **Apply for your C/QPP benefits early.** Taking them at age 60, instead of waiting for age 65, is a better choice.

- ✔ **Adjust your asset mix to generate income.** You still need growth (to handle inflation) but a source of cash flow should be your first concern.

Get Started Early

- ✔ **Open an RRSP as soon as you can.** Even if the idea of retirement sounds as remote as booking a vacation on Mars, the benefits of planning for it are too good to ignore. And the earlier you begin, the bigger the benefits become.

- ✔ **Maximize your RRSP contribution whenever possible.** It can actually pay to borrow money for your RRSP contribution.

- ✔ **Don't just save your RRSP contribution — invest it.** The difference between the two becomes enormous as time goes by.

- ✔ **Name your spouse or dependent children as your RRSP beneficiary, not your estate.** Your spouse can transfer assets directly into his/her plan.

Maximize the Value of Your RRSP

- ✔ **Choose a self-directed plan.** Managing your own RRSP requires little more than quick glances at your monthly statement and semi-annual reviews with an adviser.

- ✔ **Obtain professional financial advice.** If you place your self-directed RRSP with a full-service brokerage, a financial adviser will be assigned to you. Financial advisers may focus more on making money for the brokerage than on building your RRSP. When you are confident enough, consider a discount brokerage and consult an independent fee-for-service adviser.

- ✔ **Avoid making emotional decisions.** Markets and interest rates will rise and fall over time. If you are at least five years from retirement, don't panic. Review your progress, confirm your decisions, and stay cool.

- ✔ **Adjust your balance as time goes by.** The closer you come to needing the assets of your RRSP, the more concerned you should be about security. Gradually raise the percentage of your bonds and GICs over the years.

CDG BOOKS CANADA

...For Dummies®: Bestselling Book Series for Beginners

RRSPs & RRIFs

FOR DUMMIES®

2ND EDITION

by John Lawrence Reynolds

CDG BOOKS CANADA

Best-Selling Books • Digital Downloads • e-Books • Answer Networks • e-Newsletters • Branded Web Sites • e-Learning

◆ Toronto, ON ◆

RRSPs & RRIFs For Dummies® 2nd Edition

Published by:
CDG Books Canada, Inc.
99 Yorkville Avenue
Suite 400
Toronto, ON M5R 3K5
www.cdgbooks.com (CDG Books Canada Web Site)
www.hungryminds.com (Hungry Minds Web Site)
www.dummies.com (Dummies Press Web Site)

National Library of Canada Cataloguing in Publication Data

Reynolds, John Lawrence
    RRSPs & RRIFs for dummies

2nd ed.
Includes index.
ISBN 1-894413-36-9

1. Registered Retirement Savings Plans. 2. Retirement income—Planning. 3. Finance, Personal. I. Title.

HD7129.R49 2001   332.024'01   C2001-901626-3

Printed in Canada
2 3 4 5 TRI 05 04 03 02
Distributed in Canada by CDG Books Canada, Inc.

For general information on CDG Books, including all Hungry Minds publications, please call our distribution centre: John Wiley & Sons Canada, Ltd. Tel: 1-800-567-4797. For reseller information, including discounts and premium sales, please call our sales department at 1-877-963-8830.

This book is available at special discounts for bulk purchases by your group or organization for resale, premiums, fundraising, and seminars. For details, contact CDG Books Canada, Special Sales Department, 99 Yorkville Avenue, Suite 400, Toronto, ON, M5R 3K5; Tel: 416-963-8830; Email: spmarkets@cdgbooks.com.

For press review copies, author interviews, or other publicity information, please contact our marketing department at 416-963-8830, fax 416-923-4821, or e-mail publicity@cdgbooks.com.

For authorization to photocopy items for corporate, personal, or educational use, please contact Cancopy, The Canadian Copyright Licensing Agency, One Yonge Street, Suite 1900, Toronto, ON, M5E 1E5; Tel: 416-868-1620; Fax: 416-868-1621; www.cancopy.com.

 is a trademark under exclusive licence to CDG Books Canada, Inc., from Hungry Minds, Inc.

About the Author

John Lawrence Reynolds is a graduate of McMaster University who began his writing and financial career in advertising. After walking away from a senior executive position with a major advertising agency in the mid-1970s, he pursued a career in film directing, feature writing, and photography. Soon he was balancing business and promotional writing assignments with travel articles for major magazines — he has sailed the Nile, Rhine, and Amazon rivers; dived off Australia's Great Barrier Reef; hiked through rice paddies in Bali; and stalked perfect dim sum in Hong Kong.

The author of a dozen books, John has won two Arthur Ellis awards for best crime writing by a Canadian. His most recent book, *Free Rider*, details the escapades of a Bay Street investment broker who managed to defraud his clients of more than $20 million.

During his career, John has performed writing services for all the major Canadian chartered banks and trust companies, as well as financial giants like Merrill Lynch Canada, Trimark Funds, Templeton Funds, Equity Funds, and other investment-related firms. He has also been a faithful RRSP contributor and investor for more than 25 years.

John Lawrence Reynolds lives in Burlington, Ontario, with his wife, Judy, and an exceptionally self-indulgent cat.

Dedication

To Larry, Donna, Louise, and everyone else at Wade & Partners who implanted in me the wisdom and reward of faithful RRSP investing.

Author's Acknowledgements

This book grew out of discussions with Joan Whitman and Robert Harris of CDG Books Canada, Inc. I thank them for their encouragement and their confidence in me. For this second edition, Melanie Rutledge and Kelli Howey added their special eagle-eyed magic to my revisions and additions. They achieved what all good editors achieve: they made this a better book.

The joy of preparing this book was heightened by the presence of Charm Darby, who reviewed the book for technical accuracy. Her practical advice and sheer exuberance improved the text immensely.

Publisher's Acknowledgements

We're proud of this book; please register your comments through our On-line Registration Form located at www.hungryminds.com.

Some of the people who helped bring this book to market include the following:

Acquisitions and Editorial

Editorial Director: Joan Whitman

Associate Editor: Melanie Rutledge

Copy Editor: Kelli Howey

Production

Director of Production: Donna Brown

Production Editor: Rebecca Conolly

Layout and Graphics: Darlene Eiler, Heidy Lawrance Associates

Proofreader: Allyson Latta

Indexer: Liba Berry

General and Administrative

CDG Books Canada, Inc.: Ron Besse, Chairman; Tom Best, President; Robert Harris, Vice President and Publisher

Hungry Minds Consumer Reference Group

Business: Kathleen Nebenhaus, Vice President and Publisher; Kevin Thornton, Acquisitions Manager

Cooking/Gardening: Jennifer Feldman, Associate Vice President and Publisher; Anne Ficklen, Executive Editor; Kristi Hart, Managing Editor

Education/Reference: Diane Graves Steele, Vice President and Publisher

Lifestyles: Kathleen Nebenhaus, Vice President and Publisher; Tracy Boggier, Managing Editor

Pets: Kathleen Nebenhaus, Vice President and Publisher; Tracy Boggier, Managing Editor

Travel: Michael Spring, Vice President and Publisher; Brice Gosnell, Publishing Director; Suzanne Jannetta, Editorial Director

Hungry Minds Consumer Editorial Services: Kathleen Nebenhaus, Vice President and Publisher; Kristin A. Cocks, Editorial Director; Cindy Kitchel, Editorial Director

Hungry Minds Consumer Production: Debbie Stailey, Production Director

Contents at a Glance

Introduction 1

Part I: The Hows and Whys of RRSPs 9

Chapter 1: RRSP Basics: How They Work and Why They're Important 11

Chapter 2: Let's Get Started 29

Chapter 3: What to Expect from Your RRSP 41

Chapter 4: Fitting an RRSP into Your Financial Future 53

Part II: Getting the Most from Your RRSP 61

Chapter 5: Taking Charge 63

Chapter 6: Finding Help in Making Decisions 77

Chapter 7: Your Strategy 83

Chapter 8: Finding Your Perfect Formula 93

Part III: Guaranteed Investments 101

Chapter 9: Minimizing the Risk 103

Chapter 10: Saving Accounts, GICs, and T-bills 109

Chapter 11: Bonds 117

Part IV: Mutual Funds: A Recipe for RRSP Growth 129

Chapter 12: What Are Mutual Funds and Why Are They Important? 131

Chapter 13: Choosing Funds for Your Future 153

Chapter 14: Equity Funds 171

Chapter 15: Bond, Money Market, and Mortage Funds 195

Chapter 16: Balanced, Specialty, and Exotic Funds 207

Chapter 17: Managing Your RRSP Portfolio 229

Part V: As Time Goes By 243

Chapter 18: Tracking Your Progress 245

Chapter 19: Your Financial Adviser and You 259

Chapter 20: Resisting Temptation 265

Chapter 21: Death, Divorce, and Other Disasters 273

Part VI: Understanding RRIFs 277

Chapter 22: The Time Has Come to Cash In!.............................279
Chapter 23: How a RRIF Works 289
Chapter 24: Looking at the Whole Picture 299

Part VII: Where to Go from Here 307

Chapter 25: Sources of Help and Information.............................309
Chapter 26: Your Personal RRSP Planner.............................319

Part VIII: The Part of Tens.............................321

Chapter 27: Ten Ways to Maximize Your RRSP Growth.............................323
Chapter 28: Ten Mistakes to Avoid at All Costs.............................329
Chapter 29: Ten Things to Know about Your Financial Adviser.............................335

Glossary.............................341

Index 349

Cartoons at a Glance

By Rich Tennant

page 9

page 61

page 101

page 129

page 243

page 277

page 321

page 307

Fax: 978-546-7747
E-mail: the5wave@tiac.net

Table of Contents

· ·

Introduction 1

About This Book 2
Foolish Assumptions 2
How This Book Is Organized 3
    Part I: The Hows and Whys of RRSPs 3
    Part II: Getting the Most from Your RRSP 3
    Part III: Guaranteed Investments 4
    Part IV: Mutual Funds: A Recipe for RRSP Growth 4
    Part V: As Time Goes By 5
    Part VI: Understanding RRIFs 5
    Part VII: Where to Go from Here 6
    Part VIII: The Part of Tens 6
Icons Used in This Book 6
Where to Go from Here 7

Part I: The Hows and Whys of RRSPs 9

**Chapter 1: RRSP Basics: How They Work and
Why They're Important** 11

The Basic Principles and Benefits of RRSPs 13
Tax-Sheltered Savings 14
    Never too early, (almost) never too late 15
    We're retiring earlier and living longer 17
    Tax-deferred, not tax-free 20
    Understanding risk and reward 20
    Group RRSPs 21
The Power of Independence 22
Basic Principles of RRSP Investing 23
    Who sells RRSPs? 24
    Where to go 24
Excuses, Excuses 25

Chapter 2: Let's Get Started 29

Determine Your Maximum Contribution 29
    Canada Customs and Revenue Agency limits 30
    A little room for going over the limit 32
    A second chance to contribute 34
The Foreign-Content Factor 34

Monthly Contributions versus Lump-Sum Payments 36
    Deductions at source 36
    Borrowing to save 37
    RESPs 38
    Catching up big-time 39
Claiming Your Deduction 39

Chapter 3: What to Expect from Your RRSP 41

Growth Expectations 42
The Spectre of Inflation 43
How Much Will You Need? 45
Paying Attention 46
Spousal RRSPs and Income Splitting 47
Pledging Your RRSP as Collateral 49
What Happens in the Event of Your Death 50
Leaving the Country 51

Chapter 4: Fitting an RRSP into Your Financial Future 53

Canada/Quebec Pension Plan 53
Old Age Security 55
Company Pension Plans 55
Personal Savings 56
Real Estate 57
Reverse Mortgages 58
Your RRSP as a Basic Foundation 59

Part II: Getting the Most from Your RRSP 61

Chapter 5: Taking Charge 63

You're Not Buying Underwear 63
A "Balanced Diet" 64
Self-Directed RRSPs 65
    Choosing where to place your self-directed RRSP 67
    Getting professional advice for your self-directed RRSP 68
    Transferring funds 70
Decisions to Make 71
    Understanding risk and reward 71
    Your risk threshold 73
    When to make adjustments 74

Chapter 6: Finding Help in Making Decisions 77

Who Can Get You Started? 78
    Professional advice 78
    Choosing and working with professional assistance 79
    Paying for professional advice 80
    Your own knowledge and abilities 81

Chapter 7: Your Strategy 83

Your Contribution Plan 84
Short-Term and Long-Term Goals 84
Over-Contributing and Under-Contributing 85
Putting too many eggs in your basket (or, you can never
have too many eggs) .85
Putting too few eggs in your basket 86
Review Your Progress 86
Adjust Your Program 88
When It Makes Sense to Invest in Your Employer 88
Things Not to Worry About 89
How to Stay Calm 89
Things to Worry about Maybe a Little 90

Chapter 8: Finding Your Perfect Formula 93

Investments Suitable for Your RRSP 93
Matching Your Investment Mix to Your Goals 94
Savings accounts 96
GICs 96
Bonds 96
T-Bills 96
Stocks 97
Mutual funds 97
Mortgages — Yours and others 98
Contributions in kind .99

Part III: Guaranteed Investments *101*

Chapter 9: Minimizing the Risk 103

Laying the Groundwork 103
The risk of being too conservative 104
Examining alternatives 105
Looking for bigger returns 107
Bill and Buffy: A Cautionary Tale 107

Chapter 10: Savings Accounts, GICs, and T-bills 109

Savings Accounts 109
GICs: For Mature Readers Only 110
Things to keep in mind when buying GICs 111
New breeds of GICs .112
T-bills: Ottawa Needs a Loan 114
Frank and Frances: A Cautionary Tale 115

Chapter 11: Bonds **117**

Defining Bonds 117

What a bond represents 119

Gilt-edged, blue-chip, and junk 120

Why strip bonds are a good choice 122

Short-term or long-term? 123

How to Buy Bonds 124

The "No Free Lunch" Rule Rides Again 125

Sam and Susan: A Cautionary Tale 126

Part IV: Mutual Funds: A Recipe for RRSP Growth 129

Chapter 12: What Are Mutual Funds and Why Are They Important? . .**131**

Mutual Fund Facts 131

Fact #1: Mutual funds invest in investments 132

Fact #2: Mutual funds are professionally managed 132

Fact #3: Mutual funds deliver wide diversification 133

Resources and Clout 136

What You Own in a Mutual Fund 138

Different Kinds of Mutual Funds 139

How Mutual Funds Make Money for You 142

How Mutual Funds Make Money for Themselves 144

Front-end Load, Back-end Load, and No-Load at all 146

Front-end load funds 146

Back-end load funds 147

No-load funds 148

Other Fees 150

Chapter 13: Choosing Funds for Your Future **153**

Performance Is the Key . . . Kind of 153

Avoiding the Losers 157

Funds within Families 159

What about Bank Funds? 159

How to Understand a Prospectus 161

1. The fund's investment objectives 161

2. The fund's costs 164

3. The fund's financial performance 166

4. The fund's annual-returns record 167

Matching the Fund's Objectives to Your Own 168

Chapter 14: Equity Funds **171**

What's an Equity Fund? 172

Management Style 173

Value fund managers 173

Growth fund managers 175

Top-down and bottom-up fund managers 178
Market-timing fund managers 178
What Does All of This Mean to You? 180
Is Bigger Better? 180
Where your money goes 182
The companies they keep 184
Canadian Stocks: Large and Small-Cap 185
Index Funds 186
Foreign Equity Funds 189
Types of foreign-equity funds 189
Foreign investment beyond the 30-percent limit 191
Sample Portfolios: Ted, Terri, and Thomas 192

Chapter 15: Bond, Money Market, and Mortgage Funds **195**

Bond Funds: Trading in Dollars and Promises 196
Management Style 198
Foreign Bonds that Aren't 199
Money Market Funds 201
Mortgage Funds 203
Sample Portfolios: Judy, Jane, and Jerry 203

Chapter 16: Balanced, Specialty, and Exotic Funds **207**

Balanced Funds 208
The Bottom Line 209
Exotic Funds 211
Dividend funds 211
Special equity funds 211
Precious metals funds 212
Resource funds 212
Real estate funds 213
Emerging Markets 213
Social Responsibility or Profit? 215
Labour Funds 217
Segregated Funds 220
New Dogs, New Tricks 223
How Many Funds Do You Really Need? 223
Sample Portfolios: Rick, Ralph, and Rhonda 226

Chapter 17: Managing Your RRSP Portfolio **229**

Dollar-Cost Averaging 229
Tracking Your Progress: Read (but Don't Agonize Over)
Your Statement 231
What Are Your Relatives Like? Trying Out Other Funds from
the Same Family 233
Beware the Dreaded Drift 234
Throwing in the Towel 236
Sample Portfolios: Michael, Melissa, and Maureen 240

Part V: As Time Goes By 243

Chapter 18: Tracking Your Progress 245
How to Read Your RRSP Statement 245
Heeding Warning Lights and Road Signs 249
When Should You Lock in Your Profits? 250
Should You Trade Stocks? 251
In Case You Try This at Home 254
Full-service or discount brokerage? 254
Covering your assets 256

Chapter 19: Your Financial Adviser and You 259
In Your Best Interest 259
Reviewing Your Portfolio 261
Are You Still Compatible? 261
Changing Advisers 263

Chapter 20: Resisting Temptation 265
Your RRSP Is Not for a Rainy Day 265
Combining RRSPs and RESPs 267
The Lifelong Learning Plan and Your RRSP 268
The Home Buyers' Plan and Your RRSP 269
Bowing Out Early 271

Chapter 21: Death, Divorce, and Other Disasters 273
Family Law and Your RRSP 273
Your Will and Your RRSP 274
A Financial Checklist 275

Part VI: Understanding RRIFs 277

Chapter 22: The Time Has Come to Cash In! 279
Congratulations or Condolences? 279
The End of Your RRSP as You Know It 280
Moving from RRSP to RRIF 281
RRIFs 282
Annuities: Their Time May Have Passed 282
Should You Choose an Annuity for Your Retirement Income? 286

Chapter 23: How a RRIF Works 289
An RRSP in Reverse 289
Remember That Deadline 290

Rules for RRIF Withdrawals 291
LIFs and L-RIFs 292
Look for Income, but Keep Your Eye on Growth 293
The Difference Down the Road 293
Where to Start When Adjusting Your RRIF Asset Mix 294
Follow the Rule of Thirds 295
A Step-by-Step Approach to Making Decisions 296

Chapter 24: Looking at the Whole Picture **299**
Other Income Sources 299
Your C/QPP benefits 299
Your home 300
Estate Planning 302
A Long and Happy Life 305

Part VII: Where to Go from Here...............................***307***

Chapter 25: Sources of Help and Information **309**
Don't Be Conned 309
Information Sources 312
Canada Customs and Revenue Agency 312
C/QPP and OAS 315
Banks, trust companies, and credit unions 316

Chapter 26: Your Personal RRSP Planner **319**

Part VIII: The Part of Tens.......................................***321***

Chapter 27: Ten Ways to Maximize Your RRSP Growth **323**
Contribute as much as you can afford to your RRSP,
  as early as possible 323
Keep your RRSP investments well balanced 324
Contribute to a spousal RRSP if it's to your advantage 324
Take charge of your future with a self-directed RRSP 325
Maximize your foreign content 325
Avoid having too many RRSPs and too many different funds ...326
Arrange to make regular monthly contributions via
  pre-authorized chequing 326
Call on professional advice but make your own decisions 326
Keep your eye on the horizon 327
Remember that borrowing to save can really make sense 327

Chapter 28: Ten Mistakes to Avoid at All Costs 329
   Waiting until the last minute to make your RRSP contribution 329
   Thinking only of your tax refund instead of your RRSP growth 330
   Choosing inappropriate investments 330
   Panicking at market volatility 330
   Withdrawing money from your RRSP 331
   Making excessive RRSP contributions 331
   Ignoring the benefits of an RRSP loan 332
   Failing to file an income-tax return while still a student 332
   Believing you can do it all on your own 332
   Misunderstanding the rules of risk and reward 333

Chapter 29: Ten Things to Know about Your Financial Adviser 335
   Is he or she paid by commission, by salary, or by direct
      fees from you? 336
   What is his or her hourly rate, if on a fee basis? 336
   What formal qualifications does he or she have as a
      financial adviser? 336
   How much effort does he or she put into discovering things
      about you? 337
   Can you obtain references from clients with needs and
      assets similar to your own? 337
   Will he or she provide a brief opinion of your current RRSP
      plan components? 337
   If the financial adviser will be handling trades, has he or she
      explained the "Know Your Client" form? 338
   Who else can you call on at the adviser's firm, if necessary? 338
   What can you tell from his or her lifestyle? 338
   How often will you receive statements of your account? 339

Glossary *341*

Index *349*

Introduction

● ●

*A*s the year 2001 proved, you can never be sure of anything – which makes planning for your retirement even more vital than ever. Exerting as much control as possible over your financial future and being prepared, both financially and emotionally, to deal with the unforeseen, are two ways to deal with inevitable change. For the vast majority of Canadians – those of us who are neither permanently nor outrageously wealthy – an RRSP is perhaps the best way of preparing financially for the future. That's been the goal of this book from the start, and it's in even sharper focus here in the second edition.

This book is for people who want down-to-earth guidance on accumulating enough money via an RRSP to live reasonably well through their retirement years. It's about building your RRSP, the largest, most liquidable asset you and most other Canadians will ever own. And it's about helping you avoid mistakes by alerting you to their presence before you encounter them.

All the information is here in this second edition, updated to include new data plus reflect changes in the rules dictated by Canada Customs and Revenue Agency (the CCRA), which used to be Revenue Canada. Besides all that, there's another big change for you to deal with . . .

The first edition of this book appeared in the midst of the Great Internet & Tech Stock Extravaganza. You didn't have to be an investment addict to know that companies such as Nortel and Amazon.com were being praised as the next IBM, Xerox, Coca-Cola, and General Motors combined. They represented, we were told, "The New Economy," usually displayed in flashing red neon lights. Everyone with a portion of their RRSP money invested in these companies would spend their retirement driving Jaguars and wintering in Barbados.

Reality changed things. The slide began in March 2000, and a year later Canadians who were relying on companies like Nortel and others in its field to enrich their retirement discovered that 60 percent or more of their money was playing hide-and-seek. And the World Trade Centre disaster shook our confidence in long-term security of a different kind.

Two words: *Things change*. Here are three more words: *Prepare for it*. That's what an RRSP is all about, and that's what this book is about as well — preparing for the change in your working years, from active and stressful to relaxed and enjoyable. The hard questions about investing in The New Economy are all here, along with easy-to-follow answers. And guess what? It's not that difficult. The two most important rules are these: Start early and take charge.

About This Book

This is neither a novel nor a school text, so it's not necessary to absorb it from cover to cover or even to read it in the proper sequence. And there's no final exam to cram for.

Think of it as a reference book you can dip into whenever your needs exceed your knowledge. You want to know how to choose between growth and value-based mutual funds? Skip ahead to that section and it's all there. You're curious about calculating the effects of inflation over the long term? Pull this book off the shelf and check the index.

Unlike most reference books, however, this one avoids taking some things too seriously. Sure, investing for your retirement is a serious business, but I assume that you have a life beyond that particular concern. So you may encounter (I hope) a chuckle or two amid all the nuts-and-bolts advice. And why not? Nobody, except a particularly nasty grade five teacher I recall, ever said that having fun and improving your knowledge were incompatible.

Foolish Assumptions

You and I have never met and are unlikely ever to meet, but I have made a number of assumptions about you as a reader of this book. I assume that

- ✔ You are a Canadian.

- ✔ You are employed, or expect to be.

- ✔ Your Uncle Max did not leave you either a working gold mine, a producing oil well, or a Tahitian resort in his will, which means that you will require some means of financial support in the future.

- ✔ You do not intend to maintain full-time employment for every day of your life. In fact, the sooner you can enjoy the lifestyle you prefer without working, the better.

- ✔ You have sufficient grasp of financial matters to open and maintain a bank account, either chequing or savings.

- ✔ You are not, and are not married to, a financial adviser, financial planner, investment counsellor, chartered accountant, or someone with similar skills who will assume this role in your life out of love, affection, and future considerations. In other words, you need some help in planning your financial future.

How This Book Is Organized

In the beginning, life is simple. You eat, you sleep, you look around, and that's about it. Only when you grow older and begin accepting responsibilities does life grow more complex, and this book follows the same pattern. I start with absolute basics, and things grow more detailed as the pages get turned.

The book consists of eight parts, with each part building on information contained in previous parts.

Part I: The Hows and Whys of RRSPs

This part covers the ABCs of saving for retirement and the ultimate goal of living off the assets when your full-time working days are over. It reviews basic principles, rules, and benefits, such as the formula used by the Canada Customs and Revenue Agency (CCRA) to calculate your maximum annual RRSP contribution. Included are suggestions on how to open your first RRSP; estimating how much you'll need to retire in the style to which you are entitled; and the role of other sources of retirement income — Canada/Quebec Pension Plan, Old Age Security, private pension plans, and other assets you may accumulate, such as the value of your home. If you've been contributing to an RRSP for some time, you'll breeze through this part.

Part II: Getting the Most from Your RRSP

If you're the kind of person who thinks of an RRSP as a government-sponsored piggy bank, this section is written especially for you. It is both amazing and depressing to discover Canadians who salt their RRSP contribution away in a daily interest savings account, gloat over the tax refund their contribution earns, and assume that's the total extent of their retirement planning.

Well, it's not. But this kind of thinking is easy to understand, since virtually all of us have soared through nearly 20 years of education without once encountering classes on investment and financial planning. I'm as strong a proponent for studying Shakespeare, understanding the *British North America Act*, and being able to locate Moncton on the map as anyone, but I also believe there should be room in our educational system for real-world events that affect our lives daily. This includes at least an awareness of certain business practices such as stocks and bonds.

Without this awareness, many of us stumble around in ignorance of their implications — and, as any psychologist will confirm, ignorance leads to fear and prejudice. This part of the book won't qualify you as a savvy stock trader by any means. It should, however, perform part of the job the education system should have assumed when you were back scuffing your Reeboks in the schoolyard. It includes the relationship between risk and reward, the long-term advantages of taking charge of your RRSP's growth, suitable investments to provide that growth, and suggestions on measuring your progress over the years.

Part III: Guaranteed Investments

These are investments that we Canadians adore because they appear to reduce risk. There's nothing like the word *guaranteed* to make us feel comfortable, after all. But believe it or not, risk can raise its ugly head even among a forest of guaranteed investment certificates (GICs), government treasury bills (T-bills), and savings accounts.

Bonds are included in this part as well. Bonds are like a financial card trick to many people — mysterious at first encounter but simple once you understand how it's done.

This part deals with these investment options and provides suggestions for including them in your RRSP. It also introduces the first series of real-life vignettes showing how people like you and me can win or lose according to the wisdom of our decisions. All right, they're not all real-life (although some are based on actual personal experiences) — but, like Aesop's fables, each tale ends with a moral you can apply when making RRSP investment decisions.

Part IV: Mutual Funds: A Recipe for RRSP Growth

Financially speaking, Canadians are divided into two groups: Those who know and understand mutual funds, and those who fear and avoid them. If you are in the latter group, don't miss this section, because over the long term the proper use and wise selection of mutual funds can make the biggest positive impact on the growth of your RRSP.

This does not mean you should avoid fear (let's call it "caution") entirely. Two types of people out there love to get their hands on your RRSP money. One type manages mutual funds; the other type sells them to you. Ideally, all three of you will grow wealthy together. Of course, you are outnumbered two to one. This part will help balance the odds for you.

It begins with fundamentals, such as defining a mutual fund and its operations. It covers the methods used by mutual fund managers to make money for you and for themselves; how to assess the performance of different funds; and how to select a combination of funds for your RRSP according to your goals, comfort level, investment sophistication, and even your social values.

Once you become familiar with the characteristics of mutual funds, you may find yourself growing fascinated with the smorgasbord of selections available. The danger of holding too many of the wrong kinds of mutual funds is included here, along with ways to deal with limits on foreign investments permitted in your RRSP. Each chapter ends with a "real-life" tale of RRSP owners and their experiences, both positive and negative, with mutual funds.

Part V: As Time Goes By

When you go shopping for CDs, you don't (or won't — trust me on this) head for the same display rack when you are in your 40s as you did in your teens or 20s. More will change with time than your taste in music, and this will include your expectations from your RRSP investments.

There are many things about your RRSP that need your attention when you're nudging middle age, and they are included in this part. Plotting your progress, checking your future income needs, ensuring that you are receiving the best investment advice, and dealing with life's inevitable surprises — both pleasant and unpleasant — are covered.

Part VI: Understanding RRIFs

An RRSP doesn't stretch forever toward the horizon, apparently ending at the foot of a rainbow that's always just beyond the next hill. It has a conclusion dictated by the CCRA, and at some point you have to deal with that finale. This part reviews the alternatives you will face — lump-sum withdrawal, annuities, or conversion to a Registered Retirement Income Fund — with the expectation that a RRIF will be your best choice.

Managing a RRIF is no more complex, and much more rewarding, than managing an RRSP. Included in this part are strategies to earn maximum income from your RRIF, a review of restrictions and requirements, and how to fit a RRIF into your overall retirement plans.

Part VII: Where to Go from Here

Many complexities of RRSP/RRIF planning and rules can be solved and explained by the friendly folks at the CCRA tax service offices, and an up-to-date list is included here along with Web site addresses. Also included is a do-it-yourself RRSP/RRIF planner, courtesy of Scotiabank.

Part VIII: The Part of Tens

Top-ten lists are popular these days, so why not for RRSP owners? Included here are three top-ten question and suggestion lists to guide you in RRSP investing and planning.

Icons Used in This Book

Part of the fun gained from reading a book like this is picking up information you can use with your snobby sister-in-law — the one who says things like "But of course, everybody knows that," when she knows you have no idea what she is talking about. You can absorb this stuff to put her in her place at the next family soiree . . . or you can just skip it and drop her from your Christmas card list instead.

This is practical information you can apply right away. If the technology permitted, the words would appear in red neon letters.

Not that you would do anything as risky, foolish, or downright silly as described here, of course. But it's worth repeating that, if anyone says he or she can double your RRSP value in six months with no risk, you should picture them with a burning fuse emerging from their head and, clever as you are, run in the opposite direction. That's the kind of stuff this sign refers to.

Though I've tried to keep this book as jargon-free as possible, these are terms that are helpful to know.

Always wear clean underwear, always look both ways before crossing the street, and always remember the information repeated wherever you see this icon. Your mother may not have been an investment genius, but if she had a way of drilling some basic rules into your head, think of her dispensing this kind of advice, over and over.

Where to Go from Here

I hate to be pushy, but the first rule of RRSP investing is to start early. In fact, teenagers with their first paying jobs but with no income tax to pay can actually benefit from RRSP advantages. It's true, as you're about to read. Of course, persuading a teenager to think about retirement income is like teaching a cat to take a shower, but the rule holds true nevertheless.

Time to get started!

Part I
The Hows and Whys of RRSPs

"We were told to put our money into something that got more interest, so we started sticking it into this mason jar that's got some dang thing in it we bought from a traveling freak show."

In this part . . .

In this part, you get the basic rules of RRSPs and discover how to enjoy their benefits. The mechanics of opening your first RRSP and earning your first tax refund (hooray!) are included, along with important guidelines for growing your RRSP's value over the years. Finally, you encounter other sources of retirement income that are in the picture . . . more or less.

Chapter 1

RRSP Basics: How They Work and Why They're Important

In This Chapter

▶ Understanding the basic principles and benefits of RRSPs

▶ Assigning RRSPs a role in your financial future

▶ Taking charge of your financial future

*I*n the next ten years, Boomers will become Geezers, which means retirement will no longer be just a distant idea but an immediate reality. Having set the pace for key social values such as owning a BMW and promoting disco, Baby Boomers who arrived in the world between 1947 and 1966 are now stimulating the growth of Registered Retirement Savings Plans. The value of RRSPs tripled in the ten years from 1988 to 1998, to more than $240 billion. That'll cover a lot of shuffleboard bets among the Geritol set — even after the stock market's imitation of an absent-minded skydiver who forgot his parachute in 2000, the assets now exceed $250 billion and keep climbing.

Okay, maybe the Boomers blew it with disco music. But they've turned the benefits of RRSPs into something much more valuable and lasting.

A hundred years ago, the only retirement plan most working people relied on was their children. Assuming one of your kids settled down and accepted their responsibilities — which included looking after you and your spouse — you could count on having a roof over your head and food on your table when your working years were over.

Later, the idea of company pensions took hold. Assuming your employer accepted *his* responsibilities, he would provide a pension to guarantee at least a roof over your head and so on. Later, the federal government got into the act with something called Old Age Security, which was sort of Ottawa's reward for paying your taxes all those years.

But something happened over the past generation or two. For better or worse, Canadians no longer rely on either our kids or our government to provide a retirement income. What's more, the concept of dedicating our entire working career to one company has faded for most of us, along with prospects for a healthy private pension. Working for three, four, or more companies during our working years reduces the pension benefits we could expect from one career-long employment.

Many companies no longer try to entice employees with healthy pension plans, and those who do tend to choose pensions with *defined contributions* over the older *defined benefit* design. A defined contribution pension fixes the amount you and your employer will contribute toward your plan each year, with no formula for the amount you'll receive when you retire. A defined benefit pension uses a formula based on your years of employment and salary level. Accountants are more comfortable with defined contribution plans ("We know how much we'll be paying this year") than with defined benefit plans ("We don't know how much we'll be paying in 20 years"), and, since senior corporate executives try to avoid making their accountants nervous, the choice is overwhelmingly in favour of defined contributions.

But guess what? A defined contribution pension plan is just an RRSP hiding out in the boardroom. They both depend on a flexible level of contributions and shelter from taxation until they're needed to generate a retirement income.

Defined benefit or defined contribution?

Many members of private pension plans know disturbingly little about the design and operation of their program. If your employer provides pension benefits, try answering each of the following questions before looking at the brief description following each. If you're not confident in your answers, meet with your plan administrator or someone in your human resources department who is qualified to discuss pensions.

Is it a defined benefit plan?

Defined benefit plans determine your retirement benefits according to one of three different formulas.

If it's a defined benefit plan:

✔ **Is it a flat-benefit formula?** (Based on your years of service)

✔ **Is it a career-average formula?** (Based on income levels during your entire working career with the company)

✔ **Is it a final-average formula?** (Based on your income level during your past few — usually five — years with the company)

Is it a defined contribution plan?

Defined contribution plans — sometimes called *money purchase plans* — fix the contribution levels. The benefit levels are unknown, since they depend on the performance of investments held in the individual plans.

Note: Some firms shift their plan design from time to time, so you may be dealing with a combination of plans and formulas.

Of course, we all contribute to the Canada/Quebec Pension Plan. But, as you may have heard, many experts doubt whether the C/QPP will be as healthy as we expect to be ourselves when we reach age 65. Besides, C/QPP benefits are minimal at best. If you hope to live well in your retirement years, don't rely on C/QPP benefits to pay for it.

The Basic Principles and Benefits of RRSPs

Canadians may grumble about many government decisions, but Ottawa deserves a round of applause for creating the Registered Retirement Savings Plan way back in 1957.

By the way, let's define RRSP right up front. An RRSP is not an insurance plan. It is not a savings bond. It is not a pension plan. And it is not a ticket that you buy today and present to the government when you are 65 years old, in return for a cheque and a pat on the head for being a good citizen.

An *RRSP* is an investment. Like all investments, it demands your attention from time to time. Also, an RRSP is not guaranteed to deliver X amount of money if you contribute Y dollars to it every year for Z years. Its growth will vary over the years, and the amount you have when you retire will be based on the amount of money you put into it, the number of years you keep adding to it, the attention you pay to managing it, the quality of advice you receive in caring for it, and, like it or, a smattering of good luck.

You cannot walk into a bank, trust company, credit union, stock brokerage, or hot dog stand, plunk your money on the counter, and say, "Give me your best RRSP in a plain brown wrapper." Things just don't work that way.

An RRSP provides us with the opportunity to invest money during our working years and use the built-up savings to provide an income for our retirement years. The key word here is *registered*. Registering your retirement savings with the government involves a contract between you and Ottawa. In this contract, you agree not to touch the money in your RRSP until you choose to finish, or at least cut back substantially, your full employment. Ottawa agrees not to count your annual RRSP contribution when calculating each year's income tax, and not to tax the money as it grows inside your RRSP.

The whole idea is based on the concept of *deferred taxation*. Note that it's called *deferred* and not *avoided*. Here's a rundown of the basic principles:

- During your working years, you set aside money — up to a maximum amount annually, based on your previous year's income level and any private pension benefits — which is subtracted from your taxable earned income. "Earned income" includes salaries, commissions, and bonuses; money you make from being self-employed (after expenses); supplemental unemployment insurance benefits; disability payments from the Canada/Quebec Pension Plan; taxable alimony or support payments; royalties; net research grants; and net rental income from property you may own. Pension income, investments outside an RRSP, and inheritances are excluded.

✔ Subtracting your RRSP contribution from your earned income reduces the income tax you must pay, producing that bundle of joy that Canadians call a tax refund.

✔ The money you invest in your RRSP grows year by year, free of taxes. It remains tax-free as long as it is inside the plan.

✔ You can choose to invest your RRSP contributions in many ways, from dull-as-dishwater daily interest savings accounts to some stock market tricks as risky as anything Las Vegas offers. The choice is yours. (In case you're wondering, I advise neither. For recommended investments, see Chapter 8.)

✔ When you retire, your RRSP shifts into reverse. Now it pays you, which is when Ottawa claims a portion as income tax.

Those are the bare bones of RRSP philosophy. Everything else, as important as it may be, is strategy.

RRSP or RSP? Many people dispensing financial advice drop one of the *R*s in RRSP, reducing it to simply "RSP." The idea, I suppose, is to save one keystroke every time they write about Registered Retirement Savings Plans. It's a little like all those computer programmers back in the 1980s who decided to use only the last two digits of a year, writing "98" instead of "1998," and launching the whole Y2K crisis — which, you'll recall, cost billions to repair. Dropping one *R* from RRSP won't create that kind of damage, but I have never figured out which *R* they were dropping — "Registered" or "Retirement." So I use the full moniker all through the book. It will probably cost me 1,000 extra keystrokes, but I can afford it.

Tax-Sheltered Savings

At first glance, the one thing that makes RRSPs attractive to most people is the idea of a tax refund. That's understandable — there's nothing like near-instant gratification to generate enthusiasm in people.

But the true value of an RRSP isn't the amount of money it saves you in tax this year; it's the amount of money the RRSP can make for you next year . . . and the year after . . . and so on, right up to the day you retire. That's because your RRSP is *sheltered*, which is another way of saying that it's protected from the clutches of Canada Customs and Revenue Agency (CCRA) (which we used to know more succinctly and accurately as Revenue Canada). Sheltered investments result in a neat trick known as *tax-free compound interest*, which means they earn money on the money you contribute, and then make money on the money they made. Over a number of years, this process can produce dramatic returns when compared with unsheltered savings or investments held outside an RRSP.

Look at it this way:

From every taxable dollar that you earn over $30,000, you pay about 40 cents to the federal and provincial governments. It varies somewhat depending on where you live, but essentially you get to keep only 60 cents from each hard-earned dollar over that amount. So if you earn an extra $1,000, taxes eat up $400, leaving just $600 for you to spend as you choose.

If you're a prudent 35-year-old Canadian and decide to save $600 each year for 30 years, earning 10 percent annually in an *unsheltered* (taxable) investment, at age 65 your net savings will be $47,435. Each year, the CCRA will ask you to calculate the amount of money your investment earned and — *zap!* — about 40 percent of it will disappear in the general direction of Ottawa. The $47,435 is all that's left after taxes.

Now consider doing the same thing inside a sheltered RRSP. First, instead of investing $600 each year you could invest $1,000, because, as an RRSP contribution, the CCRA pretends that you never made the money in the first place. If everything remains the same — your money earns 10 percent annually for 30 years — you will discover a nest egg of not $47,435 when you retire but $164,494, or almost four times as much. Why such a big difference? Obviously, saving more money each year — $1,000 versus $600 — accounts for part of it. But the biggest difference resulted from sheltering your earnings from tax.

Financial people find it helpful to talk about two kinds of dollars; one is more valuable than the other. An *after-tax dollar* is what's left of a loonie when federal and provincial income tax has been deducted. A *before-tax dollar* is the money you've earned and expect to keep. Since income tax eats about 40 percent of your taxable income over $30,000, an after-tax dollar is really worth only about 60 cents.

The lesson? Generate as many before-tax dollars as you can, because they're worth almost twice as much as the other kind. And the best way for most Canadians to get their hands on before-tax dollars is with an RRSP.

Never too early, (almost) never too late

If tax-free compound interest is the most rewarding benefit of an RRSP, it stands to reason that the longer your money remains inside your plan, the more you'll benefit. In fact, while age 69 is the maximum limit for RRSP contributors, there

Ignore the skeptics — An RRSP is still your best bet

Some people in the financial community have begun to question the emphasis on RRSPs for Canadians in certain jobs. A high-school teacher who is around 40 years of age and earning $60,000 annually can expect to receive a pension of $36,000 annually, indexed to inflation. Assuming the teacher's spouse is employed and will enjoy retirement benefits as well, this could produce a reasonable income past age 55 or 60, especially if their mortgage is paid for and they are no longer incurring major expenses such as raising children and contributing to their pension plan. Do they really need an RRSP?

Generally speaking, the lower your earned income, the less you need an RRSP to maintain your lifestyle. A fully employed married couple can look forward to receiving total government benefits of around $30,000 annually when both are age 65 or older (based on both Canada/Quebec Pension Plan and Old Age Security benefits). If their total family income during their working years averaged between $40,000 and $50,000 annually, they may not need an RRSP at all.

But there are too many "what ifs" in this scenario, including the following:

✔ What if C/QPP and OAS benefits are sharply reduced, or fail to keep pace with inflation?

✔ What if one or both of the spouses lose their jobs or become unable to work before reaching age 65?

✔ What if the couple hopes for an active retirement, enjoying treats such as travel and foreign vacations they could never afford before?

✔ What if neither spouse has a pension as generous as the one enjoyed by teachers and other public-service employees?

✔ What if they earn a total of $80,000 annually? How much of their lifestyle can they retain with a $30,000 income?

✔ Finally, what if the spouses ignored one of the most generous breaks on income taxes available from the government over their entire lifetime — a break that, even with an investment as small as $50 monthly, could produce $100,000 or more after 30 years? Wouldn't they be kicking themselves for passing up a nest egg of $100,000 when their entire income consisted of shaky government benefits?

Someone, somewhere will always find something negative to say about a cute puppy, a sunny day in June, and RRSPs. This does not make any of them less attractive.

---

is no minimum age as long as the contributor earns income. This means that your son or daughter working summers or weekends at *McDonald's* can enjoy the same RRSP benefits as you. Now, it's admittedly a challenge to convince a 16-year-old to set aside a few hundred bucks and forget about them for the next 40 years or so. But if you succeed, you'll teach them a major lesson in financial management and investment. And you just might be able to persuade them with this example:

If a 16-year-old puts $500 in an RRSP earning an average 10 percent annually and leaves it there for 50 years, that same $500 will have grown to $64,000 without any further contributions. I'll bet you're impressed. I know I was impressed. But the 16-year-old? He'll take the money now.

It's only after we obtain full-time employment that the idea of retirement, which still seems eons away, enters our consciousness. Even then, it competes with other more tempting and important matters, all of which involve money. They include enjoying a social life, buying a home, raising a family, taking vacations, and other duties and distractions. Just like the 16-year-old in the example, we all pay more attention to today's temptations than to tomorrow's rewards. But the impact of an early start on your RRSP is nothing short of amazing.

Consider someone 21 years of age, in her first full-time job, who contributes $2,000 each year to her RRSP. That's a big chunk of coin at that age, especially when cars, fashions, dance clubs, and winter vacations are all tempting her to spend the money on them. But perhaps she realizes that her RRSP contribution generates a few hundred dollars in income tax refunds, which is something a new Honda or a new set of skis can never match. So she goes for it.

Suppose that she manages to contribute $2,000 each year for just seven years, stopping when she reaches age 28, and her RRSP investment earns an average of 10 percent annually. At age 65, the total value of her seven years' contribution will be $664,000, even though she hadn't added another penny to her plan since she turned 28! Here's the real shocker: If she waited until age 28 to *begin* contributing $2,000 each year, and she did so right up to age 65, the total value of her RRSP would be $660,000. In other words, *seven years of contributions starting at age 21 netted her more than 37 years of contributions starting at age 28!* That's the magic of tax-sheltered compound interest.

If you're well into your 30s or 40s and still without an RRSP, this kind of stuff can be a little disturbing because you're suddenly made aware of lost opportunity. But don't let that stop you from beginning right now. You may have fewer years to build your retirement nest egg with an RRSP, but I suspect you have more total income and more determination to save. Whether you have 3 or 30 years to go before retirement, you can still enjoy the advantages of tax-free compound interest with an RRSP.

As long as you're earning an income, you can continue contributing to your RRSP until you reach age 69.

We're retiring earlier and living longer

It's a good news/bad news situation. The good news is that Canadians are living longer than previous generations and remaining healthier as well. For most of us, retirement no longer means a rocker on the porch; it means a chance to travel, learn new skills, make new friends, and experience the kind of life we always wanted when we were busy making a living, raising children, and paying off debts. Not only that, but age 65 is no longer the target age for retirement these days; many of us are choosing 60, 55, or even younger.

Don't count on luck or lotteries

It's pleasant to go through life believing that things always turn out for the best. But when it comes to your retirement, it's also darn foolish. Yet 11 percent of the people responding to a CIBC survey on RRSPs and retirement planning hoped that "winning a lottery" would provide most of their income when they stop working. What's more, 7 percent of them consider winning a lottery to be "very much" a part of their financial planning. If we project this figure on the 15 million Canadians currently employed full-time, this means that more than a million Canadians are expecting to finance their retirement years by hitting a lottery jackpot. Others are depending on a substantial inheritance or just plain luck.

Unrealistic? Of course it is. But not much less realistic than the 24 percent of Canadians who, according to another survey, believed that their Canada/Quebec Pension Plan will provide most of the retirement income they'll need. The maximum payout from C/QPP is currently less than $750 monthly, assuming you retire at age 65. Obviously, luck, lotteries, and the government are not reasonable substitutions for good planning.

The bad news? Too many of us are unprepared to make our retirement dreams come true because we are not adequately prepared to meet our financial needs. This is the result of either insufficient planning or underestimating the money we'll need, or a combination of both.

If you are in good health at age 55 and plan to retire at that age, you can expect to live another 30 years or so. For some people, this is almost as long as their working careers! To put it another way, you could easily take almost as much money out of your retirement nest egg as all the money you earned when you were employed.

While it's true that your RRSP won't have to bear the entire burden of generating your income, it will make the difference between fulfilling your retirement dream and struggling with bare necessities.

So don't ignore the benefits of maximizing both your contributions and the growth of your RRSP. You could be living with the consequences for a quarter-century or longer.

The whole idea of retirement is to maintain your current standard of living without having to work for it. But what percentage of your current income will you need to do it? Probably more than you think.

If you save 15 percent or more of your earnings, are in a high income-tax bracket, and own your own home free of mortgages and other debts, you'll need 65 percent of your pre-retirement income to sustain your standard of living when you retire.

Is the good news in capital gains bad news for RRSPs?

In October 2000, the federal government announced changes in the income tax rules that brought joy to the hearts of every Canadian with a spare loonie or two to invest.

The change affects the way capital gains are taxed. A *capital gain* is the difference in the price you pay to purchase an investment and the price you receive when you sell it. If the price you receive when you sell it is lower than the one you paid to acquire it, that's a *capital loss*. (See? Who said high finance was complicated?)

Under the new rules, only 50 percent of a capital gain is subject to income tax (it used to be 66 percent). This means that you pay no tax at all on half of your capital gains. What's more, you can deduct capital losses from your taxable income, something you can't do with an RRSP. Just to complicate things further, remember that the money you withdraw from an RRSP is 100-percent taxable, basically twice as high as the rate at which capital gains are now taxed.

This news made some financial pundits jump for joy just like Dorothy and the Munchkins did after they heard the Wicked Witch was dead. In this case, the pundits were saying that RRSPs were dead as a retirement strategy. But they were wrong. In an RRSP, your money is taxed only once. For the vast majority of Canadians, an RRSP is still the best way to build personal wealth. Here's why:

Suppose your annual income is $50,000 and you pay income tax at a 35-percent rate. If you contribute $5,000 annually to your RRSP for 25 years, and your RRSP investments average 10-percent annual growth, you will accumulate $540,000 in 25 years' time. Withdrawing this amount at the same 35-percent tax rate puts $350,000 in your pocket. I'm assuming you withdraw it in reasonable portions, say, $40,000 annually, and I am not allowing for growth from the balance remaining inside your RRSP.

If, on the other hand, you choose to invest $5,000 a year outside your RRSP, looking for the capital-gains benefit, you have to start with $6,750. Why? Because you are investing with after-tax dollars, and at a 35-percent tax rate you need to earn $6,750 first. The $5,000 you might have put into your RRSP is worth only $3,250 after income tax, and, using the same 25-year/10-percent annual growth formula, you're left with $304,000 after taxes instead of $350,000. Another thing: The $5,000 RRSP contribution will earn you an income tax refund of, say, $1,500, so the $5,000 contribution costs you $3,500, or barely half the $6,750 you need to put $5,000 a year into a capital gains savings plan.

In an ideal world, you would contribute $5,000 each year to your RRSP and invest your tax return to generate capital gains. And somewhere over the rainbow, bluebirds fly . . . .

If you save between 5 and 10 percent of your earnings and either still have a mortgage on your home or rent to pay, you'll need 75 percent of your pre-retirement income.

If you save 5 percent or less of your earnings and still have a substantial mortgage on your home or major rent to cover each month, you'll need 85 percent of your pre-retirement income.

Tax-deferred, not tax-free

Remember that an RRSP enables you to defer taxes, not avoid them entirely. This is still an important benefit because it accelerates the growth of your RRSP investment over the years. What's more, since your retirement income will almost certainly be less than your income when you were employed, your taxes will be calculated at a lower rate.

When your RRSP finally begins to generate income for you, Canada Customs and Revenue Agency considers this money equivalent to any other earned income and taxes it accordingly. Keep this in mind when considering how much of your retirement income you will be able to keep for yourself. If your RRSP is able to pay you $30,000 annually, for example, taxes will eat up a substantial amount of it, just as they did when you were employed. That's another reason to maximize your RRSP and generate more retirement income.

Understanding risk and reward

Like raising anything else, from your children to the flowers in your garden, growing your RRSP requires a little attention now and then. But it needn't occupy much of your time and, unlike your children, it shouldn't make you lose sleep at night.

The most important thing to understand about growth inside your RRSP is the concept of *risk and reward*. Risk and reward are like Mary and her little lamb — wherever one goes, the other is sure to follow. So if you seek larger rewards from your RRSP investment — meaning more money for you when you retire — you have to accept greater risk.

Does this mean your RRSP becomes nothing more than a pile of chips on a casino craps table? Not in the least. In fact, the biggest danger faced by most RRSP owners isn't the result of being too risky. It's the result of being too careful. Far too many people leave their entire RRSP investment in "safe and secure" *guaranteed investment certificates* (GICs) and savings accounts that earn, these days, perhaps 4 percent annually. For marginally little more risk, and virtually none at all over a period of ten years or more, they could be at least doubling their earnings to 8 or 10 percent or more.

Understanding risk does not mean avoiding it altogether. It means making risk work to your advantage. Chapter 5 covers this topic in detail.

Things you can and cannot hold in an RRSP

Under current RRSP rules, you can choose from a vast number of ways to invest your RRSP contributions, building it over the years faster than any savings account.

Here is a list of qualifying investments for RRSPs. Don't be alarmed if some appear strange and unfamiliar. You'll probably never use all of them anyway. Chapter 8 covers the important qualifying investments in detail.

Qualifying RRSP investments include

✔ Cash deposits, in Canadian dollars, held in a bank, trust company, or credit union account, or surplus cash in a mutual-fund account

✔ GICs (guaranteed investment certificates) and term deposits

✔ Canada Savings Bonds

✔ T-bills (treasury bills)

✔ Mutual funds registered with Canada Customs and Revenue Agency

✔ Debt obligations — bonds, debentures, mortgages, and so on — issued by a Canadian Crown corporation or a Canadian federal, provincial, or municipal government

✔ Bonds and similar debt instruments issued by foreign governments

✔ Shares and bonds from corporations listed on a recognized Canadian stock exchange

✔ Shares listed on a qualifying foreign stock exchange

✔ Shares in qualifying small businesses

✔ Shares in a labour-sponsored venture-capital corporation (except for residents of Alberta, New Brunswick, and Newfoundland)

✔ Mortgages and shares in mortgages on real estate property located in Canada, including the mortgage on your own home

✔ Really bizarre things such as limited partnership units, rights, warrants, and call options — which, unless you consider Las Vegas to be the world's centre of high culture, you don't need to worry about

You are not allowed to hold the following in your RRSP: foreign cash, antiques and collectibles, gold and silver bars, precious stones, U.S. mutual funds (unless they are registered with the CCRA), real estate, foreign stocks traded on an unrecognized exchange, commodities, and weird stuff like futures and put options. *Put options*, by the way, are derivatives of stock market trading. Remember Barings, the U.K. firm that went broke back in 1995 thanks to the dealings of a junior trader in Singapore? He was investing in derivatives. Need I say more? Oh yeah, you also cannot hold uncovered call options in your RRSP.

Group RRSPs

Your company may use a *Group RRSP* to provide retirement benefits instead of a traditional company pension plan. A group RRSP is like cross-breeding a pension plan with an RRSP — you get a little of each.

In a Group RRSP, you and your employer contribute to an RRSP held in your name. While the company administers the plan, investment decisions are made by you, choosing from a range of options provided by your employer. Your total contributions each year are limited according to other RRSP rules, which means if your total Group RRSP contributions do not reach your limit you can still "top up" by adding the difference each year either to the group plan or to a separate RRSP.

The principal advantage of a Group RRSP is that your contributions are automatically deducted from each paycheque. This makes your contributing relatively painless, and you enjoy the tax benefits immediately instead of waiting for a tax-refund cheque each year.

The Power of Independence

Of all your sources of future income, your RRSP is the most secure. Most Canadians are aware of the shaky foundation for the Canada/Quebec Pension Plan, and Ottawa already "claws back" the few dollars it dispenses through Old Age Security payments.

If you're fortunate to have a long-standing company pension plan, its benefits are likely based on paper promises written by actuaries, lawyers, and other people who tend to treat English as a dead foreign language. So you may not fully understand exactly what your benefits are until the time comes for you to claim them. From time to time, you hear horror stories of pensioners who discover much of their future security has been a sham. And it's unwise to depend on your house as a future source of security.

A healthy RRSP, however, remains all yours and *you* are in charge. At any given time, you can measure its value and control its future, preferably with the support of a financial adviser who is looking out for your interests. The value of your RRSP may not be as high as you would like, and you have a responsibility to make decisions and pay attention to it from time to time. What's more, not all of your decisions will return maximum growth. But the money in your RRSP is real — it's not based on promises, and it's not hidden in legal terms.

Now and then someone raises the prospect of the federal government slapping a tax on RRSP earnings. This is a highly remote possibility. Not only would it effectively destroy the whole premise of Canadians saving for their future income, it would trigger an uprising from the entire financial community and virtually every RRSP owner in Canada. So consider your RRSP basically safe from taxation until you withdraw the funds.

Basic Principles of RRSP Investing

One of the joys of managing your RRSP is the satisfaction you gain from taking control of your financial future. This needn't be as complicated as you might expect.

It begins with three basic principles of investing. You can apply variations to these according to your own interest and comfort level, but understanding and applying these three concepts is the secret of investing success:

- **Diversification.** This is just another way of saying "Don't put all your eggs in one basket." If you invest all of your RRSP contributions, for example, in five-year GICs paying 6 percent annually, you might feel pretty smug . . . until you discover at the end of the five years that the stock market rose an average 12 percent annually over the same period. And if you sank every RRSP penny into shares of a South Korean manufacturing company, the Asian financial crisis of 1998–99 would have had you lying awake at night in a cold sweat, watching your hard-earned dollars sink in value.

  The solution is to *diversify* your RRSP among various investment alternatives including GICs, bonds, equity-based investments (meaning you own shares in companies traded on the stock market), and other alternatives. Diversification adds security to your RRSP and lets you sleep better at night. You need a minimum amount in your RRSP to take advantage of diversification — $10,000 say — and a formula based on your own comfort level, which is covered in Chapter 19.

- **Liquidity.** Having a $1,000 diamond ring on your finger is not the same as having a certified cheque for $1,000 in your pocket. While their value may be identical, the cheque is much more *liquid* than the diamond ring, which means it can be converted into cash more easily. Keeping a portion of your RRSP in liquid investments makes it easy to withdraw money from your RRSP to meet an emergency or for certain qualified reasons. Liquidity grows more important as you near retirement, but it also enables you to change the recipe of your RRSP investment, which means you can diversify your investments more easily.

  Savings accounts, short-term GICs, and certain kinds of mutual funds provide high liquidity. You pay for this convenience with generally low returns from your investment.

- **Growth versus income.** Think of two kinds of trees — an oak tree and an apple tree. If you plant the oak tree and I plant the apple tree, we'll each benefit in different ways over the years. You can watch the oak grow steadily taller until it becomes a strong, sturdy source of shade and, eventually, wood that you can use to heat your home or build furniture. Meanwhile, I'll be harvesting apples each year.

Some investments are like that — one provides long-term growth, and the other rewards you on a regular basis over the years. Generally, the younger you are, the more focused you should be on growth. Combining both, by the way, is one more kind of diversification.

Who sells RRSPs?

Or, more correctly, who doesn't? Banks, trust companies, credit unions, caisses populaires, insurance companies, stock brokerage houses, and mutual-fund companies all welcome your RRSP questions and guide you through the application form and other paperwork. They also provide the receipt you need to obtain a tax refund from Canada Customs and Revenue Agency when you file your income-tax return.

An early word of warning: Having so many choices does not mean you should have multiple RRSPs — one with your bank, another with your insurance company, another with a mutual-fund company, and so on. Avoid confusion and cost by consolidating your RRSP investments with one or two sources.

Where to go

If you currently have no RRSP, start by visiting a branch of the bank, trust company, or credit union where you maintain a chequing or savings account. The location is likely convenient to you, the staff already know something about your financial situation, and they can easily arrange monthly deductions or even a loan to launch your RRSP.

Remember that *you* are in charge of your RRSP and your financial future. At any time, you are permitted to move your RRSP to somewhere else that provides better service, bigger returns, more convenience, or for any reason at all. In the beginning, the key decision is not *where* you go for your RRSP, but *when*. The correct answer is this: the sooner the better.

Middle age has enough traumas without your worrying about generating maximum funds for retirement as well. So here's a little guidance if you find yourself behind schedule on building your RRSP value:

If you and your spouse are age 45 and your RRSPs total only $50,000 or so, all is not lost. But you will have to buckle down a little. Assuming you both have sufficient income, an RRSP investment of $10,000 each year in each of your RRSPs, earning 9 percent annually, will produce about $1,400,000 in 20 years. That's major coin in anyone's book.

Such high levels of contributions can be a stretch, but remember the all-important tax refund. An annual salary of $60,000 puts you into the

---

Sobering statistics in spite of those Boomers

The value of RRSPs may be growing, but as late as 1997 only one out of three Canadians eligible to make contributions to an RRSP actually did so, contributing a record total of $27.4 billion.

The average age of an RRSP contributor is 42. People in the 45-to-54 age group are the most faithful RRSP contributors: 44.5 percent of them make contributions each year.

Albertans are the most loyal RRSP contributors, with 33.8 percent in that province adding to their RRSP each year. Newfoundland has the lowest participation at 17.5 percent.

Source: Statistics Canada, Feb. 1999

50-percent tax bracket, which means the $10,000 contribution costs you only $5,000. And that's a bargain.

Excuses, Excuses

In spite of the benefits of an RRSP, many people choose to ignore them. It's always easy to find reasons for justifying this attitude. How many of the following excuses have you heard . . . or used?

- ✔ I'm too young
- ✔ I just got married
- ✔ I just got a mortgage
- ✔ My house is my retirement plan
- ✔ My spouse/partner has an RRSP
- ✔ We're starting a family
- ✔ I can't afford it
- ✔ RRSPs are too confusing

Here are my responses:

"I'm too young." No, you're not. If you are old enough to read this book and have any source of income, you're old enough to make an RRSP contribution. Sure, retirement is many years away. But look at your RRSP contributions as a form of savings. Over the years you'll receive great satisfaction in having those funds tucked away where the CCRA can't get at them, and where they'll eventually grow by leaps and bounds.

"I just got married." Now that the honeymoon is over, let's face reality. The CCRA, you may have noticed, didn't send you a wedding gift and doesn't offer special breaks to married couples. For example, unlike U.S. citizens, Canadians cannot file a joint tax return, dividing their income and lowering their marginal tax rate. But you can both benefit from an RRSP, beginning right now. If one of you is earning substantially more than the other, consider a spousal RRSP. (See Chapter 3 for details.)

"I just got a mortgage." That's a long-term financial commitment. Over the years, your mortgage will slowly decrease with each payment. If you are able to set aside even a small amount — as little as $50 each month — you can begin building an RRSP, which will move in the opposite direction as your mortgage, growing in value as the mortgage shrinks. Imagine the day when your mortgage is finally paid off and your RRSP is in the six-figure range, ready to provide you with a comfortable income. Imagine the good feeling you'll have. (And don't forget those tax advantages.)

"My house is my retirement plan." The first time I heard this statement, I thought it was a joke. A house isn't a retirement plan — it's shelter and warmth, with a little pride thrown in. The real-estate boom of the 1980s (along with a few aggressive real estate agents) convinced many Canadians that their home wasn't just their castle but the foundation of their investment portfolio. This is nonsense, as anyone who purchased a home in Metro Toronto around 1988 can attest. Houses selling for $400,000 or $500,000 in 1988 lost at least 20 percent of their value within two years. This is not a warning against owning your own home, by any means. But as a source of retirement income, it doesn't compare with an RRSP. Remember the difference between before-tax and after-tax dollars? You buy your home with after-tax dollars; you invest in an RRSP with before-tax dollars.

"My spouse/partner has an RRSP." All right, let's get brutal about this. First, it's lovely to assume that you and your partner will spend the rest of your lives together, but that's still just an assumption. Canadian family law provides for an even distribution of assets, including an RRSP. This means that, in the event of a separation, each of you owns half the RRSP benefit you need. Next, if both of you have earned income, you are jointly enjoying only half the tax benefit available to you. Here it comes again: Everyone with earned income should have an RRSP. There's plenty of upside and virtually no downside.

"We're starting a family." Somewhere amid expenses for diapers, toys, clothing, day care and other associated costs, try to find a few dollars for an RRSP. Parents do themselves and their children a favour by acquiring a savings habit and sharing it with their kids. When your offspring are old enough, you can explain how the money is contributed and invested, and together you can watch how it grows over the years. This will make it easier for your children to pick up the habit for themselves, including opening their own RRSP. Besides, think how much peace of mind they'll enjoy knowing Mom and Dad will face retirement with adequate assets . . . meaning you won't be a burden to them in the future.

"I can't afford it." This is one we can all relate to. Each of us has limits on the amount of money left over after taxes, rent or mortgage payments, food, transportation, and so on. Here are three ways to deal with this particular excuse:

- ✔ It doesn't take much to get started — as little as $50 each month, for example, will enable you to invest in mutual funds. That's equivalent to the cost of a coffee and doughnut each working day. Invest the same amount in a mutual fund, and you'll improve your financial outlook and (probably) reduce your waistline.

- ✔ Arrange an automatic RRSP contribution through your employer (called a *source deduction*), bank, trust company, or credit union and reduce the impact on your budget. If you prefer to have your employer handle the paperwork, call your local CCRA office and ask for a source-deduction form. You and your employer complete the form and your employer forwards it to the CCRA.

- ✔ If taxes are the biggest single bite out of your income each month, isn't that the best place to begin saving money? An RRSP enables you to reduce your taxes while saving money. What's more, if you qualify for a tax refund, you can use it for part of next year's contribution.

"RRSPs are too confusing." Not anymore. That's why you're reading this book, remember?

Buying a home with RRSP funds

The federal New Home Buyers' Plan permits you to withdraw up to $20,000 per person, or $40,000 per couple, tax-free from your RRSP to help purchase a home. You pay no withdrawal tax on the amount, and you have 15 years in which to repay your withdrawal. Tempting? Perhaps. But remember that the withdrawn funds are not increasing in value while they are outside your RRSP, and if you fail to repay the borrowed money after 15 years, Canada Customs and Revenue Agency will consider it taxable income. This is spelled *ZAP!*, right in the wallet.

Chapter 2

Let's Get Started

In This Chapter

▶ Calculating your maximum contribution

▶ Maximizing foreign content

▶ Making contributions regularly

▶ Borrowing to save

▶ Claiming your tax benefit

*B*y now you have some idea of the importance of investing in an RRSP and getting started as early as possible. RRSPs are remarkably free from the rules normally associated with government programs, but you should be aware of a few basics before launching your own plan, and keep them in mind when making future choices about your RRSP.

Determine Your Maximum Contribution

The federal government places no limits on the amount of money you can accumulate tax-free inside your RRSP, but it limits the amount you can contribute each year. This amount is based on your earned income for the year in which the RRSP contribution is credited. Because many people don't know how much income they have earned until the year is over, RRSP rules permit contributions made up to the end of February to be claimed against the previous year's income. This fits neatly between the end of the calendar year and April 30, the deadline for filing your income tax return. Most Canadians don't get around to making their RRSP contributions until around Groundhog Day, which is why everyone living between Newfoundland and Nanaimo cannot escape being bombarded with RRSP information from banks, trust companies, mutual funds, and probably Cousin Fred between Christmas and March 1.

Of course, you needn't wait until the end of February to make your RRSP contribution. You can actually put money in your RRSP as early as January 1 of the year in which you claim an RRSP deduction from your income. That gives you 14 months to act — from January 1 of one year all the way to February 28 the following year. By acting sooner than the deadline, you avoid the traditional rush and panic. And by investing the funds 14 months earlier, you get an extra year's growth. Over 25 years or so, the benefits of this extra year can mean literally tens of thousands of dollars more in your RRSP.

The current calculation for maximum RRSP contributions is 18 percent of earned income to a maximum of $13,500. This is expected to remain in effect through the 2003 taxation year. Then it climbs to $14,500 for 2004 and $15,500 for 2005. After the 2005 tax year, the maximum contribution will be indexed to inflation.

If you are a member of a company pension plan or deferred profit-sharing plan, your maximum RRSP contribution is reduced, because it would repre- sent a major unfair advantage to you over those Canadians who are unable to participate in such plans. This includes people such as wretched ink-stained freelance writers, for example, which means this is one Canada Customs and Revenue Agency ruling with which I have absolutely no problem. . . .

Canada Customs and Revenue Agency limits

Each spring and summer, Canada Customs and Revenue Agency sends all taxpayers a *Notice of Assessment,* which establishes the maximum contribu- tion you are allowed for the current year. So an assessment you received in June 2001 would show the maximum you are able to contribute and deduct from your 2001 income for tax purposes. Remember, you will have until the end of February 2002 to make the contribution and until the end of April 2002 to file your tax return.

The CCRA's Notice of Assessment includes their evaluation of any retirement benefits you earned from being a member of a company pension plan or *deferred profit-sharing plan (DPSP).* This evaluation, and its impact on your RRSP contribution limit, is called your *pension adjustment,* or *PA factor.* Subtracting the PA factor from 18 percent of your taxable income produces the maximum RRSP contribution permitted to you.

The PA factor changes according to the type of pension plan or DPSP your employer provides:

✔ A *defined benefit plan* pays you a retirement income based on your years of service with the company and your income level. Your PA factor with a defined benefit plan is calculated according to the future value of the plan, using your previous year of employment.

✔ A *defined contribution* or *money purchase plan* has no fixed benefit when you retire. You and your employer both contribute to the plan each year, and the amount of income paid to you by the plan when you retire is dependent on the total value of the plan at that time. If you belong to this type of plan, your maximum RRSP contribution will be 18 percent of your earned income less the amount contributed to the plan by both you and your employer.

✔ A *deferred profit-sharing plan* is built up from money placed in the plan by your employer, based on the company's profits for that year. Your PA factor under this plan will equal the total DPSP contribution (up to a maximum limit) made on your behalf. This will be subtracted from 18 percent of your earned income for that year.

Table 2-1 illustrates examples of income levels and contribution limits for four individuals with varying incomes.

Andy had $30,000 earned income in 2001 and belongs to no pension plan.

Allison had $40,000 earned income in 2001 and belongs to a money purchase pension plan. Between them, she and her employer contributed $2,500 to her plan in the same year.

Arthur had $75,000 earned income in 2001 and belongs to a DPSP. His company contributed $5,000 to his DPSP in 2001.

Amanda had $90,000 earned income in 2001 and belongs to no pension plan.

Table 2-1	Maximum RRSP Contributions, 2001–2003		
Name	*Income*	*PA Factor*	*Maximum*
Andy	$30,000	N/A	$5,400
Allison	$40,000	$2,500	$4,700
Arthur	$75,000	$5,000	$8,500
Amanda	$90,000	N/A	$13,500

Calculating Andy's maximum RRSP contribution is easy — 18 percent of $30,000.

Allison's maximum contribution was reached by taking 18 percent of her earned income — $7,200 — and subtracting the total contributions to her money purchase pension plan from that amount, leaving $4,700.

Arthur's RRSP contribution was reached by subtracting the $5,000 earned by his DPSP from 18 percent of his earned income (18 percent of $75,000 = $13,500), for an $8,500 maximum.

Amanda did very well — but 18 percent of her $90,000 earned income exceeds the $13,500 maximum that applies to everyone. Even if Amanda made a million dollars last year, she would be restricted to $13,500.

A little room for going over the limit

Believe it or not, the folks at Canada Customs and Revenue Agency agree that we live in an imperfect world. Mistakes can be made. Rules can be changed. Murphy's Law can still apply. And you and I, or even the CCRA itself, can miscalculate now and then and — horrors! — contribute more money to our RRSP than is allowed under the rules.

That's why Canadians are permitted to contribute up to $2,000 more than allowed in any taxation year. If this occurs, you simply deduct the over-contribution from the amount permitted in the following taxation year.

For example: If your RRSP contribution limit for one year, based on 18 percent of your earned income less any PA factor, is $5,000, you are allowed to contribute up to $7,000 without penalty. If you do so, and your RRSP limit remains at $5,000 for the following year, the $2,000 over-contribution is subtracted from that year's $5,000 contribution limit, reducing it to $3,000. If you think you can deduct the entire $7,000 from your earned income, generating a fatter tax refund, forget it. You cannot deduct more than your limit — in this case, $5,000. You can apply it the following year, however. So, for tax purposes, your $3,000 allowable contribution in 2001 becomes a $5,000 deduction from earned income in that year, because you have carried the over-contribution forward.

What happens if you over-contribute more than the $2,000 limit? Ottawa gets nasty, that's what. You must withdraw the excess funds from your RRSP before you can claim any further contributions to it. And to make its point, the CCRA slaps a penalty of 1 percent per month on over-contributions made beyond the $2,000, until you get it out of your plan.

By the way: No one under 19 years of age is permitted to over-contribute to their RRSP. One more source of adolescent angst. . . .

If you are currently employed and plan to retire in the next few years, you may be eligible to place a *retiring allowance* in your RRSP. A retiring allowance is any money awarded to you by your employer when you leave work permanently for any reason. It includes payments made to you in recognition of your years of service, as well as any unused sick-leave pay; it does not include unused vacation benefits. The formula is a little complex because Ottawa has tinkered with the rules over the years. It works like this:

For each year of service between 1989 and 1995, you are allowed to contribute up to $2,000 to your RRSP beyond your normal contribution limits within 60 days of the end of the year in which you received the retiring allowance (basically, the same time frame used for standard RRSP contributions).

For each year of employment prior to 1989 in which your employer did not make contributions to a pension plan on your behalf, or did not make deposits in a deferred profit-sharing plan, you are permitted an additional $1,500 contribution.

Here is why it will pay to see your accountant before transferring a substantial amount of money from a retiring allowance to your RRSP:

The amount of the retiring allowance transferred to your RRSP does not affect the calculation of your RRSP contributions for that year. But any portion of the allowance transferred to an RRSP and claimed as a deduction must be added back to your taxable income for the purpose of calculating the *alternative minimum tax (AMT),* which has a basic deduction of $40,000. If AMT is payable, it can be recovered up to seven years in the future to the extent, in any year, that your income tax liability is greater than the AMT liability. So you could face some unexpected taxes unless you obtain qualified advice.

Accountants know all about this stuff. Thank goodness.

Years of employment after 1995 do not qualify you for any retirement allowance contributions, and any part of a calendar year is counted as a full year. An example:

Ralph began working for a small-town daily newspaper in October 1963 and retired in March 1991. The newspaper maintained no formal pension plan but awarded lump-sum payments and credited sick leave not taken during employment. Ralph's 28 years of employment thus qualified him to contribute 28 (total years of employment) × $2,000 + 26 (years of employment without a pension plan prior to 1989) × $1,500 = $95,000. This amount, shown on Ralph's last T4 slip, will be offset by a standard RRSP contribution receipt.

A second chance to contribute

The most common problem people encounter, especially in the early years of their career, is not contributing too much to their RRSP but rather contributing too little. Fortunately, Canada Customs and Revenue Agency provides a break by permitting you to catch up with bigger contributions later. If your contribution limit for this year is $7,500 and you can only afford to contribute $5,000, the $2,500 difference isn't lost; it's *carried forward* indefinitely in something called *unused deduction room*. Next year, or at any year in the future, you can add the amount in your unused deduction room — sounds like a storage area in a mathematics warehouse, doesn't it? — to your deduction limit and increase your contribution. So if next year's contribution limit remains at $5,000, you are eligible to carry forward the $2,500 from the previous year, contribute $7,500, and deduct the full amount from your taxable income.

Wherever possible, however, it's best to maximize and start enjoying the benefits of tax-free compound interest growth from the earliest possible date.

Is it possible to justify contributing less than the maximum RRSP contribution, even when you can afford it? Perhaps. For example, you could use part of the money set aside for your RRSP to pay down a high-interest credit card balance instead. Some credit cards carry an 18-percent interest rate, and it's difficult to obtain that kind of growth from investments these days. You can always catch up in the future, using your unused deduction room.

But if you do, you are losing both the tax-deduction benefits of an RRSP and delaying the tax-free compound-interest growth. Here's an even bigger concern: Governments, you may have noticed, have a habit of changing rules that benefit taxpayers. Nowhere is it written that the carry-forward option for RRSPs will remain part of the RRSP program forever. If the federal government chooses to eliminate this rule sometime in the future, those delayed contributions will be gone and you will have no chance to catch up. Ever.

So, as Janis Joplin used to advise (in a slightly different context): Get it while you can!

The Foreign-Content Factor

In the past, one of the most vexing RRSP rules was the one that restricted the portion of your RRSP that you are permitted to invest outside Canada, in foreign bonds or in shares of foreign companies. Until 2000, the limit of foreign content in an RRSP was 20 percent, ridiculously low. This has now been raised to a more realistic 30 percent of the *book value* — the original cost of your investment — in foreign stocks, bonds, and mutual funds.

Some people believe this is still too low, and they have a point. After all, the best way to maximize long-term growth — and let's consider "long-term" to mean five years or more — is through investments in equities or shares in companies. History has proven that equity investments, over the long haul, provide the biggest returns. True, the stock market has its ups and downs, as you no doubt are aware. But the general trend is always up, and the longer you hold quality investments in equities, the higher their value can be expected to rise.

The problem faced by RRSP owners is that Canada represents barely 3 percent of the world's total value of traded stocks. What's more, stock markets in many countries have risen faster and higher than our own in the past decade. So every dollar invested outside Canada has a better chance of being worth much more, and much sooner, than a dollar invested in Canadian stock markets.

Another problem for RRSP investors is the nature of the Canadian economy. While Canada is an industrialized nation, a good deal of our industry is linked directly to resources — mining, lumber, petroleum, and similar activities. Resources are the raw material of other industries. When the economy begins to move, resources are in demand and their prices rise. As the economy flattens out, the demand for resources drops along with prices (and profits for the resource-based companies). All of this puts resource investments on a perpetual roller-coaster ride, making investment a more risky and stomach-churning exercise in Canada than elsewhere.

Some Canadians believe Ottawa should remove all limits from foreign investment in RRSPs. This may be good in theory, but not necessarily good in practice, especially as you approach retirement age. Here's why:

Foreign investment exposes you to both more opportunities and additional risk. The additional risk, in this case, is foreign exchange rates. Any change in the value of the Canadian dollar affects the value of your foreign investment, which rides the opposite end of an unpredictable teeter-totter. When the value of the loonie drops against the currency of another country, all your investments in that country are suddenly worth more in Canadian dollars. If the loonie rises, the value of your investment drops in proportion.

Currency changes are neither good nor bad news. They're simply unpredictable. If you invested every penny of your RRSP in U.S. assets, for example, and the loonie rises 5 percent against the Yankee green-back (hey, it could happen), your original investment drops by an equal amount.

So a 30-percent foreign-content limit is closing in on reasonable. Perhaps 50 percent would be ideal. No matter what limit is in place, however, you can still put 100 percent of your RRSP into foreign investments, if you wish to. Although it's legal, it's also pretty expensive. And, it may not be so wise, either. You'll see why in Chapter 14.

Monthly Contributions versus Lump-Sum Payments

The first wise decision you can make in providing yourself with future financial security is to open an RRSP, if you haven't already. The second wise decision you can make is to arrange regular contributions each month throughout the year instead of waiting to make a lump-sum contribution at the last minute — like, ten minutes to midnight on February 28.

What makes this such a wise decision?

First, monthly contributions become almost painless. It's much easier to adjust your budget to 12 relatively small amounts over a full year than absorb a major *whack!* each February.

Next, regular contributions give you an opportunity to ponder where and how to invest your RRSP contributions. Last-minute decisions tend to be second-rate decisions, and if you don't make up your mind where to invest your money until the late-February last-minute rush each year, the growth of your RRSP is sure to suffer.

Finally, monthly contributions enable you to benefit from *dollar-cost averaging*, a neat trick discussed in detail in Chapter 14.

If you must make a last-minute lump-sum contribution, by all means do so. But try to adapt to regular monthly contributions if possible.

Deductions at source

If your employer automatically deducts income tax from each paycheque, your deductions are made "at source." This is also an easy and more convenient way to make regular contributions to your RRSP throughout the year. While you won't enjoy the delicious thrill of receiving a fat tax refund each spring, unless you make a lump-sum supplementary contribution (assuming you have room in your RRSP limits) your net pay will be increased. That's because your employer will be authorized to lower your income-tax deductions to reflect your RRSP contributions.

It is up to you, not your employer or Canada Customs and Revenue Agency, to take the initiative to have your employer reduce your income tax with each paycheque, reflecting your monthly RRSP contributions. Write to the source deductions division of your district taxation office (your employer can provide the address) and ask the CCRA to authorize the lower tax level. Include details such as the full address of your employer and a copy of a receipt confirming your RRSP contributions issued by the bank, trust company, credit union, mutual fund, or other holder of your RRSP assets. Be sure to mention other sources of earned income if you have any.

When the CCRA is satisfied that your request qualifies, they will authorize your employer to reduce the income tax withheld from your paycheque each month, boosting your take-home pay.

If you belong to a Group RRSP administered by your employer, the income tax payments withdrawn from your salary already reflect your RRSP contributions, so there is no need to alert the CCRA.

Borrowing to save

The idea of borrowing money in order to save it doesn't make sense unless you save it in an RRSP. If borrowing is the only way to max out your RRSP contribution for the year, it becomes a very attractive move, *provided you pay back the loan in a year's time*. You are no longer allowed to deduct the interest on money you borrow to make an RRSP contribution. (Until 1981, you were. See what I mean about the Feds changing the rules now and then?) But borrowing the money to make your RRSP contribution is a much wiser move than making no RRSP contribution at all. And if you have put off making a contribution until the RRSP deadline, it makes even more sense.

Let's suppose it's mid-February and you want to contribute $5,000 to your RRSP before the February 28 deadline arrives. If you are in a 40-percent marginal tax bracket, the $5,000 deduction will earn you a $2,000 tax refund when you file your return in April. Hey, don't pass it up! So what do you do? You visit a local bank, trust company, or credit union, and tell them you want to borrow $5,000, which you will invest in an RRSP with their organization. You want to spread payments over 12 months, you expect to receive a favourable interest rate, and you would be especially pleased if they would delay the due date of the first payment by three months. If you are a local resident, steadily employed, and have a credit rating at least as good as your dog's, the financial institution will agree to these terms. If they don't, walk out the door and visit another bank/trust company/credit union where you ask for the same terms. You'll get them.

When the paperwork for the $5,000 is finished, assign it to an RRSP with the same people who loaned you the money. They will issue a receipt entitling you to deduct the entire $5,000 from your tax return. (You may have to wait two weeks or more for the receipt to arrive.) Based on your 40-percent marginal tax rate, this will generate a $2,000 refund from Canada Customs and Revenue Agency — which, if your timing is good, arrives in the mail around the same time your first loan payment is due. Apply the entire amount to the loan balance, and you now have $5,000 in your RRSP and owe just $3,000 to the bank.

There's more. You'll be paying interest on the balance, and the annual interest percentage will likely be more than your RRSP earns over the year. But *you are paying interest on a declining balance for your loan*; each monthly payment reduces both the amount you owe and the interest you pay. Meanwhile, *the $5,000 in your RRSP is earning interest on a rising value*. After six months, for example, the balance of your loan could be just $1,500 (assuming that you applied your tax refund to the original amount) and the value of your RRSP could be $5,125. In another six months your loan will have vanished. But the $5,125 in your RRSP is like that pink bunny with the drum. It keeps growing and growing and growing. . . .

Will two people, contributing exactly the same amount of money to their RRSP and investing it exactly the same way, have identical RRSP values? Not necessarily.

If you make a lump-sum payment at the end of the year in December, and your twin sister contributes the same amount 12 months earlier in January, you both qualify for the deduction in the same year. But your sister's 12-month head start means her RRSP will grow faster as time goes by. How much faster?

Assuming that you each contribute $1,000 annually and earn interest at 10 percent, at the end of five years your RRSP is worth $6,105 and your sister's will have a balance of $6,715. After ten years, your sister has $17,531 in her RRSP while you have just $15,937. And if you both maintain the same contribution level and earn the same annual interest, after 30 years your sister's RRSP will have a value of $180,943 compared with your $164,494. The difference? The 12-month head start she took each year. And that $15,000 advantage could generate enough retirement income for your sister to enjoy a few weeks in Florida each winter, leaving you back in Canada to shovel snow and read her gloating postcards.

RESPs

A recent Canada Customs and Revenue Agency wrinkle provides another source of RRSP contributions to some people under certain circumstances. It concerns *Registered Education Savings Plans* (RESPs), created to help parents and grandparents save for a child's education. RESPs have been around for a few years, but a change in the rules now benefits RRSP holders.

Previously, if funds in an RESP were not used by the designated child for post-secondary educational purposes, the contributor to the plan could recover only the money invested in it; all other funds went to the government. As of 1999, if the RESP beneficiary chooses not to obtain a post-secondary education, contributors can roll the entire value of the plan, up to $50,000, into their RRSP or a spouse's RRSP, provided the plan is at least ten years old and sufficient contribution room exists in the designated RRSP.

Catching up big-time

Some banks offer RRSP loans that enable you to catch up on the unused contribution room you may have created over the years. You can actually get your hands on as much as $50,000 for this purpose, although $15,000 to $20,000 is more realistic. What's more, you can take up to 15 years to repay the loan. Is this a good idea?

It depends. If you are in a 40-percent tax bracket, a $15,000 catch-up contribution — making up for several years when you failed to make the maximum contribution permitted each year — will produce a $6,000 tax refund. If you apply this to the loan and reduce the balance to $9,000, if the bank or trust company agrees to charge interest at *prime rate* (say around 7 percent), and if you stretch the payments over 15 years, your monthly payments are a tolerable $173. Meanwhile, your RRSP balance is immediately $15,000 fatter and grows free of tax.

Sounds good. But remember that you'll be paying back $1,876 in loan interest over the years, which is $1,876 unavailable for future RRSP contributions. Remember too that a bank's prime rate can fluctuate. Any significant rise in interest rates will boot your monthly payments higher, which could put a strain on your cash flow.

The bottom line? Weigh your options, measure your confidence level about future earnings, and be sure to shop around. RRSP loans to people with good credit ratings are considered very low risk, so you have a right to demand the lowest available interest rate.

Claiming Your Deduction

Making an RRSP deduction makes you feel good twice. First you feel good soon, when you receive your tax-refund cheque from Canada Customs and Revenue Agency. Then you feel good later, when your RRSP contributions have grown over the years into a healthy nest egg.

But believe it or not, there is a way to feel even better about your refund. Here's how it works:

The CCRA does not insist that you submit your RRSP contribution receipt, qualifying you for lower taxes, in the same tax year in which you made it. You can, if you wish, tuck the receipt into your sock drawer and leave it there for a few years. Why in the name of the Minister of Finance would you want to do this? Because it could earn you a bigger deduction later.

Suppose your earned income was $30,000 this year, and you made a $2,000 contribution to your RRSP. That income level puts you in the 28-percent tax bracket, so the $2,000 contribution produces a $520 tax refund ($2,000 × 28 percent). But you're confident that your income will rise to $40,000 over the next year or two, placing you in the 40-percent tax bracket. Now the $2,000 contribution produces an $800 tax refund ($2,000 × 40 percent), or $280 more. That's not a bad deal.

People who take time from work to enjoy a sabbatical or to have children can also benefit from delaying their deduction. While taking time off and earning little if any income, there is limited benefit in filing a deduction. But back at work again, when the income level jumps, the RRSP receipt pays off with a bigger deduction.

Both of these situations — a potentially much larger annual income in a year or two, and a return to full employment — can justify a delay in claiming your RRSP deduction.

Is there a downside? There is always a downside in life. Instead of waiting, you could claim your deduction now and use an immediate tax refund to pay down high-interest credit card balances — always a smart move — or invest the money outside your RRSP. There is also the danger of falling prey to the dreaded "Close the loophole!" cry from Ottawa, which means they yank back something they awarded you in the past before you have had a chance to enjoy it — in this case, the opportunity to claim delayed deductions.

Chapter 3

What to Expect from Your RRSP

● ●

In This Chapter

▶ Calculating growth over the years

▶ Dealing with inflation

▶ Determining how much you should accumulate

▶ Finding out what's attractive about spousal RRSPs

▶ Using your RRSP as collateral

▶ Knowing what happens to your RRSP if you should die

● ●

Contributing as much as you can afford to your RRSP year after year is one heck of a good idea, as you have probably figured out if you have read this far. But growing your RRSP isn't like raising mushrooms in your basement; you can't just toss a shovel or two of goodies at it from time to time and assume it'll take care of itself.

Making regular contributions is only the first part of your plan. The second part is finding ways to maximize the growth of your investment, year after year. This is the part that makes many Canadians nervous or confused, and perhaps a bit of both. Unless you already have some investment experience, the very mention of terms such as *diversification*, *debt instruments*, *asset allocation*, and *equities* can make your eyes glaze over.

The responsibility of making decisions about their RRSP frightens some people. Mention mutual funds or stock markets to many Canadians, and they picture a giant neon sign flashing "Risk! Risk! Risk!" in red letters. Too bad they can't see the other side of that sign. It glows in a rich, gold colour and spells out "Reward! Reward! Reward!"

Don't be intimidated by the fear of risk. You can't avoid it entirely. But you can manage it to your benefit. How? First, by learning some basic rules. The investment options you face are not all that complex, and the principles are easy to grasp by anyone who can read a bank statement. Second, by understanding the rudiments of basic investing. Using this knowledge to make wise decisions can make an astonishing difference to the value of your RRSP. Third, by realizing that taking charge of your investments can be both satisfying and fun. You can take comfort in the rewards of making good decisions, and gain experience when your decisions don't pay off quite as well as you hoped.

Actively managing your RRSP by applying basic investment principles, supported by qualified professional assistance, will produce results far richer in the long term than an RRSP that consists entirely of cash savings, guaranteed investment certificates (GICs), and guaranteed bonds. Count on it.

Growth Expectations

When RRSP owners realize the impact of long-term growth, they become enthusiastic about taking charge of their investments, seeking an extra 2- or 3-percent advantage each year. Perhaps a 2-percent improvement doesn't sound all that impressive to a baseball player's batting average. But over the long term, an RRSP that earns 12 percent annually instead of 10 percent can make the difference between a "getting by" retirement and a near-luxurious lifestyle.

How much difference can your RRSP decisions make to the amount of money you have when you retire? Check out Table 3-1.

Table 3-1	Impact of RRSP Investment Decisions		
	Original Investment: $5,000		
Investment	Percentage Growth	10 Years	30 Years
Canada Savings Bonds (CSBs)	6.5%	$9,385.69	$33,071.83
Canadian mutual funds	8.8%	$11,621.41	$62,782.25
International mutual funds	11.0%	$14,197.10	$114,461.48

If you had invested your RRSP in eligible Canada Savings Bonds in 1991, your RRSP would have produced growth of 6.5 percent each year since then. Not bad? Consider this: Money invested in an average Canadian equity-based mutual fund would have returned growth of 8.8 percent each year, a 2.3-percent annual improvement. And the same amount of money invested in an average international equity-based mutual fund would have awarded you a whopping 11.0-percent average annual return.

A $5,000 investment growing at 6.5-percent annual compound interest would grow to $9,385.69 over the ten years from 1991 to 2001. The same amount of money growing at 8.8 percent annually over the same ten-year period would be worth $11,621.41.

And if you could earn 11 percent from your $5,000, you would have $14,197.10. The difference over 30 years is even more impressive.

So don't consider a 2- or 3-percent improvement in your RRSP growth insignificant. Over the long term, that kind of advantage can be a gold mine.

The Spectre of Inflation

Back in the days of the voyageur fur traders, North American native tribes believed an evil spirit prowled the northern woods. On the coldest, darkest nights of the year, the spirit would emerge from the forest and devour all the food gathered by the tribe to sustain them through the winter. If it were famished enough, the spirit would begin consuming the people themselves. Only when the beast was satisfied did it return to its hiding place. The tribes would take a long time to recover, and they would never forget the evil spirit, lurking somewhere in the darkness, ready to creep back into the village at any time.

Economists and investors fear a similar legendary beast, called inflation. From time to time the inflation beast arrives, and the devastation is massive. Its last appearance was in the early 1980s, when interest rates shot beyond the 20-percent level, leading to business failures, mortgage foreclosures, and financial disaster for anyone living on a fixed income. Inflation leads to higher prices for goods and services, which triggers demands for higher wages and salaries, which produces higher prices . . . and the merry-go-round keeps spinning.

Large-scale inflation is created by a number of factors that are fascinating to economists and as interesting as a pile of bricks to the rest of us. Fortunately, the 1990s saw relatively low rates of inflation, averaging 2 percent per year. The world economy may be able to sustain these low rates indefinitely. Let's hope so.

But inflation is always around in small amounts, and even low levels can affect your long-term RRSP goals. Just as the 2-percent difference is a long-term shot in the arm to the growth of your RRSP, a steady 2-percent rate of inflation means you'll need substantially more money in the future to enjoy the same degree of comfort you experience today.

An inflation benchmark

It's difficult to measure the impact of inflation because so many products we buy have changed over the years. How, for example, do you accurately judge the price of a new car in 1977 versus a new car in 2002? The standard features and gadgets on today's cars were unheard of a quarter-century ago.

So think of postage stamps. In 1977, it cost 8 cents to mail a first-class stamp in Canada. Today it costs 47 cents to mail the same letter. (The letter probably arrived sooner in 1977 too, but that's another story. . . .)

Suppose that you plan to stop working in 20 years, and you estimate that a retirement income of $40,000 a year should do just fine. Sounds good. But you're measuring that income with *today's* dollar value. Over time, inflation lowers the value of every dollar you earn or accumulate each year. If inflation averages 3 percent annually over the next 20 years, the lifestyle you can enjoy today with a $40,000 annual income will cost you $72,244 a year when you retire. If inflation jumps to an average of 5 percent annually between now and then, you'll need $106,132 to enjoy a life that costs $40,000 today (see Table 3-2). By the way, historically our economy has suffered from an average 5-percent annual inflation rate.

Table 3-2	Income Growth to Match Inflation			
	Amount Needed to Match $40,000 Income Today			
Inflation Rate	*5 Years*	*10 Years*	*15 Years*	*20 Years*
3%	$46,371	$53,757	$62,319	$72,244
4%	$48,666	$59,210	$72,038	$87,645
5%	$51,051	$65,156	$83,157	$106,132

Don't fret — inflation also brings a few investment advantages with it. But the long-term impact of even relatively low levels of inflation should alert you to two rules of life, retirement, and the whole darn thing:

- Maximize the contribution level and growth of your RRSP.

- Actively manage your RRSP so you can respond to unforeseen events and opportunities.

How Much Will You Need?

Of all the questions asked by RRSP investors, this is perhaps the most difficult to answer. Why? Because it involves so many variables, including

- ✔ **Your lifespan.** How long do you expect to live after retirement? (Note: "As long as possible" doesn't count.)

- ✔ **Your age when you will retire.** Will you be 55? 60? 65? Older?

- ✔ **Your retirement lifestyle.** Will you read and garden? Travel often as globetrotters? Remain in your own home, or sell it and move to smaller, less expensive quarters? Do you plan to work part-time?

- ✔ **Your financial situation.** Will your home be mortgage-free, or will you still be making those pesky payments? Will you be facing substantial balances on high-interest credit cards?

The answers to these questions are yours to determine. There is no "one size fits all" secret to estimating the retirement income you'll need. All you can do is accept some basic assumptions and proceed from there, making adjustments as you go along.

Let's begin by dealing with a few guidelines that most economists and financial advisers agree upon.

- ✔ **Expect that you will need only 70 percent of your current income to sustain the lifestyle you enjoy today.** Some advisers say 80 percent, and others suggest as low as 40 percent, depending on the lifestyle you choose. Remember, you'll be spending less on job-related expenses such as clothing, commuting, and lunches. A paid-up mortgage and grown children will cut your living costs even further. So 70 percent of what you currently earn makes a reasonable figure for a comfortable retirement.

- ✔ **Assume at least some income from government sources.** Current maximum C/QPP benefits for those retiring at 65 are about $10,000 annually. Start drawing benefits at age 60 and it drops to around $7,000 a year; delay retirement to age 70 and it rises to the $13,000 level.

- ✔ **Plan on living to the ripe old age of 90.** A few generations ago, this was a rare life expectancy for average Canadians. But given better medical care and the awareness of maintaining a healthier lifestyle — no smoking, regular exercise, annual check-ups, and improved diet — it's not such an outrageous goal. If you retire at age 55, this means 35 years of retirement ahead of you, which may be longer than your entire working career.

✔ **Assume a conservative return on your RRSP balance after retirement of 8 percent annually and an average annual inflation rate of 5 percent.** This will generate an average 3 percent in annual growth after inflation. Now estimate the retirement income you'll need — let's say $40,000 per year, plus any government benefits listed above — and multiply by 25.

Hang on, because the answer is $1 million. But depending on your age and your determination, this is not quite as unreachable as you may think. If your current age is 25 and you are able to generate a conservative 8-percent growth from your RRSP, it takes an annual contribution of $3,860 to reach that magic million at age 65. Earn 12 percent each year from your RRSP — not an unreasonable level over the very long term — and you need only $1,300 each year in your plan.

If you're currently 35 years old, you'll need to sock away $8,830 each year earning 8-percent annual growth, or $4,140 each year if you can obtain 12-percent annual growth, to reach a million dollars at age 65. If you hold off until age 45 to launch your RRSP program, it will take $21,850 (at 8 percent) or $13,380 each year (at 12 percent) to accumulate a million.

✔ If the prospect of generating a million bucks in today's dollars sounds too daunting, make some adjustments. Do you really want to live in a large urban house when you retire? If your home is mortgage-free, you'll manage to keep virtually every penny of its value when you sell it, which helps to make up any shortfall between your RRSP value and that magic million. Your annual income needs will drop even lower by eliminating all the maintenance costs associated with your house.

✔ If you're married, and either you or your spouse earns substantially more income than the other, you can reduce the retirement income you'll need by cutting your income-tax level through a spousal RRSP, described in the upcoming section, Spousal RRSPs and Income Splitting.

To calculate the amount you need to sock away to reach a million dollars, see Chapter 26.

Paying Attention

If the biggest RRSP mistake made by most Canadians is failing to maximize their contribution each year, the second biggest mistake is not paying attention to the health of their investment. Like any growing thing, from carrots to kids, RRSPs thrive with attention, guidance, and general TLC. And who benefits? You do, with a larger nest egg to generate more retirement income.

Don't make the mistake of assuming your RRSP task ends with your annual contribution, or that your tax-refund cheque is the biggest benefit you enjoy. Paying attention to the growth of your RRSP, with a review every six months, can make an immense difference over the years. And you don't need a financial guru standing at your elbow, either. All it takes is a basic understanding of a few rules, a strategy you can follow, and a little advice now and then from a qualified adviser.

Spousal RRSPs and Income Splitting

If you are married or in a common-law relationship, it pays to understand spousal RRSPs and their benefits. Canada Customs and Revenue Agency provides few breaks for married couples, but one pops up in the RRSP rules. It provides the option of contributing to a *spousal RRSP*, which doesn't generate benefits today but delivers major reductions in income tax down the road.

A spousal RRSP permits you to place your RRSP contribution into a plan belonging to your partner. This cannot be used to increase your qualifying RRSP contribution limit; if your limit is $5,000 and you place it all in an RRSP belonging to your spouse, there is none left over for your own plan in that year. So why bother? Because a spousal RRSP favours couples in which one spouse earns significantly more income than the other. If the high-income spouse contributes only to his or her RRSP, it will produce substantially more income when retirement day arrives *and* attract substantially more tax to be paid. Here's an example:

Jeff and Jean are the same age and have been married for 12 years. Jeff is a sales executive, and Jean is an artist. Each year, Jeff makes his maximum contribution to his RRSP — about $15,000 on average. Jeff and Jean feel this substantial investment is all they will need to build a hefty RRSP balance when they retire at age 55, and they are correct. If the plan is wisely invested and grows at a reasonable 10 percent annually, Jeff's RRSP will sport a healthy $900,000 balance by the time he is 55 years of age. They expect the $900,000 to produce 5 percent of its total value annually as retirement income, which means they will be earning — and paying tax on — $45,000 each year. But this entire amount will be earned in Jeff's name, and will be taxed accordingly. Using current income-tax rates, this will mean returning $14,465 to Ottawa every year as income tax, leaving them $30,535 as net income.

But if Jeff divides his annual $15,000 contribution into equal amounts, putting $7,500 in his RRSP and $7,500 into Jean's, they would still have the $900,000 nest egg, divided equally between the two plans, with each plan valued at

$450,000 (assuming the same 10-percent average annual return for both plans). Instead of one income, the two plans generate separate incomes for each spouse, producing a different tax picture. The two separate incomes still total $45,000, but the total family income is taxed at $22,500 for Jeff and $22,500 for Jean. The lower figure triggers a lower tax rate; each spouse now pays about $6,000 in income tax each year, leaving them with a $33,000 net income — which will be like getting a $2,500 annual gift from the CCRA. Over 20 years, that's $50,000 in income-tax payments Jeff and Jean will avoid.

There's more. Every Canadian with pension income can claim an annual $1,000 pension income tax credit. If both spouses earn income from their own RRSP, the couple can claim $2,000 total instead of $1,000 if only one partner has RRSP income.

Having a spousal RRSP may also help you avoid the Old Age Security (OAS) clawback (see Chapter 4). If your spouse is younger than you, and you expect to have earned income beyond age 69 — the age limit for making RRSP contributions — you can contribute to your spouse's plan and still claim the tax benefit because your individual incomes will be sufficiently low.

The CCRA's definition of a spouse is "a person of the opposite sex to whom the individual is married or with whom the individual has cohabited in a conjugal relationship for a period of at least one year, or less than one year if the two individuals are the natural or adoptive parents of a child." This, however, is currently under review and may change. Check with the CCRA to confirm the definition if you are unsure of your situation.

Here are some things you should know about a spousal RRSP:

✔ One more time: Having a spousal RRSP does not increase the total amount of the contribution you are allowed to make. If your limit is $5,000 and you place $4,000 in a spousal plan, this leaves only $1,000 for your plan.

✔ The money you contribute to your spouse's RRSP belongs to your spouse. But if he or she withdraws the funds from the spousal plan within three years, it is taxed as your income. For this reason alone, it is wise to keep your spouse's RRSP separate from his or her own plan, if one exists.

✔ If you and your spouse separate, the existence of a spousal plan will have no bearing on the division of assets if you reside in a province with family law provisions. Under these provisions, all shared assets accumulated during the relationship are divided equally — including both personal and spousal RRSPs.

✔ Income splitting to reduce taxes on your retirement income is a key benefit of a spousal RRSP. How big is the benefit? It depends on these factors:

- What will be the taxable income and income-tax rate of the contributing spouse after retirement? (If it is less than that of the owner of the spousal plan, there is no benefit to be gained; you are simply dancing in circles, which may seem like fun but doesn't get you anywhere.)

- What will be the annual income generated from the spousal RRSP?

- How stable is the marriage?

Pledging Your RRSP as Collateral

The value of your RRSP represents an important asset to you, one that you can expect to grow substantially with time. Banks, trust companies, credit unions, caisses populaires, and other organizations love folks with assets. In fact, people with money to lend favour people with assets so much that they charge them a lower interest rate on borrowed money, as long as the loan is backed with *pledged assets,* or *collateral*.

So. Can you pledge some or all of your RRSP as collateral for a loan and qualify for lower interest rates? And if you can — should you?

Canada Customs and Revenue Agency says you can pledge some or all of your RRSP as collateral for a loan, but they do not encourage you to do it. If you pledge any or all of your RRSP assets as collateral, the fair market value of those assets held in your RRSP will be added to your taxable income for the year. If you assign $10,000 of your RRSP's value to a bank as collateral for a loan, the CCRA acts as though you had withdrawn the same amount (or fair market value) in cash, and taxes you accordingly. When the loan is paid off and you no longer need the assets as collateral, you can deduct the amount previously included in your income minus any losses suffered over the term of the loan.

It's all very complex and fraught with danger — too much, in fact, to justify unless the reduced interest rate earned by using your RRSP is substantial. Besides, most financial institutions will not accept RRSP assets as collateral. They do, however, consider anyone with a good-sized RRSP balance to be a better-than-average credit risk, and adjust the interest rate charged on the loan downward to reflect this.

Here's one situation where it makes sense to use your RRSP assets as collateral, if you can find a financial institution to go along with it:

Suppose that you find yourself suddenly unemployed for a short time. You may be tempted to withdraw money from your RRSP to cover essentials such as mortgage or rent, food, utilities, and so on. Unfortunately, once the funds are out of your RRSP, they cannot be put back in again when you find a new job. But if you borrow enough money to carry you over and pledge a portion of your RRSP as collateral, you can begin paying the loan back when you are employed again. When the loan is repaid, the pledge of your RRSP as collateral is lifted, you claim the deduction and any losses, and you haven't lost a thing.

This is probably the only time when using your RRSP this way makes sense. And only for a very short time.

What Happens in the Event of Your Death

A healthy RRSP means you may have substantial assets to protect in the event of your death. In fact, it is conceivable that your estate could actually pay more income tax to Canada Customs and Revenue Agency than you paid them during your entire working life. Unless this sounds attractive to you, here are some suggestions to follow:

- ✔ **Name your spouse as beneficiary.** If you should die, all the assets in your retirement savings account are transferred directly to his or her plan. This, by the way, is another reason to ensure that both you and your spouse maintain an RRSP. Do not name your estate as the beneficiary, assuming that your spouse will inherit it anyway. If you do, the CCRA will treat your RRSP as though you had cashed in your plan on the day you died (the CCRA's term for this is *deemed disposition*), making it fully taxable.

- ✔ **If you have minor dependant or infirm children or grandchildren, leave it to them.** A minor dependant is someone under the age of 18 with an income under $7,000 annually who is financially dependent on you. Minor dependants can, upon turning 18, convert the RRSP inherited from you into an *annuity,* paying them a fixed income for an extended period of time — the rest of their lives, if they choose it. The annuity funds, of course, are taxable. A child suffering from a physical or mental infirmity can choose to transfer the RRSP to his or her own plan, or purchase his or her own annuity to generate income.

> ✔ **If you have other descendants whom you wish to receive an inheritance, leave them assets that won't receive such a massive tax swat.** Leave life insurance proceeds or money market investments. Cash is always nice too. . . .
>
> ✔ **It goes without saying that you need a will.** Just be certain that the will protects your assets from heaviest taxation.

A word of advice: These taxation questions can become very complex and, if handled incorrectly, trigger substantial taxes. Executors of estates with these provisions in the will should obtain professional advice before approving any transfers or withdrawals of assets.

Leaving the Country

What happens to your RRSP and all those tasty tax benefits if you leave Canada for employment in another country, such as the United States? It depends on where you go, and whether the move is considered temporary or permanent.

If you leave the country to accept temporary employment in the U.S., you can continue to make RRSP contributions as long as you are still considered a Canadian resident under the Canada/U.S.A. tax treaty. Your employer or a tax accountant can provide the necessary documentation. If you commit to full residency and employment in the U.S., and you pay income tax there, you can no longer make contributions to your plan. Nor, by the way, can you transfer its assets to an Individual Retirement Account (IRA), roughly the U.S. equivalent to an RRSP. You can, however, continue to maintain your RRSP in your absence, and its value will continue to grow free of Canadian tax. To escape U.S. tax on the growth of your RRSP assets, you need a special tax form obtainable from a qualified tax accountant.

What about cashing in your RRSP while living in the U.S.? Only if you're a glutton for tax punishment. First, Canada Customs and Revenue Agency will slap a 25-percent withholding tax on the proceeds. Then Uncle Sam will tax you on all the value your RRSP earned between the day you left Canada and the day you closed your RRSP. You may even be subject to U.S. income tax as well.

Chapter 4

Fitting an RRSP into Your Financial Future

· ·

In This Chapter

▶ Counting (or not) on other sources of income

▶ Making room for C/QPP, OAS, and other assets

▶ Using your RRSP as a financial foundation

· ·

*O*ne adjustment you will need to make when considering your retirement needs is getting accustomed to having several sources of income instead of one big salary cheque. Each source comes with its own rules and limitations, and almost no one will have the same recipe of ingredients in the same proportion as another.

Canada/Quebec Pension Plan

Every working Canadian is required to contribute to the C/QPP (Canada/Quebec Pension Plan). If you work for an organization, both you and your employer make C/QPP contributions from every paycheque you receive. If you are self-employed, you pay both the employer and employee portion. In return, you expect to receive a monthly benefit beginning as early as age 60 and continuing for the rest of your life. The current C/QPP monthly payment at age 65 is $775, providing an annual income of $9,300. Start at an earlier age, and the benefit declines by ½ percent for every month before you reach 65. Defer the C/QPP payments and they rise by ½ percent monthly to age 70.

C/QPP payments are indexed for inflation, and are adjusted each January to a maximum increase of 2 percent annually. With current inflation rates expected to remain very low, this works. But if inflation rises above the 2-percent level, Q/CPP benefits will begin falling behind the cost-of-living growth. Either way, don't expect benefits to increase substantially in the near future.

Should you start receiving C/QPP payments earlier rather than later? Most advisers reply with an emphatic yes. Start at age 60 and you will obtain 70 percent of the standard age 65 benefit (5 years = 60 months × ½ percent = 30 percent, leaving 70 percent of the full benefit). If you delay the benefit until age 65, even though you receive more money each month, it will take about 10 years to catch up in total benefits with someone who started collecting benefits at age 60.

If you claim C/QPP while still earning an income, any benefits paid that exceed your income in the first year must be returned. But "first year" is the calendar year, not a full 12-month period. So if you have other income, apply for your first C/QPP benefit to be paid in November or December. Those will be reclaimed by Ottawa, but beginning in January it's all yours to keep.

The biggest concern of most working Canadians is not how much they will receive from C/QPP, but for how long. The problem lies with the plan design. Instead of building a massive nest egg set aside for future use — the way you build your own RRSP, for example — the C/QPP is basically supported by current workers, using the cash flow generated by their paycheque deductions. Instead of "sock it away for a rainy day," the C/QPP operates on a "pay as you go" basis.

Back in the mid-1960s, when the Canada/Quebec Pension Plan was launched with great fanfare, this was a reasonable idea because there were seven contributing workers for every retired Canadian. Today, there are only five of us working folk for everyone collecting C/QPP benefits, and by the year 2030 there may be only three working Canadians for each retired person. That means a bigger crowd of people taking money out of a smaller pot, and that is why some experts predict the plan will be bankrupt by 2015.

Along with monthly payments, the C/QPP also includes disability, survivor, and children's benefits. These have caused their own problems. Disability benefit payments, for example, were four times larger in 1994 than they were in 1985.

What's the solution? No one is sure. It may mean ever-larger employee/ employer contributions to the plan. It could lead to a means test — if you don't need the benefits, you don't receive them — or a rollback in eligibility age from 65 to 70.

C/QPP benefits will no doubt continue, and those who made contributions through their working lives will probably receive some return. The question is this: How much, and for how long?

It's up to you not only to choose when you begin receiving C/QPP benefits, but also to launch the whole process. Don't expect the benefit cheques to show up in your mailbox on your 65th birthday. Inform Health Canada (in Quebec, it's the Quebec Pension Plan) of the date on which you want to start drawing your benefits. Allow substantial time for the wheels to start turning — at least two months and probably closer to six months will be needed.

Old Age Security

Don't you hate that description? You probably won't be impressed by the benefits either.

Old Age Security (OAS) benefits were designed to generate only a subsistence level of income, and at $413.06 per month (the average benefit in December 2000), it won't have you gorging yourself on champagne and caviar. Everyone is automatically eligible for OAS payments at age 65. That's the good news. The bad news is that if you worked hard, invested wisely, and your annual retirement income reaches $55,309, you encounter the dreaded OAS claw-back, a voracious beast that starts consuming 15 cents out of every dollar earned above that figure. If your annual retirement income reaches the magic amount of $89,948, there's not a penny of the OAS benefit remaining.

Fortunately, two spouses can avoid the clawback through careful planning. Since the figure is applicable to individual and not family income, each partner in a marriage or common-law relationship can earn up to the $55,309 level and continue to receive the OAS benefit. The best way to ensure this is through spousal RRSPs, with each spouse generating an equal income from separate sources. Thus, you and your spouse could share a total retirement income of $110,618 before the clawback strikes.

These figures are effective as of June 2001 and are adjusted for inflation each January.

Company Pension Plans

Your parents probably counted on a pension plan from their employer to produce virtually all of their retirement income. You probably don't. In some regions of Canada, and some types of companies, pension plans are becoming as rare as Atlantic cod, for a number of reasons, including the following:

✔ **They're too expensive for employers.** This is especially true for defined benefit plans, which promise to pay a lifetime income based on your years of service.

✔ **Other alternatives exist.** These include Group RRSPs and deferred profit-sharing plans (DPSPs). They require no locked-in long-term commitment by employers, which helps the company's shareholders sleep better at night.

✔ **Pensions were designed for long-term, even lifetime, workers.** These days we may be employed by several different companies during our working years, so pensions become less important to both employers and employees.

If you changed employers several times during your working career, think back to the companies for whom you worked. If any had pension agreements, you may be fully *vested* — that is, entitled to receive full benefits from the plan, based on your years of service, when you reach age 65. Becoming vested doesn't take as long as you may think. Federal public-service employees, and private-sector employees in Ontario, Nova Scotia, Prince Edward Island, Quebec, and Saskatchewan, are now fully vested after just two years of full-time employment. In Alberta, British Columbia, Manitoba, and New Brunswick, it takes five years. In Newfoundland, you need ten years.

If you change employers, your pension may be based on a *locked-in RRSP*, which means that, unlike a regular RRSP, the funds cannot be withdrawn before retirement age; then they are transferred to a *Life Income Fund* or LIF. Many provinces add yet another alternative called a *Locked-in Retirement Income Fund*, or L-RIF. Both provide regular payments based on the value of the investment when you retire. For details on LIF and L-RIF rules, see Chapter 23.

LIFs and L-RIFs are not the product of federal thinking. They are the result of tinkering by the provinces creating their own pension legislation.

Personal Savings

With all the other demands on your budget, can you still set aside money in a savings account and expect it to provide money for your retirement?

That's up to you, your income, and your lifestyle. Certainly it pays to have cash available for unexpected emergencies. Some financial experts recommend putting two months' salary in a savings account just to carry you through various crises. Some of these experts don't have a mortgage, three kids, and car payments to meet, of course.

Who can knock the idea of socking away money for a rainy day? But before you start socking, take these steps:

✔ **Maximize your RRSP contributions.** You've heard it before on these pages, but it still makes sense. Saving your money in this fashion generates tax benefits that are unavailable to Canadians in any other way.

✔ **Pay down or eliminate credit-card balances.** A thousand dollars in a savings account these days will earn you perhaps $25 in one year. Whoopee. Maintaining a thousand-dollar debit balance on most credit cards will cost you $180 or more over the same year. Best plan: Pay down your credit-card balance and eliminate the heavy interest charges.

✔ **Make your money earn higher interest.** If you can set aside a chunk of change on a regular basis, make it work harder for you than the 2.5-percent annual interest currently paid in savings accounts. Consider a money market mutual fund or a series of laddered GICs, explained in Chapters 5, 10, and 16.

Real Estate

You can build a retirement nest egg two ways with real estate. One is by using the equity in your principal residence. *Equity* is the difference between the market value of your home and the amount you owe on it. *Principal residence* is basically your home address, or where you live most of the time. If you own a cottage somewhere in addition to your home, it is not your principal residence. This makes a major difference when you sell either or both residences, because the sale of your principal residence is not subject to tax on *capital gains.* Any profit you make on selling your cottage or residence is defined as a capital gain and taxed by Canada Customs and Revenue Agency.

Does a summer cottage represent a logical retirement investment? Not really. Face it — during your working years you'll probably spend 10 percent or less of your time there. Most financial advisers consider cottages not as financial investments but as financial drains, eating chunks of your income. If you earn rental income from your cottage, the CCRA not only taxes the net income, but also places severe limits on any maintenance expenses you try to deduct. And when you finally sell your cottage, the capital gain becomes taxable. You can, however, plan to sell your principal residence and retire to your cottage, avoiding tax on the sale of your home.

If you can afford it, and it fits your lifestyle, by all means enjoy your cottage. But don't assume you're making a major investment toward your retirement.

Many people see the equity in their principal residence as a source of retirement income, and it can be. Danger lurks if you plan to use the equity in your home as your *only* source. Remember the difference between before-tax and after-tax dollars? You contribute to your RRSP with before-tax dollars; you pay off your mortgage with after-tax dollars. Thus, an RRSP will lower the income tax you pay, but mortgage payments will not. Any way you measure it, an RRSP is a far wiser investment than home equity.

Pay down your mortgage faster or maximize your RRSP contributions — which is the better choice? The answer depends on your income level and age, along with the state of the economy. Example: Through most of the 1990s, mortgage rates hovered around 6 or 7 percent while many mutual funds were earning 12 and 15 percent or more each year. Under these conditions, it paid to carry the mortgage and earn twice as much from mutual funds inside an RRSP. Best all-Canadian middle-of-the-road solution: Maximize your RRSP contributions and use your tax refund to make a lump-sum payment on your mortgage, when you can do it without penalty — usually on the mortgage anniversary date.

Reverse Mortgages

In recent years, *reverse mortgages* have become popular among many retired people. On the surface, it sounds like a good idea: After spending years paying your mortgage, your mortgage begins to pay you. Under an agreement with a reverse-mortgage lender, you receive monthly payments based on your age and the equity in your principal residence. Between 10 percent and 40 percent of your equity can be unlocked in this manner. For example, if you have $200,000 worth of equity in your home, as much as $80,000 could be released to you. You continue to live in your home, and the regular payments are a valuable addition to any other sources of income. Upon your death the payments can be made to your surviving spouse. The loan is repaid only when neither spouse is still living. What's more, because the payments are considered a loan, they are not subject to income tax.

Sound good? Hold on a minute, and consider these potential drawbacks:

- ✔ It may be difficult to give up control over the equity in your home after all those years of paying for it.

- ✔ You are still responsible for all the costs associated with owning your own home, including maintenance and taxes.

- ✔ If your home represents a major portion of the inheritance you've planned for your children, there will not be as much left for you to pass on to them.

Reverse-mortgage lenders assume you will live for a very long time, which is very nice of them. But this spreads the equity in your home over many years, reducing the monthly payments substantially.

Reverse mortgages can appeal to people for many reasons. Before you assume they represent the perfect solution to your extra retirement income needs, however, get all the facts and discuss the idea in detail with your spouse, your family, your lawyer, and a trusted financial adviser.

The other way to provide for your retirement with real estate is through buying and selling land and buildings, or making a down payment on a home and using tenant rent to pay off the mortgage.

Real estate is not an easy way to build wealth, and it certainly is no "armchair investment." The real estate market can drop as dramatically as it rises, wiping out your entire initial investment. What's more, by investing in rental property, you become a landlord responsible for collecting rent and solving problems such as backed-up toilets and leaking roofs. Are you sure you want to do that? Give it some careful thought.

A married couple I know who invested in rental income property have regretted it for years. They made little or no money, and dealing with difficult tenants actually affected their health and relationship. Unless you have knowledge, stamina, strength, and perhaps a smidgen of unacknowledged masochism, leave rental investments to other people.

Your RRSP as a Basic Foundation

Any way you measure it, an RRSP provides the best opportunity for long-term personal investment. Other sources remain available, including government programs and private sources. But consider your RRSP as the foundation of your plan to provide future financial security. Maximize your contributions, pay attention to your plan's health, and give your retirement goals some thought from time to time, to put everything in perspective. Start by asking yourself and your spouse these questions. You can modify your answers later, if necessary, but these will provide an important first picture:

- ✔ When would you like to retire? In 5 years? In 20 years?
- ✔ Where will you live? In your current home? In another location?
- ✔ Do you plan to be mortgage-free? Still paying a mortgage? Renting?
- ✔ How do you picture your lifestyle? Relaxed? Pursuing a new career? Travelling a good deal?
- ✔ Will you have a part-time job?
- ✔ How much income will you need, in today's dollars? What percentage of your current income does this represent?

Four steps to a retirement strategy

1. Estimate your retirement income, less RRSP earnings. This is a guesstimate at best, but it gets things started. Your basic retirement income will be a combination of earnings from the Canada/Quebec Pension Plan, Old Age Security, employer pension (including deferred profit sharing plan and Group RRSP), plus income from rental properties, investments, and part-time post-retirement employment. Remember to account for income tax, which you still pay even when retired.

2. Estimate your retirement income needs. Your age and anticipated lifestyle (travel costs money; relaxing on your front porch doesn't) are two important considerations. Others: restaurant meals, wardrobe costs, transportation expenses, house maintenance, and recreation activities will all change upon retirement. Decide by how much.

3. Establish your savings objective. Subtract #2 from #1. The difference represents the shortfall, to be made up by earnings from your RRSP investments.

4. Determine your RRSP investment program. One suggestion: Multiply the shortfall by 20 to obtain the total amount you should have in your RRSP at retirement. If this is unrealistic, you may have to adjust the figures in #2.

Part II

Getting the Most from Your RRSP

In this part . . .

In this part, you discover that it pays to be in charge of your own financial future with a self-directed RRSP. This takes some professional assistance, but help is on the way. You see the value of an investment strategy and how to set one, and encounter the idea of assembling investments inside your RRSP like ingredients in a cake recipe. Some things don't belong in cakes or RRSPs. In this part, you find out which ones are best left out of your retirement nest egg.

Chapter 5

Taking Charge

· ·

In This Chapter

▶ Applying the "balanced diet" theory of investing to your RRSP strategy

▶ Managing a self-directed RRSP

▶ Understanding risk and reward

▶ Accounting for your risk threshold

· ·

*I*f you believe retirement planning begins and ends with making an RRSP contribution, you could be tossing tens of thousands — even hundreds of thousands — of dollars away. That's the difference between a passive RRSP investment strategy and the potential benefits of an informed and active strategy. So don't assume your RRSP contributions will take care of themselves. And don't be concerned that managing your plan will devour great gobs of your valuable time and energy, either. It needn't involve more than an hour or two's review and evaluation every three months or so.

You're Not Buying Underwear

Don't choose investments for your RRSP the way you might go shopping for some necessary article of clothing. Maybe it will last for years, has a familiar brand name, is priced right, and feels comfortable, but you're not choosing underwear. You're choosing the means of generating an income for yourself that has to last 30 years or more. Besides, not even underwear manufacturers promise "One size fits all!"

Some RRSP owners think *guaranteed investment certificates (GICs)* are the solution to everything. They're easy to buy, simple to understand, and guaranteed by banks, trust companies, and credit unions. They should be a part of your RRSP investment risk for precisely those reasons — but just a part. Don't make the mistake of placing all your RRSP funds in GICs, because you will become vulnerable to their two most glaring weaknesses:

✔ **Poor liquidity and flexibility.** Try moving any money tied up in a GIC before it matures, to invest elsewhere, and you're in trouble. You could lose every penny of interest you expected to gain from it.

✔ **Long-term risk.** Not the risk of directly losing your original investment, but of losing it indirectly through inflation. For example: Place $10,000 in a five-year GIC, and it's there for the entire period. If the GIC earns 6 percent, that's not a bad deal, assuming inflation remains around 1.5 to 2 percent annually. But a lot can happen in five years. If inflation leaps back to its historical level of 5 percent annually, you're basically earning nothing. And if it tops 6 percent, you are actually losing money. That's the guaranteed risk with long-term guaranteed investment certificates.

GICs have a place in everyone's RRSP strategy. But they should never represent the entire investment value of the plan.

Here's one simple but effective measurement of the role of GICs and other fixed-income long-term investments in an RRSP: *The percentage of your entire RRSP invested in GICs and similar investments should approximate your age.* If you are 25, don't put more than 25 percent of your RRSP in these investments. If you are 50, you can justify having half of your RRSP in GICs and similar alternatives. Why? Because when you're young, you're seeking *growth* — you have a long way to go before you need the money. As you approach retirement age, you begin to focus on *security* — you want to hold on to the assets you have built. GICs are high in security and low in growth.

There are exceptions to this rule, based on circumstances. For example, a 50-year-old woman in good health with no mortgage, no major debts, and substantial assets outside her RRSP would likely profit by reducing her GIC content to 25 percent and increasing her equity investments (shares in public companies) accordingly. After all, she may well live into her 80s or 90s and not need to tap the money for 25 or 30 years, which is distant enough to justify higher-risk investments.

The "age = GIC percentage" guide is just that — a guide. It's a good place to start, adjusting as time passes to reflect your own investment skills and risk threshold.

A "Balanced Diet"

Some people are overwhelmed and confused when they begin considering all the investment alternatives available for their RRSP strategy. So let's simplify everything by forgetting about your RRSP and talking about your eating habits. Just for a paragraph or two.

Potatoes are fine vegetables and good for you, right? You may have heard this since you were old enough to toss a bowl of Pablum across the kitchen. As a result, you probably eat potatoes from time to time. But if you ate nothing but potatoes for breakfast, lunch, and dinner, every day, every week, and every month, you would become pretty bored with your meals. More to the point, your health would suffer. Potatoes are good for you, but they ain't perfect. They lack many things essential for your body's health, which is why you have also been advised to eat a *balanced diet* composed of various food groups *because each member of the group provides you with essential ingredients that other members lack.*

Investing has "food groups" as well, and there are three of them:

- **Liquid investments** include cash or the equivalent to cash, such as Canada Savings Bonds, treasury bills, and mutual funds that invest in them. There will always be people willing to exchange cash for these kinds of investment. That's what makes them "liquid." Whether the cash you receive is more or less than the cash you paid is another matter. The fact remains: Liquid investments are easily convertible to loonies, and represent a basic "food group" in your mix, because, among other things, they help you sleep better at night.

- **Income investments** are designed to generate loonies over a year or more. They include GICs, term deposits, dividends (a portion of the profits made by companies to people who own shares in the companies), and mutual funds investing in bonds and mortgages. Income investments provide potentially more profit than liquid investments, and they also aid a good night's sleep.

- **Equity investments** include Canadian and foreign shares (stocks) in companies, and mutual funds investing in them. Over time, equity investments can be expected to increase in value. They are the super-vitamins and steroids of a balanced investment diet, helping your RRSP grow like a beanstalk in good times, and they are especially important when you're younger and need this growth. But they also bring their own risk. The idea of a balanced diet is to counter this risky ingredient with the stability of the other two groups.

Okay, health class is over. Let's go back to business school.

Self-Directed RRSPs

The best way to apply the "balanced diet" concept to your RRSP is with a self-directed plan. Unfortunately, many Canadians become frightened about the idea of handling their own self-directed RRSP, as though an airline pilot has just asked them to take the controls of a 747 and fly it to London. Perhaps they feel that the management of their RRSP is too important to trust to themselves. In reality, the opposite is true: *It is too important to trust to anyone else.*

Self-directed RRSPs operate under the same rules as RRSPs managed by a bank or trust company. The big differences are these:

- ✔ A self-directed RRSP provides extra qualified investment options, including stocks, bonds, a wider range of mutual funds, and much more.

- ✔ In a self-directed RRSP, you choose and adjust the investment mix to suit changes in the economy, the performance of your investments, and your own comfort level.

The discomfort many Canadians feel about self-directed RRSPs is usually a combination of misunderstanding and fear — misunderstanding what a self-directed RRSP involves, and fear of making bad investment decisions. Yet even the most security-conscious RRSP owner can benefit from a self-directed RRSP, because this type of plan permits investments that tend to earn more than a traditional GIC while delivering virtually the same high security.

Self-directed plans have other advantages too, including these:

- ✔ If you have several RRSPs, consolidating them in one self-directed plan makes it easier to keep track of your progress.

- ✔ Concentrating all your investments in one place helps you maximize the foreign-content level of your plan, which will almost certainly increase its growth rate.

- ✔ With a self-directed plan, you can use a wider variety of investments as tax-deductible contributions. For example, if you own some RRSP-eligible Canada Savings Bonds (CSBs) and you're short of cash to maximize your RRSP this year, use the CSBs instead. You'll receive a reduction in your taxable income equal to the value of the bonds on the day you transfer them into your plan, and probably trigger a tax refund.

- ✔ Owners of self-directed RRSPs can draw on professional investment advice, often free of special fees. Major banks and trust companies provide this service, as do investment firms such as Merrill Lynch Canada.

If you're still getting used to the basic ideas behind an RRSP, you're not ready for a self-directed plan. But when you have absorbed the lessons in this book, familiarized yourself with basic investment concepts, and reached $30,000 in the value of your RRSP, you're ready to look at a self-directed plan seriously. In any case, a self-directed RRSP should be your goal, as measured by the value of your assets and your ability to understand the ABCs of investment decision-making.

Choosing where to place your self-directed RRSP

Banks, trust companies, credit unions, brokerage firms, and investment houses can set up and administrate a self-directed RRSP for you. Besides handling transactions in your plan, they will issue regular statements updating the value of your RRSP. Brokerages (including spin-offs from chartered banks, such as Royal's RBC Dominion and Scotiabank's Scotia McLeod) will also assign an investment professional to advise you and respond to your investment directives. These investment houses require a minimum investment of $20,000 to $25,000 and charge an annual fee of around $125 to manage things.

This is strictly an administration fee, by the way, covering the costs of issuing statements and general handling expenses. Investment professionals — who may be identified as an account executive, investment adviser, or some other similar title — are licensed to provide advice and make recommendations to you. They earn commissions when you buy or sell investments in your RRSP, including GICs, stocks, bonds, and mutual funds.

Chartered banks, trust companies, and credit unions can perform similar services as brokerages, usually with much lower minimum and management fees. Be aware, however, that their staff may be licensed to process security transactions for you, such as buying and selling bonds and mutual funds, but may not be permitted to give advice or make recommendations. This can give some new investors a severe case of the Financial Frets when they realize they're flying solo. In contrast, using a full-service brokerage, bank-owned or independent, means you can expect research on your investment ideas, execution in buying and selling your investments, and monitoring the progress of your RRSP to ensure it's still on track. When your RRSP approaches $50,000 in total value, you should look for the best financial advice you can get — and $125 a year to pay for it is a bargain.

Once you become confident enough in your own decision-making, you may choose to transfer your RRSP to a *discount brokerage*, which is like a self-serve bargain basement for investments. The administration fees for self-directed RRSPs are similar to those at full-service companies, but you pay lower commissions when you buy and sell investments in your RRSP, and you don't have a professional adviser watching over your plan. (For more data on discount brokerages, see Chapter 18.)

Every financial institution offering self-directed RRSPs looks for ways to separate their services from the competition. This tells you two things:

 ✔ Self-directed RRSPs are important business to them.

✔ It pays to shop around for the best deal, the highest comfort level, and any available perks. TD Bank, for example, offers a low-cost Green Line RRSP. With no minimum balance needed, this plan enables you to invest in more than 800 different mutual funds, GICs, bonds, and other investments. Build your Green Line RRSP up to a $25,000 balance, and you can move up to a full-service Green Line Focus self-directed RRSP. This not only enables you to invest in stocks and mortgages, but also eliminates the $25 annual administration fee charged on the basic RRSP.

Other Canadian sources for self-directed RRSPs have similar programs, and since each is constantly jockeying with others for incentives to attract RRSP customers, they are not listed here in detail. But with $25,000 or more in your plan, you're in a buyer's market. Call bank and trust company branches near you, and ask about their self-directed RRSP services. Compare the administration fees and commissions charged when you buy and sell investments for your plan. Ask friends with self-directed RRSPs about their experience. Make a hard-nosed decision. But don't base it entirely on dollars and cents, because the next factor is important as well.

If you have at least $10,000 in a savings-based RRSP, consider moving it to a self-directed plan in the future. If you have $25,000 or more in your plan, start moving it now.

Getting professional advice for your self-directed RRSP

All the chartered banks operate investment houses that can provide you with literally every self-directed RRSP service. More important, they offer resources that investors such as you and I rarely have access to, including research facilities, staff economists, industry specialists, and foreign offices reporting on far-away activities that affect Canada.

Open a self-directed RRSP with these firms, and you have access to all the professional advice you'll need to make good RRSP investment decisions. Is it free? Not quite, but then what is? Brokerage houses expect to earn a profit from your RRSP through commissions whenever you buy or sell investments for your RRSP. This is hardly new and not unreasonable. Just remain aware of it if, when managing your RRSP, you are tempted to treat your investments like items at a flea market.

With a self-directed RRSP, you have a right to know and meet the individual assigned to provide you with important investment advice. In many cases, especially when your RRSP reaches the six-figure bracket, the quality of service and advice you receive from your account representative can be much more important than the fees charged. Nobody enjoys paying a $125 annual administration fee, for example. But on a $25,000 RRSP, this amount

---

You know what she does . . . but what is she called?

People working for brokerage houses and other firms handling self-directed RRSPs work under a number of titles. Some are called financial advisers (or advisors, depending on the dictio- nary you own), while others call themselves investment counsellors or account executives. I call anyone assigned to your RRSP account by the brokerage house a *financial adviser.*

---

represents just ½ percent of the plan's total value. If the professional advice adds an extra 2 percent in annual growth to your plan, you're well ahead. When your RRSP reaches $100,000 or more, the difference is dramatic.

The representative assigned to your self-directed RRSP should

- ✔ Create a feeling of comfort and security for you. This is usually a combination of chemistry and instinct. It is never foolproof, but it should always be heeded.

- ✔ Ask questions about your investment knowledge, your goals, and your peace-of-mind level when it comes to dealing with risk.

- ✔ Propose, in broad terms, an investment strategy reflecting your goals and comfort level regarding investments for your RRSP.

- ✔ Provide details of his or her personal background regarding training and experience in investment counselling.

Working with a representative from an investment firm or brokerage is like having a dedicated professional adviser on your side. This is very different from bank staff, who may be able to sell you certain RRSP investments but cannot offer advice or make specific recommendations. Until your RRSP reaches the $50,000+ level, stay with the financial adviser provided by the brokerage firm. When your RRSP assets begin to approach $100,000, consider seeking an independent financial adviser.

Financial advisers have a darker side. See Chapter 6 for details on choosing the best one for you.

Do not assume that the people who administrate your self-directed RRSP will make your investment decisions. They won't, and you shouldn't consider letting them. They will offer advice, but unless you provide them with something called *discretionary power*, they will make no decisions for you. Discretionary power provides someone else with the authority to buy and sell investments within your RRSP without consulting you or obtaining your approval. There may be times when it's wise to give someone this kind of power. So far, I haven't heard of any. . . .

Transferring funds

Whether you have one or a dozen RRSPs scattered around town, it pays to consolidate them when you choose a self-directed RRSP. Yes, you can have more than one self-directed RRSP if you want. In fact, Canada Customs and Revenue Agency places no limit on the number of individual RRSPs you can hold. Having multiple RRSPs is a little like having multiple spouses. It can be fun for a while, but eventually the cost and complications, among other sources of pain, make it not worth the effort.

Moving your current RRSP from one home to another is easy. Following your orders, the new RRSP administrator completes a transfer form directing the old RRSP administrator to move all the assets in your RRSP to its new home. Simple as that. Except. (There's always an "except.")

You'll pay an administration fee of between $25 and $125 per transfer, which may be waived if your account is substantial enough (the rich get richer . . .). If your RRSP includes GICs, and you move the GIC before its maturity date, you may pay a penalty. In fact, you could lose every penny of interest the GIC earned, leaving you with a net loss after the administration fee is paid. So it's a good idea to wait until a GIC has matured before moving it. Some banks and trust companies don't permit GIC transfers under any conditions. You're theirs for the term.

Don't expect the transfer to take place overnight, even though it could, in theory. Transferring your RRSP assets from a financial firm to its competition doesn't necessarily throw the old financial company into a snit, but it doesn't fill them with glee either. They're losing your business, and nobody hurries to complete a transaction that costs them money. In the best of times, expect the transfer to take two weeks, leaving your RRSP assets in financial limbo while everything is wrapped up. In the worst of times, such as January and February when the RRSP frenzy hits its peak, it could take significantly longer.

Be sure to discuss the transfer in detail with whoever will be handling your RRSP at its new home. Unexpected glitches have a habit of showing up in the investment game, and can hold up the transfer. Here's one: If you hold one bank's mutual funds in your RRSP, you may not be able to transfer them to an investment house owned by another bank. So accounts with Wood Gundy, which is owned by CIBC, cannot hold mutual funds managed by Scotiabank. You would have to sell the Scotiabank funds in your RRSP before moving it to Wood Gundy or another bank-owned brokerage. Also: Transfer your RRSP "in kind," which means they are not to be sold, except to accommodate that rule about bank-managed mutual funds.

So here's the lesson: Before transferring RRSP funds, check the maturity date of any GICs and consider waiting until they mature first. When they mature, do not renew the term but transfer the funds directly into an RRSP savings account and make the transfer from there. Consult the organization receiving the transfer to ensure they can accept the investments. And try to avoid making a transfer in January or February.

Decisions to Make

Once you move your hard-earned (but tax-deferred) RRSP dollars to a self-directed plan, it's up to you to decide how to build your balanced diet of investments.

Start with your age. The older you are, the more concerned you should be about security. Remember the concept about using your age as a measure of the percentage of secure investments such as GICs, bonds, and T-bills in your RRSP mix? It's a good rule to follow. At age 33, about one-third of your total RRSP assets should be in GICs and bonds — but, before you make any quick decisions, read more about them in Chapter 8.

Understanding risk and reward

Canadians are not big risk-takers, and that's no surprise. When you live in a country subject to two or three months of below-zero weather, you put some extra effort into ensuring that you'll have shelter, heat, and food year-round. Unlike in the South Sea Islands, you can't sleep on a beach and pull breadfruit from a tree 12 months of the year.

Avoiding risk of any kind means never becoming familiar with it, so it's worth reviewing the whole idea of *investment risk*. When you understand it, the concept of risk becomes more tolerable. Besides, risks bring rewards, and the more of one you accept, the more of the other you may harvest.

You need to deal with four kinds of investment risk when you plan your RRSP mix, as described in the following sections.

Principal risk

Principal risk means the danger of losing your entire original investment. This kind of risk is virtually nonexistent with cash deposited in a chartered bank, trust company, credit union, or financial institution that holds membership in the Canada Deposit Insurance Corporation (CDIC). Their membership guarantees replacement of any deposits on hand if the bank goes bankrupt. Other investments that protect your principal are Canada Savings Bonds and various bonds guaranteed by the federal or provincial governments. Some principal risk is involved with other types of bonds, as well as shares in companies and mortgages. The highest risk of losing your principal occurs with commodity trading, futures, and options. These are not only unsuitable for RRSP investors, but are actually prohibited from being held in an RRSP by Canada Customs and Revenue Agency. So don't worry about them.

Banks, trust companies, and credit unions make a big thing about the CDIC insurance they carry on their depositors' money. If the bank or trust company should fail, CDIC will pay you the money (up to the legal limit) you deposited in the firm.

CDIC coverage is limited to $60,000 per account, so if you have more than that amount on deposit you should split it into two or more accounts, each worth less than $60,000, to guarantee full coverage. Even then, if the bank should fail, it could take years for all the paperwork to settle and you would almost certainly lose any interest owed you. All you are likely to receive is your original deposit.

If you're dealing with a brokerage house that is a member of the Canadian Investment Protection Fund, the assets in each RRSP are guaranteed up to $500,000 (possibly $1 million by the time you read this) against the brokerage becoming insolvent — producing a broke brokerage, I suppose. This does not cover losses resulting from poor investment decisions you made, even those recommended by your financial adviser.

Insurance is a fine thing, but whether or not your RRSP investment has CDIC coverage should not be a consideration when you're deciding where to invest your RRSP funds.

Interest-rate risk

Interest-rate risk is the chance you take that GICs, bonds, and similar investments will not continue paying the same levels they currently pay. A genuine risk exists that they will pay lower interest. In the late 1980s, you would have had no trouble earning 11 percent annual interest from your GIC investments. With returns like that, your RRSP would double every seven years — an attractive prospect. But a decade later, GICs were earning less than 5 percent annual interest, so if you were counting on similar growth from GICs you were seriously out of luck.

Wise investors counter interest-rate risk with a technique called *laddering* or *rolling GIC strategy*. You "ladder" your investments by staggering the maturity date of several GICs over time. For example, if you plan to invest $5,000 in GICs for five years within your RRSP, don't opt to spend the entire amount on one GIC maturing in five years. Instead, purchase five GICs of $1,000 each, maturing in five successive years. This creates one of those rare events known as a win-win situation. If interest rates rise during the first year, you roll the GIC maturing in that year to a new GIC at the higher interest rate. If interest rates decline, you have already locked the majority of your GICs into the higher rate.

Liquidity risk

Liquidity risk involves not being able to convert your investments into cash when you need it. The best example of liquidity risk is real estate. You could own real estate property worth a million dollars today, but if you need that million in cash tomorrow or next week, or even next month, you are unlikely to get it without suffering a major loss.

This kind of risk is not a serious concern to most RRSP owners, but it demonstrates the importance of flexibility in your planning. The more flexibility you maintain in your investments, the more you will be able to take advantage of new opportunities or respond to a changing strategy.

Currency risk

Currency risk occurs when the value of the Canadian dollar fluctuates versus other currency — especially the U.S. dollar. This affects only the foreign-content portion of your RRSP, which, you'll recall, is currently limited to 30 percent of your plan's total value.

Currency risk has an upside and a downside. If you have invested in U.S. stocks or bonds and the loonie declines in value against the U.S. dollar, you're on the upside because your U.S. investment is now worth more (it's valued in U.S. dollars, remember). When the loonie recovers its value, you suffer on the downside because the value of your U.S. investments has dropped accordingly.

By the way, forecasting which direction the Canadian dollar will move is a mug's game. Nobody knows for certain. Best plan: Spread your foreign investment among several countries to soften the blow of any major currency devaluation.

Your risk threshold

Sophisticated investors have all kinds of ways of measuring a risk threshold, and even more ways of addressing it. That's nice, but these are also the kind of people who believe that The Meaning of Life is buried in the Dow-Jones average.

Let's put it in perspective:

The risk threshold for most RRSP owners is the one that either lets them get a good night's sleep or nudges them awake at 4 a.m. with nightmares of spending their retirement in an enlarged outhouse, living on roots and road-kill. A risk threshold is built on two kinds of fear: Either fear of losing all those years of RRSP contributions, like a craps player with one bad roll of the dice, or fear of not amassing enough RRSP growth because the investments were too conservative, which usually means too much money in dull, boring, and stingy GICs.

It doesn't take a Jacques Cartier to discover that comfort lies somewhere between these two extremes. By combining different kinds of investments — mixing safe-but-dull GICs with more adventuresome mutual funds — you can raise your risk threshold no matter what's keeping you awake at night. This is diversification in its simplest form, and permits you to earn a higher rate of return on your investment for a given level of risk.

Diversifying the investments in your RRSP requires you to pay attention from time to time. If every penny is in GICs, the money is essentially sleeping, and who wants to disturb a sleeping loonie? But when your money is in other more active investments, such as mutual funds, you need to keep an eye on it.

Next to recognizing the importance of RRSPs in planning your future, the importance of diversification is the most significant lesson to be learned on this topic. As a matter of fact, consider having at least one of the following statements tattooed on the inside of your eyelids. Or maybe just stick them to the fridge door with a magnet:

  ✔ There is no growth without risk.

  ✔ Well-managed risk leads to maximum growth.

  ✔ Diversification cures RRSP insomnia.

When to make adjustments

Keeping an eye on your self-directed RRSP does not take day-to-day attention. In fact, this is usually counterproductive. With your money out in the world working for you, instead of dozing in a GIC, it is subject to daily jolts in the marketplace. Most of these bumps should be of no concern, as long as you keep your eye on the horizon.

Each quarter, the firm holding your self-directed RRSP will issue a statement showing the current value of all your investments. This is the time to pay attention. Sit down with a cup of coffee and scan the performance. How much has the value of your RRSP changed since the last statement? Is it up or down, and by how much? Is the movement significant?

Even if the answers to these questions are not positive — the RRSP value has actually declined, perhaps, because of events on the stock market or elsewhere — no change may be needed. Until the time comes to convert your assets into cash, you haven't lost a penny. And if that time is still distant, and your strategy is sound, you'll gain in the long run.

Remember the rule of all experienced carpenters: Measure twice, cut once. It works with RRSPs too: Plan carefully, and resist hasty decisions.

Chapter 6

Finding Help in Making Decisions

● ●

In This Chapter

▶ Seeking professional advice

▶ Understanding the role of banks, trust companies, brokerages, and so on

▶ Deciding whether you need a financial adviser

▶ Counting on your own knowledge and abilities

● ●

Managing a self-directed RRSP is not as challenging, say, as learning to play the piano on your own. First, the basic rules are not as complex as you probably believe. Second, nobody has all the answers anyway — not even those super-confident financial gurus who write newspaper columns and hold highly publicized seminars. Good financial management is more about how to avoid doing the wrong things than defining exactly what the right things are. And finally, a good deal of professional investment guidance is available from banks, trust companies, and other people who want your RRSP under their roof. Choosing which roof to place your self-directed RRSP under is a matter of cost and chemistry.

The *cost* of your self-directed plan includes an annual administrative fee charged for the necessary paperwork your plan requires, including filing the plan with Canada Customs and Revenue Agency, sending you periodic reports on its value, and the usual nuts and bolts. There is no standard industry-wide price for this service; each company essentially charges whatever the market will bear, and since you are part of the market, you'll bear it. So shop around. Brokerage houses often have lower administration fees because they expect to earn commissions when you buy or sell investments within your RRSP. Remember, however, that banks and trust companies with lower administration fees may also have discount brokerage arms, which can save you money when you trade investments.

Chemistry is more difficult to define, and it is highly personal. You are relying not just on the firm to administrate your RRSP investment, but also to provide you with advice and guidance. If your RRSP is large enough, and you choose either a brokerage firm or the investment arm of a chartered bank, you will be assigned a specific individual to provide this service. In other words, you begin a relationship and, like all relationships, this one is built on trust and confidence. That's the chemistry side of things.

Should you attend a financial seminar to get started? Of course you should, if the seminar is being presented by a legitimate investment firm, hosted by a licensed financial adviser discussing basic investment principles, and offered at a reasonable sum ("Free!" is reasonable). It can be a very educational experience, especially for the investment novice. Remember, however, that these seminars are held primarily to obtain your business, so keep your ears open and your chequebook closed — at least until you're satisfied that the cost and chemistry are right.

Who Can Get You Started?

Launching a self-directed RRSP is no more complex than opening a bank account. In fact, you might start by talking to the manager at the bank, trust company, or credit union where you currently maintain a chequing or savings account, or the firm holding your mortgage. Banks and their relatives in the financial community place a high premium on keeping customers, because it costs a great deal to attract new customers from the competition. If your experience with your current banker has been good, begin there — but don't end there.

Talk to friends who may have self-directed RRSPs and ask about their experiences. Pay special attention to the assistance they receive — or don't receive — in managing their plan.

In other words, do your homework. And remember that you are in a buyer's market. Banks, trust companies, credit unions, and brokerage houses offering self-directed RRSPs want your business, and to get it, they will often bend the rules with lower fees and commissions.

Professional advice

Once you have a self-directed RRSP you are a bona fide investor, on a small scale perhaps. All wise investors seek advice, and you shouldn't be any different. That's why you should make use of professional expertise wherever possible.

What's the difference between a financial adviser, a financial planner, and a financial consultant? There are no cut-and-dried definitions, but most people in the industry agree on definitions similar to these:

> ✔ **A financial planner** tackles the management of all your assets, looking for benefits wherever they may be found. This can mean developing a retirement strategy, setting goals and objectives, and coordinating the work of specialists such as estate lawyers, tax

accountants, insurance agents, and investment brokers — all to maximize your wealth and reduce your taxes. Financial planners usually have CFP (Certified Financial Planner) or RFP (Registered Financial Planner) after their names, indicating they have successfully completed several relevant courses and have at least two years' practical experience in the field.

✔ **A financial adviser** works in a more narrow field, focusing on your investment activities — which, in this case, involves decisions you make regarding your RRSP assets. The best-qualified financial advisers are identified by the letters FCSI (Fellow of the Canadian Securities Institute), provided by the Canadian Securities Institute. To earn an FCSI designation, advisers must complete the Canadian Securities Course plus courses in Canadian investment management, and pass a conduct and practices exam. But someone can be an exceptional financial adviser without an FCSI after their name. More important than a bunch of letters are things such as experience, wisdom, empathy, and communication skills — plus a roster of satisfied clients.

✔ **A financial consultant** can, unfortunately, be anyone who hangs a shingle in front of his office or runs an advertisement in the *Yellow Pages*. A financial consultant may or may not be licensed to sell securities.

Best suggestion: Choose your financial adviser from a large firm that's prepared to stand behind the decisions of its staff. Check out their background, ask for references, and talk to friends or relatives who may be able to recommend a financial adviser based on their own satisfaction.

Should you employ a mutual fund specialist as your financial adviser? Along with banks, trust companies, and others, many mutual fund companies also provide the services of qualified financial advisers. Does it make sense to obtain your advice from them? Here's how one financial writer replied to the same question: "If you were feeling ill, who would you go to for unbiased advice: your family doctor, or the person who sells him the pills he prescribes?"

Me, I'll stick with the doctor.

Choosing and working with professional assistance

Here's what to look for during your first meeting with a financial adviser:

✔ He or she establishes a sense of trust and credibility. This takes time to build, perhaps. But your first impressions are worth paying attention to.

✔ The adviser does more listening than talking. After all, this is about your future, not the adviser's ego.

✔ You feel comfortable discussing your goals and objectives. Try to keep them realistic, but even if they are extreme they should not be ridiculed or sneered at.

✔ If your objectives appear unrealistic, the adviser suggests attainable goals in their place.

✔ At the end of the conversation, you feel empowered to start making decisions regarding your self-directed RRSP, relying on the expertise, empathy, and advice of the adviser.

Financial advisers can prove their worth not just by the things they advise you to do, but by the mistakes they encourage you to avoid. Some of the following may sound simplistic, but they are common mistakes made by all investors, and they can be avoided by heeding the wisdom of an adviser looking out for your financial interests:

✔ Buying at a high price and selling at a low price.

✔ Making your investment decisions on fees and sales charges instead of potential returns and suitability for your needs.

✔ Reacting to yesterday's "hot" news instead of today's reality.

✔ Waiting for "the best time" to invest while missing real opportunities.

✔ Making investment decisions that don't match your strategy.

✔ Putting all your eggs in one basket by not diversifying your RRSP investments.

✔ Losing sight of your goal by reacting to short-term events.

✔ Letting your emotions override facts when making an investment decision.

Paying for professional advice

Most financial planners and advisers are nice people, but they're not saints. With all that training and responsibility, they expect to be paid for their services, and rightly so. While not a sure-fire guide, the way they are paid can be used to assess the quality of their advice.

✔ **Fees only.** This is similar to a lawyer's method of making money. You describe your situation and your needs, and the professional makes recommendations and submits a bill. That's it. You can choose to follow or ignore the proposals. Either way, the adviser gets paid. It's a bare-bones arrangement, but it also ensures a high degree of neutrality by the adviser, who is not counting on you to follow the advice in order to earn a living.

✔ **Fee plus commission.** The fee charged to you is generally lower, because the adviser will be earning commissions from any investments you trade. Will the prospect of a large commission from one investment alternative influence your adviser to choose it over other alternatives? They will, of course, say no. You can, of course, say "Yeah, right."

✔ **Salary.** Large financial institutions may brag about their advisers being on salary, suggesting they have no axe to grind when providing advice. But if the financial institution has "house brands" of mutual funds or GICs, the adviser may favour them over others.

✔ **Percentage of assets.** When your assets are in the seven-figure range, you may pay for financial advice with a percentage of your portfolio's value. This can encourage special attention because the more your assets increase in value, the more money the adviser earns.

A wise man (I'm sure it was a man) once said: Whether you marry or remain single, at some point in your life you will regret it. You might feel that way if you rely upon the advice of a financial adviser working with a full-service brokerage, such as Merrill Lynch Canada, Scotia McLeod, Wood Gundy, and others. Why? Because, while their advice to you is well-intentioned, it will always be coloured by their need to make money for themselves and their employer. And here's the catch: *Some of the very best investments available for your RRSP do not generate income for the brokerage via commissions or other forms of payment and as a result will not be recommended by your adviser.* Most of these are mutual funds (covered in Part IV). You almost need to hold a gun to a commissioned adviser's head (speaking figuratively, of course) before these will be placed in your RRSP.

Advisers will deny this, but it's true: When it comes to choosing between a mediocre investment paying a commission and a first-class investment that pays the adviser nothing, the mediocre investment will win every time. Count on it.

Moral: Arm yourself with as much information as you can when discussing your plan with an adviser. Listen carefully but skeptically. Ask the tough questions. Remember, it's your money.

Your own knowledge and abilities

The more you understand fundamental investment principles, the more confident you'll be in the decisions you make based on the advice of the financial adviser. Remember, you don't need to understand all the details of various investment options, especially at the beginning. Start by focusing on these basics, all of which are covered in the book you're holding in your hand:

- The difference between debt investments (bonds, GICs, T-bills, and so on) and equity investments (stocks, most mutual funds, real estate, and so on).

- The value of compound growth: Money you make on your investment this year makes more money on its own next year, and so on.

- Before-tax dollars and after-tax dollars.

- How mutual funds work.

- Growth versus income (remember the analogy in Chapter 1 about the oak tree as growth and the apple tree as income?).

- The importance of diversity: debt and equity, short-term and long-term, foreign and domestic, and so on.

Chapter 7

Your Strategy

- -

In This Chapter

▶ Making a plan

▶ Setting your goals

▶ Measuring your progress

▶ Adjusting your program

▶ Things not to be concerned about

▶ Things to worry about . . . a little

- -

A self-directed RRSP will provide you with either a small sense of exhilaration — hey, you're in charge of your own future! — or a substantial dose of anxiety ("Hey, I'm in charge of my own future!").

The best way to make the most of it is by setting a strategy to maximize your RRSP growth over the years. Relax, you're not planning the D-Day invasion of Europe. You're just evaluating some basic facts, such as your age, the number of years remaining before you retire, the amount of annual contributions you'll be able to make, and the *risk threshold* that makes you comfortable while building the value of your RRSP.

Planning for your retirement income is like plotting a long journey. You start by deciding where you want to go and when you want to arrive there. Then you determine any stops you may need to make along the way, including a few to ensure you're still on the right course. That's really what an RRSP strategy is all about. Start with a goal (the total value of your RRSP when you retire); choose your route (the contributions and investments you'll make over the years); decide on some overnight stops (short-term goals); and schedule a pause now and then to confirm your progress (periodic investment reviews).

Of course, the RRSP journey for some people is a 30-year-plus excursion, which is not exactly a weekend trip to the cottage. But let's get started anyway.

Your Contribution Plan

The most difficult thing to do right now is predict how much money you'll have on hand to put in your RRSP before the deadline. (Or maybe it's the easiest, because the answer is usually "Not enough.")

So if you haven't already, start making monthly contributions to your RRSP. If it makes you more comfortable about your cash flow, keep the total annual amount of your monthly contributions below your maximum limit. For example, if you are permitted to contribute $6,000 this year but $500 per month seems a bit steep, make it $250 per month and top it up later. If your RRSP contributions produce a substantial tax refund, use it as part of next year's contribution.

Short-Term and Long-Term Goals

Your RRSP goals can be as simple as this:

✓ **Short-term goal.** Maximize your RRSP contributions this year.

✓ **Long-term goal.** Strive for 10-percent annual growth of your RRSP over the next seven years. Do this, and the value of your RRSP today will double by then, not counting the new contributions you add year after year.

✓ **Foreign-content goal.** Reach and maintain the 30-percent ceiling on foreign content in your RRSP, to take advantage of worldwide growth.

✓ **Diversification goal.** Review all the investments in your RRSP to ensure they are sufficiently diversified to avoid the dreaded too-many-eggs-in-one-basket risk.

Don't make the mistake of confusing a safe strategy with a sound strategy, especially if you're under 35 or 40 years of age. You may think that investing all your RRSP contributions in guaranteed government bonds and GICs at 5-percent annual interest, for example, is a safe strategy. And it is. But, with 20 years of growth ahead of you, it's not a sound strategy. Between 1954 and 1998, the Canadian stock market rose by an average of 11 percent. In spite of short-term gyrations in the market, the growth of stocks over a decade or two will always outpace earnings available from bonds, GICs, T-bills, and similar investments. So it's possible to be both safe *and* sound.

Over-Contributing and Under-Contributing

Some RRSP rules are set in concrete. Others kind of float on foam rubber. If you have the cash available, and if you enjoy shaking things up a little, this is one area where you can bend the rules to your benefit.

Putting too many eggs in your basket (or, you can never have too many eggs)

If you believe in taking every advantage offered you, consider the benefit of contributing more to your RRSP than Canada Customs and Revenue Agency officially allows.

Tax regulations allow you to exceed your contribution by up to $2,000 at any time up to retirement. This is cumulative, by the way, not an annual limit. When you retire, you adjust the balance of your RRSP by claiming the excess as part of your final RRSP contribution. If in your final year of making RRSP contributions your limit is $8,000, you must subtract any over-contribution from that amount to arrive at your actual maximum contribution limit.

The idea was to provide RRSP owners with a margin of error, so they could avoid the severe penalty of 1 percent per month on excessive RRSP contributions, which doesn't kick in until the $2,000 limit is exceeded.

Over-contributing to your RRSP has benefits. You'll have an extra $2,000 growing tax-sheltered within your plan for several years. If it grows at an average 10 percent annually, after 20 years your $2,000 will be worth about $15,000, which is $15,000 more than if you had strictly abided by the rules.

Drawbacks? There are always drawbacks.

First, this assumes that you are young enough to wait 20 years before collecting this particular bonus. Trouble is, people in their mid-30s are often too strapped for cash to even meet their maximum permitted annual contribution, so going $2,000 over it, even once, could be a stretch.

Next, use the $2,000 up and you have no margin for error. Every loonie you happen to contribute over your limit in the future brings with it a penalty of 1 percent per month.

Should you over-contribute? Sure, if the extra dollars are available and you are careful to monitor your contributions in the future, avoiding that nasty penalty.

Putting too few eggs in your basket

In contrast with excess contributions, most Canadians find they don't have enough funds on hand to reach their RRSP limit. This creates carry-forward amounts, which appear on the CCRA's Notice of Assessment sent to you after you file your income tax return.

Making up some of this unused contribution room is a good idea — but where can you find the money? Here are four possible sources:

- **Year-end bonuses.** If you receive year-end bonuses from your employer, as much as $10,000 can be contributed directly to your RRSP tax-free, providing you have contribution room.

- **Contributions in kind.** You can use RRSP-eligible investments held outside your plan, such as stocks, bonds, and mutual funds, to make up unused contribution room. (For details, see Chapter 8.)

- **Your tax refund.** Roll it into your RRSP immediately to absorb at least some carry-over and start building your plan balance.

- **Borrow the money.** (See Chapter 2.)

Review Your Progress

The administrator of your self-directed RRSP will issue statements either each month or each quarter. This is not junk mail — take a few moments to review each statement and file it away with others for reference. Here's what your statement will include, and what to review:

- **A summary of your account.** Look for: any change in asset value (the total value of everything in your RRSP). Is your RRSP worth more or less than on your previous statement? If more, how much (if any) was generated by new contributions? If less, did you expect a drop due (almost exclusively) to fluctuations in the value of your mutual funds?

- **A summary of your contributions,** both since your last statement and the year to date. Look for: confirmation that your contributions are being registered.

✔ **Plan growth.** Look for: the increase in the value of your self-directed RRSP since placing it with the bank, trust company, investment firm, or other administrator.

✔ **Foreign content.** Look for: maximum (30 percent) foreign investment through bonds and mutual funds.

✔ **Transactions.** Look for: a record of all transactions in your RRSP since you received your last statement. This would include new contributions, any buying or selling of investments (bonds, mutual funds, and so on) held in your RRSP, and any "roll-over" of GICs or T-bills that have matured since your last statement. Did you authorize these trades or renewals? Do you understand why they were made?

✔ **Account valuation.** Look for: both the book value (what you paid for them originally) and current value (what you would get for them if you sold them on the date of your statement) of all the individual assets held in your RRSP, including GICs, T-bills, bonds, mutual funds, and other investments. Which ones have risen since the last statement? Which ones have fallen in value? How comfortable are you with this?

✔ **Cash balance.** Look for: excessive amounts of cash. A few hundred dollars is probably not worth being concerned about. If it approaches $1,000 or more, find better ways of earning money from it through the purchase of T-bills, which are almost as good as cash but earn more interest. (Cash can build up in your account from various sources, including dividends from stocks you own in your RRSP, unallocated contributions, or other reasons.)

Draw on your adviser's knowledge and skills, but try not to be a pest about it. If investments in your RRSP based on the stock markets have fallen in value, and you're aware that the market itself has slipped downward over the past few weeks, *c'est la vie*. The market has never climbed in a straight line. Never will. So changes in value from time to time are to be expected, and it's not worth either your or your adviser's time to discuss short-term drops, unless:

✔ The market has been rising steadily, but the value of your investments keeps falling.

✔ You don't recognize some transactions described in your statement, or transactions that you approved are not included.

✔ You and your adviser set a timetable to reach certain goals, and they have not been met.

✔ It's time for an annual review of goals and strategies.

✔ You want to increase your RRSP contribution. (Your adviser loves to get calls like that.)

Adjust Your Program

The most important lesson for owners of self-directed RRSPs to learn is this: Stay calm. If your goals are realistic and your strategy is sound, you'll almost certainly be better off doing nothing than you would be by tinkering with it. Your bonds are outperforming your mutual funds? Remember that it's not a horse race, and your money is not riding on one in a race with the other. Assuming you've chosen quality investments, and you're still several years from retirement, it doesn't matter which is ahead as long as you're the winner in the end.

If you feel an adjustment is necessary — for example, to increase the foreign content of your RRSP — discuss it with your adviser. Explain your concern, ask for a recommendation, and be aware of any unexpected costs. Selling some bonds and mutual funds may trigger unexpected charges or sales commissions, leaving you with less than you expect.

Transactions within your RRSP can be achieved with a simple telephone call. No special form is needed, and the sale or purchase will be confirmed with you by mail.

When It Makes Sense to Invest in Your Employer

Should you hold shares of the company you work for, inside your RRSP? Some employers encourage this idea, but beware the possible consequences of investing too much in one place. Spending a large portion of your RRSP on shares in your employer's firm means you are relying on the company for income, benefits, and retirement funds. If the company has bad times, you could lose all three.

It makes sense to spend your RRSP contributions on shares of your employer's company under these conditions:

- ✔ You are totally confident that the company is well-managed and maintains a strong market position.

- ✔ The company offers you shares at a discounted price. (It should be at least 10 percent to make it worthwhile.)

- ✔ The company offers you a *share purchase plan*, where it matches your contribution — usually on a 50-percent basis. So, for every dollar you spend to buy shares for your RRSP, the company adds 50 cents.

- ✔ You limit the value of its shares to no more than 25 percent of the total value of your RRSP.

"Stock market"? Sounds more like a stockyard

You might as well learn a couple of basic pieces of jargon, if you don't know them already. If the stock market continues to rise over an extended period of time, it is known as a *bull market*. If it falls over an extended period of time, it is a *bear market*. In recent years, the Canadian stock market has seemed to be moving both ways at the same time — is that a "beaver market"?

Everybody with money in stocks, or mutual funds based on stocks, smiles a great deal during bull markets. The same people grow snarly and depressed during bear markets. But the earth keeps turning and the sun keeps rising and, if your strategy is sound, your RRSP will keep growing over the long term — bulls, bears, or beavers.

Things Not to Worry About

The further you are from retirement, the more you will benefit from investing a large portion of your RRSP assets in equity-based mutual funds or shares in traded companies. This puts your investments at the mercy of the market-place, and every time a stock-market tumble makes the headlines, you may find your pulse racing and your palms sweating.

This is all very natural. The idea of your retirement nest egg dropping 20 or 30 percent is not pleasant. Nor are headlines about market meltdowns in Russia or South Korea. Many investment pundits, gurus, and similar creatures make a living by playing up these events and impersonating Chicken Little, shouting, "The sky is falling!" This helps sell a bunch of books, but you may have noticed that the sky remains in place, even if the stock market slips now and then.

Every time the market falls into a hole (the usual term is *market correction*), it eventually crawls out and starts climbing higher than before. As long as you're five years away from needing the money in your RRSP, a goodly portion of it should be in equities. Nobody, not even the person who wrote one of the best-selling books of the mid-1980s, titled *The Coming Crash of '89*, which predicted the 1990s would be a repeat of the 1930s, disagrees with that opinion.

How to Stay Calm

Blips, fumbles, and lurches in the market (otherwise known as economic downturns) can encourage all of us to run for cover now and then.

Here are four ways to calm yourself during these short-term upheavals.

- **Focus on your long-term goals.** If you hadn't planned on tapping your RRSP investments for another 15 years last week, it's still 15 years away this week.

- **Look at the big picture.** So much can happen in 15 years. For example, the Toronto Stock Exchange (TSE) 300, the measure of Canadian stocks, lost money in only four of the 15 years from 1982 to 1997. The only double-digit loss was in 1990, when it dropped almost 15 percent. But the TSE 300's rise in 11 of the positive years was measured in double digits, growing 35.5 percent in 1983 and 32.5 percent in 1993. Imagine if you had bailed out of equities in 1990. You would be sadder and poorer, but maybe wiser, today. The meltdown in high-flying tech stocks that occurred in mid-2000 panicked new investors. Old hands simply shrugged and began looking for bargains. Two years from now, guess who will be wealthier? The moral: Don't panic.

- **Stay diversified.** This becomes even more important as you grow older. (But don't overdo it. See Chapter 15 for some guidelines.)

- **Keep your expectations realistic.** Take every advantage available to make your plan grow, but temper it with realism. The rising bull market of the late 1990s made some people believe that 20- to 25-percent annual growth was normal. By 2001, they realized it was not. Over the long term, steady growth is closer to 12 percent, which means a few corrections will occur. But hey — watching your RRSP grow at an average of 12 percent a year with stock market investments is a heck of a lot more fun than watching it struggle at 5 percent a year with GICs.

Things to Worry about Maybe a Little . . .

Remember inflation, the beast that hides in the bushes and emerges to devour everyone's stash? There has been no sign of it in years, but the danger exists that it may come out of hiding in the future. When it does, interest rates climb (to account for increased costs), the stock market tumbles (people pull money out of the market to invest it in bonds and GICs at higher interest rates), and the value of your bonds drops (they are sold at a discount to earn a higher interest rate).

Boy, that's an economic poke in the eye with a sharp stick, isn't it?

Should you be concerned? A little. Should you panic? Definitely not. Here's what the smart money does in such a situation. (The "smart money," by the way, is a stockbroker term referring to an individual who always makes the best possible decision, no matter what the market conditions may be. The smart money, of course, is about as genuine as the tooth fairy.)

Because they've used "laddered" dates on their GICs (see Chapter 5), the smart money's money is reinvested at the new higher interest rates as their old GICs mature. Similarly, lower stock prices mean an opportunity to buy when the price is right. The smart money also knows that quality long-term bonds will recover when interest rates stabilize again.

Inflation should mean a rise in your income to keep pace with the higher cost of living. If so, concentrate on increasing your RRSP contributions accordingly.

Chapter 8

Finding Your Perfect Formula

· ·

In This Chapter

▶ Creating the right "recipe"

▶ Choosing investments for your RRSP goals

▶ Defining the most suitable choices

▶ Evaluating mortgages as RRSP investments

· ·

*L*ike a kitchen recipe, your self-directed RRSP will be made up of a mix of various ingredients, each chosen for the particular "flavour" it brings to the entire dish. Like all recipes, none is actually "perfect" for everybody. You may like a little more salt, and I might prefer a little more cayenne (we're talking chili here, not chocolate cake). Who is to decide which is best?

If it's your recipe, you're the ultimate judge. Start with basics, familiarize yourself with the qualities of each ingredient in the recipe, and adjust things as you go along. This works as well for RRSPs as it does for chili. So the best way to begin is by getting to know the qualities of basic ingredients, and figure out how to blend them to your needs.

Investments Suitable for Your RRSP

Remember the three groups of investment types: Liquidable (cash and its equivalent), income (bonds, GICs, and mortgages), and growth (stocks and mutual funds). Almost any investment based on these characteristics is accepted by Canada Customs and Revenue Agency for use in your RRSP.

Things you *cannot* hold in your RRSP (the CCRA prevents it):

- Foreign cash
- Collectible items such as coins, artwork, stamps, and antiques
- Mutual funds not registered with Canada Customs and Revenue Agency
- Commodities, futures, and complex options

✔ Real estate

✔ Investments in small, privately held companies

Things you *shouldn't* hold in your RRSP (common sense prevents it):

✔ **Annuities.** Annuities produce a steady income over a fixed period of time, purchased with a single large payment. They're a possible alternative to other options when you eventually retire, but they have no place inside an RRSP. Their tax-free growth status carries no benefit because everything in your RRSP grows free of immediate taxation anyway. What's more, annuities pay hefty commissions to the people who sell them, and they carry large administration fees. Avoid them. (For more on annuities, see Chapter 22.)

✔ **Limited partnerships.** Some investment salespeople may propose a limited partnership (LP) as a suitable RRSP investment. Some people may suggest removing your own appendix too. For the record, an LP enables managing partners of a company or real estate development to use Other People's Money (in this case, yours) as capital. Later, when the term of the agreement is up, the investors and partners share in the profits.

Sounds like a good idea? It's not. LPs are sold through brokers and financial consultants who earn commissions as high as 10 percent, skimmed off the top of your initial investment. Management fees and other expenses are deducted from the operation each year, and the LP managers — who are paid by these fees and expenses — decide the amount to pay themselves. Sound bad? It gets worse. Unlike mutual funds, you can't vote with your dollars, because LPs are not liquid. Their term is usually from seven to ten years, and you cannot take your money out — whatever may be left of it — before the term is up.

If an adviser seriously proposes an LP for your RRSP investments, do two things: Say no . . . and consider looking for a new financial adviser.

Matching Your Investment Mix to Your Goals

The ideal RRSP does not match the opinions or reflect the preferences of anyone. Instead, it meets the unique needs of its owner — which is you.

Your RRSP should change with time, just as you will. As you age, your priorities shift, you grow wiser in the ways of the world, and you tend to conserve your energy a little more. That's a good way to describe the changes you'll want to make to your RRSP over time. All of these changes, of course, will be influenced by your personal comfort level, your investment sophistication, and your risk threshold. That's what makes the ideal mix of liquidable, income, and growth investments unique to you.

Let's tackle your concerns, and the changes to your RRSP basic recipe you may want to make, decade by decade.

- ✔ **Up to age 25, you're fancy-free.** Retirement is an eon or two away, your income is limited, and your attentions are elsewhere. Still, this is the time when you can earn maximum rewards from every RRSP dollar you invest. This is the time to go for growth. You don't need income from your RRSP, and you don't need much liquidity. The vast majority of your investments should be growth-oriented, even if they are subject to wide fluctuations in value. For example, you may want to choose sector funds, which are mutual funds investing in specific industries, such as entertainment, communications, and health care. These are subject to wild swings in value, but if the underlying quality is good, they are a route to maximum RRSP growth.

- ✔ **From age 25 to 35, you acquire commitments.** You may be married with children and a mortgage, and deeply involved in your career. You have more income, but more expenses as well. The needs of your RRSP reflect your new commitments, now geared for steady growth to maturity. Some of the riskier growth investments that appealed to you ten years ago aren't as attractive, and a little liquidity in your plan, enabling you to obtain cash if needed, wouldn't hurt at all.

- ✔ **From age 35 to 45, the word is *reality*.** You are approaching your maximum income level, and your RRSP contribution limits have risen accordingly. Most of all, your RRSP is now worth a fair amount of money — and that's good, because all those people who appear in advertisements promoting retirement benefits start looking like you and your friends. Your major concern is holding onto all the money your RRSP has earned over the years, and that means more income and security. You still need growth, but now you prefer sure and steady improvements rather than fast-paced, jerky motions — kind of like your changed taste in music.

- ✔ **From age 45 to 55, the horizon draws closer.** Perhaps you're an empty nester by now. In any case, you relish each increase in your RRSP's value and look for all the guarantees you can get. It's a time of consolidation and preparation. Income investments are especially attractive, and GICs you once sneered at for their low earnings now find a place in your plan. After all, they are guaranteed and predictable, which is something you have come to learn that life is not.

- ✔ **From age 55 to 65, it's harvest time.** You focus on both "topping up" your RRSP before converting its assets to retirement income and locking in as much as possible with reduced-risk investments. Growth and liquidity are still factors, but you are more conscious about holding on to what you have.

Keeping the three basic investment groups in mind — liquidable, income, and growth — let's examine the various options that deliver these qualities in various proportions. These are the raw ingredients of your recipe. Later, we can add a little spice if you like.

Savings accounts

You may have had one of these since you were a child. Besides being safe, they are also highly liquidable, as you know if you ever took a hammer to your piggy bank. But money in your piggy bank tended to grow mouldy, and not much else. Savings accounts provide not much more than that these days, yet too many Canadians open an RRSP savings account, plunk their loonies into it, and call the whole process "retirement planning." It's not. Savings accounts pay little more than the rate of inflation, which means no growth and no income. A little liquidity in your RRSP goes a long way, but you can enjoy its advantages in better places than a savings account.

GICs

Along with savings accounts, *guaranteed investment certificates (GICs)* are one way for a bank, trust company, or credit union to borrow money from you. In return, they generate interest payable either when the GIC term, from six months to ten years, is up, or on a regular basis — monthly, semi-annually, or annually. These are known as *fixed-income* investments.

Some RRSP owners believe in GICs the way people believe in heaven, convinced that nothing better exists. Sorry. Until you build substantial funds in your RRSP or approach retirement, there are many things better for your RRSP than large quantities of GICs.

Bonds

A bond is basically a GIC with more class. Bonds pay higher interest, can be sold with relative ease (for high liquidity), and some even come with a guarantee. They are admittedly more complicated than GICs, but it's worth learning about them in detail. To do so, read Chapter 11.

T-Bills

The *T* stands for treasury, which means your government needs a short-term loan to get it through the weekend. T-bills, bought and sold by brokerage houses, pay rates comparable to guaranteed bonds. They are not intended for long-term investments, which makes them both highly secure and very liquid. You can obtain longer-term benefits from T-bills by investing in money market mutual funds trading in T-bills and selected high-quality bonds issued by large corporations. See Chapter 10 for more information.

Stocks

Here's where we enter sweaty-palm territory for investment novices. Too many Canadians associate the words *stock market* with the word *Crash!* That's because a slow and steady rise in the TSE and other stock markets never makes the front page of most newspapers, but a major drop in stock prices suddenly becomes big news.

The facts: Nothing provides better long-term growth prospects for your RRSP than a mix of shares in quality companies, in Canada and around the world. Choosing the companies in which to invest, however, demands knowledge, experience, patience, and a little luck now and then. The best advice when you're just starting your RRSP is, don't try this at home. That's what mutual funds are for. (See Chapter 16.)

When you purchase a *common stock*, you own a piece of that company and are investing in its future prosperity. The price of the stock will fluctuate with the financial successes or setbacks of the company, influenced by the economy and the sentiments of the market. Some companies, like some people, are more popular than others, even though they share similar characteristics with the less popular companies. Popular companies see their stock value rise and remain more immune to world events and the state of the economy.

Many companies issue two kinds of stock: *common shares* and *preferred shares*. They're a little like flying economy or first-class. Owners of preferred shares are first in line when the dividends are handed out. Owners of common shares have to wait. (For more detail, see Chapter 9.)

Mutual funds

Suppose that you had $25,000 in your RRSP, and you liked the idea of having someone manage it for you on a continuous basis. Every day this manager would review your account before deciding which stocks, bonds, or other investments to buy and sell, based on the manager's knowledge, experience, and access to huge volumes of research information. In return, you would pay the manager about 2 percent of the value of your RRSP each year.

It's a nice idea, except that 2 percent of $25,000 won't get the job done. But if a thousand people like you pooled their RRSPs, the total would amount to $25 million, and 2 percent of that is $500,000 annually. Now you have a manager's attention — and, with a little tweaking here and there, you also have a *mutual fund.*

In reality, $25 million is a tiny mutual fund these days. Many Canadian mutual funds reach several billion dollars in *managed assets,* the money entrusted to them by investors. The skills of the fund manager should produce a substantially higher annual return for investors than they could earn on their own, more than making up for the annual fee paid to the manager. This is why the amount of money invested by Canadians in mutual funds exploded from a few hundred million dollars in 1980 to more than $400 billion by 2000.

Mutual funds provide the best opportunity for inexperienced investors to build their RRSP value over time. They also provide an excellent way to diversify your investments in several different ways. But they are not foolproof, and choosing the best fund for your needs takes some investigation by you, as well as some consultation with your financial adviser. (See Part IV.)

Mortgages — Yours and others

A mortgage is a legitimate investment for an RRSP, as long as it is secured by real estate within Canada — such as your own home, for example. Does this mean you can use cash from your RRSP to finance the mortgage on your home and actually pay yourself with monthly mortgage payments? As a matter of fact, it does. Hey, why doesn't everybody do that? Here's why:

- ✔ It's a complex operation involving a mortgage trustee, real estate appraiser, legal counsel, and mortgage insurance.

- ✔ It involves several high-priced people, all of whom expect to be paid, to set up the mortgage inside your RRSP. It also involves a separate self-directed RRSP fee each year.

- ✔ You need at least $50,000 in cash or liquidable assets (plus that much room in your mortgage) to make it worthwhile, and at least $75,000 to make it attractive.

- ✔ You cannot charge an excessive interest rate on the mortgage to build your RRSP. Canada Customs and Revenue Agency says the interest rate must be "comparable" to current rates in the marketplace. If your bank offers you a 10-year mortgage at 7.5-percent interest, that's the amount you should set for your RRSP mortgage.

Yet there are some advantages. Mortgage rates are always a few percentage points above GICs, with similar security. And you can also use RRSP cash to fund a mortgage for someone else, including a son or daughter. But do you want to?

If your RRSP plans are just getting rolling, the mortgage option is not for you — at least, not for a few years. When the value of your RRSP hits six figures, you may want to review it, however. (For information on mortgage-based mutual funds, which enable you to invest your RRSP in other people's mortgages, see Chapter 15.)

Contributions in kind

Until now, the focus has been on making contributions in cash to your RRSP. But there is another alternative, called *contributions in kind*. A contribution in kind simply means transferring any eligible investment held outside your RRSP into your plan, where any earnings it produces are subject to deferred taxation, just like other RRSP investments. If you own, inherit, or otherwise acquire some Canadian bonds (including CSBs), mutual funds, eligible mortgages, or shares in Canadian companies (or in foreign companies, up to 30 percent of your total RRSP value), you can move them into your RRSP and claim a deduction.

This is even better than it sounds. Suppose you've been purchasing Canada Savings Bonds over the years instead of contributing to your RRSP, and you have accumulated $5,000 worth of CSBs. Now you want to begin your RRSP, but don't have cash on hand to make a contribution. No problem. Launch your RRSP with the CSBs as your opening contribution, and claim a $5,000 deduction from your income for the year (assuming you have that much contribution room, of course). If you're in the 40-percent tax bracket, this produces a $2,000 tax refund, and you have another $2,000 to add to your plan.

You can enjoy the same benefits if Uncle Herbie decides to give you a gift of his shares in Gold Brick Mining, Inc. Assuming that they qualify as an RRSP investment, you can roll them into your plan and earn a tax refund. The amount you can claim is equal to the value of the shares, or any qualifying investment, on the day you transferred them into your RRSP.

Here's where things can get tricky. If Uncle Herbie paid ten dollars per share for the gold mine stock, and each share was selling for 20 dollars on the day you transfer them into your RRSP, a light goes on at Canada Customs and Revenue Agency. After all, the value of the shares has doubled since Herbie purchased them. That's a capital gain, and capital gains are taxable even though you have not sold the shares for a profit. Thus, you'll be assessed tax on the increase in the share value as soon as the shares are transferred to your name. The CCRA calls this *deemed disposition*. If the shares also increase in value between the day they are transferred and the day you put them in your RRSP, this will be taxed as well. It's probably still wise to make the contribution this way; just be prepared for the tax it triggers.

You can even use your RRSP as a form of pawnbroker, in times of need. No, it won't loan you 20 bucks against your watch or wedding ring. But if you own eligible securities such as stocks, bonds, or mutual fund shares outside your RRSP, and you're strapped for cash on a fairly short-term basis, you can transfer the securities into your RRSP and withdraw an equal amount in cash. Your securities continue to grow in value, but now the growth is tax-deferred. You have the cash you need to tide you over and, when the cash crisis is past, you can buy the securities back again. This gets a bit tricky, so you'll want a little professional assistance. But it can be done.

Part III

Guaranteed Investments

The 5th Wave — By Rich Tennant

"ANNUITIES? EQUITY INCOME? TAX-FREE MUNICIPALS? I SAY WE STICK THE MONEY IN THE GROUND LIKE ALWAYS, AND THEN FEED THIS GUY TO THE SHARKS."

In this part . . .

You discover good news and bad news about reducing the risk of your hard-earned RRSP contributions. We take a new look at old standbys like savings accounts and GICs, and strip away (sometimes literally!) the mystery of bonds, revealing their true nature. You grasp the concept of Ottawa asking you for a short-term loan until payday (called a T-bill), and how the government's need for a loan can affect your RRSP strategy.

Chapter 9

Minimizing the Risk

● ●

In This Chapter

▶ Building a secure foundation

▶ Comparing RRSP-eligible investments

▶ Looking for bigger returns

▶ Learning from Bill and Buffy's different investment styles

● ●

*T*here is no free lunch, even in a tax-sheltered RRSP. That's a basic rule to keep in mind when it comes to making decisions on your RRSP investments.

Do you want your RRSP to grow over the years to astonishing values? It's possible. There are several million-dollar RRSPs around today, and more arriving each year, as Canadians grow savvy about investing for the future.

Do you want minimum risk? That's understandable. Nobody wants to lie awake at four in the morning worrying about budget deficits and the state of the TSE.

This is where the "no free lunch" rule comes in: You can't have both. Maximum growth involves some risk. Minimum risk limits growth. So it's best to take a position somewhere in the middle, which, after all, is something we Canadians are supposed to be good at doing. . . .

Laying the Groundwork

Professional investors and economists often refer to *capital*, as in *capital reserves* and *preservation of capital*. It's a two-dollar word for money — in this case, money spent to purchase investments.

One way to ease the four-in-the-morning "Are my investments safe?!" willies is to place a portion of the capital in your RRSP in a secure fixed-income investment. This portion should vary with your age and your risk threshold. As your age increases, your risk threshold should drop, meaning you are less comfortable with the prospect of losing some of your capital.

Some people wear both a belt and suspenders. Some insist on a constantly filled pantry and freezer. And some people can't relax unless every last penny in their RRSP is guaranteed safe. This attitude approaches paranoia, especially when the RRSP owner is under the age of 40. Nothing is 100-percent guaranteed in life, including RRSP investments. And no one who follows basic investing principles should fear losing 100 percent of their RRSP investment, or even a majority of it, in any circumstance.

By the time you are 30 years of age or older, or have more than $25,000 in your self-directed RRSP, you may want to give some thought to preservation of capital if it helps you sleep better. Here's the guideline again: The percentage of "guaranteed" investments — GICs, T-bills, bonds, and so on — held in your RRSP should not exceed your age until you are within sight of retirement. It's just a guide, of course, but a good one to remember.

The risk of being too conservative

There is an irony in being too conservative about your RRSP decisions. An overly conservative approach is the result of trying to avoid risk. Actually, it doesn't eliminate the problem entirely; it just changes the *kind* of risk you face. (For a more detailed explanation of different types of risks, see Chapter 5.)

Whenever you reduce your risk of losing capital, you increase the risk of not having sufficient money in your RRSP down the road. Here's one more example of the growth differential between overly conservative and controlled-risk investments:

In 2001, a combination of GICs and savings-account interest might generate an annual return of 4 percent for your RRSP. But RRSP-eligible mutual funds, investing in quality companies in Canada and elsewhere, average a 12-percent annual return over a typical ten-year period. If you are overly conservative, with $5,000 to invest in your RRSP, you might choose the GIC/savings-account combination. If you are careful with your investment but want at least reasonable long-term growth, you could choose a well-managed equity mutual fund. Table 9-1 outlines the difference, in five-year periods:

Table 9-1	4-percent versus 12-percent Annual Growth		
$5,000 growing at 4-percent average annual returns:			
After 5 Years	*10 Years*	*15 Years*	*20 Years*
$6,063	$7,401	$9,005	$10,956

$5,000 growing at 4-percent average annual returns:			
After 5 Years	*10 Years*	*15 Years*	*20 Years*
$14,099	$24,847	$43,789	$77,170

So . . . who took the bigger risk?

It's fair to mention that "average annual return" for mutual funds, while accurate, does not guarantee future performance. The value of a mutual fund could decline to less than your original investment, something that happened to mutual funds invested in Internet-based stocks in 2000. But these declines have historically been followed by increases in value that more than offset the loss. Remember: 12 percent is an average among all mutual funds; some well-known funds have averaged 15-percent growth annually for 20 years or more.

Examining alternatives

Table 9-2 provides an at-a-glance introduction to various RRSP-eligible investments. Each is covered in detail in subsequent chapters, but this provides a quick assessment of three key qualities: liquidity (how fast you can convert it to cash); safety (how certain you can be that you won't lose most of your investment); and earnings (how the investment grows over time). Here are other terms worth understanding:

- ✔ **Capital growth** is the increase in value of your original investment over time.

- ✔ **Dividends** are payments made to shareholders by corporations based on earned profits and agreed upon by the company's board of directors.

- ✔ **Preferred shares** are similar to common shares but are first in line to receive any dividends in return for not giving the share owners any voting rights in the company.

- ✔ **Currency values** refers to any fluctuations in value between the Canadian dollar and foreign currency used to purchase the investment. An investment in a U.S. company, for example, will rise in value if the value of the loonie decreases against the U.S. dollar; if the loonie's value rises compared with the U.S. dollar, the U.S. investment is worth less.

You may be impressed by the wide range of investments available, but don't be confused. Many RRSP owners include no more than four or five in their plan and still manage to create substantial earnings over the years. This list is merely an introduction to the choices available when you're seeking the best balance between meeting your risk threshold and maximizing the value of your RRSP over time.

Table 9-2	Comparing Investment Alternatives		

Fixed-Income Investments *(You loan them your money)*

	Liquidity	Safety	Earnings
Canada Savings Bonds	Very high	Very high	Interest
Corporate bonds	Medium/low	Medium	Interest
GICs/term deposits	Low/medium	Very high	Interest
Mortgages	Medium	Medium	Interest
Savings account	Very high	Very high	Interest
Strip bonds	Medium	Very high	Interest
Treasury bills	Very high	Very high	Interest

Equity Investments *(You invest your money in their company)*

	Liquidity	Safety	Earnings
Common shares (in Canadian companies)	High	Medium/low	Dividends/ capital growth
Foreign stocks	High	Medium/low	Dividends/ capital growth/ currency values
Preferred shares (in Canadian companies)	High	Medium/low	Dividends/ capital growth

Mutual Funds *(Your money is professionally managed according to the description of the fund)*

	Liquidity	Safety	Earnings
Balanced funds	High	Medium	Dividends/ capital growth
Bond funds	High	Medium	Interest/growth
Canadian stock funds	High	Medium/low	Dividends/ capital growth
Foreign stock funds	High	Medium/low	Dividends/ capital growth/ currency values
Money market funds	Very high	High	Interest
Mortgage funds	High	Medium	Interest/growth
Precious-metals funds	High	Medium/low	Dividends/growth
Real estate funds	Low	Medium	Interest/growth

Looking for bigger returns

Whenever you give your RRSP serious thought, you should be looking for ways to increase its value and maintain your comfort level. This isn't greed; it's just good sense. Remember that your self-directed RRSP is the one source of future income over which you exercise control. Your job, your government benefits, and the value of your home, among other things, may slip away in the future. Maintaining the value and security of your RRSP is a good way to add financial security to life, and you shouldn't feel greedy about doing it.

Bill and Buffy: A Cautionary Tale

Bill and Buffy are each 30-something with good jobs and self-directed RRSPs. Both earn $50,000 annually, have $25,000 in their RRSP, contribute $3,600 each year, and retirement is about 30 years away. But when they get there, Buffy will have almost half a million dollars more than Bill to finance her retirement.

The difference? Investment styles.

Both consider themselves active managers of their RRSPs. Buffy, however, keeps her eye firmly on the far horizon. By making quality choices, she knows that time is on her side, and time is also her security. Sudden drops in the stock market don't faze her. She knows that next week, next month, next year, the market will rebound and earn back any losses she suffered, plus more.

She also knows that interest rates on GICs and savings accounts, while perhaps not swinging as wildly as the stock market, tend to even out over time. Unless she can "lock in" a high interest rate in a guaranteed investment for an extended period, short-term changes in interest rates hold little interest for her.

Finally, Buffy retains the services of a financial adviser employed by the firm that administers her self-directed plan. She trusts her adviser's viewpoint, listens closely, considers the options, and makes up her mind. Buffy works according to a plan.

Bill, however, works according to instinct, plus a pinch of panic. Instinct may help a rabbit in a forest, but it can seriously cripple an investor.

When Bill learns the stock market has shot up in value, he moves his money into equity-based mutual funds and common shares. But by the time Bill reacts, others have begun to sell, which reduces prices, and Bill panics as the values fall. "Once bitten, twice shy" is Bill's philosophy, so he sells his mutual funds at a loss to buy long-term GICs and CSBs. Okay, they're only paying 5 percent or so, but that's 5 percent guaranteed for five to ten years, right?

Well, kind of. Within a few months, interest rates start rising past 6 percent, past 7 percent, and are soon crowding 8 percent. Taking inflation into effect, Bill's 5-and-a-bit-percent GICs and CSBs are barely making a profit. Now Bill wants to get out of his GICs before they mature, but if he does he'll pay a penalty in lost interest. And he wants to sell his CSBs, but they're now worth less money than when he bought them because their interest rate is so low compared with current rates. Poor Bill.

The moral? Avoid impulsive behaviour. Do your homework, stick with quality, monitor your progress, weigh your decisions, keep your eye on the horizon . . . and then go catch a movie and relax.

Chapter 10

Savings Accounts, GICs, and T-bills

In This Chapter

▶ Waking up to why you should avoid savings accounts

▶ Matching GICs to your needs

▶ Outlining a GIC investment strategy

▶ Assessing special kinds of GICs

▶ Explaining T-bills and their place in your RRSP

▶ Learning from Frank and Frances's different investment styles

*B*uilding an RRSP isn't a matter of saving. It's a matter of investing. Unfortunately, this basic idea hasn't filtered down to all RRSP owners, which means thousands of Canadians will spend their retirement with much less money than they could have. Millions of RRSP dollars are sleeping in savings accounts and GICs when they could be working hard for their owners in other prudent and eligible RRSP investments.

Is there a place in your RRSP for savings accounts and GICs? Yes. But when you're young, it's a small place. Over there in the corner.

Savings Accounts

Here's a fact you may find surprising: Your bank or trust company doesn't want to handle your savings account. In recent years, they've been proving it by charging outrageous fees on these accounts unless you maintain a cash balance big enough to buy downtown Moose Jaw. Savings accounts with low balances are expensive to administer, and a time-waster for bank staff. Your bank or trust company would prefer that you purchase a GIC with the money, because GICs need no passbook, no statements, and less general administrative upkeep. Just leave your money for a few years and go away, thank you very much.

Add this to the very low interest your RRSP will earn in a daily interest savings account (DISA) these days — averaging 3.0 percent in mid-2001 for balances between $10,000 and $100,000 — and it's evident that you pay a price for both the security and liquidity that a DISA offers.

At the same time, Canadian T-bills were earning about 4.5 percent for their investors, with virtually the same level of security and liquidity. Is there a time and a place for a DISA in your RRSP? Perhaps, when and if

✔ You have just opened an RRSP and want to build up its value to the point where you can consider other alternatives. (But note that you can immediately begin investing in some mutual funds with as little as $500 initially and $50 monthly. Why wait to transfer a bundle from the bank?)

✔ It's late in February and you want to make a lump-sum contribution to your RRSP in order to claim the tax deduction, but you're unsure where to put the money for a long-term RRSP investment. Instead of making a frantic last-minute decision in haste, you choose to place your contribution in a DISA and wait a few weeks until the RRSP panic season subsides. This is known as "parking," and generally is a wise idea. But don't wait too long.

✔ You have substantial RRSP assets and would like a little liquidity, so you move some of your money to a savings account. But it shouldn't total more than 2 or 3 percent of your assets. (Money in T-bills is also considered "cash" and can represent a substantially larger share of your plan, especially as you approach retirement age.)

When "unparking" your money, it may be wise not to yank it out of your savings account all at once, especially if you plan to invest in equity mutual funds during a period of high volatility. A *volatile market* is one with wide swings in prices: up today, down tomorrow. Two other alternatives:

✔ Move the balance to T-bills or a money market mutual fund, where the liquidity is almost as good and the earned interest is a little higher, leaving it there until things become less volatile.

✔ Arrange to transfer the money in equal amounts over a few months. This tends to "flatten" volatility.

GICs: For Mature Readers Only

Guaranteed investment certificates (GICs) are secure, but they are not very liquid. With a standard GIC, you lock your money in for periods ranging from six months to five years. While it's true that the longer the term, the higher the interest earned by a GIC, a high rate of very little is still not much. Even worse, most GICs are not very liquid. Try to withdraw cash from a standard GIC before its *maturity date*, which is the day the bank or trust company promises to give you back your money plus interest, and you could lose several months' worth of earned interest. Some GICs don't allow you to withdraw any funds at all, which makes you wonder whose money it really is — yours or the bank's?

There are as many breeds of GICs as there are of domestic dogs, and almost as much variety. Some firms offer "cashable" GICs that let you withdraw funds without penalty. But, since these GICs tend to pay a full percentage less than standard GICs, you pay a penalty in reduced earnings.

Once you retire and convert your RRSP into an income-producing plan, it makes sense to place a portion of your total in GICs, which will generate regular payments to you. Most banks and trust companies can arrange monthly interest payments on GICs of $5,000 or more. The interest rate still won't knock your socks off, but it's guaranteed, and your *principal* — the amount you spent to purchase the GIC in the first place — remains intact.

Until then, the biggest attraction of GICs is the "guaranteed" part, which helps you sleep better as your RRSP grows older and fatter. This makes GICs suitable for a portion of RRSP investments among the over-50 set. But there are other ways to enjoy both bigger returns and much better liquidity in your RRSP, no matter what your age.

Things to keep in mind when buying GICs

Before you pick up the phone and call your financial adviser to investigate your GIC investment options, though, remember these points:

- ✔ Financial institutions selling GICs price them according to their need for your money; the more they want your cash, the higher the interest you earn. So it pays to shop around. Example: If you had $5,000 or more in your RRSP in April 2001, the average GIC would pay you about 3.5 percent interest for one year. But the same $5,000 was earning 4.46 percent at one trust company that was more desperate for your money.

- ✔ GIC rates are tiered; as a general rule, the more you invest and the longer the term, the higher the interest rate you earn.

- ✔ Non-redeemable GICs pay higher rates than redeemable versions. In a non-redeemable GIC, the money in the GIC cannot be accessed (except to settle an estate) before the term is completed. The GIC can, however, be transferred or sold at market value under certain conditions.

- ✔ Remember the laddering principle: Purchase GICs in staggered maturity dates to protect against wild interest-rate fluctuations. Instead of buying one five-year GIC for $10,000, choose one, two, three, four, and five-year GICs of equal value, providing access to 20 percent of your money each year.

- ✔ Investigate other options that provide guarantees similar to those of a GIC but with more liquidity and the prospect of better earnings, such as strip bonds (see Chapter 11).

New breeds of GICs

To their credit, banks and trust companies have acknowledged the drawbacks of GICs for use inside an RRSP, and introduced a few crossbred versions worth investigating.

Index-linked GICs are GICs based on various market indices, such as the TSE 35 or the TSE 100. The TSE 35 includes 35 different companies listed on the Toronto Stock Exchange whose prices are used as a benchmark to indicate the general movement of stock prices. The companies making up the TSE 35 are considered to be blue-chip and represent a cross section of the economy, so the list includes banks and financial institutions, manufacturers, mining companies, retailers, and so on. The TSE 100 is more diversified; it includes 100 companies and industries.

If Canadian stock-market prices rise during the term of your GIC, you earn growth in proportion to the increase of the index, with a couple of exceptions.

The growth may be limited by something called the *market participation rate,* or MPR. This can vary from time to time, but it hovers around 85 percent and is locked in when you purchase the index-linked GIC. The MPR is the fund operators' way of ensuring that they get to keep some of the profits. With an MPR of 85 percent, their share is 15 percent

In practice, the growth of the index used to measure your GIC's earnings is multiplied by the MPR as a percentage. So, for example, if your TSE 35 index-linked GIC is for a two-year term, and the TSE 35 index rises from 7,000 to 8,500, that's an increase of 21 percent. This is reduced by the MPR (which, if it is set at 85, equals 85 percent of 21, or 17.85 percent), which is the amount of interest your indexed GIC pays when the term is up. Spread across a two-year GIC, that's 8.925-percent annual interest, which ain't bad these days considering there was no risk of any capital loss.

Sound good? It gets better . . . sort of. Some index-linked GICs permit you to "lock in" any growth before the GIC term is up. So if the index rises 21 percent in the first year, you can "lock in" that growth (less the MPR) and renew the GIC at the higher value for an extended term. If the index is worth less when the GIC term is up, you get back the locked-in amount — you haven't lost a thing.

The choice of index-linked GICs keeps widening every year, providing the benefits of diversification along with the guarantee against loss of principal. TD Bank, for example, calls its index-linked investments TD Market Growth GICs, which stretches things a little because nobody guarantees growth, they can only guarantee the safety of your initial investment. Three of TD's products are linked to stock markets — Canadian, U.S., and global. The latter two are both 100-percent eligible for your RRSP, which means that they avoid the dreaded 30-percent limit on foreign investments. That's an important plus.

Three other TD products are linked to the bank's Green Line Mutual Funds instead of to stock-market prices. Growth in value of the three mutual funds is reflected in the interest paid on the GICs.

Okay, now for the "no free lunch" rule. First, index-linked GICs are not easily liquidable; you are in for the full term. Second, while you can't lose your principal, neither can you win if the index has not risen while your funds were invested. If the index on which the GIC is based hasn't moved over the term of your GIC, you earn nothing. What's more, index-linked GICs without a market participation rate (MPR) are usually *capped.* This is like a Vegas casino setting a limit on your winnings. If the cap is set at 20 percent annually and the index rises 25 percent in a year — an unlikely but not impossible event — the house keeps the extra 5 percent and pays you no more than 20 percent. Now, 20-percent annual interest on a guaranteed investment is nothing to sneeze at. But it proves the "no free lunch" rule is always hiding somewhere. Just be aware of it from the beginning. (For an interesting alternative to index-linked GICs, see *index-linked notes* in Chapter 15.)

Finally, index-linked GICs are not always available from all sources; like certain kinds of seasonal wines and candies, they're for sale one day and withdrawn the next. TD Bank, for example, withdrew its TSE 100 index-linked GICs from sale in early 2001, promising to reintroduce them at a later date.

In May 2001, Scotiabank continued to offer its Stock-Indexed GICs, or SIGICs. Table 10-1 shows a demonstration of a $10,000 SIGIC versus a $10,000 standard GIC, using Scotiabank's posted rates. The Scotiabank SIGIC is for three years and is linked to the TSE 35 index, with no MPR but with a 20-percent cap. The three-year standard GIC pays 3.7-percent interest annually.

Table 10-1	**Index-Linked GICs**
Index-Linked (Scotiabank's SIGIC)	*Standard*
If the TSE 35 index is lower at the end of the three-year period, the GICs are worth:	
$10,000	$10,712
If the TSE 35 index is up 15 percent, the GICs are worth:	
$11,500	$10,712
If the TSE 35 index is up 25 percent, the GICs are worth:	
$12,000	$10,712

Money market GICs, like the index-linked varieties, reflect monthly changes in the bank rate, either up or down. Interest is paid monthly, creating potential compound growth. These usually are limited to one-year terms and may be converted to cash, with earned interest, after 90 days.

Convertible GICs are offered by mutual fund companies such as AIM/Trimark. Available in terms of one year to five years, they pay an interest rate that's comparable to that of banks and trust companies, but provide an interesting option during the second half of the term. At any time after the end of the first year of a two-year convertible GIC, for example, you can choose to keep your money in the GIC for the balance of the term, or convert the full amount to an eligible mutual fund.

Here's the advantage: If mutual funds, especially those in the stock market, are not performing well when you're ready to invest, you can earn GIC rates. This guarantees you both the safety of the money you invest and the amount you will earn each year. If mutual funds and the stock market begin to rebound, you can step off the GIC and onto an eligible AIM/Trimark mutual fund.

It's a neat trick, combining both security and flexibility in one package. Convertible GICs from AIM/Trimark and other mutual fund companies are generally sold only through financial advisers. One small catch, though: The eligible mutual fund is usually a *deferred sales charge fund (DSC),* which means you could pay a redemption charge to get out of the fund. The DSC, however, declines over about five years; after that period, no DSC applies. (Read more about DSCs in Part IV.)

Other exotic breeds of GICs include the following:

- ✔ **Escalating-rate GICs.** These are typically for three-year terms, offering higher earned interest in the second and third year. You can withdraw your investment, plus interest, on the first and second anniversary date of your investment.

- ✔ **"Forced savings" GICs.** These split your investment (minimum typically $1,000) into 12 equal monthly payments deposited into a daily interest savings account. When you make the final payment, the balance is automatically rolled over into a two-year GIC earning a slightly higher rate of interest than paid to standard two-year GICs.

Specialty GICs like these are not always available. You may have to dig to find a bank, trust company, or mutual fund offering them, or wait until they appear on the market. Regular GICs, however, are always available.

T-bills: Ottawa Needs a Loan

The *T* stands for treasury, which is where Ottawa goes to pay its bills. The federal treasury is a little like the chequing account you use to buy groceries, pay the mortgage, and cover your general living expenses. When your chequing account is low, you ask your bank for an overdraft, use your credit card, or borrow a few dollars from a friend. Ottawa issues T-bills.

Nobody in Canada has better credit than the federal government, even if it's already in hock for tens of billions of dollars. Because Ottawa is such a good credit risk, they don't have to pay a very high interest rate on their loans, which means they're not a good choice for building long-term growth. They are a good alternative for cash in your RRSP, however, and a fine place to park your money while you decide on more appealing investment alternatives.

You can purchase T-bills through a broker or your financial adviser, but unless they represent the cash portion of your RRSP (in place of a DISA), don't hold on to them for more than a few months.

T-bills can also be purchased through mutual funds, which trade in them and other highly secure investments. T-bill funds return modest earnings — around 4 percent annually — but provide a "parking area" among funds in the same family without incurring fees or extra costs. For more details on T-bill funds and other money market funds, see Chapter 15.

Frank and Frances: A Cautionary Tale

Nearing age 60, both Frank and Frances have built sizable balances in their RRSPs by following the usual guidelines of maximizing their contributions wherever possible, obtaining professional advice, diversifying their investments, and remaining loyal to their long-term strategy.

Several years ago, Frank began to consolidate his earnings, moving gradually from equity-based mutual funds into GICs. Until age 50, Frank had kept his GIC investments at a minimum — never more than 10 percent. About 20 percent of his RRSP was invested in bonds. But once each year after he turned 50, and following an annual review with his financial adviser, Frank purchased a series of one- to five-year GICs, laddering them so one-fifth matured each year. Now he has more than 40 percent of his RRSP in laddered GICs, another 20 percent in bonds, and the balance in growth-oriented mutual funds. He feels confident he can retire later this year, just as he planned, to spend time travelling with his wife each summer and building furniture in his beloved basement workshop over the winter.

Frances followed the same general path, except that she became enamoured with the growth available to her from her equity-based mutual funds. GICs seemed dull and listless to her. She loved watching the stock markets rise over the years, and maintained more than 80 percent of her total RRSP in equity-based mutual funds.

GICs may be dull and listless, but once purchased they remain immune to the ups and downs of stock markets — something Frances forgot, or simply ignored when her financial adviser pointed it out.

Over the past few months, stock-market values have slipped dramatically. They'll come back, Frances knows, but when? And how far? Can she afford to move now to that lakeside cottage she dreamed about, and launch a new career writing horticultural books and newspaper columns? Maybe not, after all. Should she sell some of her mutual funds now, taking a loss, and move them into those dreaded GICs . . . or wait to see if the market recovers soon? But of course, it could fall further still. . . .

It's a confusing time for someone who spent so many years methodically building an impressive RRSP balance, and who now sees it shrinking in size just when she needs it most.

The moral: GICs have their time and place. The very things that make them unexciting when you're young can make them appealing when your hair begins to grey and your primary concern shifts from growth to security.

Chapter 11

Bonds

● ●

In This Chapter

▶ Explaining bonds

▶ Identifying types of bonds

▶ Choosing strip bonds for your RRSP

▶ Matching maturity dates to strategy

▶ Knowing where and how to buy bonds

▶ Learning from Sam and Susan's different investment strategies

● ●

Next to mutual funds, bonds are the most confusing investment option for the majority of Canadians. That's because bonds have a mystique about them — with the exception of Canada Savings Bonds (CSBs), which many people use as a means of forced savings.

Bonds are not as complex as you may think, and by the time you reach your mid-30s, they deserve a place in your RRSP, in one form or another.

Defining Bonds

Bonds are a simple idea made complicated by time. Essentially, a bond is an IOU issued by a corporation or a government in exchange for cold, hard cash. Here's an easy way to understand bonds.

If a friend asks to borrow a hundred dollars from you until the end of the month, she may offer an IOU promising to pay you back on that particular day. Bonds aren't much different, especially if your friend agrees to pay you interest on the loan.

But suppose your friend wants to borrow the money for a little longer than a month — say, 30 years? That changes things quite a bit.

First, you would hope she'll still be your friend in 30 years, and that she'll be around to pay back the loan. Also, instead of waiting 30 years for the entire amount to be repaid plus interest — which would be a pile of interest — you would probably appreciate receiving a series of interest payments from time to time. That's when the one big IOU becomes a series of little IOUs, promising to pay interest on the loan once or twice a year. Each small IOU would have a date on it, indicating when the payment was due. You would agree to give each small IOU back to your friend on its date in exchange for cash payment, representing interest earned on the loan.

If you needed cash before the term of the loan was up, you could obtain it by selling the IOU to someone else. If this third person knows nothing about your friend, and has doubts about her ability to repay the loan, it will influence the price they are willing to pay for the IOU. Familiarity and trust reduces the risk and raises the price; unfamiliarity and distrust increases the risk and lowers the price. All bonds work essentially the same way.

The date on which a bond/IOU must be paid is called its *maturity date*, and the difference between the price paid for the bond and its value at maturity, divided by the number of years between then and now, equals the annual interest (see Table 11-1).

Table 11-1	Interest Calculation on Bond's Issue Date
Price you pay for the bond:	$1,000
Value of the bond at maturity:	$2,000
Difference in value:	$1,000
Number of years to maturity:	10
Annual interest earned ($1,000 divided by 10):	10%

These days, 10-percent guaranteed interest is pretty appealing for a high-quality bond. In fact, if the *issuer* of the bond — whoever borrowed the money in the first place — is well-known, with a good credit rating, people would pay more for this bond if you were selling it, lowering the actual annual interest rate. If you offered me this bond, I might pay you $1,400 for it, earning you an immediate $400 profit (see Table 11-2).

Table 11-2	Interest Calculation If Rates Drop
Price I pay for the bond:	$1,400
Value of the bond at maturity:	$2,000
Difference in value:	$600
Number of years to maturity:	10
Annual interest earned ($600 divided by 10):	6%

But if interest rates suddenly skyrocket, as they did in the 1980s when I could earn 14 percent a year from money in my savings account, your 10-percent annual interest will be almost an insult. So I'll pay you *less* for the bond than you paid in order to earn *more* in annual interest (see Table 11-3).

Table 11-3	Interest Calculation If Rates Rise
Price I pay for the bond:	$500
Value of the bond at maturity:	$2,000
Difference in value:	$1,500
Number of years to maturity:	10
Annual interest earned ($1,500 divided by 10):	15%

Notice three things here:

- Nothing about the bond has changed except its selling price. The company or government issuing the bond is the same; the maturity date is the same; the face value of the bond is the same. The only difference is the current interest rate available from other sources.

- You can make money from bonds in two ways. First, from the interest they earn for you, and second, from buying and selling bonds just as you would buy and sell any other item.

- Bond prices and interest rates are opposite riders on the same teeter-totter — when one goes up, the other drops. So the bond you buy today for $1,000 may be worth substantially less next month if the interest rate climbs higher. If the interest rate on bonds you hold is high enough, and the life of the bond is long enough, this shouldn't be a major concern to you. But it illustrates that a risk exists even with so-called "guaranteed" bonds.

What a bond represents

When a government or corporation issues bonds — basically a batch of IOUs borrowing money to expand the business, pay debts, improve facilities, and for other practical reasons — it is faced with a number of decisions:

- How much money do we need to raise? (Always a prime concern)

- How long can we take to pay it back? (Usually from 5 to 30 years)

- How much annual interest will we have to pay? (Determined by current interest rates and the level of risk involved)

Government-guaranteed bonds are not always issued by governments. Back in the early 1980s, when interest rates soared through the stratosphere, you could purchase Ontario Hydro bonds, guaranteed by the Government of Ontario, that paid *14-percent annual interest for 25 years!* Since mortgages were earning close to 20 percent in annual interest, this wasn't quite as dramatic as it sounds. But interest rates go up and down over time, and clever (or well-advised) RRSP owners like me stocked up on Hydro bonds. When interest rates dropped, the other end of the teeter-totter took off. I sold the bonds at a fat profit and moved the money into equity-based mutual funds. None of this is rocket science among sophisticated investors, of course. But you don't have to be sophisticated to take advantage of these opportunities. You just have to read books like this one to understand the basics. So keep reading!

After bonds are issued by a company through an investment dealer, they are traded the same as any other commodity, from pork bellies to uncut diamonds. The price people will pay to obtain the bonds is based, as with commodities, on how much profit the buyer believes he can make and how much risk is involved.

For example, bonds issued or guaranteed by a government are low risk because most governments can always find a way to pay their debts — they simply raise taxes. But since government-guaranteed bonds carry minimum risk, they don't have to pay high interest to attract your money.

Bonds issued by a corporation whose reputation is less than perfect, or whose coffers are not filled with gold bars, must pay higher interest to match the risk involved.

Gilt-edged, blue-chip, and junk

Bond trading services are companies that employ experts who spend their career evaluating bonds and the firms or governments issuing them, assigning each a rating based on the risk involved. A bond whose likelihood of being paid at maturity is about as certain as the sun rising tomorrow morning is rated AAA. A niggling doubt might reduce it to A+ or A. Serious concerns will topple a bond down to a C or D rating.

- ✔ **AAA- and AA-rated bonds** are considered high-grade, with little risk of default. They include bonds guaranteed by federal and provincial governments as well as the bluest of blue-chip companies.

- ✔ **A- and BBB-rated bonds** represent moderate risk, and are usually issued by large corporations.

- ✔ **BB- and lower-rated bonds** carry a more serious risk of default, meaning you could lose your entire investment in them. Bonds in this category are marketed as high-yield bonds, more familiarly called *junk bonds*.

A bond's rating has a direct impact on the price the market will pay for the bond, and the amount of interest the bond must earn to attract investors. In that sense, bond rating services are like handicappers at a horse race, telling you which nag is likely to finish in the money. If you go along with their views, your odds of winning may be better, but the amount of money the cashier pays for your ticket will be lower.

Gilt-edged bonds are rated AAA or AA. These are issued by federal or provincial governments and large, well-managed companies with excellent reputations, usually referred to as *blue-chip* firms. In Canada, this includes corporations such as Bell Canada, Bombardier, IBM Canada, Loblaw Companies Limited, and chartered banks. It can also include corporations whose reputations may have been tarnished in recent years, such as the former Ontario Hydro, but whose payment of their bonds is guaranteed by the government.

The bonds that most Canadians are familiar with are Canada Savings Bonds (CSBs), which may seem like a wise addition to your RRSP. Except that they weren't eligible for an RRSP unless they were called *Canada RRSP Bonds*. Then their name was changed to *Canada Premium Bonds*. Isn't government wonderful?

Whatever their current name, CSBs for RRSPs pay compound interest (the interest you earn this year earns its own interest next year), are 100-percent guaranteed by the Government of Canada, and can be purchased by anyone who has had a permanent residence in Canada for at least six months. The minimum purchase for RRSP-eligible bonds is $500, and they are available in denominations of $500, $1,000, $5,000, and $10,000.

Junk bonds — or *high-yield* bonds, as they are known in more polite circles — are at the other end of the risk scale from CSBs. These IOUs, which tend to have short maturity dates and pay very high interest rates, may be issued by companies as a means of financing the takeover of another firm. The odds of the company covering these bonds may still be in your favour, but the risk of losing your entire investment remains.

Between these two extremes are bonds issued by lesser corporations that may or may not be around with the money they owe you when the bonds reach maturity. These include smaller but solid companies such as Domtar and Interprovincial Pipeline, and it's worth obtaining professional advice before deciding to risk your RRSP funds in them.

The lower a bond's alphabetical rating, the higher the interest it pays. In mid-2001, bonds rated BB, which is edging into junk-bond territory, averaged 7.92 percent, or almost 3 percent more than top-rated bonds. Bonds three notches lower, at the CC level, were averaging 17.95-percent interest. Pretty tempting? Yes, but if the company issuing the bond defaults, you are left holding a very pretty piece of paper in your RRSP — and nothing more.

Junk bonds can pay *very* impressive interest rates. It may be appealing, when everyone else is promising a paltry 5-percent annual interest for their bonds, to invest a few bucks in a junk bond promising annual interest of 12 to 16 percent. If faced with this opportunity — probably not by a qualified professional financial adviser, by the way — take a long walk around the block before reaching your decision. If you still want to throw your money at some junk bonds, take another walk . . . and another. In the end, the decision is yours. But don't make it without a lot of thinking and a lot of walking.

Why strip bonds are a good choice

A bond's small IOUs, which pay interest once or twice a year, are called *coupons* and come attached to the bond itself. The world is filled, or so we are told, with cackling millionaires whose days consist of removing bonds from their vaults and clipping off the coupons, which they can spend like cash. Let's try not to think about them right now. . . .

Bonds consist of coupons, which represent the scheduled interest to be paid over the life of the bond, and the *residual,* which is the original (or *par*) value of the bond. If you own a $100 (par value) Government of Canada bond paying 8-percent annual interest and maturing on January 1, 2020, it includes coupons dated December 1 and June 1 for each year between the date it was issued and its maturity date. Each coupon is worth $4.00, representing 4 percent of the par value; two coupons each year produce 8-percent annual interest.

But nobody says you must have all the coupons and the residual in one piece on the bond. Each can be removed and traded at whatever value buyers and sellers agree upon for them.

When coupons and the residual have been removed from a bond, the bond is undressed. It's actually called *stripped* — but bonds can be dull stuff for some people, so think of them as naked if it makes them more interesting. (Even *strip* sounds a bit risqué in some tonier circles, where you may hear them referred to as *zero-coupon bonds.*)

Actually, coupons are no longer physically stripped from a bond. Instead, they are *book-based,* which means they exist only as an entry in a centralized financial registry system called the Central Depository System (CDS).

Both the coupons and the residual have a fixed value on their maturity date. Will you pay that price to purchase them before that date? Of course not. How can you make money by paying $100 today for something that will be worth $100 in 5, 10, or 20 years? You will pay *less* than the amount shown on the coupon or residual. The difference between the price you pay today and the price it will be worth on its maturity date, divided by the number of years between now and then, equals the annual interest earned. In other words, it works precisely like a regular bond, but without regular interest payments.

Strip bonds are popular choices as RRSP investments for a bunch of reasons, and they belong in the RRSP of anybody over age 35. Here's why:

- ✔ Strip bonds pay higher interest than guaranteed investment certificates.

- ✔ You know exactly how much interest you will earn between now and the bond's maturity date.

- ✔ Strip bonds are more liquid (you can sell them when necessary) than GICs, which lock you in for periods from six months to five years. Try cashing in your GIC before it comes due and you'll pay a fat penalty.

- ✔ Government-guaranteed strip bonds are even more secure than a GIC. GICs are guaranteed by the Canada Deposit Insurance Corporation to a maximum of $60,000 per account. But federal and provincial governments guarantee their bonds for the full amount.

- ✔ Strip bonds represent extra value for RRSP holders, since they hold no appeal for investors who buy bonds as a source of regular income. Hold a strip bond outside your RRSP and you are required to declare the increase in value each year on your income-tax return. This means you'll pay tax on the profit, even though you are years away from actually pocketing it! In a tax-deferred RRSP, this doesn't apply. The result: Strip bonds appeal to a smaller section of the market, which lowers their price and raises the interest they pay.

- ✔ When you purchase strip bonds, you'll receive a disclosure document indicating limits on their liquidity, marketability, tax implications, custodial arrangements, and safekeeping issues. None of these is critical to RRSP owners who plan on keeping the bonds within their RRSP until maturity.

Short-term or long-term?

Short-term bonds, maturing in two years or less, provide you with flexibility. The interest they produce will be relatively low, but they'll be converted into cash fairly soon, opening up new opportunities.

Long bonds, shorthand for "long-term," are the same size as short models — "long" indicates a maturity date far into the future. They pay higher interest rates than short-term bonds, because long-bond buyers want protection against the danger of inflation between the day they buy the bond and the day it matures. The longer the term, the higher the risk of inflation.

Long bonds are almost as flexible as short-term bonds, since there will always be a market for quality bonds. The question is, at what price? A rise in interest rates will reduce the price you can get for your bonds if you decide to sell them.

Facts to know about bonds

Here are some facts about bonds you can use to impress your financial adviser, spouse, or bowling league partners:

✔ When long interest rates are higher than shorter-term interest rates, this is called a *normal yield curve*. Example: Bonds maturing in two years are paying 5.2 percent annually and bonds maturing in 20 years are paying 5.95 percent. That's a normal situation.

✔ When the difference between long- and short-term interest rates is large, this is called a *steep yield curve*. Example: Bonds maturing in two years are paying 5.1 percent, and bonds maturing in 20 years are paying 8.95 percent. Steep yield curves occur when credit and money are both readily available, which usually means the government is trying to kick-start the economy out of a recession. So short-term interest rates are sharply reduced.

✔ When short-term bonds earn higher interest than long bonds, this is called a *reverse* or *inverted yield curve*. Example: Bonds maturing in two years are paying 7.95 percent, and bonds maturing in 20 years are paying 6.25-percent interest. A decision by the federal government to place tight restrictions on money is usually behind this kind of bond market. The restriction raises short-term interest rates because more people want access to less money. Long-term bond buyers believe interest rates will fall eventually, so they settle for lower earnings down the road.

Most investment professionals believe "Be long or be wrong" when it comes to high-quality bonds. As an RRSP owner, here are your concerns:

✔ How much of your RRSP should consist of fixed-income investments such as quality bonds? (The older you are, the more you'll value the security that bonds provide.)

✔ How does this fit your current strategy? (Is the balance between growth and security correct? Does it help you sleep at night?)

✔ What alternatives promise similar returns? (Perhaps a mutual fund investing in bonds — see Chapter 15.)

How to Buy Bonds

Bonds are available from banks, trust companies, credit unions, caisses populaires, brokerage houses, and licensed financial advisers. Strip bonds are a little more difficult to obtain, although your self-directed RRSP administrator can purchase them for you. TD Bank sells strip bonds. So do independent and bank-owned investment brokers such as BMO Nesbitt Burns and Merrill Lynch, and full-service financial planners including The Financial Planning Group, Money Concepts, Financial Concept Group, and others.

Although it's wise to hold good bonds to maturity within your RRSP, there may come a time when you want their cash value before that date. This means you will be selling your bond on the secondary market, which is like a used car lot for bonds. The price you receive for your bond will depend on a number of factors, all as variable as the wind. These include the following:

- ✔ **Current interest rates.** If they have risen since you purchased the bond, you will receive less than you might expect. If they have dropped, you'll make extra profit.

- ✔ **The bond's maturity date.** Short-term bonds tend to earn lower interest.

- ✔ **Bond features.** Some bonds come with extra features (or, as they might say in a used-car lot, "optional extras"). These include callable bonds — the lender reserves the right to pay you back before the maturity date — and extendable bonds, which means you could wait a little longer than you thought.

- ✔ **The creditworthiness of the lender.** If a company's fortunes have fallen since the bond was issued, the bond's price will drop to reflect this.

The "No Free Lunch" Rule Rides Again

No matter who sells you a bond — stripped, well-dressed, or junk — they are not doing it because they like your curly hair and sweet smile. They're doing it to make a profit. This probably does not qualify as headline news, but it should concern you because the profit margin charged by the bank, trust company, or broker selling you the bond is both hidden and negotiable.

Most brokers, if you ask about commissions on bonds, will claim they don't charge any. They may say something like "We agreed on a ten-year stripped bond at 4.87 percent and that's what you received, with no commissions charged." Trouble is, when the brokerage firm purchased it on your behalf, the bond didn't pay 4.87 percent; it paid perhaps 5.25 percent. The difference? The broker paid *less* to buy the bond so the lower purchase price would have produced *more* interest earned between now and the bond's maturity date. How much more? That depends. But pay attention: If you sell the bond before its maturity date, your broker will pay you less than full market price, producing a lower earned annual interest than you might expect. So you pay a commission buying the bond and a commission selling it. Or, to put it succinctly: You lose coming and going.

All in all, you could wind up losing 2 full percentage points from the interest earned on your bond, without even knowing about it. Instead of earning you 7 percent annually, the bond earns you little more than 5 percent annually.

Does this make your broker, financial adviser, or self-directed RRSP administrator crooked? No, it's just the way things are done in the bond market. Bonds for small investors like you and me are bought and sold according to the interest they earn, not according to the actual purchase price.

But losing as much as 2 percent in annual interest should concern you — especially since you can do something about it. Here's what to do:

- Get details on the recommended bond from your adviser or investment counsellor. Write down the name of the company or government that issued the bond, the date of issue, its value, the maturity date, and, if possible, the series number.

- Ask your financial adviser or the counsellor who purchases the bonds for you to provide information on her firm's bond-commission policy. Refuse to believe that a policy does not exist. Every major investment dealer has guidelines on bond commissions. If your adviser stonewalls you, inform her that you're prepared to ask other firms the same question, looking for the best deal. Make it a threat and follow through. (It's always a buyer's market for RRSP owners.) Hey, it's your money, not theirs.

- Contact a discount brokerage such as TD Waterhouse. Ask for the price and point spread of the bond recommended by your adviser, providing all the data you have. The difference will be your adviser's commission rate.

- Demand that your broker or adviser confirm the commissions being earned on the bond she wants you to purchase, and the amount by which it reduces your earned interest. A difference of 0.50 percent between the two yields is acceptable. You owe your adviser something for her service, after all. Just don't overpay. Example: The bond price paid by your adviser's firm yields 5.75-percent annual interest; at the price you pay for it, the bond earns 5.25 percent. That's reasonable. Anything greater than 0.50 percent is like having your pocket picked.

 All these demands and action by you will not generate unbridled delight from your financial adviser. Tough. It's your money, your future, and you have every right to know what something is really costing you. Simply remind your adviser that she is supposed to be working for and with you — not against you.

Sam and Susan: A Cautionary Tale

For Sam and Susan, strip bonds were an ideal way to lock in some of their RRSP earnings and obtain long-term growth. Just entering their 40s in 1992, they had both accumulated six-figure RRSPs and heeded the suggestions of their financial advisers, who suggested that each place about $100,000 in a series of guaranteed strip bonds with maturity dates starting in 2005. Each year, another series of bonds matured, carrying them to 2012, earning an average 8.75 percent annually.

Five years later, interest rates had declined dramatically and guaranteed strip bonds were paying less than 6 percent annually. That's when both Sam and Susan received phone calls from their advisers. "Since interest rates have dropped, your strip bonds have shot up in value," their advisers said. "If you wanted to sell them now, you could make a big profit."

Sam liked the sound of the *P*-word and agreed to sell his bonds, making a 50-percent profit on his purchase price, or about 10 percent for each year since he had purchased the bonds. "Not bad for a guaranteed investment," Sam said smugly.

Except that now Sam had to decide what to do with his profits. Buy GICs at 4 and 5 percent? Not very attractive. Put everything in equity-based mutual funds investing in the stock market? The balance of Sam's RRSP investment was already there. What's more, the market was going through some wild gyrations and this was not a time to have most of his RRSP invested in equities. In other words, Sam had lots of cash but few places to put it.

Susan, however, listened to her financial adviser's comment, asked about alternative investments, and decided to stay put. She wasn't looking for a fat profit from selling her bonds. She was looking at long-term guaranteed profits instead. Besides, where else could her money earn 8.75 percent a year from a guaranteed investment?

The moral: It's the financial adviser's job to suggest options. It's your job to make the final decision, based on your long-term investment strategy. So change it at your peril.

Part IV

Mutual Funds: A Recipe for RRSP Growth

The 5th Wave By Rich Tennant

@RICHTENNANT

Being Dracula's slave didn't pay much, but Renfield always found extra money to invest.

In this part . . .

You see that mutual funds aren't so mysterious after all, and should be included as part of every RRSP strategy. You meet various fund families, with each family member having a quirk in its personality that either appeals to you or doesn't. Here you uncover the many alternatives for mutual fund investments — shares in companies, bonds and T-bills, and funds investing in exotic companies and places. This is where you gain the knowledge and confidence to reach basic investment decisions, helped along the way by Patience and Prudence, the singing sisters.

Chapter 12

What Are Mutual Funds and Why Are They Important?

In This Chapter

▶ Defining mutual funds

▶ Understanding their benefits

▶ Finding out how funds make their money: front-load, back-load, no-load, and MERs

*T*wo decades ago, you could have listed all the mutual funds sold in Canada on the back of a business card, and the total amount invested in them was perhaps $10 billion. Today, more than 3,000 different mutual funds are available for Canadians to choose from, representing over $400 billion in money entrusted to them by people like you and me. A billion, in case you missed it in math class, is a thousand million bucks. Or, to put it another way, more than $16,000 for every man, woman, child, and cocker spaniel in the country is invested in mutual funds sold in Canada.

Yet many Canadians remain fuzzy about what mutual funds are, how they work, and what they can and cannot do. What's more, people invest in mutual funds without fully understanding how much money they may be making (or losing) in the fund, or how to maximize their investment — which, of course, is the whole point of being in a mutual fund in the first place.

Mutual Fund Facts

Learning the basics of mutual fund operations, and how to use them to generate optimum returns for your RRSP, may be the most complex part of this book. It may also be the most valuable, so I promise to make things as simple as possible. Stick with this section, because your RRSP needs both growth and diversity to maximize its value over time. Mutual funds are far from perfect, and they need to be chosen carefully and monitored. But nothing exceeds a well-chosen mix of mutual funds when it comes to building your RRSP's value over the long term.

I want to begin with three facts about mutual funds.

Fact #1: Mutual funds invest in investments

Every mutual fund invests money in the same things you might choose to invest in yourself, assuming you had a hundred million dollars or more when you went shopping for bonds, T-bills, and shares on the stock market. Most mutual funds don't deal in exotic stuff you can't buy on your own. They just buy and sell more of the same things you might, except that they tend to do it better.

Fact #2: Mutual funds are professionally managed

Here's the real benefit of mutual funds for the kind of person who thinks the TSE is a sports TV channel and "long-term bond" describes a golden wedding anniversary.

Suppose you have $10,000 in your RRSP to invest in shares of well-run companies listed on a stock exchange. Owning shares in well-run companies is a good way to make the most money over the long run. Trouble is, you know as much about evaluating and trading stocks as you do about breeding and raising camels. You need professional help from someone who knows the best companies to invest in. They could tell you how well each company is managed, how much profit they make each year, how tough their competition may be, and much more. This person could decipher a company's balance sheet in less time than it takes you and me to scan a menu at McDonald's, and they could spot a phoney profit-and-loss statement from across a crowded boardroom. He or she would not only study each prospective company, but would have access to information on entire industries, with a herd of research people digging up facts and statistics.

If you found someone like this, you might want them on the job every day, watching over your investment and making decisions in your best interest, leaving you free for more important work — like painting the kitchen, or driving the kids to their soccer game.

Think you can do this with a mere ten grand? Think pigs can fly?

But hold on: If 10,000 people like you each put their $10,000 together, there would be $100 million to invest on behalf of you and your 10,000 partners. That kind of money generates a lot of attention. If all of you agreed to pay a small amount each year — say, 2 percent — for someone to provide professional management of your investments, this would generate $2 million annually, which is more than enough to cover a professional investment manager's annual bar tab, with a chunk left over for a Mercedes or two. And now you have a mutual fund.

In a mutual fund, the person who makes the buying and selling decisions is called the *fund manager*. (See? The jargon isn't that weird . . . yet.)

To protect your investment, the fund manager does not have direct access to all the money you and other investors have trusted him or her to manage. That money is *segregated,* which means it is held by a bank or trust company serving as a *trustee* or *custodian.* The custodian, operating under the *Bank Act,* is severely limited by what either it or the mutual fund can do with the money, which prevents the fund manager from skipping off to Rio with all the cash, never to return. The fund manager can use the money to purchase investments according to the mutual fund's guidelines, but cannot get his or her hands on it. There. Feel better?

Fact #3: Mutual funds deliver wide diversification

Ah, the *D*-word again. Diversification, you'll recall, reduces wide swings in the value of your investments, a disturbing process called *volatility.* Volatility needn't be a major concern in your younger years, but it becomes something to avoid from your mid-40s on. A well-diversified RRSP reduces volatility, and is more likely to deliver maximum growth with minimum risk. It can also produce income from interest (bonds, money markets) and dividends (shares in profitable companies), which can be reinvested to generate more money.

Diversification is part of every well-structured RRSP, especially one whose value is in excess of $25,000 and whose owner is over 40 years of age. A mix of mutual funds is an excellent way to obtain diversity in every imaginable flavour.

Mutual funds invest in one or a combination of four types of investments: bonds, money markets (primarily T-bills), mortgages, and *equities* or shares of common stock in companies. Combining a few different types of fund in your RRSP creates immediate diversification. But that's just the beginning, because funds provide not just basic diversification but different *kinds* of diversification. Like this:

Mutual funds investing in bonds may focus on Canadian or North American bonds exclusively, or widen their scope to include Europe or the entire world. Combining two or more bond funds diversifies your investment further.

Money market funds and mortgage-based funds are another measure of diversification, although money market funds are best suited for either parking your money or as the cash component of your RRSP.

The widest opportunity to diversify your RRSP is with mutual funds investing in *equities,* or shares of companies listed on stock exchanges. Each mutual fund invests in dozens, even hundreds, of companies. These companies, depending on the fund's design, can be either restricted to Canada or a small region of the world, or be as far-flung as the fund manager wants to go in pursuit of a good investment. That's *geographic diversification.*

This does not mean that someone who promised to invest in Canadian bonds can suddenly put your money into Brazilian hot-dog stands and Australian kangaroo ranches. Fund managers are guided by restrictions on where and how they can use your money to purchase investments. (These restrictions are explained in Chapter 13.) There is usually some leeway in their decision-making, but a fund manager who finds herself straying too far from the guidelines will be in hot water. Unless, of course, she doubles the fund's money within a few months. Then she becomes a genius. But this hardly ever happens.

In addition to geographic diversification, mutual funds can focus their investments on specific industries and specialized sectors, such as entertainment, real estate, mining, pharmaceuticals, and more. Combine a specialized fund or two with other, more broadly based funds, and you have *sector diversification.*

Does size matter? It does for mutual funds that limit their investments to smaller companies, avoiding the multibillion-dollar behemoths. Smaller companies tend to be more flexible and able to react more quickly to changes in the marketplace. On the upside, this produces more growth opportunities; on the downside, it means greater volatility. The companies for these funds are selected according to limits on their *capitalization* — the total value of all the outstanding shares of the company — so they are called *small-cap* funds. This is not to be confused with small businesses. A "small cap" company may be valued up to $500 million, making it not exactly a mom-and-pop operation. Anyway, small-cap funds provide *asset-size diversification.*

Finally, fund managers tend to be very individualistic people, with such strong convictions that they are convinced they qualify for membership in the Masters of the Universe Club. It's all ego-driven, but if you woke up every morning with control over a few hundred million dollars to spend wherever you please, your ego might be as large as Baffin Island, too.

Big egos produce strong personalities, which means fund managers stubbornly tend to follow their own unique path toward the same goal. Give any three fund managers the same data on the same choice of investments with the same amount of money to spend on them, and each manager will propose a different combination. Will all three be correct? Perhaps, if they all deliver equally high returns. Will each feel his or her route was the only way to go? Undoubtedly.

Mutual funds are grouped in "families" of funds, and family members usually follow a similar investment philosophy subject to the personalities of the various fund managers. Some of the largest, best-known fund families available to Canadians are AIM/Trimark, Fidelity, Templeton, Mackenzie, AGF, and various bank-managed mutual funds. Just as fund managers have their own investment style, fund families like to adhere to their own investment philosophies. Templeton's philosophy is different from AGF's, and both are different from any of the bank-managed funds. Between the individual fund manager's style and the fund family's basic philosophy, you can achieve *management-style diversification.*

Are mutual funds risky? Here's a straight answer: yes and no. Yes, there is risk in losing a large portion of your investment, as anyone who invested in Internet-based companies in 2000 discovered. Losses can occur with any mutual fund, even money market funds investing in rock-solid T-bills. The risk grows higher in bond funds, higher still in equity funds, and highest of all in funds limiting their investments to specific industries or far-flung corners of the world. But there is virtually no risk of losing your entire investment with any mutual fund. No mutual fund in North America has ever gone bankrupt, which is not something you can say about banks and insurance companies. Nor is any mutual fund likely to go bankrupt. Here's why:

Banks are permitted to loan out more money than they have on hand to pay their depositors. If a majority of the bank's loans are left unpaid all at once, and the depositors suddenly want their money back, the bank is history. This not only can happen, it *has* happened, on several occasions. And if an insurance company is hit with more claims than it expects to pay, or, like Confederation Life in the 1990s, burns up its cash in bad investments, it's out of business too.

 Neither scenario can happen with a mutual fund, because for every dollar a mutual fund holds for its investors, it has a dollar's worth of redeemable securities on hand, including cash — which, of course, is the most redeemable of all. The only way you could possibly lose every penny you invested in a mutual fund is if every investment in every company held by the fund became suddenly worthless. Your odds of winning a lottery are infinitely better than that.

There are many things to be concerned about when choosing mutual funds for your RRSP, but losing your entire investment shouldn't be one of them.

Mutual funds are easy to invest in. Most, including almost all of the bank-managed funds, require an initial investment as little as $500, with minimum additional investments of $50. Some mutual funds demand higher levels of contributions — as high as $250,000 or more to participate — but the selection of minimum investment funds is wide enough to meet everyone's needs.

Bread, milk, eggs ...
Oh, and six units of mutual funds

If you don't think mutual funds are becoming commodities among some Canadians, you haven't visited a Loblaws grocery store recently. In February 2001, the chain announced it would begin selling CIBC mutual funds through its President's Choice Financial Services outlets. By mid-2001, Loblaws had about 200 of these "pavilions," as they are called, across Canada.

Sticking with its high quality–low cost policy, Loblaws promotes CIBC Index Funds (see Chapter 14 for a description of these funds) because they carry lower fees and generally score high on performance.

So the next time you're shopping at a Loblaws for your weekly staples, consider adding mutual funds to your list.

Resources and Clout

Managers of mutual funds have at least two qualities you and I lack: a dawn-to-dusk focus on investment opportunities according to the kind of fund they manage, and the resources to investigate and evaluate these opportunities.

Their focus on investments usually comes honestly. Many fund managers begin their careers as chartered accountants (CAs) handling financial investments for banks, insurance companies, and giant corporations. They combine their CA training or economics degree with a talent for spotting things that escape the eye of other people. What kinds of things? Perhaps it's a bond paying higher interest than it needs to, given the low risk involved. Or a company with outstanding management, an exceptional product, a dominant position in a fast-growing market, or (hallelujah!) all three, yet whose stock share price doesn't reflect these advantages.

Spotting these kinds of opportunities requires a special knack, equivalent to that Wayne Gretzky had from the day he first laced up his hockey skates. Not every fund manager is a Gretzky, of course, but they know how to skate and stickhandle.

Mixing our metaphors for a moment, fund managers are a combination of football quarterbacks and master chefs. Like a quarterback, they have to plan and execute strategy, sometimes improvising as they go along, but working within certain restraints. They're also like chefs, because they blend various ingredients to create certain effects. And as with quarterbacks and chefs, good fund managers may move around, attracting fans that follow them wherever they go. Some mutual fund fans play Follow the Manager, moving their investments to wherever the fund manager travels. This is not necessarily wise investing, but it illustrates the high esteem achieved by top people in the business.

The other quality fund managers possess that you and I lack is an array of valuable resources.

Each day, the fund manager and his staff review the performance of all the investments held in the fund. They must make decisions to buy, sell, or hold an investment according to their opinion on how well it will perform in the future and how much profit or loss they can expect from it.

The fund manager also needs resources to gather every bit of data on investments being considered for the fund. Successful fund managers and their staff perform more analyses on companies and markets than your physician will ever perform on you during a routine physical. Consider this partial list of activities to evaluate a company's investment value and ask yourself if you could, or would even want to, do them yourself:

- **Analyze the financial statements.** Every company issues financial statements reporting how much it earned, how much it spent to keep operating, how much was left over as profit, how much the company owes, and how much the company is worth. That's complicated enough, but it takes several pages to explain it all, and the people who prepare these financial statements are very good at minimizing bad news and maximizing good news. Can you understand a balance sheet, or calculate a price–earnings ratio, or recognize an accrued interest payable if it pops up in your cornflakes tomorrow morning? Most people can't.

- **Rub elbows with senior executives.** What would you ask the president of Petro-Canada or the Hudson's Bay Company or Inco if you sat across from them at their boardroom table? ("How's business?" doesn't count.) Knowing what to ask, and of whom, before investing in a business takes a special skill. So does deciding how much of their answer is true and how much may be questionable. Fund managers and their researchers discuss a company's health and prospects with the people who run things. Then they ask tough questions that you and I would never think of asking. They may also tour factory and mine sites, inspecting equipment and getting their hands dirty, just to confirm what the top brass has told them.

  Sometimes corporate bigwigs don't wait for mutual-fund managers and staff to visit their offices — they'll visit the mutual fund offices themselves, where they do everything but grovel at the feet of the managers. (Or maybe they do that too. Who knows what goes on behind closed doors?) Do you think the president of a billion-dollar company will sit down in your living room and explain his company's prospects? And if he did, is your stemware clean and free of spots?

- **Investigate markets and competitors.** Great Lakes Widgets Inc. may look like a winner as a prospective investment, but perhaps its chief competitor, Maritime Widgets Ltd., is winning over more customers. Or maybe the entire widget market is shrinking. The only way to know for sure is by looking beyond Great Lakes Widgets Inc. at the whole picture.

✔ **Meet with customers, suppliers, and industry observers.** All corporate managers put a positive face on their company's operations. The real story, however, is usually found by talking to the people who buy (or don't buy) the firm's products or services, and the people who run companies supplying raw materials. Has quality slipped in recent months? Is the company taking longer to pay its bills? Are the managers in touch with the Real World beyond their office windows? The answers all serve to give a true picture of the company's value and future prospects.

✔ **Attend trade shows and read trade magazines.** Are you interested in wandering the aisles of Industrial Equipment Expo, or reading several years' copies of *Plastics in Canada*? Probably not, even if you had the time. But if you're considering an investment in a business connected with these industries, you need to know the latest developments in machinery or plastic technology or widget design. Immersing themselves in various industries is the sometimes unenviable role of mutual-fund researchers.

What You Own in a Mutual Fund

The fund uses your money to purchase bonds, stocks, T-bills, or other investments, according to the fund's goals and objectives and the limits placed on the fund manager. You don't actually own these investments, because they are registered to the fund itself. Instead, you own *shares* or *units* in the fund. These are valued according to the total assets of the fund divided by the number of shares owned, and the price is called the fund's *net asset value,* or *NAV*.

The math is easy: If mutual fund PDQ has investments and cash totalling $100 million and its investors own 10 million shares, each share is worth $10. If the investments and cash of mutual fund XYZ total $500 million and its investors hold 10 million shares, each share is worth $50.

A mutual fund's share or unit price is always fluttering up and down like a leaf in the wind because it is affected by many factors. The prices of investments held in the fund change from day to day, and these will move the unit price accordingly. In addition, units of the fund are bought and sold by investors like you and me. When we buy units in a mutual fund, this temporarily increases cash held in the fund. The cash stays there until the fund manager decides where to invest it. When we sell units in the fund, the cash reserves drop, creating another change in the unit value. And when the fund pays its unitholders their profits (called a *distribution*), these are usually taken as new units in the fund; the fund's assets have more value, but the additional shares dilute the value of each unit.

Different Kinds of Mutual Funds

At the beginning of 2001, more than 3,300 mutual funds were available in Canada and each was different from the others, especially when it came to making money for investors in the fund. Don't let this bewilder you. All mutual funds can be grouped into one of seven broad categories. Understanding the different categories is the beginning of eliminating the mystery from mutual funds.

- **Money market and T-bill funds** invest in government and other high-quality securities. Units in these funds tend to be both highly secure and very liquid, which makes them ideal for the cash component of your RRSP. They earn perhaps 2 to 3 percentage points more than you could earn from savings accounts, and their objective is to create income.

- **Fixed-income and bond funds** invest either exclusively, or in combinations of, bonds, mortgages, T-bills, and other relatively secure investments. They also create income, but by buying and selling bonds and mortgages at a profit they produce some growth in their value too.

- **Equity funds** invest in shares of companies in Canada or elsewhere. As long as the shares of foreign companies represent no more than the current 30-percent limit on foreign content, the entire amount of the fund is 100-percent eligible for your RRSP. These funds aim for long-term growth, which means you should be planning to hold your investment for at least five years to ensure a good return.

A major difference between equity funds is their focus on either value (the companies are selling at a bargain price) or growth (the companies aren't turning much profit now, but just you wait!). Read more about the difference, and the influence it can have on both your RRSP and your peace of mind, in Chapter 14.

- **Balanced funds** are a crossbreed of equity and fixed-income/bond funds. They can hold both kinds of investments in the fund, either to generate both income and growth or to provide the fund manager with more options. When the bond market rises, the fund may hold a larger proportion in fixed-income investments to take advantage of the opportunity. When stocks begin to rise, the emphasis may shift to them for greater profit. In changing market conditions, like the ones we saw in 2001, an actively managed balanced fund is a rather nice place to be.

- **Special equity or sector funds** limit themselves to investing in gold, real estate, science and technology, and almost any other industry according to the fund's guidelines. These funds tend to vary widely in value because they are not as diversified as other equity funds. In fact, some advisers consider them almost speculative in nature, and question their value inside an RRSP. Generally, these should make up no more than 5 or 10 percent of an RRSP's total value, and then only if you are a) young, b) ready to accept possible losses in your investment, c) preferably both.

- ✔ **Dividend funds** invest in common and preferred shares of companies expected to pay high, long-term dividends. Some capital growth can be expected as well, but these funds primarily represent an opportunity to generate income.

- ✔ **Global or international funds** mirror other funds described previously in this list, except that they function almost exclusively outside of Canada. This makes them ideal for the foreign content of your RRSP, but beware: International funds may limit themselves to one country or region, such as India or Japan. They may also focus exclusively on developing or emerging markets, which includes Latin America and some Asian countries. Focusing on one region, or one type of country, defeats the prime purpose of investing beyond Canada, which is to build as much diversification as possible into your RRSP. Better to choose funds that invest anywhere the fund manager finds the best prospects.

    There are always exceptions, of course. Funds investing in the U.S. performed exceptionally well during most of the 1990s, reflecting that country's strong economic growth. But all well-managed global equity funds, such as AGF International Value, Spectrum Global Growth, CI Global, and others, had already invested heavily in the U.S. market. They profited from the U.S. market's growth. Unlike funds investing exclusively in the U.S., however, these global funds will be able to move elsewhere when the U.S. market is not performing as well as others.

- ✔ **Open** and **closed funds** describe the structure of the fund, not the investments they hold.

    An *open fund* is the most common fund structure. It enables you or any investor to buy or sell shares in the fund at any time at the current unit price, which is based on the total net assets of the fund at the end of the day divided by the number of units in the fund. That's the price you'll receive per unit if you sell and the price you'll pay if you buy, and it's fixed by the market value of the fund's investments. Open funds have to keep a fair amount of cash or liquidable assets on hand in case more people want to sell their units than buy them. (There are other reasons as well, but this is a practical requirement.)

    A *closed fund* is really like a separate company investing in other companies or securities on the market. Managers of closed funds invest money from shareholders just as they would in an open fund. But once the fund reaches its target investment limit, no further shares are issued. Instead, the fixed number of shares are bought and sold just like shares in IBM, Royal Bank, and Stelco. As a result, the

TIP

Three main courses

Here are three favourite recipes for mixing investments inside your self-directed RRSP. The possible variations are virtually endless, but these provide typical examples of mixing security and risk/reward to match changing needs:

An aggressive mix for investors up to age 35 to 40 seeking maximum long-term growth:

Cash and cash equivalents including RRSP-eligible Canada Savings Bonds, T-bills, and mutual funds investing in them: 5 percent to 10 percent.

Fixed income including strip bonds, GICs, and mutual funds investing in bonds and mortgages: 20 to 25 percent.

Equity mutual funds investing in a wide range of large domestic and foreign (to maximum allowed) companies: 55 to 65 percent.

Special equity or sector mutual funds investing in specific growth-potential areas such as small-cap funds, emerging markets, industry sectors, and so on: 5 to 10 percent.

A conservative mix for RRSP owners age 35 to 50 or for anyone seeking more stability in unsettled economic times:

Cash: 15 percent.

Fixed income: 40 percent.

Equity-based mutual funds or company stocks: 45 percent.

A cautious or mature mix for RRSP owners age 50+:

Cash: 15 to 20 percent.

Fixed income: 50 to 60 percent.

Equity-based mutual funds or company stocks: 25 to 35 percent.

price of the shares does not reflect the actual asset value so much as the *perceived* value of people who may want to own them. Units in closed funds are not as liquidable as open funds, so they're suitable for folks who limit their investments primarily to their RRSP. Until you build your investment knowledge, it's best to stay with open funds.

Other types of funds you may encounter include the following:

- ✔ **Pooled funds,** generally created for wealthy, sophisticated investors. If this includes you, why are you reading this book?

- ✔ **Segregated funds,** which are a combination of mutual fund and insurance policy, to prevent any loss of capital. Chapter 16 covers segregated funds.

- ✔ **Labour venture funds** are designed for labour unions to use when investing in smaller companies just starting up. They offer attractive tax incentives and have finally begun producing reasonable results. They are also covered in Chapter 16.

- ✔ **Royalty trusts** are a closed version of mutual funds that disperse income earned from their investments to the fund shareholders.

How Mutual Funds Make Money for You

Your investment will shrink or grow in a mutual fund according to its *return,* which is the measure of how much the fund has increased or decreased in value over a given period of time. Most people assess a mutual fund's return over one year, which is understandable. But annual returns over periods of three, five, and ten years provide a better picture of performance, if the fund has been around that long.

Returns are calculated two ways. The first is by any *distributions* made by the fund to its unitholders after the fund has earned money from interest (generated by any bonds or T-bills held by the fund); dividends (paid by companies whose shares are owned by the fund); or capital gains (by selling investments at a profit). Distributions are similar to dividends, except that mutual funds inside your RRSP do not pay you in cash, but rather in additional units of the fund added to your plan. If you own 1,000 units of the PDQ Fund valued at $10 per unit, and your share of the fund distribution is $200, you will receive 20 more units of the fund. Now you own 1,020 units of PDQ still valued at $10 per unit.

Notice how this prevents you from calculating your return by comparing the new unit price, or net asset value (NAV), with the price you originally paid. The two prices could be identical, yet you made more money because you own *more* units at the *same* price.

You have the option to accept distributions in cash instead of more units, which is one way a mutual fund can provide you with retirement income, as described in Part VI.

The second way mutual funds generate return is through changes in the value of each fund unit. If a $100-million mutual fund has 10 million units valued at $10 per unit, and the fund's investments rise 10 percent, the calculated unit value rises by the same amount to $11. When the fund distributes this profit to its investors in the same proportion, the unit value will fall because the 10 million units have been swelled 10 percent to 11 million units.

All of this may be fascinating to you, or you may have fallen asleep somewhere in that last paragraph. No matter. You don't need to follow the complex calculations required to determine return. In fact, it's probably a good idea if you don't. Novice investors who track every daily change in their investments risk riding an emotional roller coaster. A jump in unit price can make you euphoric, and a similar slump may throw you into either a panic or a funk — or even both at the same time.

"They're at the post ..."

Choosing to invest your money in a savings account, a T-bill, or a quality bond usually results in a difference of perhaps 2 percent a year in the earnings you make. But it's a whole new horse race when you move into mutual funds, where your decision can amount to a difference of 50 percent or more in earnings over just a single year. Now that's a race worth entering.

Consider how different types of mutual funds made out in 2000. If you put your money on thoroughbred funds, such as those investing in Canadian dividends or real estate, you were a winner. If your bet was on funds investing in emerging markets or companies in the Asia-Pacific region, your money's still somewhere up the track. But have heart — there's another race tomorrow.

Average Fund Return by Investment Category, 2000

Investment Category	Return
Canadian dividend	20.9%
Real estate	16.1%
Natural resources	14.5%
Canadian large companies	12.0%
Canadian equity	10.1%
Canadian bond	8.4%
Canadian balanced	7.9%
Canadian mortgage	6.7%
Canadian small companies	5.1%
Canadian money market (T-bills)	4.5%
U.S. equity	–4.6%
Global equity	–5.0%
Precious metals	–10.8%
Science & technology	–11.9%
Latin America	–14.5%
Emerging markets	–28.4%
Asia-Pacific	–32.0%

Source: Morningstar Research Inc.

Think of managing your RRSP the way you drive your car. Keeping your eyes on the road just a few metres in front of your car's hood is a very risky way to travel. You need a medium view — not too close, and not too far ahead. The same goes for handling your RRSP, especially when it comes to mutual funds. Plotting changes in the value of your mutual fund every day may be bad for your blood pressure. Check fund performance perhaps once a month. Look at total returns, not unit prices.

How Mutual Funds Make Money for Themselves

No one expects a mutual fund to perform all its necessary chores free of charge. It needs money to cover rent, staff salaries, marketing expenses, and much more, with a few million dollars left over for profit. To generate money for themselves, mutual fund companies hold back a small percentage of your investment each year.

This is called the *management expense ratio,* or *MER,* and in recent years it has developed into one of the most controversial aspects of Canadian mutual funds.

The MER is expressed as a percentage of the fund's total assets. Remember the previous example, where you and 10,000 of your closest friends each trusted a fund manager with $10,000 to be invested on your behalf? This produced a pool of $100 million and everyone agreed to pay the fund manager a paltry 2 percent of the total each year, which seemed a fair deal. The 2 percent represents the MER, and is the source of the fund company's income.

Each business day, a portion of the MER is removed from the total assets of a mutual fund, providing cash for the fund company to carry on its business. So when the time arrives for you to dispose of your units in the fund, you needn't worry about being dinged for the MER all at once; it's been accounted for day by day.

If your mutual fund investment earns 10 percent for you each year and the fund's MER is 2-percent, the investments in the fund were actually returning 12 percent annually — the 2-percent MER was deducted before the earnings were paid to you. Look at it this way, and the 2 percent of assets now becomes about 16 percent of the profits earned, because the 2-percent MER is $\frac{1}{6}$ of the 12-percent growth actually produced by the fund.

"So what?" you say. "If I had left the money in a bank or GIC, I might have made just 5 percent. If somebody can double my money, they should be paid for it."

No doubt about it. The more successful the fund is at making money, the bigger the reward for the fund manager and her staff, since the MER is subtracted from the total value of the fund's assets. Building the size of the assets builds the fund's profits in the same proportion. But some things concern people about mutual fund MERs, and while the concerns shouldn't prevent you from including mutual funds in your RRSP, they can help you make the right decision in choosing among various funds. Just be aware:

✓ **Funds collect their MER whether they earn it or not.** While it's true that a mutual fund's income rises and falls with the fund's value, the MER is collected even when you're losing money. Consider the $100-million fund described earlier. If the total value of the fund drops 10 percent in one year, which is not unheard of, the value of your investment drops accordingly. Now the $100-million fund is valued at just $90 million and your original $10,000 investment is worth just $9,000. You made nothing and actually suffered a paper loss of $1,000. But the fund itself earned $1.8 million (2 percent of $90 million).

✓ **MERs vary widely, and have little or no direct relationship to each fund's success.** If you invest a portion of your RRSP in a mutual fund dealing in Canadian equities, which is probably a good idea, the MER could be as low as 0.08 or as high as 4.73, as stated in the *Globe and Mail's Mutual Fund Report*. The median MER is 2.43, so there are as many funds above 2.43 as there are below it. From 0.08 to 4.73 represents a range of almost 60 to 1 — the highest MER is 60 times bigger than the lowest. Does the fund with the 4.73 MER do 60 times better than the one with the 0.08 MER? Hah! As a parallel, imagine one plumber charging $10 an hour to fix your sink and another charging $600 an hour for the same chore, and neither promises to do a better job than the other.

✓ **MERs for Canadian mutual funds are higher than for similar U.S. funds.** There are several reasons for this, some more valid than others. Canadian mutual funds tend to be much smaller than U.S. funds, which reduces certain economies of scale. In Canada, funds must obtain regulatory approval from each province and produce their documents and marketing materials in both French and English, a bilingual expense. Almost half of U.S. mutual funds are sold directly by the fund company to its shareholders, while most Canadian funds are sold through financial advisers, who receive commissions and other payments for their services. It all adds up.

✓ **Perhaps the biggest reason for the wide gap in Canadian versus U.S. MERs is that we Canadians have simply ignored the topic.** As a whole, Canadians know little about mutual funds, so we hire financial advisers to make selections and recommendations for us. The advisers expect to be paid, and their commission payment comes out of the MER. If we knew more about mutual funds and how to select them, we wouldn't need advisers nearly as much, and we would be far less tolerant of high MERs.

✔ **MER earnings have been used for questionable purposes.** A few years ago, some Canadian mutual fund companies were rewarding financial advisers and brokers who recommended their funds with luxury perks, such as vacations in Hawaii. Where did the money come from to pay for all those mai-tais and hula bands? From the MER, of course, which means from the fund shareholders, ultimately. If an adviser or independent broker didn't sell the funds hosting the luaus, she didn't get the perks, and this bordered on bribery. Even worse, it put the advisers in the position of working for the mutual fund companies instead of the advisers' clients. Things have tightened up since then, but there is still room for many funds to reduce their MER size without affecting their quality of service. Just don't expect it to happen without pressure from people like you and me.

Front-end Load, Back-end Load, and No-Load at all

The individual who sells mutual fund shares to you expects to be paid in commission, which is reasonable. As with MERs, the more you know about this part of mutual funds, the less you pay.

A sales commission paid to mutual fund salespeople is called a *load,* and funds are categorized according to the load, or lack of it.

Front-end load funds

Front-end load funds knock a commission from your investment as soon as you hand money to the salesperson, leaving the fund less money to purchase bonds, shares, or whatever the fund invests in for you. The salesperson's commission can be as high as 9 percent, although 5 to 6 percent is more common these days. Should you pay the up-front commission asked for? No, especially if the fund's rate of commission includes the words "maximum" or "up to," which indicates the rate is negotiable with the salesperson. Truth is, front-end load rates are almost always negotiable anyway. Assuming that you have sufficient funds to make the purchase worthwhile — say, $5,000 or more — you shouldn't be paying more than a 3-percent front-end load. If the salesperson or adviser asks for more, start shopping around.

Look at the difference the load can make in your $5,000 investment:

If you pay a 3-percent front-end load, your initial $5,000 investment is reduced to $4,850.

If you pay a 6-percent front-end load, it is reduced to $4,700.

If you pay a 9-percent front-end load, it is reduced to $4,550.

Is there a benefit to funds with a front-end load? Just this: They tend to have lower MERs than other funds. Over the long run — perhaps five years or more — this can more than make up for the lower initial investment you have, and the longer you hold the fund, the bigger the difference. So front-end load funds are not necessarily bad. Just keep the load to a minimum.

Back-end load funds

Back-end loads are charged not when you purchase the fund shares, but when you sell them sometime in the future. Back-end loads are usually reduced by a percentage each year you hold the fund, until the load disappears entirely, which encourages you to hold on to the fund, or at least keep your investment within the same fund family. Back-end loads often are not applied if you switch funds within the same family, such as moving your investment from the PDQ Bond Fund to the PDQ Equity Fund. A back-end load for a fund charging a 6-percent fee might be reduced by ½ percent each year you remain in the fund, until five to seven years have passed, at which time the fee is waived entirely.

Back-end load funds are very popular with investors because, unlike front-load funds, they put 100 percent of your investment to work from the very first day. That's appealing. But remember two things about funds with back-end loads:

✔ Back-end load funds tend to have higher MERs than front-load versions. The fatter MER generates money to cover those sales commissions you thought you were avoiding. In other words, with front-load funds you pay the commissions; with back-load funds the fund pays the sales commission, then collects it from you each year, a little at a time. This is yet another version of the No Free Lunch Rule.

✔ If you decide to redeem your investment in a back-end load fund, the load may be charged against either your initial investment or its market value when you want out. Obviously, it's better to choose a fund whose load is applied to the initial investment, assuming the load is the same size.

Suppose that you invest $5,000 with two funds, each using back-end loads. Fund A applies the load against your initial investment, and Fund B applies it against the market value of your investment if and when you choose to cash in your units.

Both funds manage to average 10-percent annual growth over five years, producing a market value of $7,500 for each fund. By this time, the declining back-end load is down to perhaps 4 percent for both funds. If you choose to take your money out of Fund A, you'll pay 4 percent of $5,000 (your original investment), or $200 subtracted from $7,500, leaving you with a net of $7,300. Fund B will apply its 4-percent load to the $7,500 market value, leaving you with $7,200.

Table 12-1 lists the major companies selling mutual funds in Canada and their policy regarding back-end-load redemption charges.

Table 12-1 Back-End-Load Redemption Charges Charged Against:		
Fund Family	*Initial Investment*	*Market Value*
AGF Management Limited	X	
AIC Limited	X	X*
AIM/Trimark	X	
CI Funds	X	
Dynamic Mutual Funds		X
Fidelity Investments		X
Global Strategy Funds	X	
Guardian	X	
Investors Group		X
Mackenzie Financial		X
Spectrum Investments	X	
Templeton Funds	X	

* Redemptions calculated on initial investment for funds purchased prior to July 1, 1998, and on market value for funds purchased after July 1, 1998

No-load funds

No-load funds are very popular because they can claim that you don't pay going in (as with front-load funds) and you don't pay going out (as with back-load funds). You may think this is the best idea since the invention of sunlight, but remember the No Free Lunch Rule. These funds, for the most part, simply jack up their MER, producing more income to cover their sales commissions. Larger MERs usually translate into lower net returns over the long run.

Here's a practical demonstration of the difference a lower MER can make over the long term. AIM/Trimark manages two international equity funds: the original Trimark Fund, and its young sister, the Trimark Select Growth Fund. The management style and philosophy of both are virtually identical, but the Trimark Fund is a front-load fund with an MER of 1.62 while the Trimark Select Growth Fund is essentially a no-load arrangement with an MER of 2.5.

(Note: In 1998, the Trimark Fund's MER was 1.52 and the Trimark Select Growth Fund's MER was 2.36. Do you think AIM/Trimark trumpeted their increased MER to the world, letting everybody know they were keeping more of their investors' money for themselves? Do you think you can grow bananas in Yellowknife?)

The no-load feature obviously has broad appeal to investors, because the younger Select Growth Fund holds almost twice the assets of its older sibling ($5.4 billion versus $2.9 billion in mid-2001). Yet, over the five-year period ending March 31, 2001, the Trimark Fund's annual earnings averaged 2 percent higher than the Select Growth Fund. Year by year, the lower-MER Trimark Fund tends to outpace its Select Growth version. The difference in annual earnings of 2 percent will produce substantial advantages over ten years or more, long after the relatively small front-end load has been accounted for in the Trimark Fund.

Table 12-2 lists Canadian mutual fund companies, their total assets, and what kind of load they have.

Table 12-2	Load/No Load Policies of Major Canadian Mutual Fund Companies (As of May 2001)	
Company	*Assets*	*Policy*
AGF Management Limited	$21.8 billion	Load
AIC Limited	$14 billion	Load
AIM/Trimark	$26.8 billion	Load
Altamira Investment	$7.2 billion	No load
Bank of Montreal	$12.3 billion	No load
Bank of Nova Scotia	$10.1 billion	No load
CI Funds	$27.6 billion	Load
CIBC	$23.9 billion	No load
Dynamic Mutual Funds	$6.2 billion	Load
Fidelity Investments	$21.8 billion	Load

(continued)

Table 12-2 *(continued)*

Company	Assets	Policy
Global Strategy Funds	$6.4 billion	Load
Investors Group	$43.1 billion	Load
Mackenzie Financial	$34 billion	Load
MD Management Ltd.	$9.8 billion	No load
Phillips, Hager & North	$9.6 billion	No load
Royal Bank	$34.2 billion	No load
Spectrum Investments	$6.2 billion	Load
Templeton Funds	$19.6 billion	Load

Other Fees

Mutual funds are closely linked to banks and trust companies (some are actually owned and managed by the banks) who have learned how to apply charges here and there . . . and there . . . and there . . . .

These are admittedly for services you'll rarely encounter if you choose your funds carefully and hold on to them for several years. But the best surprise is no surprise, so here are a few expenses that may or may not be included in the funds you choose. Note that not all of these fees are charged by all fund companies, and they can vary widely. In many cases the fees can be waived under certain conditions (one of these conditions is simply asking them to be waived before you hand over your money).

- **Redemption fees.** If you decide to sell back your shares in a fund within 90 days of acquiring them, most funds will charge you this fee, which can range from a flat charge of $100 to as high as 2 percent of the original investment.

- **Distribution fees.** Watch for this one. It's charged on some back-load funds and is paid annually to the individual who sold you the fund in the first place. (These are also called trailing fees.) Distribution fees, usually between 0.25 and 0.5 percent of the value of your investment, represent the salesperson's commission and extend as long as the back-end load is in effect, usually seven years. But some funds charge them for as long as you keep your investment. The percentage is not very high, but every $10,000 in a fund charging a 0.5-percent distribution fee earns the salesperson 50 bucks a year, directly out of your pocket.

- ✔ **Switching fees.** Almost every fund company manages a "family" of funds to cover various investment options such as Canadian equities, foreign equities, bond funds, balanced funds, and so on. Most companies do not charge a fee for switching from one fund to another inside the same family, but don't take it for granted — there are exceptions. You shouldn't have to pay a switching fee, ever.

- ✔ **Set-up, closing, and handling fees.** You may be charged $50 or so to open or close an account with a mutual fund company, and a similar amount to open a no-load fund with a broker. Once again, fund companies and brokers have been known to waive these charges just for the privilege of working hard to make you rich. So why not ask?

Converting all this MER and front-load/back-load/no-load stuff into cold, hard cash helps put things in perspective.

Suppose that you are faced with a choice of three different mutual funds, all following the same basic investment formula and with similar management expertise. You invest $10,000 in each fund, and each fund manages to average a 10-percent annual return before applying the MER.

The PDQ Fund has an MER of 1.75 percent and a front-end load of 4 percent. The XYZ Fund has an MER of 2.65 percent and a front-end load of 2.5 percent. The Honest John Fund has an MER of 3.35 percent and no load, front or back. Hey, no-load sounds good, right?

At the end of ten years, your $10,000 investment in the PDQ Fund will have a value of $20,870.06 — you've more than doubled your money. The same investment in the XYZ Fund will be worth just $19,431.78, while the Honest John Fund produced only $18,447.84.

Remember that each fund held the same investments, which generated 10 percent each year. But less money filtered down to investors in two of the funds.

The longer you hold money in a fund, the more impact the MER makes. Let's take the same $10,000 investment, but this time we'll hold it in the same three funds for 25 years, earning 10-percent annual return before applying the MER. Over that period, $10,000 in the PDQ Fund will be worth $66,896.34, the XYZ Fund's value will be $55,255.29, and when you cash in the Honest John Fund you'll get back just $46,223.58.

None of the funds achieved true 10-percent annual earnings for their investors, because the MER had to be deducted first. But notice that loads, either front or back, don't make the same impact as higher MERs over the long term.

Note also that the records of these funds would not indicate annual average earnings of 10 percent, because *the earnings statements are made only after the MER has been accounted for.*

The moral? It's not impossible for a mutual fund with a high MER to return more money for its investors. Just more difficult.

(For a way to ensure a low MER, see the section on index funds in Chapter 14.)

Chapter 13

Choosing Funds for Your Future

· ·

In This Chapter

▶ Measuring a fund's performance

▶ Spotting (and avoiding) one-hit wonders

▶ Steering clear of funds that don't meet your standards

▶ Reading a prospectus

▶ Deciding if a fund fits your RRSP

▶ Making your own best choice

· ·

Trying to choose among thousands of mutual funds, all qualifying as components of your RRSP, can be overwhelming. A financial adviser in tune with your needs and expectations can help, but until advisers provide a guarantee along with the advice they dispense, the ultimate decision is your own.

When you are familiar enough with mutual funds and confident in your own abilities, you can manage your self-directed RRSP within a discount brokerage, save hundreds of dollars a year on fees, and ensure that the decisions are made in your best interests, not your broker's.

Performance Is the Key . . . Kind of

Imagine you have to get from Toronto to Vancouver as quickly as possible, and two airlines are willing to fly you there. One airline uses planes that travel at 800 kilometres an hour, and the other uses aircraft travelling at 500 kilometres an hour. The fares, seat size, safety record, and flight dates are identical. Which airline would you choose?

Choosing the mutual fund to build the value of your RRSP as fast as possible should be as easy, but it's not. Why? Because mutual fund growth doesn't travel at the same predictable rate. Even while mutual funds brag about their growth performance over the past year or five years, they are required to insert the caveat *"Past performance is no guarantee of future results."*

This makes choosing a mutual fund similar to driving a car by watching the road through your rearview mirror. The view may be fine, but it's no guarantee that the road ahead won't be bumpy.

Still, every mutual fund investor is attracted by high returns, especially if someone else was making big money while their RRSP was limping along with single-digit growth. And the differences can indeed be massive. During the one-year period from May 1, 1998 to April 30, 1999, the average Canadian equity-based mutual fund lost 10.4 percent. Bummer, right? Okay, everyone knows you need a long-term view for investing in equities. Historically, the average return is close to 10 percent for Canadian equities, so hang on.

But people who invested during the same period in the Trans-Canada Value Fund, managed by Vancouver-based Sagit Management, weren't hanging on. They were out buying mink coats and drinking 60-year-old cognac because their investment had earned 50.6 percent, while you and I and the rest of The Great Unwashed were crying in our Molsons (see Table 13-1).

Table 13-1	Trans-Canada Value Fund Performance (April 30, 1999): 1 to 5 years			
	1 Year	*2 Years*	*3 Years*	*5 Years*
Trans-Canada Value	22.7%	6.0%	6.5%	6.4%
Bissett Cdn. Equity	−11.4%	11.7%	16.8%	15.4%
Phillips, Hager & North Cdn. Equity	−5.2%	9.6%	12.8%	12.8%
First Cdn. Equity Ind.	−7.8%	8.8%	11.5%	11.1%
Green Line Cdn. Equity	−6.7%	10.8%	14.3%	11.7%

Source: Globe and Mail Report on Mutual Funds, May 20, 1999

Compare the Trans-Canada Value Fund's one-year performance with two of the most highly regarded independent mutual funds investing in Canadian equities — the Bissett Canadian Equity Fund and the Phillips, Hager & North Canadian Equity Fund — plus two of the best bank funds, from Bank of Montreal and TD Bank, in the same category.

Should you have rushed out to sell your units in under-performing mutual funds and buy every share you could afford of the Sagit fund? Hold on to your pen, Rockefeller, and take another look at those performance figures. Over five years, the minimum horizon you should use when choosing equity funds for your RRSP, the fund's average annual return is well below the average for all Canadian equity funds.

Contrary to first impression, the Sagit fund was *not* outpacing the competition over the years but actually lagging behind. It enjoyed one Roman candle–like burst of success that, when added to a decade-long mediocre performance record, booted its "average" into the stratosphere. If you had purchased the Trans-Canada Value Fund in September 1998 and sold it in March 1999, you would have made a killing. If you bought it earlier and sold it later, you could have been a loser. In the vernacular of the music business, Sagit was a one-hit wonder, guesting on Letterman this month and working a bar in Thunder Bay next month.

This is a fine demonstration of *volatility*, or wide changes in price over a relatively short period of time. Volatility is a two-edged sword that's suspended like a pendulum, and it can cut you and your investment down to size with one wild swing. The more volatile an investment, the more speculative it tends to be, and vice versa.

A closer investigation of Sagit's Trans-Canada Value Fund revealed that more than 50 percent of the fund's total assets (a mere $4.18 million, by the way) was invested in one company: a 20-employee waste disposal firm located in Coquitlam, British Columbia, that managed to triple its sales in one year, creating similar leaps in the value of its stock. It didn't take a lot of detective work to track down this reason behind the Trans-Canada Value Fund's burst of glory. But you shouldn't have to be a detective. When looking at average returns, beware of high volatility, and be very suspicious of short-term stratospheric growth.

Take a look at the shorter-term performance for these same funds (see Table 13-2). Notice anything remarkable?

Table 13-2	Trans-Canada Value Fund Performance (April 30, 1999): 1 to 6 Months		
	1 Month	*3 Months*	*6 Months*
Trans-Canada Value	−16.9%	33.1%	65.1%
Bissett Cdn. Equity	3.2%	−0.8%	6.1%
Phillips, Hager & North Cdn. Equity	6.0%	6.8%	14.0%
First Cdn. Equity Ind.	6.3%	4.3%	13.1%
Green Line Cdn. Equity	4.6%	6.8%	20.2%

Source: Globe and Mail Report on Mutual Funds, May 20, 1999

The Sagit Trans-Canada Value Fund achieved better-than-average performance over the past five years, even with an unusually high (3.52) MER, but only if the astonishing recent performance — 65.1-percent growth in the six months ending April 30, 1999 — is factored in. Interesting fact: Sagit also manages the Cambridge Growth Fund, which invests in Canadian *small-cap* companies (the total value of all the company's shares is less than $500 million). Average annual returns for that fund were –38.6 percent for one year, –29.2 percent for three years, –18.7 percent for five years, and –3.7 percent for ten years. Yes, those are minus signs in front of the performance figures. (For more on small-cap companies, see Chapter 14.)

This is a dramatic example of extreme volatility and the effect it can have on both your selection of funds and on their performance within your portfolio. Funds achieving exceptionally high performance usually involve substantial volatility and a good deal of risk. Don't forget that risk and reward go hand in hand. So how much risk are you willing to take?

Making wise choices in mutual funds for your RRSP is not so much a matter of picking winners as avoiding losers. This can be difficult to remember when a co-worker meets you at the copying machine to brag about making huge gains in his RRSP from some mutual fund you've never heard of. It becomes even more painful when you open the business section of the newspaper and there it is in black-and-white: Standback & Duck's Canadian Equity Fund actually made 63.5 percent for its investors last year. Wow! If your RRSP could earn 63.5 percent a year, you'd be a millionaire in no time.

Okay, come down to earth for a moment.

One-year performance results don't mean all that much. In fact, they may be the result of luck as much as skill. Equity-based mutual funds work best when chosen as long-term investments, not as one-year wonders. A U.S. study examining outstanding mutual fund performers for one-year periods discovered that the top-performing stock and bond fund in each year of a 15-year period actually did worse than the average fund in its category over the next three to ten years.

If you could foresee any fund achieving number-one status a year ahead of time and purchase units before its meteoric rise, you could make millions. Of course, if you could foresee the next card handed to you in every game of blackjack, or the next number coming up on every turn of the roulette wheel, you could put all of Las Vegas out of business too. But you can't. And you won't. So keep your eye on the horizon.

Does this sound like sour grapes from someone who has never ridden a high-flying mutual fund to 50-percent-plus annual earnings? Darn right. But it's true nevertheless.

Avoiding the Losers

If "avoiding losers" sounds suspiciously like the lament of a single person looking for a prospective mate, that's a fine parallel with choosing the best mutual funds for your RRSP. Beyond the euphoria of romance lurks the reality that there is probably no perfect partner for you among the 5 billion or so other souls on the planet. But there is probably at least one that's better than the others.

Take the same approach when choosing mutual funds for your RRSP. Start by eliminating those that don't measure up to your standards. Your standards when you are younger are different from the ones you value in later years. When you're young, you don't mind a little excitement and a few wild times, but as you grow older and wiser you're more attracted to stability, maturity, and steady, if unspectacular, companionship . . . sorry, growth.

Your mother (or father) might have advised you when choosing a mate to "Look for a good family." Your parents meant a family whose majority of members weren't in jail, or something like that. In mutual funds, it means looking for funds with a familiar name and several healthy siblings. Large, well-established funds may not deliver the exceptional returns you prefer, but they're not as likely to be at the bottom of the barrel, either. Being able to choose from several funds within the same family provides flexibility to move all or a portion of your investment from one fund type to another without penalties or fees, although this benefit isn't really as appealing as some mutual-fund promotional materials may make it sound.

Table 13-3 shows the top five and bottom five families of 41 mutual fund families sold in Canada in 2000. "Outperformers" are the funds within the families that beat the average returns for other funds in the same categories. Some fund families, like some fund categories, are more volatile than others. A year earlier, for example, 88 percent of AIC Funds outperformed their competition; AIC overplayed its investment in the financial category and when this group slipped badly in 1999 the bottom dropped out of most AIC funds.

Even the best of families has its black sheep, and this includes families of mutual funds. Don't assume that a company scoring good returns with its Canadian equity fund will outpace others in bonds, money markets, or other investments.

Table 13-3	Family Performance (December 31, 1999)	
Company	*Total Funds*	*Outperformers*
Top 5		
Bank of Montreal	40	73%

(continued)

Table 13-3 (continued)

Company	Total Funds	Outperformers
Clarington Funds	13	85%
HSBC Bank Canada	14	93%
McLean Budden	6	83%
Synergy Mutual Funds	8	75%
Bottom 5		
AIC Limited	10	20%
Ethical Funds	8	13%
Saxon Funds	5	0%
Sceptre	7	29%
Templeton Funds	20	25%

Most important of all, keep your feet on the ground when reviewing average annual return figures provided by the mutual fund companies and listed in virtually every mutual fund review you'll encounter. Remember the mantra: *Past performance is not necessarily indicative of future earnings.* High levels of return, especially if they are reasonably consistent over at least five years, are worth your attention but not necessarily your money. Use these performance figures as a first measure. Then begin comparing volatility — the lower the better — and the fund's performance versus all other funds in its category. This is the only way to use performance figures with any degree of confidence.

Finally, be realistic about your investment goals. During the mid-1990s, equity mutual funds posted annual returns of 20 to 30 percent. Through the spring of 2000, high-tech funds were shooting up by 60 or 70 percent a year. All of this made some investors feel like kids with the key to the candy store. "Hey!" they shouted, opening their wallets and selling their boring old bonds, "Feed me some more of those funds, and which way to the Jaguar dealership?" Reality arrived a few months later, and the same investors felt like they were disembarking an aircraft ten minutes before it landed.

If you're young, optimistic, and enjoy the thrill of Saturday night singles bars and skydiving, investment volatility is just another of life's kicks. But when the face in the morning mirror looks suspiciously like your parents', you'll be more willing to accept the widespread reality of comfort and predictability, such as annual returns of 10 to 12 percent over several years.

Funds within Families

Most mutual fund companies want to operate like an investment department store. You want bonds? Second floor, just past the money market funds. Equities? Any special kind, madam? Canadian equities are on the main floor, small-cap equities on the third floor, and we're having a special on emerging-market equities, currently in the bargain basement. . . .

The major benefit of choosing from a large family of funds is the opportunity to move easily within the family as your needs change. Some fund families, of course, do better with some investments than others. The Templeton Growth Fund, for example, has a superb reputation as an international equity fund, averaging over 13 percent annual return over ten years with low volatility. Templeton's record for choosing investments for its Canadian Stock Fund is not nearly as impressive, however, and its Canadian Bond Fund has shown abysmal performance.

Because each fund family follows a general investment philosophy or style, each fund under the same umbrella will retain some aspect of that approach. Look for wider diversification by selecting funds from two or more families, once your mutual fund investments break through the $10,000 level.

As you add different funds to your portfolio, don't make the mistake of spreading your RRSP assets as though you're seeding a lawn. No matter how large your RRSP may be, you don't really need more than five or six different funds to meet your needs. If you have ten or more funds in your portfolio, you're probably adding more confusion than growth to your plan.

What about Bank Funds?

The explosion of mutual funds in Canada is due at least partly to the entry of our chartered banks into the mutual-fund market. When the Big Five banks began promoting and selling their own mutual funds in the mid-1980s, it changed the market completely. Suddenly mutual funds weren't those esoteric things sold by brokers and run by Bay Street barons. They were legitimate alternatives to savings accounts and GICs, available from that nice young man in your own bank branch, the one who sells you your traveller's cheques.

The psychological impact was enormous for many people. Natter and grumble as they may about the chartered banks, Canadians consider them to be pillars of stability and conservatism. Seeing the banks selling mutual funds was like watching a bunch of Jesuits dance the samba — hey, if they can do it, it must be okay. When equity-based funds began piling up 20- and 30-percent annual returns in the mid-1990s, Canadians everywhere looked at the paltry 5- to 7-percent interest earned from GICs sold by the banks and began running after the mutual fund bandwagon.

Should you consider a bank-managed mutual fund for your RRSP? This raises a point of discussion among financial commentators in Canada, who generally reveal a bias against mutual funds offered by the banks. The view of the financial gurus seems to be "Let the banks do the banking and let the mutual fund companies do the investing," based on the premise that any endeavour, from plumbing to parachuting, benefits when specialists are running things.

Even though CIBC, Scotiabank, TD Bank, Royal Bank, and Bank of Montreal hire qualified people to manage their funds, they operate within a chartered bank environment, suggesting that the bank funds are too conservative in their outlook and too burdened with corporate bureaucracy. But the reality is that many bank funds perform very well compared with other funds, and a few manage to beat the average.

Table 13-4 shows how the major Canadian equity funds sold by Canada's five chartered banks, plus Hongkong Bank of Canada (now HSBC Bank Canada), performed over one, three, and five years as of March 31, 2001. Canadian equity funds should represent the core of your RRSP's mutual fund holdings, so this is a good area to review. The Bank of Montreal and HSBC funds invest in larger companies only; the other bank funds are more broadly based.

Table 13-4	Bank Funds Performance (March 31, 2001)			
Fund	*MER*	*1 Year*	*3 Years*	*5 Years*
BMO Equity (Bank of Montreal)	2.34	−4.9%	6.1%	13.8%
CIBC Core Cdn. Equity	2.00	−11.3%	1.2%	9.7%
HSBC Equity (HSBC Bank Canada)	1.96	−14.6%	4.1%	11.6%
Royal Cdn. Equity (Royal Bank)	2.08	−7.9%	3.6%	9.8%
Scotia Cdn. Growth (Scotiabank)	2.13	−8.4%	2.1%	9.0%
TD Cdn. Equity (TD Bank)	2.27	−7.1%	6.2%	13.9%
Average of bank-managed equity funds	**2.13**	**−9.0%**	**3.88%**	**11.3%**

Two other Canadian equity funds widely available where you might do your banking are National Bank Canadian Equity Fund, from National Bank branches, and Ethical Growth Fund, sold through a network of credit unions.

The National Bank fund is smallish (about $300 million in mid-2001) with performance figures close to the average of the larger banks. Ethical Growth Fund, a favourite with tree huggers (for more on this one, see Chapter 16) has slipped badly in recent years. Its three- and five-year averages, as of May 2001, were –1.41 percent and 7.83 percent, respectively.

The consensus? You are not likely to enjoy extraordinary performance from broadly based bank funds, but you may have a better chance of avoiding bottom-feeders and wild volatility. Don't ignore them just because they're bank-owned.

How to Understand a Prospectus

A mutual fund *prospectus* is like the instruction manual that comes with disassembled bicycles, folding garden furniture, and computer software — which means that hardly anybody reads one until they get in trouble.

Every mutual fund, by law, is required to publish a prospectus, and you, as a potential investor in the fund, are expected to read it with interest, if not with heart-pounding delight. The role of the prospectus is to provide all the information you need, and much more than you want, about the fund — how it will be managed, how its fees are structured, where it will invest your money, and virtually everything else except the fund manager's shoe size.

Since it is required by law, a fund prospectus is usually written by corporate lawyers whose concept of a gripping writing style is to use *whereas* and *therefore* in the same sentence. Yet some of the most valuable information you need when selecting a fund is buried in the prospectus, so it's worth obtaining one for every fund you're considering and pulling out the nuggets of data.

Obtaining a prospectus is easy. Simply contact the fund office or ask your financial adviser or broker for a copy. Fund companies and brokers love sending out a copy of their prospectus, responding to what they see as serious interest by investors.

Here are the four most important things to read in a fund prospectus (you can skip the rest of the stuff unless you are a mutual fund junkie or somebody who reads every word in their insurance policy):

1. The fund's investment objectives

This explains what the fund is attempting to accomplish on your behalf. It describes the kinds of investment the fund will make, the type of return it hopes to generate (capital growth, income, or a combination of the two), and the type of investor it seeks to attract. It should also be up front about risk, where appropriate.

As an example, here is the way Scotia Mutual Funds describes its Canadian Growth Fund:

> "The Fund invests in well-run, well-financed companies with above-average growth potential, complemented by under-valued blue chip stocks to provide the portfolio with adequate liquidity and sectorial balance. It is suitable for investors seeking long-term capital growth and who accept the volatility of a diversified portfolio of Canadian stocks."

There's a bit of jargon in there ("sectorial balance"? Sounds like a Vatican acrobatic team. . . .) but you get the general picture: The fund will not focus on a small number of industries or one geographical area; it is best-suited for long-term investors; and it hopes to deliver growth, not income.

Can you judge a mutual fund by its name? You should be able to, but don't count on it. Some fund managers take more freedom with their fund's objectives than you might expect. This doesn't mean that a fund manager can suddenly shift a fund from Canadian equities to international bonds, for example. But one well-known Canadian fund calling itself a mortgage and income fund held most of its assets in equities and only a dollop or so in bonds and mortgages. This gave it very good long-term performance, since equities tend to outperform mortgages and bonds over several years. But anyone looking for low volatility and steady income from the fund was disappointed.

How does the Scotia Canadian Growth Fund live up to its objectives? Not badly at all. For the five years ending December 31, 2000, the fund returned an average 13 percent annually, above the median for all funds in its Canadian equity category.

For a contrast, compare the objective of the Scotia Canadian Growth Fund with that of another growth fund in the same family, the Scotia Latin American Growth Fund:

> "The Fund invests primarily in companies based in Latin America and listed on recognized stock exchanges. The Fund holds securities denominated in a number of currencies to hedge against foreign exchange risk. It is suitable for investors seeking long-term capital appreciation and who understand the volatility of Latin American equity markets. The unit price is sensitive to changes in foreign exchange rates, relative to the Canadian dollar."

There are more red lights in that objective than you'll find on the average Ferris wheel. "Hedge against foreign currency risk," "volatility of Latin American equity markets," and "sensitive to changes in foreign exchange risks" all suggest this fund should be considered only if you have a solid knowledge of regional political and economic realities in your head, or an economy-size box of antacid in your hand. Or maybe both.

To the fund's credit, it has outperformed others in its category, returning an average of 8.2 percent annually over five years (ending December 31, 2000). Differences in objectives are not always so clear-cut. Here's the objective of another growth fund from the same family, the Scotia Canadian Blue Chip Fund:

> "The Fund holds a well-diversified portfolio of high-quality, listed Canadian common shares. It is suitable for investors seeking long-term capital growth and who understand the volatility of a diversified portfolio of Canadian equities."

With minor variations, this describes the same objective as the Scotia Canadian Growth Fund. Comparing the top holdings in both funds — the companies in which the funds own the most shares on March 31, 2001 — confirms the similarity (see Table 13-5).

Table 13-5 Comparing Holdings in Two Funds (March 31, 2001)	
Scotia Canadian Blue Chip Fund	*Scotia Canadian Growth Fund*
Bank of Montreal	Bank of Montreal
BCE Inc. (Bell Canada Enterprises)	BCE Inc.
Bombardier Inc.	Bombardier Inc.
Nortel Networks	Nortel Networks
Royal Bank	Royal Bank
TD Bank	TD Bank
Alcan Inc.	Anderson Exploration Ltd.
CIBC	CAE
Canadian Pacific Limited	Nexen Inc.
Manulife Financial	Quebecor World Inc.

(It's interesting how all the Canadian chartered banks invest in each other, isn't it?) These top ten companies represent a relatively small proportion of each fund's total investment: the Blue Chip Fund had 95.7 percent of its total assets in 61 different companies, and the Growth Fund had 91.7 percent of its assets in 82 different companies. The rest of the assets for each fund were in short-term bonds and T-bills.

Neither fund has been a whiz-bang performer, but the Scotia Canadian Blue Chip Fund was the slightly better choice over the five years ending February 28, 2001, averaging 10.07 percent annually, compared with the Scotia Canadian Growth Fund's 9.86 percent.

The Scotia CanGlobal Income Fund is in sharp contrast to either of the funds described above. Here is its objective:

> "The Fund invests primarily in high quality, foreign-currency bonds issued by Canadian or foreign governments, corporations and supranational entities, such as the World Bank. This Fund is suitable for investors seeking higher interest income and global diversification for their income-generating investments."

Notice the absence of the terms "growth" and "blue chip," and the emphasis on interest income and global diversification. In spite of the global diversification, this fund remains RRSP-eligible because it invests in bonds valued in foreign currency but issued by Canadian sources. This is one of several dance steps that mutual funds can perform to overcome the limits on foreign investment in your RRSP. Unfortunately, the fund managers need a few dancing lessons, or maybe they just lack a sense of rhythm, because Scotia's CanGlobal Income Fund has consistently under-performed all other funds in its category since its inception.

Here are things to note when reading about objectives in the fund's prospectus:

- ✔ What are its prime investments: stocks, bonds, mortgages, T-bills, or a combination?

- ✔ Where are they located?

- ✔ What special qualities do the investments have: blue-chip, small-cap, sector, and so on?

- ✔ How much, if any, of its investments are foreign? (If the foreign content in the fund exceeds 30 percent, it is not 100-percent RRSP-eligible.)

- ✔ What will the fund deliver: growth, income, or a combination of both?

- ✔ What special knowledge or risk appreciation should an investor have regarding this fund?

2. The fund's costs

This should be self-explanatory, although the fund prospectus may not include its management expense ratio (MER) alongside the description of its expenses. Here's a sample reference to fees and expenses:

> "The Fund is offered on a No-Load basis, which means you pay no sales commissions or marketing fees. You will, however, incur expenses for investment advisory, management, administration and distribution services, which are included in the Management Expense Ratio."

That's very clear, except that it does not indicate the MER for the fund, which is buried somewhere in a section usually titled Fund Expenses. Once again, it's wise to have a benchmark by which to judge a fund's MER.

Keep in mind that some types of funds understandably cost more to manage than others, according to the kind of investment being traded. Money market and index funds are the least costly to manage, because all the fund manager's decisions can be made while sitting in front of a computer screen. Equity funds, however, involve digging and probing into companies. Fund managers and researchers often travel to far-off towns named Dismal Seepage or Upper Rubberboots, where they scuttle through mines and avoid being struck by swinging whirligigs just to get a hands-on assessment of a company's true worth and prospects. That takes money and guts, but mostly money.

Naturally, the MER will be higher for Canadian equity funds than for money market and bond funds, and higher still for international equity funds. Indexed equity funds require no such travel or investigation because they slavishly follow the TSE 35, S&P/TSE 60, TSE 100, TSE 300, or some other stock index.

Table 13-6 shows some general guidelines on measuring appropriate MERs for various fund categories. If the fund you're considering has an MER higher than these, your investment may be earning more for the fund managers than it is making for you and your RRSP. By the way, all of the funds outperformed others in their categories over the three-year period ending December 31, 2000, including funds with MERs three times or more the level charged by these winners.

Table 13-6	Funds with Low MERs	
Fund Type	*MER Range*	*Look At*
Money market	0.50 to 1.0 (median MER: 1.0)	Beutel Goodman Money Market Fund; Bissett Money Market Class F; Phillips, Hager & North Cdn Money Market Fund; TD Canadian Money Market Fund; Sceptre Money Market
Cdn. bonds	0.57 to 1.65 (median MER: 1.9)	Altamira Short-Term Canadian Income Fund; Desjardins-Laurentian Bond Fund; Equitable Life Segregated Accum.; Phillips, Hager & North Bond Fund; Scudder Canadian Bond Fund; TD Canadian Bond Fund

(continued)

Table 13-6 *(continued)*

Fund Type	MER Range	Look at
Cdn. equity	1.0 to 2.5 (median MER: 2.5)	Bissett Canadian Equity Fund; Fidelity True North Fund; Phillips, Hager & North Canadian Equity Fund
Cdn. balanced	1.0 to 2.0 (median MER: 2.46)	AGF Canadian High Income Fund; Beutel Goodman Balanced Fund; National Bank Moderate Diversified Fund; Saxon Balanced Fund; Scotia Canadian Balanced Fund; TD Balanced Index Fund
Global equity	1.0 to 2.0 (median MER: 2.68)	CDA Global Fund (AIM/Trimark); Hartford Global Leaders Fund SC; MB Global Equity Fund; Templeton Growth Fund

One way funds can keep their MERs low is by insisting on larger opening balances. So you may need as much as $25,000 to invest in funds administered by companies such as Phillips, Hager & North. Check the minimum opening balance needed, shown in the prospectus.

3. The fund's financial performance

This is really what it's all about. Let's face it, you don't care if the fund manager is a two-headed goat whose investment strategy involves chicken entrails and astrology — if the fund can deliver exceptional performance with low volatility and virtually no risk, it gets your money, right? Well, fund managers aren't, and they don't, and it can't. So take just a moment or two to check these financial figures from a fund's prospectus:

The *net asset value* (NAV) or *net asset value per share* (NAVPS) tracks the value per unit of a fund and is practically useless because it does not reflect distributions converted into new units. Since the vast majority of Canadian mutual funds are held in RRSPs, distributions from the fund's earnings are converted into new units, which effectively lowers the individual unit value. (See Chapter 12.) So tracking the NAV is a fruitless exercise.

Net assets or *total assets* represents the total value of all investments held within the fund and gives you some idea of the fund's size and clout. The range in size is enormous; in Canadian equity funds alone, they extend from a handful of new funds with barely $500,000 in total assets to the giant Ivy Canadian with almost $6.3 billion to watch over.

Generally, bigger is better. Smaller funds may have more flexibility to spot outstanding opportunities, but their expenses tend to be higher and their operating efficiencies lower. Larger funds are less volatile, but they can have difficulty spending all that money wisely. All things considered, however, for a novice mutual fund investor there is safety in numbers. For the core of your mutual fund holdings, which should be Canadian equities, it's best to join the crowd at the most popular funds.

Portfolio turnover rate is an indication of how often the fund sells one investment and purchases another. The figure represents the percentage of the entire fund's holdings traded each year. A low figure — 25 percent or less — indicates a "buy and hold" strategy for long-term growth. A high figure — 75 percent to more than 100 percent — reveals a fund manager who is wheeling and dealing, selling to take profits here and buying new shares to chase new profits over there. This is not necessarily bad, depending on your expectations. But the higher the figure, the more volatile the fund is likely to be — and that means higher risk.

4. The fund's annual-returns record

Performance figures are the meat and potatoes (or tofu and bean sprouts, for you vegans) of a fund's measure, but don't expect to find them in the prospectus. And remember that past performance can't be used to judge future results — it simply provides a measure against a benchmark, such as the returns of other funds in the same category. Request a prospectus from a mutual fund company and expect to receive some glitzy promotional material with it. This is where the performance records are found, and these should be expressed in two ways. One is historical rates of compounded returns; the other is calendar-year returns.

Historical rates of compounded returns provide an average annual return over a period — usually one, three, and five years. *Calendar-year returns* are just what they say — the return, or growth, of your original investment, within one calendar year. Both sets of figures are revealing about a fund's performance, especially its volatility. Tables 13-7 and 13-8 compare these figures for three Canadian equity funds as of March 1, 2001.

Table 13-7 Compounded Returns (percentage to March 2001)			
Fund	*1 Year*	*3 Years*	*5 Years*
AIM/Trimark Select Canadian Fund	21.8%	6.8%	9.5%
Altamira Capital Growth Fund	−36.7%	6.0%	7.9%
Clarica Premier Blue Chip Fund	−12.7%	−0.8%	6.0%

Table 13-8	Calendar-Year Returns				
Fund	*2000*	*1999*	*1998*	*1997*	*1996*
AIM/Trimark Select Canadian Fund	15.2%	18.0%	−6.5%	3.4%	23.3%
Altamira Capital Growth Fund	1.2%	51.5%	9.2%	7.8%	10.5%
Clarica Premier Blue Chip Fund	−9.0%	19.8%	11.9%	10.1%	26.4%

All three of these funds are 100-percent eligible for your RRSP, which means they won't affect your 30-percent limit on foreign investments. The Altamira Capital Growth Fund has been around since 1937, but it's relatively small — less than $300 million. It invests in larger, well-established Canadian companies, as does the Clarica Premier Blue Chip Fund. Trimark has used a "bottom-up" investment style, meaning it looks for low-priced companies and ignores, for the most part, specific industries.

In spite of the fact that all three funds go shopping in the same marketplace, the differences in their performance are remarkable. Trimark's much larger size ($3.7 billion) provides less volatility than do the smaller companies, as both charts reveal.

Every mutual-fund investor must memorize and repeat a mantra — *Past returns are not necessarily indicative of future performance* — when examining a fund's performance over any period, from one month to ten years. The returns, in percentages, are often compared to the interest earned from a GIC, bond, or savings account over the same period, so a 10-percent "average annual return" on a $100 investment is expected to produce $10 annually. Trouble is, while the interest earned on a bond or savings account is fixed and predictable, the returns from a mutual fund are neither. A fund can return 45 percent this year and lose 20 percent next year — and some do. Throughout all the discussion of mutual funds, past returns will be used as a primary measure of a fund's performance. Just remember the mantra.

Matching the Fund's Objectives to Your Own

Now that you know what the fund is trying to do, and how well it's doing it, you can decide if it fits your RRSP at this point.

✔ If the fund is equity-based, growth-oriented, and 100-percent RRSP-eligible, it may qualify as the core fund in your portfolio, providing long-term growth.

✔ If the fund has relative low volatility — its returns fluctuate less than average over as many years as you can track them — the steady if unspectacular returns it generates will appeal to you if you have a low risk threshold or you are somewhere past the age of 40.

✔ If the fund invests in specialized sectors of industry, it could represent the high risk/high return component of your RRSP, supplementing your core equity investment. Unless you are under 40 or have an exceedingly high risk tolerance, keep your total investment in the fund to no more than 5 to 10 percent of the total value of your RRSP.

✔ If the fund is foreign-based and not 100-percent RRSP-eligible, it could represent part or all of the 30-percent foreign content of your RRSP. Be sure to evaluate its other qualities as though you were considering a domestic fund: Is the MER reasonable? Does the value fluctuate wildly? Are the investments giant international blue-chip companies or high-risk new ventures? Does the fund manager shop the world for the investments or focus on a defined area?

✔ If the fund consists of bonds and similar investments, it could replace all or part of your RRSP that is security-based, including bonds, strip bonds, GICs, and others.

Chapter 14

Equity Funds

In This Chapter

▶ Defining an equity fund

▶ Managing equity funds — various styles

▶ Choosing funds to help you sleep well

▶ Understanding the importance of fund size

▶ Determining the companies they keep

▶ Examining special kinds of equity funds

▶ Comparing portfolios: Ted, Terri, and Thomas

Some people go to casinos and toss dice. Others invest in the stock market. This is a reasonably acceptable comparison of two ways of making money. So what, you may be asking, is it doing in a book on RRSPs?

You can live a full and even reasonably affluent life without ever entering a gambling casino — in fact, there could be a direct relationship between how well-off you are and how often you manage to avoid casinos entirely. This doesn't hold true where the stock market and your RRSP are concerned. Over the long term, avoiding the stock market entirely will prevent you from enjoying the same level of retirement benefits as someone who invests in it with reasonable expectations, professional assistance, and their eyes on a long-term horizon.

If you can't help equating the stock market with Vegas, here's a way to get over it: Imagine that the person running the casino is a friendly in-law. Whenever you visit, the in-law guides you gently past the slots and keno tables, escorting you to games where the odds are most in your favour. The in-law buys your chips, chooses your cards, decides when to hold and when to fold, and trades winks with the dealer now and then. Most of all, the in-law encourages you to be patient and not try to double your money with just one roll of the dice, one turn of the wheel, or one shuffle of the cards.

That's the role of an equity-fund manager. He or she is someone who knows both the system and how the game is played, and who makes critical decisions for you. This may take some of the thrill out of the game, but as time passes you realize you're going to leave the casino with your shirt still on your back and more money in your jeans than when you entered the place.

With that in mind, unless you're on your way out the door to apply for your Canada/Quebec Pension Plan benefits, you should make equity mutual funds part of your RRSP assets. Choose the funds carefully, forget about short-term ups and downs, ignore anybody who proposes "timing" the market, and relax. Time is now on your side, and the more time you have, the wealthier you'll become.

Back in the 1950s, a couple of too-cute-for-words sisters scored some major hit parade songs. Their singing talents were minuscule and the song titles were meaningless and long forgotten, but the names of the twin girls carried a message. They were called (and, as Dave Barry likes to say, "I'm not making this up") Patience and Prudence. Whenever I'm pondering an equity invest-ment, either as a mutual fund or as shares in a company, I imagine those melodic brats sitting on my shoulder repeating their names over and over in my ear. Patience — give an equity investment time to grow. Prudence — there's enough risk in equities without adding more by investing in unknown companies making unknown products for an unknown market.

You might want to try listening to them. Just don't let them start to sing. . . .

What's an Equity Fund?

Equity mutual funds invest your money and the money of other fund shareholders in publicly traded shares, or *stock,* of companies. This explains why they are sometimes referred to as "stock funds." To make their investment decisions, equity-fund managers wade through more data about companies than you probably know, or even care, exists. They per-form analyses of a company's total value, examine the growth of the firm, forecast its future prospects, measure the cash flow generated by its sales, evaluate the management staff, assess the competition, and on and on.

These are the same things you would do — or should do — before investing your money in a company, if you had the time, the knowledge, the facilities, and the interest. You haven't, and they have.

Here's another advantage of equity-based mutual funds: our old friend diversification. If you agree that equities provide the best long-term growth prospects (nobody seriously disagrees with this fact), and you have $10,000 to invest in shares, over how many different companies could you effectively spread your money? Five? Seven? Ten at the most? That's not much diversification by either company or industry. If you invest $1,000 in each of ten different companies and one of them goes bankrupt, you will lose 10 percent of your original investment.

In contrast, $10,000 in an equity mutual fund gets you portions of 40, 50, or perhaps 100 or more companies covering a wide range of industries. Sure, one of them can still go belly-up. But with 50 companies in your fund portfolio, you only stand to lose 2 percent of your original investment. A mutual fund that invests wisely across a broad range of industries, from banks and telecommunications to mines and manufacturing, also reduces the risk of a severe long-term decline in one sector dragging down the value of your investment.

Management Style

Two things set all equity funds apart from each other. One is *where* they invest your money. This includes the size and type of companies as well as the geographical area, which may cover Canada only, North America exclusively, one region (Latin America, the Pacific Rim, Europe), or anywhere in the world the fund manager spies a prospect.

The other thing that sets mutual funds apart is less obvious, especially to novice investors in mutual funds. This is *how* the fund manager chooses investments, or the *management style,* and it can differ from one fund to another. Choosing funds with contrasting management styles for your RRSP adds another dimension of diversification to your plan.

The idea of contrasting management styles can be difficult to grasp, so try thinking of fund managers as musicians, each playing a different instrument. If you gathered four pianists and their instruments in one room and had them all play at the same time, you might get music, but you wouldn't get much variety. Replace three of the pianists with a bass player, a drummer, and a guitarist, and now you have a more pleasing range of sound — assuming, of course, that the pianist isn't Elton John and the guitar player isn't Liona Boyd, proving there's a limit to analogies like this. . . . Anyway, the idea is not to duplicate styles, but to *contrast them* in your portfolio of mutual funds — especially funds based on equities.

Value fund managers

When assessing which mutual fund management style is best suited to your needs, start with a very clear distinction between *value* and *growth*. Some fund companies may claim they use both approaches at the same time, but almost all favour one over the other, and the more you understand the impact this has on the fund's performance, the better your chances at matching a fund to your needs.

Value managers shop for shares in companies the same way you shop for groceries. Suppose your grocery list includes canned peas, and when you reach the canned goods section, six different brands face you on the shelf. If you're a value shopper with little or no brand loyalty, you check the size of each can and compare the prices, deciding which brand is the best buy according to its cost and contents.

You also look for specials, or discounted brands temporarily priced lower than the competition. Their price could be reduced for any number of reasons irrelevant to the contents, such as a label that's not as attractive as the competition's, or an overstocked warehouse. Unless you are an inflexible fan of one brand over another you'll probably choose the discounted brand, and that decision identifies you as a value shopper. Then again, perhaps the pea crop was exceptionally small this year, which boosted the price of peas and made all of the brands so expensive that you buy corn instead. That's another definition of value — you choose price over industry.

Choosing stocks according to their value is simply a more complex way of doing the same thing. If the regular price of a 14-ounce . . . sorry, a 398-mL . . . can of peas is 89 cents, and you choose a can of similar quality for 69 cents, you've made a value purchase. With companies being a little more complicated than cans of peas, value-oriented mutual fund managers look at the following:

- ✔ **Price to earnings ratio** (sometimes called simply P/E ratio), which measures the market price of one share against the amount of money each share of the company has earned. Suppose that a company has 10 million shares outstanding, and each share is currently priced at $10. If the company's earnings reach $10 million, that's one dollar of earnings for every share, which translates into a P/E ratio of 10 to 1.

- ✔ **Price to book ratio** measures the market price of the company's outstanding shares against the value of the company according to the accountant's calculations. A company might be valued at $100 million according to all the assets listed by its accountants, including land, buildings, machinery, inventory, and so on. If the current market price of all the firm's shares adds up to only $80 million, it has a low price to book ratio — and that makes it a bargain.

- ✔ **Dividend yield**, found by dividing the share price by the dividend, measures the current market share price against the dividends paid by the company. A high dividend yield usually means good value.

If all decisions were made purely on the basis of calculations such as these, there would be little or no opportunity to find values. Anybody with a number-crunching computer could do the same thing, and searching for so-called "hidden" values would be fruitless. But emotion and misperception can play a role even among shrewd fund managers, producing stocks that are temporarily "out of favour" and undervalued. Here's an example:

From 1993 to 2000, the U.S. stock market staged the longest and steepest growth period in its history. Meanwhile, Japan was going in the other direction, suffering economic and political woes. This added an extra-warm glow to U.S. companies and put Japanese companies in a cold shadow, with similar effects on their market price. As a result, in early 1999 the U.S. electronics giant General Electric was selling for ten times the price of Japan's Sony on a per-share basis. Yet both companies were in the same industry, generating similar levels of sales, and racking up almost identical rates of earnings.

Mutual-fund managers who swung their attention from the excitement of Wall Street to far-off Japan discovered out-of-favour bargains, and picked up Sony shares as a value investment. How much difference was there between their international bargain-hunting and your decision to slide a few extra cans of under-priced peas in your grocery shopping cart? Not a whole bunch.

Growth fund managers

Growth managers take a different approach from value managers. Shopping for value is based on *what you know now*. Shopping for growth is based on *what you expect to happen in the future*. For this reason, most growth stocks are in relatively new industries based on technology and biotechnology. The explosion in share prices for Internet stocks such as Amazon.com during 1999 and early 2000 was an example of growth investing gone wild.

Over the 12 months between March 2000 and March 2001, *the NASDAQ composite index*, a measure of growth-oriented technical stocks, fell more than 60 percent. If you had $10,000 invested in companies listed on the NASDAQ on March 10, 2000, those same shares were worth less than $4,000 exactly one year later. You can lose money faster at the crap tables in Vegas, but you'll have a lot more fun doing it.

The stomach-churning drop in company shares making up growth-based mutual funds did more than slash the value of retirement accounts from Conception Bay to Coquitlam. It made many Canadians question the whole idea of investing in equity-based mutual funds to build their retirement nest egg. This wasn't necessarily a bad thing, because it injected a shot of reality into their RRSPs, if not their veins. Here are the lessons to be learned from The Great Meltdown of the New Millennium:

> ✔ **Diversify:** If you put your total RRSP assets in a growth fund investing in Internet-based companies back in early 2000, you could have lost as much as 70 percent of your money a year later. Value-based funds lost as well, but only one-third as much.

- ✔ **Don't be greedy:** It sure was nice watching some of those high-flying mutual funds rise like a rocket in the air. It sure was painful watching them fall like a bowling ball down an elevator shaft. If you insist on the possibility of making better-than-average profits, spend some of them on Gravol and tranquilizers.

- ✔ **Learn where your money goes:** In 1999, most people (including many mutual-fund managers) believed Nortel was a blue-chip stock, as solid as the Canadian Rockies. In one way, it was. But most of its customers were not. Mutual funds heavily invested in Nortel suffered more than those who recognized the true risk of Nortel's future.

- ✔ **Beware of media hype:** Many of those investing gurus who appear on TV talk shows mumbling about the TSE and the NASDAQ grew excited over Nortel and its prospects. As a result, thousands of unsophisticated investors shared the excitement and helped drive the share values up. Hear that in the background? That's the sound of gurus backpedalling and investors gnashing their teeth.

- ✔ **Stay cool:** A well-managed company with good products and a solid industry will often get dragged down by an entire industry. That's the bad news. The good news: They always rebound. So avoid panic . . . but ask yourself if you want to go through this again.

Growth stocks are chosen differently than most value stocks. In a value stock, the individual company is examined first, to measure its value. In a growth stock, the overall industry receives attention; if the industry is expected to grow, then companies serving the industry can be expected to prosper. In the late 1990s, a lot of people saw the Internet as an industry, and began buying shares in every company associated with it. Other growth-oriented industries (as seen by the Smart Money): Health and geriatric services, genetics and bio-genetics, and communications. (For a more detailed discussion of the way stocks are selected, see the section on top-down and bottom-up fund managers a little later in this chapter.)

Timing really is everything

Growth-based investments are not always small companies poised on the cutting edge of technology. A bank or trust company that is the first to introduce a new product or service, positioning it well ahead of competition, can be considered a growth stock. And although other growth stocks may be small at the beginning, they can grow to blue-chip size eventually, and any fund manager or investor who was either clever enough or lucky enough can reap massive rewards. Imagine, for example, that it is 1959 and you are asked to invest a few dollars in a small firm out of Rochester, New York, that is using an entirely new technology to make cheap, quality copies on plain paper. Would you see the future of that little company, called Xerox?

Or imagine that a brash young guy with thick glasses and a bad haircut gave you a chance to get in on the ground floor of his new company back in 1979. Would you have handed Bill Gates a few hundred bucks and trusted him to spend it wisely when launching Microsoft?

Those are two classic and very rare growth investments. If you missed them, there is always another one around the corner, and every growth-oriented mutual fund manager hopes he or she will be the first to spot it.

A cure for fiscal insomnia

So here's the dilemma: Do you put most of your RRSP in growth funds, based on warm and cozy companies such as Petro-Canada, Bombardier, and the chartered banks? Or do you rely on funds investing in companies whose markets are tied to the Internet, computers and their components, biotechnology, telecommunications, and other industries that have more pie in the sky than money in the bank? The first choice will help you sleep well. The second could make you rich.

There is a third choice to consider: Income balanced funds. These slightly illegitimate offspring of balanced funds (see Chapter 16 for a full description) base their investment philosophy on an idea you and I can understand, favour, and lust after — namely, "Show me the money!" In this case, the money is delicious cold cash paid in the form of shared profits.

The profits are generated by royalty trusts and income units. These are a little like bonds, a little like shares of common stock, but not really either. *Royalty trusts* and *income units* are issued by companies with proven income-producing assets, such as oil and gas wells, pipelines, rental real estate, and so on. The issuers sell a portion of the profits expected to be generated by these assets, and use money from the sale of these trusts to drill for more oil and gas, build more pipelines, and buy more real estate. Income balanced funds combine royalty trusts and income units with equities for a combination of cash flow (from profits) and capital gains (from expected increases in share values).

Most income balanced funds are small, but (here's the best part) every Canadian fund in this category made money during 2000 and 2001 — a time when virtually every other mutual-fund group was doing swan dives into shallow pools. Table 14-1 shows three of the best performers and their returns as of April 30, 2001.

Table 14-1 Top-Performing Income Balanced Funds (April 2001)			
Company	*6 Months*	*1 Year*	*2 Years*
Bissett Income Class Fund	17.5%	40.7%	17.0%
CI Signature High Income Fund	11.8%	27.8%	13.0%
Elliott & Page Monthly High Income Fund	12.8%	33.0%	7.5%

The Bissett fund's 40.7-percent return in one year is the stuff dreams are made of, especially if your dreams involve BMWs and condos in Maui. When you remember that the average Canadian equity fund barely made 3 percent in the same year, you may wonder why you would put your money anywhere else. Here's why.

Income balanced funds move in a contrary direction from general equity funds. When the equity guys are laughing all the way to the bank, these funds tend to languish somewhat, although the largest of the above, the CI fund, has scored a respectable 9.9-percent average return over the four years since it was launched.

When your RRSP assets pass the $25,000 mark, consider a three-pronged strategy where mutual funds are considered — perhaps 50 percent in value-based funds and 25 percent each in growth and income balanced funds.

Top-down and bottom-up fund managers

Among the various management styles encountered in equity funds are two that sound slightly risqué when written out of context: *top-down* and *bottom-up*.

- ✔ **Top-down fund managers choose the companies they invest in by looking at the "big picture."** They begin by examining the economy as a whole and deciding which areas are likely to generate the biggest growth. Then they narrow their selection down to specific industries and individual companies within those industries. For example, a fund manager may decide that the financial industry is about to do very well over the next few years. If so, she would collect data on every eligible firm in that category, including banks, trust companies, and companies that would likely share in the good times, such as mortgage lenders and service firms with a strong link to the financial industry.

- ✔ **Bottom-up fund managers ignore the so-called "big picture" and examine individual companies on their own merit.** It matters little whether good times are about to shine on the steel industry, mining, telecommunications, or any other sector. The philosophy of bottom-up management style is based on the assumption that solid, well-managed companies with a low share price will survive and prosper no matter how the overall market or individual industries perform. Bottom-up managers tend to be very value-oriented as a result, but good growth-oriented managers can use the same approach.

Market-timing fund managers

Another fund-management style is *market timing,* made both famous and successful by Altamira Funds and its manager Frank Mersch. Market timers live and die by the cliché "Buy low, sell high." They purchase company shares at a low price, hold on to them while the share value increases, then sell the shares for a profit and look around for other companies to buy. It's like riding an endless series of escalators to the penthouse, or so the theory goes. When the timing isn't right, or there are no attractive companies to purchase at a low price, market timers sit on the sidelines, parking the mutual fund's cash in T-bills.

The consensus is that market timing doesn't work, and hasn't since Isaac Newton — yes, that Isaac Newton — said, "I can calculate the motions of the heavenly bodies but not the movements of the stock market." Most people have found no reason to disagree with Newton. Now and then, the consensus is proven wrong. For a while. Frank Mersch managed to do it in the mid-1990s, when his Altamira Equity Fund outpaced virtually every other Canadian equity mutual fund for annual returns. To be fair, Mersch was no seat-of-the-pants manager. He used various technical devices, a discussion of which is beyond the scope of this book. But he was still a market timer who managed to question old Isaac's wisdom, after all. Hey, defining gravity doesn't make somebody an expert on the stock market, right? That's what many people who invested in the Altamira Equity Fund believed and, for a few years, who could prove them wrong?

Unfortunately, all market timers face two challenges that no one has ever been able to sidestep. One is the large quantity of cash that the fund may be forced to leave in low-yield T-bills because there are no satisfactory investments lying around waiting to be acquired. The problem with buy low/sell high is finding shares at sufficiently low prices. When none exist, you sit around waiting for them to turn up. Meanwhile, the fund's cash reserves may be earning less money than other equity funds.

The other obstacle to market timers is the unpredictability of world events. Did you know Saddam Hussein would invade Kuwait in mid-1990, driving up the price of oil? Could you have predicted, in 1985, the reunification of Germany less than five years later? Or the collapse of the Soviet Union? Do you know what the next Quebec referendum will bring, or where the next major gold mine will be located?

These are the kinds of events that plague market timers, because they don't see them coming. They affect other types of fund managers as well, of course. But equity funds based on distant horizons rather than a buy-and-sell timing philosophy are better equipped to ride them out.

As Isaac Newton predicted in an offhand way more than 200 years earlier, Altamira's exceptional returns based on market timing couldn't last. After a few years of outpacing the field, the Altamira Equity Fund slipped dramatically through 1997 and 1998. Mersch's timing was gone, and soon Mersch himself was gone from the helm of Altamira.

The philosophical opposite of Frank Mersch is a man named Warren Buffett, who directs the Berkshire Hathaway fund in the United States. Buffett takes a very dull approach to equity investing compared with Mersch, an approach that Buffett calls "Buy and hold." You buy shares in good companies and you hold on to them. That's it. End of story. Does it work? Last time I checked, Warren Buffett was personally worth $35 billion, which would be enough to pay off my VISA balance and leave lots of loonies for beer and chicken wings. Canadian mutual funds that reflect at least some of the Buffett belief include AIC Diversified Canada and the Mackenzie Universal Future Fund.

What Does All of This Mean to You?

The two most important fund management styles to be aware of are *value* and *growth*. With two Canadian equity funds in your portfolio, each emphasizing a different management style, you've added to the overall diversification of your fund portfolio. When your RRSP assets exceed $25,000, consider adding an income balanced fund for an extra measure of diversity.

Not all mutual funds want to identify themselves with one style or the other. They'll simply claim that they pursue "whichever strategy produces maximum potential returns for our unitholders," or some similar weasel phrase. The truth is, one philosophy will almost always dominate the other, and some fund companies, to their credit, have begun to label their funds according to their management style. Atlas, Synergy, TD Green Line, and Talvest are a few firms that offer both value- and growth-based funds, and clearly label them.

With roughly equal amounts of your equity investments in value and growth funds, plus a dollop or two in an income balanced fund, don't be surprised or dismayed if one begins outpacing the others in performance. This does not mean the fund style with the lower return is in error. In time, they will likely reverse positions. That's what diversification is all about. As one observer has wryly observed, "If all your funds are making equal amounts of money at the same time, you don't have an investment portfolio. You've got a bet."

Is Bigger Better?

Some mutual-fund observers, gurus, and columnists hold a deep-seated prejudice against large mutual funds. In Canada, this would be a fund with more than $1 billion in unitholders' investments. Unlike most other prejudices, this one at least has a basis in logic.

Successful, well-managed mutual funds tend to attract investors. This is hardly earth-shattering news. But mutual funds can grow to a critical mass, where (I can't believe I'm writing this, but it's mostly true) having too much money actually can become a problem. Imagine, for example, an equity mutual fund with $100 million in unitholders' assets. Its manager and staff follow a careful, disciplined style and a buy-and-hold philosophy. Their wisdom and hard work produces exceptional returns for their unitholders, and suddenly they are media darlings, smiling from the covers of *Report on Business, Canadian Business, Maclean's,* and maybe even *Beekeeper's Journal.* They are the new geniuses of Canadian investing, and people begin tossing money their way. Soon they have $100 million invested and twice that much sitting around as cash.

Now they have a problem: What to do with all this cash. You can't very well return it with a "Thanks, but no thanks" note attached. Nobody managing an open mutual fund ever has. You are a disciplined fund manager, so you spend much time and effort choosing only the very best investment opportunities. But few of them are lying around waiting to be picked up like apples after a windstorm. So you invest the money in a liquidable asset, such as T-bills, where you can get your hands on it as soon as you decide where and how to spend the money. This means a major chunk of the fund's assets will be earning much less than the returns that made the fund such a hit in the first place, and next year's return figures may show your fund slipping badly.

This can happen, but it is more rare than you might expect. In fact, for the ten years ending in early 1999, Canadian mutual funds with assets of $1 billion or more averaged a compound annual return of 11.5 percent. Small funds, with assets of $250 million or less, delivered a return of just 10 percent. I don't know about you, but I'll hang out with the big guys!

What made the difference? Management style, for the most part. Mutual funds set up to generate returns by aggressively buying and selling shares of neglected companies work better when they're relatively small. There aren't many neglected companies whose prices keep moving up and down the market for a large fund to benefit from, and still make an impact on the return. They need bigger trades, which is difficult to do with non–blue-chip companies, or a much better batting average, which isn't easy either.

 This does not come with a guarantee, but here's a general rule you might apply: When looking for a value-managed buy-and-hold fund, think big in terms of the fund's assets. Look for something in the billion-dollar range. When searching for a growth-managed fund, consider a smaller, more aggressive fund, closer to the $250- to $500-million range. Then take two aspirins and call me in the morning.

Where your money goes

You can learn much about a fund's investment style by reading its prospectus. Now, I'll admit that I have encountered no prospectus as well-written as *The English Patient* or as entertaining as *Gone With the Wind*. But if you choose to look beyond basic information such as MER levels and compound annual returns, some nuggets of information are lurking among that legalese. Most of them concern the fund's portfolio, which is where the fund manager tends to dole out your money.

You don't have to perform this exercise if a) it simply confuses you; b) it puts you to sleep out of pure boredom; c) you would rather find, and totally trust, a financial adviser. But it's your money and your future, and the more you know about where your money is going, the better you'll feel about the decisions you make. Besides, some people (including me) find this stuff moderately interesting.

I studied the geographic distribution and specific companies of three roughly comparable international equity funds. In other words, I discovered where and with whom the fund managers were spending the money they collected from investors like you and me.

The Templeton Growth Fund is a bit of a granddaddy in mutual funds, founded back in 1954 by Sir John Templeton. Like many grey-haired patriarchs, the Growth Fund has tottered lately. But over the ten years ending March 31, 2001, it averaged 13.3-percent annual returns to its investors, outperforming other funds in its category. Thankful investors have helped build the total assets of the fund to just under $10 billion. Think of it as a down pillow — not very exciting, but it sure helps you sleep well.

The Mackenzie Ivy Foreign Equity Fund has been around less than ten years, but it has managed to establish a solid record of performance, averaging 13.2 percent annually over the five years ending March 31, 2001 (the Templeton Growth Fund delivered 9.8 percent over the same five years). Like the Templeton Growth Fund, the Ivy fund looks for underpriced international companies, using a buy-and-hold philosophy. Okay, it's not rock and roll, but a lot of people like it anyway — enough to boost its total assets to almost $1.5 billion.

The AIM Global Theme Class Fund is roughly the same age and size as the Mackenzie Ivy Fund, but it's not nearly as successful at generating returns; its average earnings for the five years ending March 31, 2001 are just 5.2 percent.

Consider the geographic distribution of investments made by all three funds, as shown in Table 14-2. Keep in mind that these are all value-based international funds, able to search out companies anywhere in the world that appear to offer long-term returns.

Table 14-2	Distribution of Investments		
	AIM Global Theme Class Fund	Mackenzie Ivy Foreign Equity Fund	Templeton Growth Fund
USA	47.8%	57.0%	33.6%
Japan	18.3%	2.0%	6.7%
France	7.3%	2.0%	—
Germany	—	—	4.2%
Netherlands	3.4%	3.0%	3.9%
Switzerland	4.4%	—	—
U.K.4.2%		17.0%	10.3%
Hong Kong	—	—	9.1%
Australia	—	—	3.4%
Canada	4.4%	—	2.3%
Brazil	—	—	3.1%
South Korea	—	—	2.4%
Singapore	—	2.0%	—
Denmark	—	2.0%	—
Norway	—	2.0%	—
Mexico	2.0%	—	—

Just two years earlier, the Templeton Growth Fund had substantial investments in France (7.1 percent), Spain (3.6 percent), and Switzerland (4.5 percent), with relatively little in Australia, Canada, Brazil, and South Korea. Large it may be, but the Templeton Growth Fund is not immobile.

The Mackenzie Ivy fund's heavy investment in U.S. markets helped it generate impressive earnings, but should the Yankee economy tumble further into the ditch than other countries, its investors will not be amused.

The AIM fund isn't as heavily invested in U.S. markets, but unless Japan pulls up its economic socks compared with recent years, it will have difficulty keeping up with the best in its category.

It doesn't take a geopolitical genius to understand the basic differences among mutual funds investing your money around the world. Reading this corner of your fund prospectus will tell you where your money is going. Interpreting the value of this information is something you can do to maintain control of your RRSP investments in this area.

The companies they keep

Here's another example of management style and its impact on equity funds. This time we'll look at four funds investing primarily in Canada, making them 100-percent eligible for your RRSP (see Table 14-3). Three of them are thoroughbreds, and the other (based on five-year performance) is a mangy cur. Can you identify the flea-bitten bow-wow based on the companies representing each fund's top ten holdings? In alphabetical order, they are Acuity Pooled Canadian Equity Fund, AIM Canadian First Class Fund, Dynamic Focus + Canadian Fund, and Saxon Canadian Stock Fund.

Table 14-3	Top Ten Holdings of Four Canadian Equity Funds		
Acuity Pooled Cdn. Equity Fund	**AIM Cdn. First Class Fund**	**Dynamic Focus + Cdn. Fund**	**Saxon Cdn. Stock Fund**
1. Nortel	EI Financial	Loblaws	The Nu-Gro Corporation
2. CIBC	Enron Corp.	TD Bank	Canadian Pacific
3. Scotiabank	Clarica	Thomson Corp.	Agrium Inc.
4. C-Mac Industries Inc.	Bank of Montreal	Berkshire Hathaway	Manulife Financial
5. Embraer	Canadian Pacific	Bombardier	CAE
6. Sun Life Financial	Canada Life Financial	Power Financial	Goldcorp Inc.
7. Tesco Corp.	Coinstar Inc.	CanWest Global Communications Corp.	Trilon
8. Aur Resources	Rothmans Inc.	Mackenzie Financial	Cara Operations Ltd.
9. Westaim Corp.	Reliant Energy	Quebecor	Cott Corporation.
10. AES Corp.	Power Financial	AGF Management Ltd.	Industrial Alliance Life Insurance

Most of these Canadian companies will be familiar to you, and some pop up in more than one fund. The Dynamic fund is chock-full of solid blue-chippers like TD Bank, Bombardier, Quebecor, and Loblaws.

The Acuity fund is a tiny fund (less than $20 million) established back in 1993. Its small size is responsible, in part, for its high volatility. But if you had invested in this fund back in March 1996, you might forgive its wild ups and downs, because you would have averaged 22.2-percent earnings every year since then.

The AIM fund, substantially larger at almost $425 million, has consistently scored in the top quartile of its category since it was launched in 1997. In fact, its two-year annual return of 28.89 percent (as of March 31, 2001) ranked it the best of all Canadian equity funds.

The Saxon fund is almost minuscule, at $15.4 million in total assets, and what's with all those funny companies no one has heard of — Nu-Gro, Agrium, CAE, and Trilon? Is this any place to entrust your RRSP money? Well, maybe it is. The Saxon fund has consistently scored in the top quartile of its category, averaging more than 13-percent returns over the five years ending March 31, 2001. This one's a winner. So why isn't it bigger? One reason may be its stronger focus on small-cap companies, although it is not identified as a small-cap fund. More on these funds later in the chapter.

The dog here, when it comes to evaluating performance, is Dynamic Focus +. Canadians have invested well over $300 million in this one, and over three years it has managed an average loss of 2.6 percent per year. Yet some of the biggest, most familiar names in corporate Canada are in its top ten list. What's going on here?

Success in value funds requires hard work and digging here and there to find overlooked bargains. Investing in companies everyone knows about, no matter how well-managed and efficient they may be, is not the road to long-term success.

Canadian Stocks: Large and Small-Cap

What's the difference between a large company and a small-cap company . . . and why should you care? Companies are measured, for investment purposes, according to the total market value of all the outstanding shares. Ten million shares in Global Paperclips valued at $10 each gives the company a total value, or *capitalization,* of $100 million. If you owned all the outstanding shares of Global Paperclips, your brother-in-law the plumber might be impressed, but Bay Street wouldn't. Your firm would be a *small-cap* company and wouldn't join the Big Boys until its value had multiplied perhaps five times.

Some mutual funds invest exclusively in small-cap companies, and their performance tends to be markedly different from funds focusing on larger blue-chip operations. Small-cap firms, for example, react faster to market opportunities than giants; think of Apple versus IBM in the home-computer business. Smaller firms also tend to pay lower dividends than large firms, because profits are more often ploughed back into the company. This, of course, generates more growth opportunity.

Should a small-cap fund hold a place in your RRSP portfolio? Yes, assuming the following conditions:

✔ You already hold two contrasting Canadian equity funds (one value and one growth)

✔ Your RRSP is of sufficient size — perhaps $50,000 and up

✔ The small-cap fund represents all or most of your sector investment (replacing emerging markets, industry sectors, and so on)

✔ You are prepared to accept wider volatility than experienced with large-cap blue-chip funds. Small-cap companies tend to be growth-oriented, which these days suggests tech companies associated with the Internet or computer communications. What does this tell you about their performance lately? Picture an elevator shaft and a bowling ball.

Index Funds

As you have read, most equity mutual fund managers assemble a portfolio of shares in companies that reflect a broad base of the economy. This is one way they earn the MER charged to unitholders.

But wait a minute. Other people do the same thing, without charging you a penny. They're the eggheads at the Toronto Stock Exchange who assemble the stocks making up the TSE 35, TSE 100, and TSE 300 indexes.

The *TSE 35* is based on the country's 35 bluest blue-chip stocks, while the *TSE 100* adds 65 more stocks, including some mid-size firms. The *TSE 300* is the broadest of all, with 300 companies represented. Each company is weighted according to its perceived impact on the market. Nortel (formerly Northern Telecom) is just one of the 100 companies making up the TSE 100 index, but its impact is so great that instead of representing $\frac{1}{100}$ of the total index it represents $\frac{11}{100}$. So a one-dollar decline in the price of Nortel stock has the same impact on the index as a one-dollar decline in 11 other companies on the index, each of them representing $\frac{1}{100}$.

These TSE indexes serve as the benchmark for the stock market's performance. When you hear about the TSE rising more than 200 points in a day, the roar you hear in the background is the sound of Bay Street barons

Market indexes? Think thermometers

A stock-market index is a shorthand method of measuring changes in prices for the entire market or for selected corners of it. The share prices of selected companies are tracked, weighted according to their size and overall impact, and put through a number-crunching machine to produce a figure that is like a thermometer reading, indicating whether the market is hot, cold, or tepid. Other market indexes include the Dow Jones Average and the Standard & Poor's 500 Composite in the United States. The Standard & Poor's (S&P) 500 is considered a better index than the more familiar Dow Jones Average, which tracks only 30 giant firms. The S&P's 500 listings include both large and mid-size companies, providing a clearer picture.

rushing out to order another BMW. When it falls more than 200 points, the street gutters run with tears. Or sometimes blood.

From time to time, the TSE tweaks its indexes by removing companies and replacing them with others that represent the state of the market more appropriately.

Index funds mirror the index on which they are based — in Canada, that's usually the TSE 100. Since the funds move in lockstep with the underlying index, adding and dropping companies as the index does, they are considered *passively managed funds*. You or I, with access to a decent computer program, could manage an index fund ourselves. Forget about earnings ratios and top-down/bottom-up philosophies. Just follow the index.

Does it work? Consider this: Over periods of ten years or more, index funds outperform about 75 percent of actively managed equity funds.

Do they belong in your portfolio? Perhaps, but keep these things in mind:

- ✓ **Index funds are always 100-percent invested.** Actively managed funds may be only 85-percent invested, with the rest held in cash. Managers of index funds don't have to keep cash on hand in case a bargain leaps out of the bushes at them, because whatever's lurking there doesn't matter. Only companies on the index mirrored by the fund can be purchased, in the same proportion as the index. No cash is held in low-return T-bills. So when the market climbs, virtually every penny in the fund is riding with it.

- ✓ **If the market drops, there is no cash reserve to help cushion the fall.** As a result, index funds can be more volatile than actively managed funds.

- ✓ **Index funds have an immediate advantage over actively managed funds, thanks to their lower MER.** This is true, assuming the fund follows the rule. But not all funds do. Some figure they can charge whatever MER the market will bear. You shouldn't pay an MER of more than 1.0 for an index fund — in fact, you should pay much less.

Who is on the TSE 300?

About one-third of the companies listed on the TSE 300 index are associated with mining, petroleum, wood products, and pipelines. This reflects the nature of Canada's economy, like it or not. It would be wishful thinking, for example, to have one-third of the list based on computer products, movie production, or aerospace.

With so much of our economy resting on the supply and demand of resources such as gold, nickel, copper, oil and gas, and lumber, Canada does not enjoy as diversified an income as the United States — or, in fact, many other industrialized countries. This makes it all the more important for people like you and me to maximize the foreign content of our RRSP investments. When the prices of gold, oil, lumber, and nickel all drop simultaneously, as occurred in 1998 and 1999, Canadian investments begin to decline in value. In Canada, we lack giant corporations such as IBM, General Motors, and Disney. These companies, and others like them, are invulnerable to resource prices and help balance things for us. But they are not available in Canada, so

we have to look elsewhere. That's the idea behind building the foreign portion of your RRSP.

How high should you go — 30 percent? 50 percent? 100 percent?

When Ottawa increased foreign-content limits in RRSPs from 20 percent to 30 percent, it represented a major improvement. With derivative-based funds, it's possible to invest 100 percent of your RRSP outside of Canada (for details, see Chapter 17). But is this a good idea?

Probably not, because it raises the spectre of foreign-exchange risk. If every loonie in your RRSP is riding on foreign investments and the value of the loonie rises 10 percent against other currencies (hey, it could happen . . .), the value of your RRSP in Canadian dollars drops by 10 percent.

Choose your own level, but 50 percent seems like a reasonable, middle-of-the-road, vanilla-flavoured solution here. It's also easy to achieve, as I explain in the section below on foreign equity funds.

✔ **Index funds are especially sensitive to MER levels.** Over the five years ending March 31, 2001, the TSE 300 averaged 10.6-percent annual returns. TD Bank's Green Line Canadian Index Fund, with a reasonable MER of 0.85, managed to average 9.9 percent annually for the same period. Bank of Montreal's First Canadian Equity Index Fund squeezed its unitholders for an MER of 1.13 and delivered a five-year return of 9.7 percent. The difference in return reflects the difference in MER rates.

If you invest in an index fund, don't expect to see it in the Top Ten List of Performing Funds. But don't worry about discovering it among the Top Ten Worst Funds either. The conclusion: Think about an index fund as the third or fourth Canadian equity fund in your RRSP. With careful consideration, you should be able to find an actively managed fund whose manager consistently outperforms any index.

Foreign Equity Funds

Over the many years since 1987, only once has Canada placed among the top five equity markets in terms of investment growth. Going back to 1974, the Canadian stock market has trailed the world's average return level by 1.2 percent every year. For this reason, it pays to consider investing a portion of your RRSP assets in foreign equity funds.

There is no need to feel either greedy or unpatriotic about investing money outside Canada. Money flows easily anywhere these days, and if you have a million in cash right now, there is nothing to prevent you from investing it in a company stock, mutual fund, bond, or yak farm anywhere in the world, *unless it is tax-deferred RRSP money.* So you're neither greedy nor unpatriotic to seek maximum returns on your RRSP investment wherever you can find them. You're simply being realistic.

Getting in on foreign investment action starts by ensuring that 30 percent of your RRSP investment resides in companies located outside Canada. It can reside in foreign bonds and other investments as well, but this can be achieved without eating into your foreign limits, as explained in Chapter 15.

Foreign-equity mutual funds should be seen as one more measure of diversification in your plan. For this reason, many advisers suggest broadening your investment as much as possible.

Types of foreign-equity funds

Foreign-equity funds can be categorized as *global* (investments made anywhere in the world), *international* (investments made anywhere except a defined region or certain countries, such as the U.S. and Canada), and *regional* (investments made in specific geographical areas such as Europe, Latin America, Japan, the Pacific Rim, and so on). A fourth category includes *emerging markets,* which represents countries easing their way into either capitalism or major industrialization. These countries offer terrific growth potential and enormous risk, and suffer more economic turbulence than a ten-dollar bill in a tornado.

So what to do? Same old advice: If you're under 40 with a long investment horizon and a strong stomach for volatility, you might choose an emerging market fund or specific regional fund as part of your foreign-equity portfolio. If you are convinced, as many people are, that the U.S. equity market represents the best long-term investment opportunity, consider mutual funds that focus on it, or are heavily weighted toward it. Among the better-performing funds in this category are the AIC American Advantage Fund, the Spectrum United American Growth Fund, and the Dynamic Americas Fund.

I prefer to give the fund manager maximum choice when it comes to looking for good investments, which means a global equity fund. The MERs are admittedly higher — the median is 2.59 compared with 2.40 for Canadian and U.S. equity funds — but *somebody* has to visit those yak farms in Nepal.

Most global funds are weighted toward the U.S. market, often by 40 percent or more. Check the fund's prospectus to confirm this.

More than anywhere else, wisdom and experience counts when it comes to managing an international mutual fund. Only after you have witnessed the roller-coaster ride of international politics and its effect on business in countries such as Indonesia, South Korea, and Brazil can you make investment decisions with confidence. This means overlooking the new guys and choosing companies that know the back route between Kuala Lumpur and Singapore.

Two international equity funds with both long experience and attractive track records are Mackenzie's Cundill Value Fund and the Templeton International Stock Fund.

The Cundill fund, while small (about $275 million in mid-2001), has been impressively consistent and profitable over the years, scoring a 13.2-percent average return over the ten years ending March 31, 2001.

The giant Templeton International Stock Fund (total assets: $6,460 million in mid-2001) bypasses the U.S. market, with no investments there. This might have been a cause for concern over the past few years, as it lagged behind other funds with investments in the United States. Still, its ten-year average return is a comfy 14.6 percent, in spite of some recent losses. If and when the U.S. market starts dragging its heels compared with other regions of the world, these fund holders will be giggling and holding their sides.

It's a good idea to consolidate all your RRSP assets. This makes especially good sense when we're talking about the foreign content of your RRSP. The foreign-content limit is applied to each plan separately, not to your total RRSP assets. If you spread your RRSP assets among three different locations,

TIP

How do you calculate the value of foreign assets in your RRSP?

The foreign holdings in your RRSP are calculated according to their *book value*, which is the amount you paid for them. If you invest $3,000 of your $10,000 RRSP assets in foreign investments, and the $3,000 doubles to $6,000 in a year — don't try this at home, by the way — you are still within the foreign content limit no matter how much the total value of your RRSP may have risen or fallen.

requiring three separate plans, each plan cannot hold more than 30 percent in foreign assets even if you have room in other plans. It's much easier to monitor and control foreign holdings in a single large plan than to juggle them among two or more smaller plans.

Go over the 30-percent foreign limit in your RRSP and Canada Customs and Revenue Agency slaps a penalty of 1 percent per month on the excess amount.

Foreign investment beyond the 30-percent limit

Even though Canada Customs and Revenue Agency is serious about the 30-percent limit on foreign investments held inside an RRSP, it's a bit of a nudge-nudge, wink-wink rule. If you pay attention, you can bump the 30 percent up to over 50 percent of your total RRSP assets without the CCRA throwing a fit. Here's how.

The 30-percent foreign investment limit applies to mutual funds investing in Canadian equity funds and bonds as well as your own RRSP. These 100-percent RRSP-eligible funds can hold up to the same proportion of foreign investments in their portfolio as you do. If you hold 30 percent of your total RRSP in foreign investments, and the balance in Canadian mutual funds that maximize their foreign investment limits at 30 percent, you boot your RRSP's total foreign exposure up to 51 percent of the total — for those of you without a calculator, 30 percent of 100 percent plus 30 percent of 70 percent (21 percent of 100 percent) equals 51 percent.

This calls for you to pay attention to your investments now and then — once every quarter should do it. Keep your foreign-equity mutual funds as close to 30 percent of your RRSP total as you dare, and select Canadian-equity mutual funds according to their long-term average annual returns, acceptable volatility, and maximized foreign investments.

And now for the return of the No Free Lunch Rule. Index funds, as we saw, have their appeal. But a Canadian equities index fund cannot, by definition, invest in foreign equities, so it is unable to deliver 30 percent of its total assets as foreign equities. Maybe there is a place for a hybrid index fund, putting 70 percent of its assets in the appropriate index (TSE 35, TSE 100, or TSE 300) and the balance in foreign equities. Until this happens, choosing a Canadian equity index fund automatically reduces your opportunity to reach the 51-percent foreign investment goal.

Hang on. There is more than one way to skin a federal government ruling. To learn how to raise your RRSP foreign content to a true 100 percent, read about the foreign factor (again!) in Chapter 17.

Sample Portfolios: Ted, Terri, and Thomas

In mid-1996, Ted, Terri, and Thomas attended an evening financial seminar on RRSP investment strategy, conducted by a panel of local financial advisers. All of the advisers promoted the idea of maximizing foreign exposure in an RRSP. "You'll never realize the maximum growth potential from your RRSP without using every trick in the book to place as much of your money as you can outside Canada," one of them preached.

Afterward, the three friends and co-workers gathered over coffee to discuss what they had heard. "I'm sold," Ted said. "I don't see any advantage to investing everything at home when I could be making two or three times as much from investments outside the country."

"I'm a little concerned about risk," Terri said. "Somehow, I'll sleep better if my money is here in Canada."

"How can you two sit there and rave about making money elsewhere?" Thomas asked, fingering the Canadian flag pin in his lapel. "Don't you have any faith in this country?"

It went back and forth like that for a while before Terri finally proposed an idea. "Let's put our money where are mouths are," she said. "Why don't we each transfer $10,000 from our RRSP into separate plans and manage them according to our own feelings about foreign investment? Then, five years from now, we'll compare the value of our plans."

There was some hemming and hawing over extra costs and confusion with separate plans, but in the end they agreed.

The next day, each transferred $10,000 in RRSP assets to a new plan. Ted immediately placed $2,000 in the AGF American Growth Class Fund. "Yankees know how to make money," he said. For the balance of his plan, he needed a 100-percent RRSP-eligible fund, so he chose the Talvest Global RRSP Fund. Holding 80 percent of its assets in Canadian government T-bills, the fund actively traded in futures and other derivatives with the balance. About 40 percent of the companies were in the U.S. and about 12 percent in the U.K., with the rest scattered primarily among firms in European countries.

Terri believed in foreign investment for her RRSP but was hesitant about a fund based on companies she didn't know located in countries she hadn't visited, so she opted instead for foreign bonds. They seemed safer to her, so she invested $2,000 in the TD Green Line Global RSP Bond Fund. Then she looked around for a well-performing Canadian equity fund, choosing Mackenzie's Ivy Canadian Fund for the balance of her $10,000.

Thomas was determined to remain staunchly patriotic. "There are excellent mutual funds in Canada," he told himself, "and I'll trust a good fund manager to watch the foreign investment level. I have better things to do." He found the Phillips, Hager & North Canadian Equity Fund, which was 100-percent RRSP-eligible, and invested the entire $10,000 in it.

On a fine spring day in March 2001, the three gathered in the same coffee shop, clutching their RRSP portfolios purchased with the $10,000 allotment agreed upon five years earlier. Each passed copies to the others, and all three sat in silence while they compared the performance of the other portfolios to their own.

Ted's $2,000 in the AGF American Growth Class Fund had averaged a 16-percent annual return over the five-year period, converting his original $2,000 into $3,600. His Talvest Global RRSP Fund had performed not nearly as well, with an average 6.5-percent annual return. Still, this built his $8,000 balance to $10,600 in five years, so his original $10,000 investment was now worth a total of $14,200, or an increase of 42 percent over five years.

Terri winced at the figure. The Green Line Global RSP Bond Fund may have soothed her sleep but it hadn't lit a fire under the foreign investment portion of her RRSP. Bonds weren't the place to be in the latter half of the '90s, and the bond fund averaged just 6.1-percent annual return over the five years, building her $2,000 foreign assets to $2,610. Fortunately, her $8,000 balance in the Ivy Canadian Fund fared better, generating an average annual return of 11.9 percent, which meant her $8,000 Canadian investment had grown to $12,760, leaving her with a new balance of $15,370.

Thomas felt at least a little vindicated. His $10,000 total in the PH&N Canadian Equity Fund had returned an average 12.4 percent over the five years, leaving him with a new balance of $16,200. "See?" he said, waving his statement in front of Terri. "You don't need to go outside Canada for good returns."

"Yeah, but," Ted interrupted, pointing to his own statement, "if we were able to put 50 percent of our RRSP assets in foreign investments, and I had bought $5,000 instead of $2,000 in the AGF American Growth Class Fund, my balance would now be —" Born before the introduction of pocket calculators, Ted could do figures in his head, and after staring at the ceiling for a moment or two, he continued. "— $9,000 in my foreign portion plus —" He furrowed his brow for a moment. "— $6,625 from my Talvest Global investment . . ."

"Equals $15,625," Terri finished for him. With the lowest returns of all three, she would be stuck paying for the coffee.

The results:

Ted erred in emphasizing foreign investments at the expense of checking a fund's performance more carefully.

Terri earned decent returns, but she paid a price for a good night's sleep.

Thomas should stop gloating and start looking for some foreign diversifications — Canadian investments alone won't maximize his RRSP.

The moral: Maximizing foreign portions of your RRSP is an important part — but only *one* part — of your investment strategy. It still pays to do a little homework.

Chapter 15

Bond, Money Market, and Mortgage Funds

. . . .

In This Chapter

▶ Understanding bond funds

▶ Getting foreign exposure from RRSP-eligible bond funds

▶ Looking at curves and maturities

▶ Choosing a fund for your portfolio

▶ Evaluating money market and mortgage funds

▶ Comparing portfolios: Judy, Jane, and Jerry

. . . .

Should you hold bond funds in your RRSP? It's probably not a question that keeps you awake at four in the morning when your mind grows preoccupied with Life, Death, and the Whole Damned Thing. But it can generate heated debate among some financial advisers.

"Why pay a mutual-fund manager to handle your bonds," a financial adviser once told me, "when you can get all the long-term security you need from strip bonds?"

"How can you expect to get the same level of diversification from bonds as you get from equities," another adviser pointed out, "unless you take advantage of pooled investment and professional management?"

Both were correct in their basic facts, but both also committed at least one small sin of omission.

The first adviser omitted the fact that he and his firm made a direct and immediate profit on the sale of strip bonds to clients such as me. "We sell them commission-free," he said, which was true. But I paid for them with lower interest rates. (For a detailed and valuable explanation of this practice, see Chapter 11.) Besides, since the MERs on bond funds are lower than those charged against equity funds, his argument about paying a fund manager to do what I can do myself is a little weaker.

The second adviser's point about diversification is well taken. On the surface, choosing bonds seems less complicated than choosing companies to invest in. When selecting bonds, you don't have to visit far-flung factories and mines, or interview the heavies who run the corporations seeking your money, or weigh all the other what-ifs and how-abouts. You simply examine a whole bunch of fancy printed paper with fixed values and fixed interest rates, then crunch some numbers with your computer. Hey, it looks easy!

So, of course, does ballroom dancing and playing a Beethoven concerto, as long as you are standing on the sidelines, watching.

Bond Funds: Trading in Dollars and Promises

Imagine your RRSP resting on a three-legged stool. One leg of the stool is called *security*. Another is labelled *growth*. And the third is our old friend, *diversification*. A good bond fund delivers all three and manages to do it for a substantially lower MER than charged by most equity-based mutual funds. True, the growth of a bond fund will be somewhat lower, long-term, than a comparable equity fund. But security tends to be higher, and it's possible to obtain lower volatility with bonds than with equities. Diversification between the two kinds of funds is about equal, depending on the fund's objectives and management style.

- ✔ **Quality bond funds** deal only in bonds and debentures issued by federal, provincial, and municipal governments, as well as major corporations. These tend to be very secure and are often guaranteed by one level of government or another.

- ✔ **What's a debenture?** It's like a stepchild in a bond family. Both bonds and debentures are certificates to prove that a government or corporation owes you money. The amount of money and the terms of repayment are spelled out in both. But while a bond is secured by assets such as equipment and real estate — just like the mortgage on your home is secured by the house and land — a debenture's security is basically only the reputation and good name of the issuer. In effect, bonds are a "Here's my wristwatch, keep it until I pay you back" arrangement, while debentures are a "Trust me!" deal. For this reason, debentures pay higher interest than bonds issued on a similar basis.

- ✔ **Bond funds also provide a different kind of diversification,** if a substantial part of your RRSP is invested in equity funds. Stock and bond funds rarely, if ever, move in lockstep. A jump in interest rates can attract a large number of investors out of the stock market, selling their shares in order to buy bonds at the new, higher interest rates. Higher interest rates lower the price of existing bonds, but raise the average annual return. So combining a well-managed bond fund or two with an equally well-managed equity fund or two, or three, helps you cover most of the bases.

Here's a critical difference between buying bonds and buying units in a bond fund:

✔ **Bonds pay fixed interest over a fixed period of time.** If you purchase a bond paying 10-percent annual interest for ten years, that's exactly what you will receive for precisely that length of time.

✔ **Bond funds pay fluctuating levels of interest over an indeterminate period of time.** This is easy to understand when you realize that a bond fund will hold thousands of bonds paying different interest rates over different periods of time. What's more, a bond fund manager can make capital gains for the fund by trading them, using the old buy low/sell high philosophy. So there is no way to fix the returns of a bond fund.

Bond funds are loosely grouped according to the terms of the bonds they buy and sell.

- **Short-term bond funds** tend to restrict their holdings to bonds that mature in one to five years.

- **Medium-term bond funds** deal in bonds from five to ten years before maturity.

- **Long-term bond funds** focus on bonds that are at least 10 years, and as much as 30 years, from maturity.

There is no hard-and-fast rule about the kinds of bonds a fund can deal with, although it would be rare indeed to find a short-term fund dealing in 20-year bonds. But while the bonds in one medium-term fund may have an average maturity date 12 years into the future, the average maturity of another could be just 7 years. This has a major impact on each fund's returns. Here's why.

During "normal" economic conditions, longer-term bonds will generate higher returns than shorter-return bonds. (So what are "normal" conditions? Let's say they're when interest rates are no more than 20 percent higher or lower than the most recent 50-year average.) A fund whose bonds have an average maturity date 12 years in the future should be generating higher returns than a fund loaded with bonds maturing just 7 years from now. Because long-term bonds will be more volatile whenever interest rates change, this is something else to keep in mind. Both can claim to be medium-term bond funds, and if that's all you use as a measure you could choose the medium-term bond fund with the 12-year maturity date without understanding the volatility risk.

Management Style

Even though you may think the *B* in Bonds also stands for Boring, there are more tricks and turns in bond trading than I can cover in this book, which is probably more than you care to know anyway.

The many complications in bond trading create a range of bond fund management styles as wide as the styles used by equity fund managers. The most basic difference is between *passive* and *active* bond fund management.

Passive fund management occurs when a fund manager concentrates on one type of bond, such as those issued by federal and provincial governments, with a fixed maturity date — perhaps ten years. Snore. . .

Active or aggressive fund management provides the manager with wide latitude for wheeling and dealing in bonds. People who've read Tom Wolfe's novel *The Bonfire of the Vanities* will recognize the kind of character who relishes this sort of bond trading. Guessing correctly, and being in the right place at the right time, can make millions for a large-volume bond trader.

Active bond fund managers anticipate future events that will influence the price of bonds. If a bond fund manager grows convinced that interest rates are about to rise, he or she will buy shorter-term bonds, because they are less vulnerable to changes in the interest rate, and probably keep a lot of cash on hand. If the economy looks as though it is going to prosper, which means more companies will enjoy a successful year in sales and performance, the fund manager may look favourably on high-yield (or junk) bonds, which now carry a lower risk of default.

Bond funds are very sensitive to any change in interest rates. If you or a bond fund are holding a bond paying 7-percent interest, maturing in seven years, and interest rates rise just 1 percent, the value of your bond drops by 5 percent. (For a full explanation of how and why bond prices rise when interest rates fall, and vice versa, see Chapter 11.)

Short-term bonds are less vulnerable to interest-rate changes, and long-term bonds are more vulnerable (see Table 15-1).

Table 15-1	Rising Interest Rates Depress Bond Prices
Bonds Paying 7-Percent Interest	*Value if Rates Rise 1 Percent*
Short-term (2 years)	−2%
Medium-term (7 years)	−5%
Long-term (20 years)	−20%

TIP

The folly of predicting interest rates

Think it's easy to predict the direction of interest rates, especially if you are enmeshed in the financial business? Think again. Here's a true story that, besides demonstrating the folly of assuming that experts know where interest rates are heading, also proves that even ink-stained writers can move in elevated social circles.

In early 1992 I attended a large, elegant dinner party at a mansion in Toronto's Forest Hill area. The host was the president of one of Canada's biggest chartered banks, a man whose name you could drop in any financial circle in the country and gain immediate respect and open ears. During the dinner conversation, one guest mentioned that her mortgage was coming due. "What do you think?" she asked the host. "Should I take a short-term mortgage in case interest rates go lower, or lock in a longer term at today's rates?"

Our host, the eminent and highly respected heavyweight bank president, answered without hesitation. "Grab these low interest rates while you can," he said. "They won't be any lower than they are now."

Of course, interest rates began dropping like knickers at a nudist convention. The guest, who locked herself in to a ten-year mortgage at 9¾ percent on the president's advice, watched in horror as 6- and 7-percent mortgages became the norm. Taking the advice of the Pres was costing her thousands of dollars a year in extra interest payments.

Incidentally, the bank president lost a battle for the chairman's job just a few weeks later, and was pushed out . . . uh, resigned from . . . the firm. And me? I enjoyed a fabulous meal, got a peek at the select upper crust of Toronto society, and learned a lesson in the folly of believing that anybody could ever predict interest rates.

Foreign Bonds that Aren't

You have to hand it to the people who market mutual funds for RRSP owners such as you and me. They know the hot buttons to press, and one is marked Foreign Diversification.

The idea of investing large amounts of our RRSP assets in areas other than Canada is critical to maximizing growth and ensuring a prosperous retirement, as I have explained on several occasions. In order to offer Canadians more opportunity to increase the foreign content of their RRSPs and add the security of bonds in the bargain, some mutual fund companies offer funds that satisfy the need for a so-called 100-percent foreign investment opportunity without breaking any of Canada Customs and Revenue Agency's rules.

Their solution: global bond funds that really aren't. It's all parlour-table magic, with some guy in a top hat promising to deliver "unlimited foreign investment exposure with no foreign-content restrictions on your RRSP."

Sounds great, doesn't it? You invest in foreign bonds, for diversification, and the fund remains 100-percent eligible so you don't eat into the 30-percent limit. Hey, where do you sign?

Don't. Not until you realize what is really going on here.

These RRSP-eligible *global bond funds* don't trade in bonds issued by foreign countries, or corporations located in other parts of the world. They buy and sell bonds issued by Canadian governments and corporations in foreign currency, which makes one heck of a difference.

If Canada's federal government wants to attract money from Germany, it issues bonds in German marks, not Canadian loonies. These become so-called "foreign bonds" to the fund companies, but they're about as foreign as Don Cherry eating apple strudel. It's still a Canadian bond. The Ethical Global Bond Fund, for example, held more than half of its assets in Canadian government bonds in mid-1999. Wow, is that exotic or what?

In fact, the only foreign element in these RRSP-eligible global bond funds is the currencies on the face of the bonds — which, by the way, adds an element of unwanted volatility to the recipe. What happens, for example, if the value of the bond rises but the value of the underlying currency — German marks, French francs, Italian lira, or American greenbacks — falls against the Canadian dollar? Not much, obviously. Of course, the bond may rise and the loonie may fall simultaneously, which gives you a double dip. Or both the bond's value and the loonie may fall, which will give you extreme heartburn. When three things can happen and two of 'em are bad, pay the waiter and get my coat — I'm out of here.

Things get worse. Trading in global bonds costs more than doing the same thing with good ol' Canadian bonds, or so a lot of mutual fund companies claim. They use this to justify MERs as high as 3.15 percent. In mid-2001, quality global bond yields, as reported by Salomon Brothers, were 5.9 percent over five years. A bond fund with an MER of 2 or 3 percent was sucking half the expected yield from its basic investment vehicle.

Global bond funds are not, in my opinion, an answer to faster growth for your RRSP via more foreign exposure. And if my opinion doesn't count, consider the facts: Over the five-year period ending March 31, 2001, Canadian mutual funds dealing in so-called global bonds scored an average annual return of 3.7 percent. Now, that's about as exciting as cold mashed potatoes spiked with tofu, isn't it? It makes GICs look like gushing oil wells in comparison. Over the same period, mutual funds dealing in Canadian bonds averaged 6.7 percent annually, which still may not be mouth-watering, but is at least palatable.

Money Market Funds

Think of a *money market fund* as an automated teller machine for your RRSP — a handy place where you can stop to deposit or transfer money to other places.

That's how the federal and provincial governments, banks, and some of Canada's biggest corporations look at these funds. The fund managers buy and sell T-bills, guaranteed investment certificates, and "commercial paper" the same way other fund managers buy and sell stocks and bonds. (*Commercial paper* is a common term for an unsecured promissory note, or debenture, used by large corporations to borrow money for a short period of time — from a few days to a few months. If The Bay needs a few bucks to tide them over until the Christmas sales period kicks in, for example, its IOU is called commercial paper.)

For your RRSP portfolio, money market funds should be used for only two purposes: as the cash element of your RRSP (most money market units can be redeemed or transferred within 24 hours), and as a place to park your money while you make your decision among longer-term investments. You may choose to wait out a long, sharp decline in stock prices (a *bear market*) and hang around until prices start a long, steady climb again (a *bull market*). By the way, if you are able to predict the beginning and end of bear and bull markets with reasonable accuracy, please call me collect and let me buy you lunch. Or dinner. Or a restaurant or two. This is not a common talent.

Money market funds pay about 2 or 3 percentage points better than a savings account, and are just about as safe. What makes them safe? Most money market funds hold large amounts of their assets in government T-bills. Other investments depend upon the strength of the issuing corporation, but since all the securities are short-term their safety is very high as well.

There are two main differences between money market funds and bond funds:

- ✔ **Money market funds are restricted to maturity dates of less than one year.** Some hold securities that mature in just 24 hours, but most are a few weeks or months away. Shorter-term maturity dates provide more opportunity for a money market fund manager to react to any upward moves in interest rates.

- ✔ **Unlike stock and bond funds, the unit price of money market mutual funds never fluctuates.** The price is always pegged at ten dollars. Only the percentage return changes, according to the fund's performance.

Money market funds measure their performance according to their yield, which can lead to some confusion. The *effective yield* of a money market mutual fund is the amount earned by the fund in the past seven days, then projected as though the fund would generate the same return every week for a year. This is expressed as a percentage, but don't trust it too much. It's a little like watching the first inning of a baseball game with the score at 2 to 1 and projecting that the final score, after nine innings, will be 18 to 9.

Money market funds tend to deliver similar performance figures since they trade in similar securities. While there is a variation in maturity dates among T-bills and commercial paper, they all reflect the general interest level paid for high-grade short-term loans. This leaves much less room for the kind of wide swings in returns found among equity mutual funds, and should produce consistently lower MERs for these funds, right?

Right, and it should snow on Christmas Day, too. Money market mutual fund MERs vary from a suspiciously low 0.05 to a shamefully high 2.38. The median MER is a neat and round 1.00, which is the maximum you should pay for this type of fund.

While it's true that chartered banks are adept at managing money market funds, they're not always the best at it. Table 15-2 lists funds managed by the five largest Canadian chartered banks plus three independent fund companies and their average annual returns ending March 31, 2001.

Table 15-2 Selected Money Market Funds Performance (March 2001)

Fund	Assets	MER	5 Years	10 years
Bank of Montreal	$956 million	1.22	3.5%	4.5%
Beutel Goodman	$53.4 million	0.63	4.2%	5.4%
Bissett Class F	$37.4 million	0.54	4.3%	—
CIBC Money Market	$2946.5 billion	1.04	3.7%	4.5%
CIBC Premium T-bill	$3659.9 billion	0.60	4.1%	5.0%
Phillips, Hager & North	$761.5 million	0.48	4.3%	5.2%
Royal Canadian	$3399.9 billion	1.00	3.8%	4.7%
Scotiabank	$1130.0 billion	1.00	3.7%	4.6%
TD Canadian	$5889.7 billion	0.91	4.0%	5.0%

Nowhere is the impact of a low MER more apparent than with money market funds. The chartered banks, which are well equipped to handle a product like this, squeeze as high an MER as they can get away with — and in the case of Bank of Montreal, they get away with almost a billion loonies in spite of charging more than twice the MER of Phillips, Hager & North. Note that PH&N delivers better performance.

The average compound returns are only a measure of each fund's consistent performance. Unlike other mutual funds, you shouldn't plan on keeping a substantial portion of your RRSP in a money market fund for five years, or even much beyond five months. Better long-term returns are available elsewhere. Money market funds should represent the cash portion of your RRSP only.

Mortgage Funds

Bonds, debentures, T-bills, and GICs are all called *debt instruments*. They can be acquired and sold, usually independent of the issuer's knowledge or concern. Mortgages work like that, so why not have a mutual fund dealing in mortgages the same way it might deal in other debt instruments? Let's see . . . the fund could deal only in high-quality mortgages guaranteed by the National Housing Association (NHA) awarded to salt-of-the-earth Canadians buying split-levels all over the country. They would pay their mortgages on time, like hardworking Canadians do, which would generate cash flow, which would provide more money for other hardworking Canadians to borrow for their mortgages . . . Hey, this is a good idea — a really good idea!

Well, it used to be. Bank of Montreal's First Canadian Mortgage Fund is one of the oldest funds in the country, paying good returns with minimum volatility and low risk. But the success of mortgage funds is directly linked to mortgage rates, and what is good news for you can be bad news for me. The good news for you, if you're buying a house: Mortgage rates have dropped and remained there for several years. The bad news for me, if I invested in a mortgage fund: Mortgage rates have dropped, and so on. Returns on mortgage funds have been sliding down a slope for ten years, putting them as low as money market funds, savings accounts, and your basement. There are much better choices to be had.

Sample Portfolios: Judy, Jane, and Jerry

"Yikes!" Judy cried, opening her equity mutual fund statement. "What the heck happened to the stock market?"

"It's called a correction," her sister Jane said, sipping her tea. She and husband Jerry had dropped in to discuss the family Christmas party a few weeks away. It was Judy's turn to host it. "Or maybe a bear market."

"How long do these things last?" Judy said. She, her sister, and brother-in-law were all in their early 30s.

"Who knows?" Jerry replied, reaching for another shortcake cookie. "That's the fun of investing in equities. They're up and they're down, they're down and they're up. . . . "

"So what do we do about our RRSPs this year?" Judy asked, looking first at her sister, then her brother-in-law. All three were firm believers in making regular RRSP contributions and often got together to compare strategies and returns.

"Park it," Jane advised. "That's what we plan to do. Then we can let things settle out and move the money somewhere else, maybe in the spring when the market picks up again."

"*If* the market picks up again," Judy said, tossing her RRSP statement aside. "Where do you plan to put your money?" she asked Jane and Jerry.

"I'm going with a money market fund," Jane said. "I've got my equity investments with Mackenzie Financial and they have a fund called Industrial Cash Management. Later, I can transfer it to one of their equity funds I'm in."

"I don't agree," Jerry said, and his wife's expression suggested this was not an uncommon event in their marriage. "All mutual funds should be long-term. I'll stick to GICs until I decide what to do with it."

"Oh boy," Judy mused. "I'm not sure what to do. Maybe I'll play it safe and go with a bond fund. Or maybe I'll just take the long-term approach. I've been reading about index funds lately . . . ."

Each of the three made their RRSP contribution in October. "It's our Canadian tradition," Jerry smirked once. "Like Thanksgiving." In 2000, each was contributing $2,000.

Jane stuck to her guns, placing her contribution in the Mackenzie Industrial Cash Management Fund. Six months later, at the end of March 2001, she sat gazing at her statement. Her contribution was now worth $2,042, having earned 2.1-percent interest, or 4.2-percent annual return. She shrugged. "Now what do I do with it?" she mused.

Still, she had done better than her husband. The best Jerry could do with a GIC was 3.6 percent annually, which meant his $2,000 was worth just $2,036 after six months. And he still wasn't certain what to do with his money.

Judy decided nobody really knew what either the market or interest rates were going to do anyway, so she would stick to the long-term view. Deciding on a value-based mutual fund investing in Canadian equities, she chose AIM Canadian First Class. Six months later, she opened her statement to discover that her $2,000 had declined by 5.13 percent, leaving her with $1,897.40.

Naturally, Jane and Jerry smirked. Hey, they hadn't made much but they hadn't lost a penny either. But Judy noticed that the TSE 300 index had dropped more than 25 percent during the same six months. Market values return, she knew, especially the value of quality companies like the ones in her AIM mutual fund. The way she looked at it, when the markets swung back her way again, she was already 25 percent ahead.

The moral: If you are in for the long term, it usually pays to accept the ups and downs and not attempt to guess the direction. Over the long term, quality investments eventually pay off.

Chapter 16

Balanced, Specialty, and Exotic Funds

In This Chapter

▶ Understanding asset allocation

▶ Evaluating balanced funds

▶ Weighing exotic and specialty funds

▶ Searching for security with segregated funds

▶ Taking a risk on emerging market funds

▶ Considering labour and socially responsible funds

▶ Comparing portfolios: Rick, Ralph, and Rhonda

*B*eyond equity and bond/money market funds, the choice of mutual funds for your RRSP becomes both simpler and more complex. The simple alternative is *balanced funds*, a kind of blue-plate special for people who can't decide what to choose from the menu. In contrast, and keeping to the restaurant analogy, complex fund choices appeal to special tastes as appetizers instead of main courses. All of this food talk is making me hungry, so let's move quickly back to investment choices.

By the way, this chapter can be considered optional reading. Many RRSP investors will be quite satisfied, thank you very much, with the performance of their plans using a simple combination of bonds and equity funds, with a portion in money market funds as a cash reserve. Balanced mutual funds and other specialty funds discussed in this chapter will be about as fascinating to them as Egyptian hieroglyphics, and equally helpful.

But if you want information about every conceivable method of building your RRSP, you'll want to know about these alternatives — especially balanced funds.

Balanced Funds

When you invest in any mutual fund, you and all the other fund members entrust a fund manager to make investment decisions on your behalf in return for a management fee, known as the *management expense ratio (MER)*. The fund manager makes decisions to buy and sell, and her wisdom and skill are reflected in returns generated by the fund. Meanwhile, you focus on maintaining diversification in your RRSP by adding bonds, T-bills, and similar secure investments to the mix.

Like the chef who puts together a blue-plate special (or, as they say in higher French-speaking circles, a *prix fixe entrée*), the manager of a balanced mutual fund says, "Leave everything to me!" Why hold separate investments in different funds — equities over here, bonds and T-bills over there — when you can pay one fund manager to do it all, with one MER?

This provides some immediate benefits, and some not-so-obvious problems. First, the benefits:

- ✓ **A well-managed balanced fund can generate both growth and income,** all in one package. Remember our story about the two trees, and how an oak tree hangs around getting bigger until you cut it down to use the wood, while an apple tree delivers fruit year after year? A balanced fund could be like an oak tree that bears apples, which sounds like a very good idea indeed.

- ✓ **Balanced funds are diversified by nature,** since they hold both equities and bonds, with as much foreign content of each as Canada Customs and Revenue Agency permits. As a result, if you don't have a great deal of money in your RRSP, a single balanced fund could be a wise choice.

- ✓ **Balanced funds can be fine-tuned between growth and income,** emphasizing one over the other to meet your primary needs.

- ✓ **Depending on the fund's objectives and the fund manager's philosophy, a balanced fund can be like a successful hitchhiker,** catching rides with whatever vehicle is moving fastest. The stock market is booming? Hey, let's move most of our assets into equities. Interest rates are rising? Let's dump most of the equities and hitch a ride on the bond wagon. Actually, funds operating in this fashion are commonly referred to as *asset allocation* funds, which is a more correct term. But the distinction between an aggressively managed balanced fund and a restricted asset allocation fund grows very fuzzy, so let's keep them under the same moniker for now.

- ✓ **Balanced funds are substantially less volatile than all-equity funds,** which is to be expected. Yet their returns are close to equity-fund levels. The median annual return for all Canadian equity funds over the five years ending March 31, 2001, was 9.9 percent; Canadian balanced funds were a step or two behind, at 8.5 percent.

This is all very good . . . or is it? Balanced funds are not perfect. And they're not for everyone. Consider these drawbacks:

- ✔ **A balanced fund's MER is usually higher than it deserves.** Every fund company offering a balanced fund also offers both equity and bond funds. Owners of those funds already pay the salaries and expenses of the managers, whose research and expertise can be used to make decisions for the balanced fund. You would think that owners of balanced funds would pay a lower MER as a result, right? If so, you might also think a diet of cheeseburgers and milk shakes will make you slim. The median MER for a Canadian equity fund is 2.52 percent; for a Canadian balanced fund it's 2.46 percent. Balanced-fund MERs should be at least as low as those for a Canadian bond fund, or 1.9 percent. But most aren't.

- ✔ **It's a balanced fund supermarket out there.** CIBC alone lists 30 different balanced funds, from the 5-Year Protected Balanced Index Fund to the PRS Income RSP Portfolio, with two dozen strange crossbreeds among the herd. Perhaps Canadians really do need this many choices in a balanced fund from one company. Or perhaps it's all a marketing ploy, the way a soap company will market half a dozen brands of detergent in different-coloured boxes, all equally adept at washing your underwear. In any case, it can lead to major confusion and frustration when you're choosing a balanced fund for your unique needs.

- ✔ **Who knows what works?** If the fund manager of your South Sea Equity Growth Fund overestimates the future of the Bali Banana Peeling Corporation and similar industries, you can figure it out. But in balanced funds, you're never sure if the smart or dumb move was made in bonds or equities unless you track it closely. This creates a problem if you're looking for liquidity. Should too many Bali Bananas go bust, the fund's unit values could drop significantly.

The Bottom Line

Should you consider a balanced fund for your RRSP? Yes, especially if

- ✔ **You have a small amount of money in your RRSP** and want to get into mutual funds without suffering the emotional ups and downs of a volatile 100-percent equity fund. In fact, if you have less than $15,000 in your RRSP available to invest in mutual funds, one good balanced fund may be your best choice. When you pass the $25,000 mark, you can begin looking for other combinations.

- ✔ **You want the diversification benefits** of both equities and bonds without worrying about how much to hold of each.

- ✔ **You are about to retire** and seek both growth (to continue building the value of your assets in the future) and income (to provide cash).

As with any mutual fund, be sure you know what you are buying. Read the prospectus, looking for answers to these questions:

- ✔ **What is the objective of the fund?** Does it emphasize growth over income, or vice versa, and how well does this match my needs?

- ✔ **Is it primarily a balanced fund** (the fund manager will hold bonds and equities in roughly equal proportion) or an **asset allocation fund** (the fund manager will shift the balance to a wide degree between the two asset classes, depending on market conditions)? Funds in the latter category tend to be more volatile.

- ✔ **How broadly based is the asset mix?** Generally, the broader the better. It should include something from every asset category, including financial, industrial, resources, and so on.

- ✔ **What is the MER?** Low MERs are especially important in balanced funds because the returns can be modest. Avoid funds with MERs over 2.0. In fact, you should pay substantially less.

- ✔ **Do you already own a mutual fund from this fund family?** If so, look elsewhere. It's always wise to keep equity mutual funds and balanced mutual funds in different fund families. Why? Because they are almost certainly sharing the same analysis data, which means your balanced fund holds the same mix as your equity fund in the same family. That's duplication, not diversification.

Here are four exceptional Canadian balanced funds worth considering, along with their performance as of March 31, 2001:

- ✔ **HSBC Canadian Balanced Fund** has scored better than 10-percent returns over the most recent five-year and ten-year periods. At $550 million it's mid-size.

- ✔ **Phillips, Hager & North Balanced Pension Trust Fund** also boasts 10-percent-plus average annual returns. With $2853.7 million in assets, it may prove less volatile than the HSBC fund.

- ✔ **Saxon Balanced Fund,** like all Saxon funds, is small (just under $6 million in assets) but it's cleverly managed. How clever? While almost every Canadian equity-based mutual fund lost substantially between March 2000 and March 2001, the Saxon fund made 19.63 percent for its unitholders. Yes, that's a plus. Such tiny assets will make the fund more volatile than others, but the people at Saxon have racked up almost 12 percent in average annual earnings since March 1991.

- ✔ **Scotia Canadian Balanced Fund** is another chartered bank winner, with a five-year average return of 10.2 percent and a 10-year average of 9.8 percent.

Exotic Funds

Some people are content with vanilla ice cream. Others are drawn to mango-chocolate-date or coconut 'n' boysenberry. All you vanilla fans can skip this part. The rest of you should be prepared for major volatility along with a sprinkle of confusion. You might want to have a spoonful of Pepto-Bismol on hand.

Dividend funds

Dividend funds are designed to generate cash income based on profits earned by corporations and spread among their shareholders. For this reason, dividend funds hold mostly *preferred shares*. A preferred share has first call for any dividends paid by the company, in exchange for accepting no voting rights. In effect, preferred shareholders are told to shut up and take the money. That works for me.

Should you hold a dividend fund or two in your RRSP? No, because you need growth more than income. Dividend funds work best when held outside an RRSP, where the income they produce is taxed at a lower rate than other sources of income. That's right. Dig ditches, flog burgers, or push pencils all day and Canada Customs and Revenue Agency hits you with the Full Monty every April. Live off dividend cheques and you're treated with kid gloves. Ain't taxation wonderful?

Special equity funds

Special equity funds are sold at craps tables. Well, not really — but perhaps they should be. These are legitimate mutual funds appealing to people with a chunk of disposable income and an appetite for adventure. Special equity funds break industries down into little niches you probably never knew existed. Here is a sample of actual special equity funds available and eligible for your RRSP as either Canadian or foreign content:

- Global Infrastructure (very large companies operating around the world)
- All-Canadian Consumer (companies selling only consumer goods such as food, household furniture, appliances, and so on)
- Global Consumer Product (if you buy it, they may invest in it)
- Generation Wave (companies selling products aimed at tomorrow's generation, which means kids under age ten)
- World's Leading Brands ('nough said)

✔ Boomernomics (anything meeting the tastes of people who worship BMWs, sushi, and ABBA)

✔ Entertainment & Communication (Steven Spielberg meets Ma Bell)

✔ North American Long-Short (darned if I could figure this one out. Anyway, a lot of people did, because they invested in it and it's now closed)

These, and others in their category, are the most volatile of all the funds you can choose. In fact, on a commonly used volatility scale of 1 to 10 (1 = total predictability, 10 = a roller coaster), some specialty funds actually score a 9. One-year returns from Canadian specialty funds, as of March 31, 2001, ranged from 64.6 percent to –80.5 percent. *Gack!* I've seen narrower win–lose ratios at craps tables. These funds provide virtually no diversification and carry among the highest MERs as well. One specialty offering, the closed Friedberg Currency fund, charges a near-record MER of 4.59 percent. (But to be fair, its three-year average return as of mid-2001 was 24 percent.)

Should you hold a specialty fund or two in your RRSP? Perhaps, if you are young and prepared to accept volatility. If the value of your plan is already well into the six-figure range, a specialty fund could represent a small (5 to 7 percent) speculative portion of your investment. But is speculation what you really want, or need, in your RRSP? For most people, the answer is no.

Precious metals funds

Precious metals funds buy and sell metals, including gold bullion, silver, platinum, palladium, and rhodium, among others, as well as the companies that mine them. At one time, gold was considered a hedge against economic uncertainty, which qualified it as an ideal retirement investment. That day has passed, as far as the Western world is concerned. Gold prices have dropped in recent years; many economists doubt if it will ever recover, or even regain its status as a solid investment. In fact, both gold and the funds investing in it are considered highly speculative.

Should you hold a precious metals fund in your RRSP portfolio? No, except as a small portion of your assets — perhaps 5 to 7 percent. These funds are too volatile, too speculative, and too narrowly focused. Many other, and better, opportunities for growth exist.

Resource funds

Resource funds invest in raw materials such as oil and gas, metals and minerals, lumber and other forestry products, and so on. Some include gold and silver among their holdings; others don't. You may not be aware of it, but the market for these products tends to be very cyclical for reasons only economists really care about. Unlike other cycles, like those of the moon and your two-wheeler, economic cycles are less than predictable. For this reason, resource funds tend to be highly volatile and speculative.

One possible exception: Oil and gas stocks may continue on the upswing because the world needs more energy every year and, as you may have noticed, they're not making petroleum in large quantities these days.

Should you hold a resource fund in your RRSP? Only in small portions, for the same reasons listed in the preceding section on precious metals.

Real estate funds

Real estate funds treat commercial and industrial real estate as though they were corporations listed on the stock exchange. Buying and selling property produces capital gains (and losses), while rents and leases produce income. Sounds like a good idea, but the principal advantage of these funds — the tax-sheltered rental income — is lost inside an RRSP, where all income is tax-sheltered anyway. Also, it may be more difficult to redeem your investment in a real estate fund, because all the fund's properties must be appraised before the unit values are established.

Should you hold a real estate fund in your portfolio? No. There is no advantage, and there are some substantial disadvantages — including the fact that real estate funds have not performed well in recent years.

Emerging Markets

Imagine it's January 1, 1993, and we meet over Bloody Marys and coffee to toast the New Year. "I don't know where to invest my money," you moan. "Any ideas?"

"Sure," I reply. "Put everything you have into stock markets in Thailand, Vietnam, Brazil, Indonesia, and Malaysia."

Your eyes glaze over. You wanted to hear about IBM, Nortel, Petro-Canada, maybe a hot little computer outfit near Ottawa, and here I am talking about rice paddies and chopstick manufacturers, right?

If that conversation had taken place and you heeded my advice, at the end of the year your investment would have increased about 75 percent in value (see Table 16-1). That's the kind of phenomenal growth you can earn from emerging markets, where countries are rushing headlong into global-trading capitalization (preparing to sell their products worldwide), widespread industrialization, and a reasonable facsimile of democratization, sometimes all at the same time.

Table 16-1	International Stock Indexes	
Year	*Traditional Markets (Europe/Australia/Japan)*	*Emerging Markets (Indonesia/Kenya/China)*
1988	28.6%	40.4%
1989	10.8%	65.0%
1990	−23.2%	−10.6%
1991	12.5%	59.9%
1992	−11.8%	11.4%
1993	33.0%	74.9%
1994	8.1%	−7.3%
1995	11.2%	−0.2%
1996	6.4%	15.2%
1997	2.1%	−16.4%
1998	11.9%	−8.6%
5-year average	**11.7%**	**9.4%**
10-year average	**6.6%**	**19.2%**

Source: Morgan Stanley EAFE and Emerging Markets indexes

One year after our meeting described earlier, things were very different. Putting your money into Canadian equities would have earned you about 25-percent returns for the year. "Peanuts compared with emerging markets," you say? Not when you notice that the same emerging markets lost more than 7 percent in 1994.

This, as you recognize by now, is extreme volatility, and investing a substantial quantity of money in emerging-market mutual funds can be the economic equivalent of several cc's of caffeine administered intravenously just before bedtime.

I believed in emerging markets funds once. They were right up there with the Tooth Fairy and the Repeal of Temporary Tax Laws. Not anymore. Emerging markets are too small, and the countries are either too corrupt or too unstable for my hard-earned loonies. Don't get me wrong — I love Mexico, Indonesia, Egypt, and Brazil. I've vacationed in them all. Wonderful people and good times. But that's the only way I'm leaving my money there, thank you.

Emerging-markets mutual funds qualify as foreign content in your RRSP, which means their book value cannot exceed 30 percent of your total RRSP assets. But anybody who puts more than 10 percent of their RRSP assets in emerging markets probably lives in a cave, wears rat-skin underwear, and chants Barry Manilow lyrics. Or ought to.

Social Responsibility or Profit?

If you are a fiercely dedicated anti-smoker, how would you feel about loaning money to a tobacco company to help it become larger, more prosperous, and more efficient? You may not be pleased with the idea. But even if you have strong feelings about social concerns such as tobacco, nuclear power, labour relations, environmental protection, and others, you could be assisting the firms who promote these products and practices by investing your RRSP dollars in mutual funds. True, only a minuscule amount of your mutual fund investment — less than 5 percent, perhaps — may be going to companies who crank out cigarettes, operate nuclear power stations, produce weapons and other war materials, operate non-union sweatshops, and practise racial discrimination. But you are supporting them nonetheless, which may or may not rankle.

So here's a test:

If I were to invest your RRSP in my Shoot The Works! Mutual Fund, which happens to include companies such as Philip Morris (tobacco), Smith & Wesson (firearms), and perhaps Nukes 'R' Us Electric Corp., would you invest in it? Let's assume that it consistently delivered 20-percent annual returns. Would that change your mind? How about 35 percent? Maybe 40 percent? This makes the decision a little more difficult, perhaps.

I don't know any fund meeting the preceding description, but if you feel strongly enough about things like tobacco, military machinery, environmental concerns, and the rest, you can both invest your money and express your concerns with socially responsible mutual funds. These funds guarantee that your dollars won't find their way into the coffers of companies dealing with tobacco, military supplies, or nuclear power. They'll favour firms maintaining good employee relations and demonstrating concern for the environment.

The question is this: How much will it cost you in potentially lower annual returns to choose socially responsible funds (SRFs) over other less restricted mutual funds for your RRSP?

Before we get to the figures, let's review the rationale:

The promoters of SRFs suggest you could actually earn more from their funds than from less restrictive funds. Companies that maintain better employee relationships and avoid fines for environmental damage will score bigger profits than those that do not. If they also avoid the ups and downs of depending on military contracts for survival, as well as potential damages due to nuclear power and tobacco use, that's even better for their bottom line.

SRFs have their skeptics, of course. These hard-nosed investors refer to SRF fans as "tree huggers," and suggest that anything narrowing a fund manager's selection of potential companies is counterproductive. Besides, others point out, "socially responsible" means too many different things to too many people. Is McDonald's socially responsible because it supports children's charities, is a major recycler, and was a leader in hiring minorities? Not if you are opposed to the large-scale cattle ranching, with its waste of land and water, needed to support a business built on beef. And there's the whole question of the treatment of animals and health issues as well. Is a toy company socially responsible if it markets violent video games? Why isn't a fund that invests in mortgages, enabling people to buy and own their home, considered socially responsible? Finally, how do you measure your own social values against your desire for a large RRSP balance (remember the Shoot the Works! Fund)?

For a few years, Canadian-based socially responsible funds tended to slightly outperform other Canadian equity funds, generating a warm feeling all around for its investors. But when things grew testy in 2000, the limited manoeuvring room of the SRFs led to trouble. Here's how three major SRFs have fared:

- ✔ **Clean Environment Equity Fund** actively seeks out companies that focus on improving the environment. These companies are busy developing and marketing things such as alternative energy sources (solar power is a good example) and anything that promotes environmental protection. The fund's assets shrunk to half its size in two years, standing at just over $200 million in April 2001. Its one-year loss of 24 percent probably had something to do with it.

- ✔ **Desjardins Environment Fund** invests in "companies whose activities contribute significantly to maintaining or improving the environment." This Quebec-based fund uses screens to filter out non-qualifying companies, instead of the active management approach of the Clean Environment Equity Fund. Small in size (less than $115 million in assets), the Desjardins fund delivered a five-year average return of 8.7 percent in April 2001. Ho hum.

- ✔ **Ethical Growth Fund** is the granddaddy of all Canadian SRFs. Like the Desjardins fund, it uses a screening mechanism to filter out companies that do not meet its seven ethical criteria. These criteria include a North American head office, progressive industrial relations, and no major clients in military activities. Companies also must practise racial equality, follow environmentally conscious guidelines, and avoid dealing in tobacco products and nuclear power. For a while, it worked; Ethical Growth Fund posted above-average results for several years. But excessive losses during 2000 shrunk its asset base from $800 million to $625 million by mid-2001. Its five-year average return saw a similar downward slide to 6.6 percent, compared with median earnings of 9.9 percent for equity funds free to invest in the most tree-chopping, water-polluting, nicotine-spewing, slave-labour dependent companies they could find. Proving, I suppose, that sainthood comes at a price.

Ethical Funds, by the way, are sold load-free through credit unions in every province except Quebec (whose rather arcane consumer protection laws relating to investments have discouraged many mutual funds from participating in that market). You may also purchase them from investment brokers, but expect to pay a negotiated commission fee.

Investing in socially responsible mutual funds is one way of ensuring your RRSP contributions are not used to support ventures you don't agree with. Be prepared to pay the price, however, with greater volatility.

Labour Funds

Boy, did the federal and some provincial governments ever have a deal for you in the early 1990s. Here was the offer:

If you lived in Ontario, Prince Edward Island, New Brunswick, or Nova Scotia, and were in the 50-percent marginal tax bracket, you could purchase $5,000 in labour-sponsored mutual funds for only $500. That's because, in addition to the usual RRSP deduction from your taxable income producing a $2,500 tax refund, both Ottawa and the four provinces would each grant you another $1,000 deduction. (Saskatchewan joined the crowd as well, but awarded a maximum tax credit of just $700.) Bottom line: You buy $5,000 worth of these special mutual funds and put $4,500 back in your pocket. Hey, isn't investing fun?

Actually, it was too much fun. The various governments pulled back on part of their deal when they realized they were being perhaps a little too generous . . . and that the funds weren't achieving their original goal, which was to encourage new business developments that other investors chose to bypass. The funds remain, but the incentive is no longer as sweet.

These funds were created to channel investment money to new businesses, creating jobs in the process. That's why they're usually referred to as *labour-sponsored venture funds*. Promoted by organized labour, whose political clout managed to wring all those tax credits from governments, labour funds offered enough immediate benefits for RRSP investors to take them seriously. And why not? If the chartered banks were selling GICs at a 90-percent discount, wouldn't you rush down and buy a bushel-full?

Even with the catch — there's always a catch, remember — labour funds looked like an offer you couldn't refuse. The catch with these funds prevented you from selling your units for at least five years, or the governments would yank those tax credits back and a hefty redemption fee would apply. But so what? These funds were designed especially for RRSP owners whose investment horizon should be at least five years in the distance. And you could purchase new units, up to $5,000 worth each year, year after year.

Unfortunately, a few things went wrong. One was the matter of management expense ratios. The median MER for Canadian equity-based mutual funds is 2.52 percent. For Canadian labour-sponsored venture funds, it's 4.92 percent. Incredibly, one fund, the Centrefire Growth Fund Ltd., skins unitholders with an MER of 7 percent.

For the most part, the performance of the larger and longest-running RRSP-eligible labour-sponsored venture funds has been about as impressive as the lemonade stand you and your friends ran one hot summer's day (see Table 16-2).

Table 16-2	Labour-Sponsored Venture Funds Returns (March 2001) (Assets in Millions)		
Fund	*Assets*	*3 Years*	*5 Years*
Canadian Medical Discoveries	$370.9	–0.1%	1.0%
Capital Alliance Ventures	$75.1	13.9%	8.8%
Crocus Investment Fund	$109.7	0.8%	3.4%
First Ontario Labour Sponsored Investment Fund Ltd.	$55.9	0.0%	1.7%
Triax Growth	$237.4	–1.8%	1.3%
VenGrowth I Investment	$589.7	15.2%	12.6%
Working Ventures Canadian	$421.3	–3.7%	–1.6%

These are, of course, very volatile funds, as you might expect, with their relatively small asset base and their focus on struggling new companies. The VenGrowth fund, for example, had very respectable three- and five-year returns, but its return for the year ending March 31, 2001, was a teeth-chattering –20.2 percent.

In another example of the Ottawa giveth and Ottawa takcth away rule, the federal and provincial governments decided that a potential $1,000 tax credit from each for investing in qualifying labour funds was too generous, after all. Severe limits were placed on those tax credits in 1996, and when fund sales virtually collapsed at their disappearance, Ottawa relented and restored some of the credits. The federal credit is now 15 percent, providing a maximum $750 credit against a maximum annual investment of $5,000 in these funds. Ontario and New Brunswick each match the federal 15-percent credit, and Saskatchewan and Nova Scotia apply it to a maximum annual investment of $3,500. British Columbia, Manitoba, and Quebec all offer similar credits against labour funds restricted to provincial residents, such as Manitoba's Crocus Investment Fund. An Ontario resident with $50,000 taxable income who is in the 41-percent income tax bracket would earn a tax refund of about $3,500. But the five-year holding period for these funds is extended to (yikes!) eight years.

Okay, so the labour funds are not great at generating annual returns. But you can't ignore that heavy discount due to tax refunds (where available), can you? Well, yes you can. If a labour-sponsored venture fund seriously and consistently delivers much less return than funds in the same general category (that is, Canadian equity funds), those tax refunds soon disappear, as Table 16-3 illustrates. The table records returns after ten years, ending March 31, 2001, for Working Ventures (the only labour-sponsored venture fund with a ten-year track record) versus a number of other Canadian equity funds.

Table 16-3	Labour-Sponsored Venture Funds versus Canadian Equity Funds (March 2001)		
Fund	*10-Year Avg.*	*Initial*	*Final*
Working Ventures	1.2%	$5,000	$5,600
Bank of Montreal Equity Index	9.0%	$5,000	$9,500
Mackenzie Universal Future	12.5%	$5,000	$11,250
Phillips, Hager & North Cdn. Equity	10.9%	$5,000	$10,450
Saxon Small Cap Fund	13.1%	$5,000	$11,550
Scotia Canadian Growth	10.2%	$5,000	$10,100

Bank of Montreal's is a typical Canadian index fund; the Mackenzie, PH&N, and Scotia funds are typical middle-of-the road funds investing in Canadian equities. More telling is the Saxon fund, which invests in small companies closer to the size targeted by Working Ventures.

In fact, a very clever strategy might have been to invest the $3,500 tax-incentive return from the $5,000 Working Ventures fund into the Saxon Small Cap Fund. After ten years, you would have $5,600 from Working Ventures plus $8,085 from the Saxon fund (your $3,500 original investment plus $4,584 profit at 13.1-percent annual growth), for a tidy $13,685 return.

Does this make labour-sponsored venture funds more beneficial to your RRSP? Perhaps. But be sure the fund qualifies for this little bribe . . . er, perk. Then weigh the amount of foreign exposure it increases for your plan against the expectations of lower returns from the labour fund.

All in all, labour-sponsored venture funds are based primarily on good intentions — which, you will recall, is the stuff used to pave roads to an undesirable location. They may have a place in your RRSP, but only if you use the tax credits to add more traditional, better-performing investment choices.

Segregated Funds

In the summer and early fall of 1998, many people with RRSP investments in Canadian equity mutual funds became slightly nauseated whenever stock market prices were mentioned. Many saw the value of their mutual funds drop by 10, 15, or even 20 percent or more. No amount of explaining that this was a "paper loss" due to a "market correction" would mollify them. Losses and corrections never happened with good old GICs and CSBs.

Smack-dab in the middle of this came a torrent of advertisements trumpeting a cure for corrections and losses. The cure was *segregated funds* ("seg" funds), which few people understood but many wanted anyway. After all, seg funds offered the best of both worlds: The growth potential of equity funds and the guaranteed principal of GICs. Invest $10,000 this year, and you'll have at least $10,000 when you cash out in ten years, no matter how far into the tank the market has gone. If the market has risen, you win. If it has dropped, you don't lose. Well, not on paper, at least. And if the market suddenly skyrocketed, you could lock in the new value for another ten years (see Table 16-4).

Table 16-4	Segregated Fund Performance	
	Equity Fund	**Segregated Equity Fund**
	Value	**Value**
Initial investment	$10,000	$10,000
10-year 10-percent average return	$20,000	$20,000
10-year 2-percent average loss	$8,000	$10,000
First 5-year period		
10-percent average gain	$15,000	$15,000 (locked-in)
Second 5-year period		
8-percent average loss	$9,000	$15,000

Ten thousand dollars in both a regular equity fund and a seg version of the same fund would grow in value at the same rate, so a 10-percent annual return would double the value of both in ten years. But if both funds lose an average of 2 percent annually over the same ten years, the non-seg fund drops in value by 20 percent and the seg fund holds 100 percent of its value.

To sweeten the deal, many seg funds permit you to "lock in" any increase in value for another ten years. As the chart shows, if both funds grow 10 percent over the first five years of a ten-year term, you can say, in effect, "I'll take the 15 grand and roll it for another 10 years." Now you have locked in a higher rate, ensuring that you cannot lose the money you have already made.

With charts like this one, the rush was on. By early 1999, segregated funds were representing 20 percent or more of all RRSP-eligible sales for some fund companies. For the most part, the seg funds were purchased not on the basis of logic and benefits, but according to the same twin engines that propel every other investment decision: Fear and Greed.

Setting these two aside for the moment, here are the bare and bald facts about segregated funds:

- **Segregated funds are not new at all.** Life insurance companies have been offering segregated funds for decades, sometimes calling them "variable annuity contracts." The fact that these funds originated with insurance companies and not with investment brokers should tell you something about their primary value.

- **Seg funds are available in more than Canadian equities.** They can include international equities, money markets, bonds, and virtually any other class of assets.

- **Seg funds carry a higher MER.** This is needed to cover the "premium" of the insurance policy guaranteeing no loss of principal, and the difference can be substantial. The MER for the AIM/Trimark Select Canadian Growth Fund, for example, is already a hefty 2.52 percent. Choose the segregated fund version and the MER leaps to 4.35 percent.

- **Over ten years, the risk to your principal is minimal.** Seg funds are sold on ten-year terms and make sense only when your concern is a loss of your original investment, if a serious risk exists. But history says it doesn't (see Table 16-5).

  Over the 50 years from 1947 to 1996, the worst decade for U.S. stocks was the ten years from 1965 to 1974. But guess what? You wouldn't have lost money: you would have gained an admittedly minuscule 0.4 percent.

  Between 1933 and 1996 — a period covering 64 years in all — only a single ten-year period produced a loss in Canadian stocks, and then it was a mere sliver (0.2 percent), as close to breaking even as you can get. Bonds were almost as good (or just slightly worse, depending on your point of view), with only one ten-year period out of 64 chalking up a loss.

Keep in mind that these losses, as rare as they were, represent less than the difference in MERs between segregated and regular mutual funds. In other words, you could be paying as much as 1 percent to prevent the possibility of a 0.2-percent loss — which, if past history is a guide, will occur less than ¹⁄₆₄th of the time. This, friends, is not a good deal.

Table 16-5	Worst 10-Year Periods (Loss of Principal)		
	Period	*Worst 10 Years*	*Loss/Gain*
U.S. stocks	1947–96	1965–74	0.4%
Canadian stocks	1933–96	1929–38	−0.2%
Canadian bonds	1933–96	1950–59	−0.3%

Remember that seg funds originated with insurance companies, and that's where they make sense. If you're concerned about leaving a substantial part of your estate to certain beneficiaries — a favourite niece or nephew, a valued friend, or me — seg funds make sense. Putting $50,000 into a seg fund today ensures that the beneficiaries you name will receive at least that much money. If the fund performs well, they'll get even more.

But unless you are desperately afraid of suffering losses over the longer term, seg funds are not a wise choice due to the higher MERs — in effect, the insurance premium — charged to them. The two most valuable reasons for choosing a seg fund are these:

✔ Segregated funds in your RRSP provide protection from creditor seizure. If you are sued or forced to declare bankruptcy, creditors can seize the assets in your RRSP (except in Prince Edward Island, where RRSPs are exempt from creditors). Unless it is proven in court that you transferred RRSP assets to a seg fund specifically to avoid seizure by creditors, your seg fund assets are safe. Be aware that the beneficiary of your seg funds must be your spouse, a child, a grandchild, or a parent, and the transfer is considered irrevocable. This may hold some appeal for self-employed people whose risk of bankruptcy or legal action against them is relatively high.

✔ Seg-fund values can be passed on to beneficiaries without the need for a will or the payment of probate fees. They are essentially an insurance policy and are treated like one in the event of your death.

Should you have segregated funds in your RRSP? No, unless you are concerned about the risk of bankruptcy or want to use the assets outside your will.

New Dogs, New Tricks

Want to get a little exotic when searching for more foreign investment? Hey, everything's available on the Mutual Fund Smorgasbord! Down in the Hot 'n' Spicy section are mutual funds that provide virtually total foreign investment, yet remain 100-percent RRSP eligible. Wow! Talk about being able to walk and chew gum at the same time! How do they do it?

By keeping 70 percent of their assets in Canadian T-bills and investing 30 percent in *derivatives*, which are highly leveraged deals suitable only for experienced professionals and financial Evel Knievels. Detailed explanations of these little devils are not suitable for a family-oriented book like this one. It's enough to say that derivatives provide the opportunity for *high leverage*, which is a financial guru's term for shooting craps. The 30 percent in foreign derivatives stays within Canada Customs and Revenue Agency's guidelines, while the 70 percent in low-risk bonds and T-bills provides stability against the high volatility and high risk of derivatives.

Two things to file away about these RRSP-eligible funds:

✔ They should be considered only after you have maximized your RRSP's foreign content by other means, described above.

✔ You should obtain a qualified professional opinion about them before proceeding. Anything based on derivatives can quickly become cloudy and confusing to normal people such as you and me.

How Many Funds Do You Really Need?

Diversification can be overdone, especially if your RRSP assets are limited. Having a dozen or more mutual funds in an RRSP portfolio whose value totals less than six figures isn't diversification: it's confusion. Even if your RRSP value nudges the quarter-million-dollar mark and beyond, you probably don't need more than six or seven funds in all, comprising three Canadian equity funds (one each for growth and value, and a small-cap); two foreign-equity funds (a growth and a value); one sector fund (regional, emerging market, or industry); and perhaps a bond, money market, or balanced fund.

Table 16-6 provides a list of highly regarded mutual funds in each category. These are by no means your only choices, but they all bring a good performance record, reasonable MER levels, stable management, and the widespread approval of most financial commentators and observers.

Table 16-6	Recommended Mutual Funds by Category
Canadian Equity — Emphasis on Growth	
AIC Diversified Canada Fund	
First Canadian Growth Fund (Bank of Montreal)	
Green Line Canadian Equity Fund (TD Bank)	
Phillips, Hager & North Canadian Equity Fund	
Standard Life Equity Mutual Fund	
Canadian Equity — Emphasis on Value	
Bissett Canadian Equity Fund	
Ivy Canadian Fund	
Spectrum United Canadian Investment Fund	
Canadian Equity — Small-cap	
Bissett Small Cap Fund	
Fidelity Canadian Growth Company Fund	
Saxon Small Cap Fund	
U.S./International Equity	
AGF American Growth Class Fund (U.S. only)	
AIC Value Fund (U.S. only)	
Templeton International Stock Fund (excludes Canada & the U.S.)	
Fidelity International Portfolio Fund	
Templeton Growth Fund, Ltd.	
AIM/Trimark Fund	
Canadian Bond	
Altamira Bond Fund	
Phillips, Hager & North Bond Fund	
TD Canadian Bond Index Fund	

International Bond

AGF RSP Global Bond Fund

AIM Global Bond Fund

CI Global Bond Fund

Canadian Balanced

HSBC Canadian Balanced Fund

Saxon Balanced Fund

Scotia Canadian Balanced Fund

Canadian Money Market

Beutel Goodman Money Market Fund

CIBC Premium T-bill Fund

Phillips, Hager & North Canadian Money Market Fund

Sectors

CI Emerging Markets Fund

AIM Global Health Sciences

CI Global Consumer Products

Sector funds are outrageously volatile, not to mention prolific. No more than 5 percent of your RRSP assets should be invested in sector funds, and only when its value is approaching the six-figure market. The three funds shown at the end of Table 16-6 are there because they represent promising growth areas, and, as of mid-2001, were delivering better-than-average returns.

The larger your asset size, the more you can fine-tune your diversification. With less money, use a more basic diversification formula (see Table 16-7).

Table 16-7	Sample Diversification by RRSP Assets		
Fund Type	*To $25,000*	*$25,000–100,000*	*$100,000+*
Money market		Canadian	Cdn. & foreign
Canadian bonds	Bond fund	Laddered	Medium-term
		Strip bonds	(up to 10 years)

(continued)

Table 16-7 *(continued)*

Fund Type	To $25,000	$25,000–100,000	$100,000+
Canadian equity	Diversified	Large-cap	Large-cap value
			Large-cap growth
			Small-cap
			Sector
Foreign equity	International	International	Global
			Global sector
			Emerging market
Other		Cdn. balanced	

Sample Portfolios: Rick, Ralph, and Rhonda

Rick's father and grandfather had both worked in mining. Even though Rick had a white-collar job, he felt mining was in his blood and he believed he knew as much about the business as anyone. "It's a resource," he told his buddy Ralph. "Which means it's disappearing year by year, so its value will grow." He slapped the table. "That's where I'm putting my money."

It was the spring of 1996, and to cover his risk a little, Rick chose the CIBC Canadian Resources Fund. "Banks are more cautious and conservative about their investments," he muttered as he signed $10,000 of his RRSP over to purchase units in the fund. "So this should cut my risk a little."

Ralph thought Rick was foolhardy. "You need diversity, and somebody to move your money around," he told his buddy. "Balanced funds are the way to go." But Ralph also liked the idea of having a bank manage the mutual funds he owned, so on the day Rick dumped $10,000 into the CIBC resource fund, Ralph moved the same amount into the Royal Balanced Fund.

Ralph's wife Rhonda took an independent view. "Things are too mixed up in the stock market right now," she said. "Read the business papers and listen to the commentators on TV. I'm going to sit this one out until things settle down again." She chose to put $10,000 into the Standard Life Ideal Money Market Fund.

"A money market fund?" sneered Ralph. "Why not just hide it in a shoebox under the bed?"

"A mutual fund managed by an insurance company?" Rick laughed. "Are you serious?"

Five years later, in 2001, the three sat on Rick's patio sipping cold drinks. "So, how've you guys been doing with your RRSPs lately?" Rick asked.

"Hey, didn't I say balanced funds are the way to go?" Ralph responded. "The Royal balanced fund averaged 7.6 percent. Last time I looked, the ten grand was worth $13,800. Not great, but not bad either."

Rhonda smiled. "I want you to know that my money market fund run by an insurance company, which you guys sneered at, scored the highest of all money market funds."

"Yeah, a big fat 4.6 percent a year," her husband said. "That's no way to build your RRSP."

"How did you do, Rick?" Rhonda asked, ignoring her husband's teasing.

Rick shook his head. "Mining and investing are two different things," he said.

"No kidding?" said Ralph, laughing.

"You lost?" Rhonda asked. When Rick nodded his head, Rhonda said, "How much?" Rick shook his head, which meant "don't ask."

In fact, Rick's $10,000 investment in the CIBC resource fund was now worth just $7,100, because the average annual return had been –5.8 percent. Rick had chosen a good fund — the CIBC fund had outperformed other Canadian resource funds over the past three years — which meant that it had lost less than the others. But a loss was a loss, and it would take some time for Rick to recoup his investment and show a profit.

The moral: Don't invest on emotion. Ever.

LEARNING THE LINGO

What's a derivative?

Derivatives are the strange nocturnal animals of the investment jungle. Some people know they exist, few have ever seen one, and many consider them dangerous. You may know, for example, that dealing in derivatives brought down Britain's famed Barings Bank, costing its owners and shareholders billions of pounds.

Many companies use derivatives as a form of insurance to protect themselves against financial disaster. This way, the cost of the derivative is considered a premium expense, just like the premium you pay for your car insurance. You may never need the insurance coverage, but you still don't mind paying the premium to have it.

There are more forms and strategies of derivatives than you can shake a stockbroker at, but the most common and easily understandable kind are *options*. An option is just what it sounds like: It provides you with an opportunity to act on something at a later date. If you decline to act, it's no big deal. If you choose to act, it's because something has happened that will benefit you.

An option contract gives the buyer the right to buy (called a *call option*) or sell (called a *put option*) a predetermined quantity of a predetermined stock at a predetermined price for a fixed period of time. Puts and calls are sold by various players, yet buying and selling them does not transfer any assets — just the option or obligation to buy or sell.

It's something of a game, except that the money to be made or lost can be substantial. When you offer to sell a put you are *bullish*, believing that the price of the shares will not lose their value and it's worth the risk of being obligated to buy the shares. If the market price falls and the option is exercised, you are obligated to buy the shares at the higher price. When you buy a call option you are also bullish, because you believe the value of the shares will rise.

Here's the other side of the coin. When you sell a call you are *bearish*, because you believe the price is going to fall and there's a bigger fool in the market than you are. Of course, if the price does *not* fall and the buyer does not buy, you keep both the shares and the premium you earned when you sold the call option. And if the call option is used, you are obligated to sell the shares at the agreed-upon price, even if their value has risen in the meantime.

Or you can simply look at it all this way:

- When you buy a call, you have the right to buy the security.

- When you sell a call, you are obligated to sell the security if the option is exercised.

- When you buy a put, you have the right to sell a security.

- When you sell a put, you are obligated to buy the security if the option is exercised.

It gets more complex, because new variations are added all the time. Best advice you may receive all day: Never buy something you don't understand.

Chapter 17

Managing Your RRSP Portfolio

• •

In This Chapter

▶ Making regular RRSP contributions with the help of dollar-cost averaging

▶ Measuring your RRSP's performance

▶ Moving among fund family members

▶ Avoiding the drift toward equity-based mutual funds

▶ Parting company with a fund in your portfolio

▶ Comparing portfolios: Michael, Melissa, and Maureen

• •

*Y*ou have seized your financial future by its lapels, committing to making regular contributions to your RRSP and maximizing them whenever possible. You have opened a self-directed RRSP, mixed your investments for diversification, and added foreign content. You sleep well at night and spend your time on other things during the day. Do you have a right to feel a little smug?

Darn right. But not too smug. Your RRSP may have cruise control, but it lacks an automatic pilot. It still needs you to turn the steering wheel a little now and then.

Dollar-Cost Averaging

Everybody who ever invested a dollar or two has a system. From racetrack touts to penny-a-point cribbage players, they all believe they can overcome the odds by following some basic rules, and no amount of failure will persuade them that such magic doesn't exist.

I don't have a system for beating the financial market and helping your RRSP grow bigger, faster. But a neat trick called *dollar-cost averaging* comes very close.

Dollar-cost averaging means that you make your investment over a series of year-round equal payments, usually monthly, instead of one lump-sum purchase. If your RRSP contribution limit is $6,000, you contribute $500 each month. This doesn't sound like such a big deal, until you see what happens in volatile times when equity-based mutual funds, for example, are rising and falling to unpredictable degrees with unmeasurable frequency. Under those conditions, dollar-cost averaging is the only technique that makes any sense, as Table 17-1 reveals.

Table 17-1	The Effects of Dollar-Cost Averaging		
	Contribution	*Unit Price*	*Units Bought*
January	$500	$12.50	40
February	$500	$11.90	42
March	$500	$10.40	48
April	$500	$10.00	50
May	$500	$9.80	51
June	$500	$10.65	47
July	$500	$12.50	40
August	$500	$11.30	44.2
September	$500	$12.50	40
October	$500	$11.40	43.8
November	$500	$11.50	43.5
December	$500	$13.00	38.5
Totals	**$6,000**		**492**
Averages		**$11.45**	**$11.36**

Over a year, the unit price of this fund fluctuated from a low of $9.80 to a high of $13.00. Had you been wise enough to purchase all the units in the month of May, when the unit price was lowest, you would be both wealthy and wise. But no one is wise enough to recognize the bottom price of any mutual fund or common share, nor are they wise enough to know when the top price has been reached.

Dollar-cost averaging provides the best solution, because when unit prices are lower you purchase more shares, and when the prices are higher you acquire fewer shares. Over time, this actually lowers the average price you pay for the units — in this case, the average price charged for the units was $11.45 but the average price *paid* for them was just $11.36. That's not a mind-numbing bargain, but it's simple, understandable, and (almost) fail-safe.

Tracking Your Progress: Read (but Don't Agonize Over) Your Statement

Once every three months, or more frequently in some cases, you'll receive a statement from the firm holding your self-directed RRSP. The purpose of the statement is to inform you of changes in the value of your plan, and confirm transactions such as buying, selling, or transferring assets inside your RRSP. It will also record contributions and withdrawals.

I'll go into more detail on self-directed RRSP statements in Chapter 18. For now, make note of the importance of reading your statement as soon as you receive it. It is not junk mail.

One of the key purposes of your statement is to provide raw data on the growth of your RRSP. Here you need to put things in perspective with a dollop or two of good old Canadian moderation. Obviously, it is a mistake to assume that your RRSP will do fine, thank you very much, with no direction from you. It is also a mistake to scrutinize and evaluate the performance of every asset in your plan — comparing the return of every mutual fund you own with others, checking current bond yields against yours, and so on — the moment your statement arrives.

By all means, examine your statement closely. But evaluate your RRSP's performance against your own reasonable expectations. A reasonable expectation, from a well-diversified portfolio of quality investments, is an average annual growth rate of 8 to10 percent. Can you do better than that? Probably. Can you do worse? Easily. But an 8- to 10-percent growth rate means the value of your RRSP will double about every seven years . . . and then redouble after that . . . and so on.

Remember when calculating the growth rate of your RRSP to subtract contributions made by you in the past year. You are measuring the performance of its assets, not the consistency of your contributions.

With reasonable growth in your plan, you can relax a little and decide where, if anywhere, it is possible to tweak an extra percentage or two. The longer until you plan to retire, the more valuable this tweaking can be.

Earlier, I mentioned how some people can scoff at an improvement of 1 percent in annual growth of an investment. Over a year or even five years, it doesn't amount to much. But if you are 30 years from retirement the difference is enormous, as Table 17-2 reveals.

Table 17-2	How a 1-Percent Boost Makes a Major Difference in a $5,000 Annual Contribution	
RRSP Growth Rates	*at 8 Percent*	*at 9 Percent*
After 5 years	$29,333	$29,924
After 10 years	$72,433	$75,965
After 30 years	$566,416	$681,538

Here's what to watch for when measuring the progress of your RRSP:

- **Downward trends.** A sustained downward trend, unless it follows the entire market, indicates a lack of management expertise. Table 17-3 traces the average compound return of four Canadian equity funds, along with the TSE 300 index, over the same periods.

  This was not a good 12-month period for the TSE. Led by Nortel, Internet-based and tech stocks behaved like kids on a diving board in July, which explains the almost 20-percent drop in value.

  Compare that dismal performance with Mackenzie's Ivy Canadian Fund. With more than $5 billion (notice that's a *b*) in assets, the Ivy fund is Canada's largest by far. Mackenzie's fund managers actually made money in the same year that the TSE dropped significantly. Those relatively paltry losses in the one-month and three-month period should be no cause for concern. (For the record, the Ivy fund's average annual return for the five years ending March 31, 2001 was just under 12 percent.)

  The smaller Optima Canadian Equity Value Pool ($695 million in assets) scored even better, delivering more than 32 percent to its investors in a year when the TSE lost 18 percent. Is this a one-shot wonder, a volatile "roll the dice" kind of investment that makes you wealthy one year and a squeegee kid the next? Not really. Over five years, the Optima fund averaged almost 17-percent annual returns, keeping it in the top quartile of all funds in its class since it opened in April 1993.

  The Phillips, Hager & North Canadian Growth Fund is more typical of Canadian equity fund performance in 2000–2001. This is a good fund, but it slipped badly in early 2001. It bears watching — have the PH&N wizards lost their wand?

  Finally, the Trans-Canada Value Fund is like one of those kids your mother warned you against playing with. Its one-year performance, if that's the appropriate word, made it number 293 out of 299 similar funds; its seven-year record (average annual return, April 1, 1994 to March 31, 2001: –1.17 percent) earned it 81st place out of 82 funds in its class. And here's the kicker: its MER is a ridiculously high 5.31 percent! Fortunately, less than $2 million is invested in this turkey. But who *is* leaving their money in the fund? Do they get out much? Are they allowed to vote and drive cars?

✔ **Excess volatility.** The risk of excessive volatility is in inverse proportion to your age: The older you are, the less you like it. But even in your 30s and 40s, wild swings in the returns of your mutual funds should be a warning, especially if they occur in places where you least expect them, such as Canadian equities. Wild swings in returns might be expected among funds investing in emerging markets, small-cap companies, and specialty funds. In a mainstream equity fund, they are intolerable.

✔ **Your changing needs.** This has more to do with your age and expectations than with the fund's performance. Suppose you inherit a fair amount of money at age 53, or your employer dangles an early-retirement offer in front of your face. If either one convinces you that you're ready for a second career, you no longer need an emphasis on growth in your RRSP; you need a regular source of income to replace your salary. That's when to consider changing your equity mutual funds.

Table 17-3	Canadian Equity Fund Returns, Plus TSE 300			
April 1, 2000 to March 31, 2001				
	1 Month	**3 Months**	**6 Months**	**1 Year**
Mackenzie Ivy Canadian	–1.3 %	–3.6 %	–0.8 %	14.9 %
Optima Cdn. Equity Value	0.1 %	0.7 %	12.7 %	32.1 %
PH&N Cdn. Growth	–3.2 %	–10.7 %	–13.7 %	–4.9 %
Trans-Canada Value	–5.0 %	–12.5 %	–27.6 %	–40.8 %
TSE 300 index	–5.6 %	–14.5 %	–26.2 %	–18.6 %

What Are Your Relatives Like? Trying Out Other Funds from the Same Family

Most mutual fund companies attempt to cover all the bases, from tightly conservative money market funds to wildly volatile funds investing in exotic industries and even more exotic countries. The goal is to provide "one-stop shopping," suggesting that if you don't find what you want in our equities department, you'll probably locate it in our bond or emerging markets departments.

This idea is given extra appeal through back-end loads and transfer fees. Should you choose, for example, to invest in the AGF Canadian Stock Fund, you would be faced with a declining back-end load if you decided the fund's performance wasn't meeting your expectations. Redeeming your units after two years could cost you 4 percent of their value. But shifting your units from the Canadian Stock Fund to AGF's Canadian Bond Fund or Canadian Money Market Account eliminates the back-end penalty, because you're keeping it all in the family.

The drawback is that almost all fund families perform well in one investment area, and not so well in others. Templeton, for example, has scored a long-running hit with its Templeton Growth Fund, Ltd., an international equity fund. But its Templeton Canadian Bond Fund hasn't crawled out of the basement since its inception in January 1990. Any waiving of fees shouldn't be enough to encourage you to switch to another fund within the same family if its long-term returns are flatter than southern Manitoba. First, look around within the family to be sure. Then, if the family lacks a well-performing fund with the investing philosophy you're looking for, such as a switch from growth to income, look elsewhere.

Some fund companies may try to charge a *switching fee* for moving from one fund to another inside the family. This fee can usually be waived; check the fund prospectus to be sure. Others place a limit — usually four — on the number of times you can switch funds in one year. This is not unfair. If you're moving your money around that often, you're not an investor. You're a gambler.

Beware the Dreaded Drift

One reason for paying attention to your RRSP portfolio is the potential danger of drifting too far in the direction of equities. This can happen when your selection of equity-based mutual funds actually becomes too successful for your own good, especially as you grow older. Here's how.

Remember the formula for balancing equities and securities in your RRSP portfolio? The percentage of securities should roughly equal your age, with 5 to 10 percent of your entire portfolio in cash, T-bills, or other liquid assets. Trouble begins when bonds plod along at a relatively fixed rate of growth and equities suddenly spurt ahead in value, throwing your equities-versus-securities balance out of whack.

Consider self-employed Olivia, aged 40 back in mid-1994, with $100,000 in her RRSP. Her portfolio mix is ideal for her age and aims (see Table 17-4).

Following the formula, she has $7,000 in a money market fund, $32,000 in strip bonds paying 7.5 percent annually, and the balance in equity funds.

Table 17-4	Olivia's Drifting Portfolio, 1996–2001	
	April 1996	*April 2001*
CIBC Money Market	$7,000 (7%)	$8,435 (4.0%)
Strip bonds	$32,000 (32%)	$44,000 (21.2%)
AIC Advantage Fund	$24,000 (24%)	$44,280 (19.7%)
Bank of Montreal Equity Fund	$17,000 (17%)	$28,730 (13.6%)
Manulife VistaFund 1 American Stock Fund	$20,000 (20%)	$42,600 (23.1%)
Additional Contributions:		
Manulife VistaFund 1 American Stock Fund		$9,670 (4.6%)
AIC Advantage Fund		$28,770 (13.8%)
Totals:	**$100,000**	**$206,485**
	100%	**100%**

Olivia is obviously an astute investor. The AIC Advantage Fund earned an average of 16.9 percent each year from 1996 to 2001, while the Bank of Montreal Equity Fund, focusing on large-cap Canadian companies, managed an average 13.8-percent return over the same period. But it was her investment in the Manulife VistaFund 1 American Stock Fund that really paid off, with a through-the-roof 22.6-percent average annual return, boosting her $20,000 investment to $42,600 by April 2001. She was so impressed by the AIC and VistaFund performance that she divided her annual $5,000 RRSP contribution between them, purchasing $1,000 of the VistaFund fund and $4,000 of the AIC fund each year.

Olivia's foreign exposure, via the VistaFund 1 American Stock Fund, is approaching Canada Customs and Revenue Agency's 30-percent limit according to *market value*. But as long as the *book value* — the price Olivia originally paid for the units — remains under 30 percent, there is no problem.

The problem with Olivia's portfolio is one of balance. Now age 45, she should have a percentage roughly equal to this in bonds, cash, and other securities. Instead, she has just half that amount.

"So what?" you may say. "She almost doubled her original investment in five years." True, but the large gains generated by her equity investments, especially those U.S. equities, are subject to potential volatility. They may vanish even faster than they appeared; that's just the nature of the market. In fact, by March 2001 they had already declined by about 15 percent. Olivia, who plans to take semi-retirement in just five years, cannot endure a long-term bear market where stock prices — and the mutual funds holding the shares — drop steadily over an extended period.

Her RRSP has drifted out of balance, and she would be wise to take some of her equity-based mutual profits by redeeming a portion of the units she holds in each fund. Then she should invest them in bonds or a quality bond fund to increase her securities holdings to closer to 45 percent of her total RRSP value.

Throwing in the Towel

Loyalty to family and friends cannot be faulted, but excessive loyalty to a mutual fund is foolish and expensive. The trouble is, if investing in a mutual fund is ideally a long-term commitment, how and when do you decide to part company? No relationship is perfect, and no one should expect the mutual funds in his or her RRSP portfolio to deliver higher-than-average returns year after year. But riding a losing horse year after year is foolish as well. So how do you determine when your need for more performance from a fund overrides your loyalty?

Assuming that you selected mutual funds meeting your original objectives, and your objectives haven't changed drastically, stay with the fund unless two of the following occur:

✔ **The fund's performance slips more than 25 percent beneath a benchmark over a two-year period.** For a benchmark, you can use the TSE 300 index for Canadian equities, the Standard & Poor's 500 Composite Index for U.S. equities, or one of the Morgan Stanley indexes for foreign equities. Or consult mutual fund reports published monthly by the *Globe & Mail Report on Business*, the annual mutual fund review by *Maclean's* magazine or, best of all, your financial adviser or mutual fund representative. Table 17-5 tracks two-year annual returns for a number of well-respected Canadian equity funds, along with the median for the same category.

The *median* represents the location where an equal number of funds delivered higher and lower returns. An *average* would be the total return divided by the number of funds making up the total. An average return can be distorted by a small number of funds delivering excessively higher or lower returns, so the median figure more accurately reflects reality.

All of the funds in Table 17-5 managed to beat the TSE's dismal performance, which is what you should expect from an actively managed fund. The Elliott & Page fund stumbled badly, but the two-year performance remains impressive.

The Trimark fund suffered in the late 1990s when the fund manager — good ol' What's-His-Name-and-What's-He-Doing-Now? — invested heavily in resources and went light on the banks. Meanwhile, the market went the other way in both cases. Since then, it has made a turnaround. Loyal Trimark fans who stuck with the fund have become insufferable as a result.

The standout performer on the list is the CI Harbour Fund. It doesn't have the best performance in each of the three time periods, but it's wonderfully consistent. Ah, consistency. It's a virtue, young'uns.

Remember to plot your fund's progress against either an appropriate index — in this case, the TSE 300 — or a median return for all similar funds. Remember, too, that past performance, whether up or down, does not necessarily indicate future returns.

✔ **The fund boosts its MER**. Would you award a raise to a losing pitcher, a stumbling quarterback, or a chef who forgets how to boil water? Probably not. But under-performing mutual funds have raised their MER in the past, even when the fund's returns were sinking. When somebody charges you more money to make less money, it's time to flag a cab and head across town.

✔ **The fund manager loses his/her way.** Last year you chose a fund that invested in blue-chip financial firms. This year the fund is heavily into small-cap growth companies exploiting the Internet. Next year? Next year this fund should be nothing but a memory. Don't let anybody else dictate the investing style that suits you best.

Table 17-5	Slipping Returns for Canadian Equity Funds (For the Period Ending March 31, 2001)		
Fund	*6 Months*	*1 Year*	*2 Years*
Bissett Cdn. Equity Class F Fund	−6.54%	7.53%	12.75%
CI Harbour Fund	2.84%	18.61%	15.47%
Clarington Cdn. Equity Fund	−3.15%	8.39%	21.11%
Elliott & Page Cabot Cdn. Equity Fund	−22.21%	−13.37%	18.42%
Trimark Select Growth Fund	6.49%	13.49%	12.69%
Median in Group	**−6.20%**	**−4.6%**	**4.5%**
TSE 300 index	**−26.2%**	**−18.6%**	**8.8%**

Source: G&M ROB Mutual Fund report, April 19, 2001

Funds should tell you about a rise in the MER and a shift in investment philosophy, but they likely won't announce it in flashing neon lights. This is another good reason to scan all the material the fund companies send you.

The more comfortable you feel about managing your RRSP, the more you'll become aware of various investment subtleties and alternatives to boost your plan's growth. You may or may not choose to explore them, and you shouldn't feel neglectful if your RRSP remains solidly entrenched in the "classic mix" of bonds, Canadian equity funds, and foreign exposure.

Banks and investment firms continue to create new ways to add diversification to your RRSP, and many of them are designed to circumvent Canada Customs and Revenue Agency's 30-percent restriction on foreign investments. The most common solution is a *derivative-based index fund*, which keeps 70 percent of its assets in Canadian T-bills and bonds and the other 30 percent in various derivatives such as options and futures contracts. The 30 percent, representing foreign exposure via derivatives, mirrors a successful fund investing 100 percent in that market, so these funds are often referred to as *clone funds*. This recipe works surprisingly well; the solidly secure bonds and T-bills provide stability, and the derivatives give the fund much more exposure to foreign markets — usually U.S. — than their 30-percent limit may indicate.

Here are three such funds that have attracted interest from the investment community and large loads of loonies from RRSP owners:

- **CIBC U.S. Index RSP Fund** is a classic clone fund, investing up to 30 percent of its assets in a combination of S&P 500 index futures, the rest in Canadian bonds and cash. The MER is a reasonable 0.90 percent, but the fund's performance won't set your hormones humming. Over the three years ending March 31, 2001, the fund delivered a blah 5.32-percent average annual return.

- **CI Global Boomernomics RSP Fund** is an interesting way to add diversification to your RRSP. The fund exploits three different but related factors: the impact of Baby Boomers and other population groups on the world's economy; the technological revolution fuelled by satellite communications, the Internet, and similar advances; and global capitalization, wherein 85 percent of the world's economies now operate in something close to free-market conditions. If you can get past the gimmicky name and the fairly high (2.45) MER, they may have something here. But not yet: Its two-year average annual return was 7.1 percent in April 2001.

- **Mackenzie/Ivy RSP Foreign Equity Fund** is a futures-based clone of the well-performing Ivy Foreign Equity Fund. By using the foreign derivatives/ Canadian securities combination, the new fund seeks to deliver good returns while being 100-percent eligible for RRSPs. It just might succeed; launched in May 1999, the fund earned 16.32 percent during 2000.

The foreign content increase to 30 percent of your RRSP's book value reduces the need to scrounge around looking for tricks to boost your foreign exposure. Personally, I feel 50 percent should be the maximum foreign content; above that, you could suffer from currency fluctuations that devalue your investment. The 50-percent level is easily reached by investing directly in global/international mutual funds plus Canadian equity funds that, in turn, maximize their own foreign exposure.

Besides, performance of the clone funds has been slightly less than world-class, as shown in Table 17-6.

Table 17-6	Performance of RRSP-Eligible Foreign Funds		
Two-Year Average Annual Return to March 31, 2001			
Fund	*Return*	*Benchmark*	*Return*
Global Strategy Europe Plus RSP	–11.2%	MSCI Europe	–2.1%
Mackenzie Universal RSP Select Managers*	3.2%	MSCI World	–2.0%
TD AmeriGrowth RSP	–4.1%	S&P 500	–2.9%
Transamerica Growsafe Japan 225	–12.9%	MSCI Japan	–0.7%

* Eligible as foreign content only
MSCI = Morgan Stanley Capital International

The Global Strategy fund favours blue-chip European-based companies such as Royal Dutch Shell and Boots drug stores (U.K.). Good companies, not-so-good performance: the five-year average return is an unimpressive 7.6 percent.

Mackenzie's Universal RSP Select Managers Fund became a legend soon after it was launched in May 1999. Within less than a year, Canadians shovelled more than $4 billion into it, setting a record for growth in a new fund. Well, almost new; it's a clone of a Mackenzie fund whose investments are directed by five leading Mackenzie fund managers, like an all-star team. They manage to outperform the index, so maybe it works (the two-year return shown above is actually that of the original fund).

TD's AmeriGrowth Fund and the Transamerica Growsafe Japan 225 Fund couldn't beat the index over the two years. The Transamerica fund has an abysmal record, averaging an 8-percent annual loss for the past four years.

You can't tell your mutual funds without a program

Mutual funds, and the companies that run them, change their names faster than some people change their socks — or maybe it just seems that way.

In the two years between the first and second editions of *RRSPs & RRIFs For Dummies*, Canada Trust mutual funds were rolled into the TD family; National Trust mutual funds were swallowed by Scotiabank's roster of funds; BPI funds became CI funds; Global Strategy funds disappeared into the AGF maw; NN funds are now Transamerica funds; O'Donnell funds were enveloped by Strategicnova (sounds like a military spaceship . . .); 360 Capital funds now answer to Venturelink; Westbury funds are now listed under RBC Life; and there are at least a half-dozen other name changes.

Think that's confusing? Fund names change as well. The Spectrum United Canadian Equity Fund became the plain-vanilla Spectrum Canadian Equity Fund. The Dynamic Canadian Growth Fund is now the Dynamic Power Canadian Growth Fund (how many extra percentage points did that name change make for its investors?).

What's going on here? In some cases, individuals launch their own funds, and, when their investment genius pays off with good returns, sell them to a gigantic company and pocket an insufferable amount of capital gains. That's how Jim O'Connell of O'Connell Funds and Robert Krembil of Trimark managed to earn hundreds of millions of dollars.

In other cases, voracious predators (read: banks) swallow smaller prey (read: trust companies) and the mutual funds they manage. Or sometimes it's a silly marketing decision, like adding an adjective like "Power" to a fund's name. And sometimes it's a strange natural phenomenon, related to sunspots and locust plagues.

When it comes to increasing the foreign content of your RRSP, clone funds look and sound great in the promotional brochures. In real life, and with a more realistic 30-percent foreign content, they're not a very good deal. Stick with dedicated foreign funds that focus on blue-chip companies, like the Templeton Growth Fund, which will be 50 years old in 2004. It may be massive and dowdy, but by the time you're in your 50s, so are many of your friends — and perhaps even you. So maybe it fits.

Sample Portfolios: Michael, Melissa, and Maureen

Working together in the same small office gave Michael, Melissa, and Maureen lots of opportunity to discuss many matters, including the performance of their RRSPs. In fact, after Michael came in one morning to brag about being "on the sure road to becoming a millionaire" with his RRSP investments — they had returned almost 30-percent growth in the previous year — Melissa and Maureen began comparing their portfolios with their colleague's.

All three had assembled a fairly aggressive yet traditional portfolio of invest-ments, with about 35 percent in strip bonds and money market funds, the maximum 30 percent in foreign equities, and the rest in a Canadian equity mutual fund. Each had stayed with his or her Canadian equity fund for more than five years, and when they reviewed the performance they were startled to notice the wide range of different returns among them. In fact, Maureen and Melissa were bent over their most recent RRSP statements during lunch one day, when Michael walked in, clutching his own statement. "Are we millionaires yet?" Michael asked, gloating.

This led to a direct comparison of each Canadian mutual fund, and a review of the returns over five years, along with the TSE 300 index, as shown in Table 17-7.

Table 17-7	Michael's, Maureen's, and Melissa's Canadian Equity Funds (to March 31, 2001)						
1 Month	*3 Months*	*6 Months*	*1 Yr*	*2 Yrs*	*3 Yrs*	*5 Yrs*
Michael (Spectrum Cdn. Equity)						
–3.7%	–7.2%	–11.8%	–2.5%	15.0%	4.8%	11.9%
Maureen (Dynamic Power Cdn. Growth)						
–4.1%	–10.8%	–19.3%	14.5%	19.8%	7.9%	9.5%
Melissa (Mackenzie Ivy Canadian)						
–1.3%	–3.6%	–0.8%	14.9%	8.8%	5.6%	11.9%
TSE 300 index						
–5.6%	–14.5%	–26.2%	–18.6%	8.8%	1.7%	10.6%

"Hey, I made nearly 12 percent from my Mackenzie fund," Melissa said. She looked reasonably pleased with herself. Twelve percent was more than twice the interest she was earning on her GICs.

"So did I," Michael said. "But look at the losses in my Spectrum fund over the past six months. And it's still losing money. When are things going to turn around?"

"Over five years, my Dynamic fund hasn't done as well as the TSE 300 index," Maureen moaned. "What are we paying these people for, anyway?"

"Maybe we should switch funds," Melissa suggested.

"Maybe we should get out of equities," Maureen added.

"Maybe we should just be patient," Michael said.

Before making any decision, the three should examine the different investment approaches of each fund. Both the Dynamic and Mackenzie funds are invested in Canadian resources, including gold, nickel, and petroleum producers. This market segment performed poorly in recent years, dragging down the funds' performance with it, but a recent upturn produced a spurt of growth.

Michael's Spectrum fund uses a very different investment approach: its largest investment is in the dreaded Nortel, which explains why it dropped further and harder than Melissa's Mackenzie fund (see Table 17-8).

Table 17-8	Top Ten Holdings (And Percentage of Total)*		
Spectrum Cdn. Equity Fund		**Mackenzie Ivy Cdn. Fund**	
Nortel	6.4%	George Weston Limited	6.1%
BCE Inc.	3.7%	Royal Bank	5.0%
Royal Bank	3.2%	Berkshire Hathaway	4.9%
TD Bank	2.8%	Great-West Life	4.1%
CIBC	2.6%	Omnicom Group	3.8%
Bank of Montreal	2.5%	PotashCorp	3.7%
Scotiabank	2.5%	Safeway Inc.	3.5%
Bombardier Inc.	2.2%	CIBC	3.2%
Canadian National Railway	1.9%	Pepsico Inc.	3.2%
Alcan Inc.	1.9%	Loblaw Companies Limited	3.2%

As of March 31, 2001

The moral: The more you understand about the investment policies of the mutual funds inside your RRSP, the more you can make sense of their performance. This does not guarantee total success in your decision-making, but it provides a better basis for deciding whether to get rid of under-performing funds.

Part V

As Time Goes By

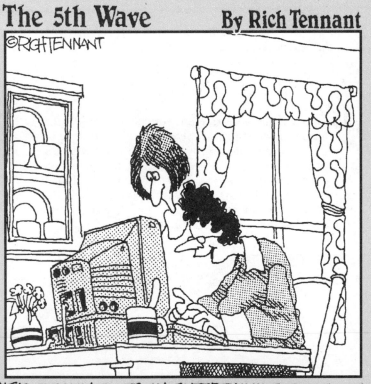

The 5th Wave By Rich Tennant

"IT'S REALLY QUITE AN ENTERTAINING PIECE OF SOFTWARE. THERE'S ROLLER COASTER ACTION, SUSPENSE AND DRAMA, WHERE SKILL AND STRATEGY ARE MATCHED AGAINST WINNING AND LOSING. AND I THOUGHT MANAGING OUR BUDGET WOULD BE DULL."

In this part . . .

You become the investment equivalent of a master gardener, weeding out the undesirables here and there and encouraging growth in your prize-winners. You discover how to spot warning signs, how to ensure that your financial adviser works for you (instead of vice versa), and how to resist the temptation of cashing in too early. Finally, you face the reality of possible bad times and how they can affect your RRSP assets.

Chapter 18

Tracking Your Progress

In This Chapter

▶ Reading your RRSP statement

▶ Spotting potential problems and getting satisfactory explanations

▶ Locking in profits

▶ Trading stocks

*A*s time passes, you'll grow more comfortable with managing your RRSP and understanding the impact of your decisions. This may not make your decisions any easier, because too many influences on the performance of your RRSP are made in faraway places by people who frankly don't give a fig for your investment concerns. That's just the way the world works.

Remember the two words that launched this book: Things change. Now that you've taken steps to fund and manage your RRSP, add two more words: *Don't panic.*

The events of September 11, 2001, were tragic and disastrous. They were also, in the grand scheme of things, transient. Other events (not, it is hoped, nearly so appalling) will occur in your lifetime, both while you're working, and after you've retired. Barring global catastrophe, things will recover. If you have diversified your investments sufficiently and taken steps to preserve capital according to your age, you'll probably ride them out unscathed. But if you panic — by selling equities just as the market bottoms, for example — you'll lose. And that's a promise.

Neither you nor I can directly predict, prevent, or change future events. As they unfold, we can simply try to understand how they affect our investments and make rational decisions in our own interests. If that sounds cynical and self-centred to you . . . well, welcome to the world of high finance.

How to Read Your RRSP Statement

Each RRSP administrator has a slightly different statement format, but they all include certain key areas of information. Please remember that *your RRSP statement is not junk mail.* It is in your selfish interest to review it briefly as soon as you receive it, and scan it in detail on a regular basis. You should also file copies in a safe place. Figure 18-1 shows the first page of an actual RRSP statement from a bank-owned brokerage to one of its RRSP customers (we've changed the brokerage and customer's name, but not the figures).

Figure 18-1:
The opening
page of
an RRSP
statement
includes
account
summary
information.

ANYBANK CANADA, INC.
2001 Walla Walla Blvd., Toronto, ON M5R 3K5

Registered Retirement Savings Plan
Statement of Account

March 2001

Currency: CANADIAN DOLLARS

ANY BANK SELF-DIRECTED RRSP
TRUST COMPANY ACTING AS TRUSTEE

Account number

This statement is for
March 1 to
March 30, 2001

Your last statement was for
February 1 to
February 28, 2001

SUMMARY OF YOUR INVESTMENTS

in Canadian dollars

	Value on Feb 28, 2001 ($)	Value on Mar 30, 2001 ($)	% of total value on Mar 30, 2001
Cash and cash equivalents	542.03	543.11	1.3
Fixed income	37,228.66	37,311.71	87.5
Equities	—	—	—
Mutual funds	5,062.00	4,766.85	11.2
Other	—	—	—
Total investments	**42,832.69**	**42,621.67**	**100.0**

SUMMARY OF YOUR RRSP CONTRIBUTIONS

	First 60 days of the year ($)	Balance of the year ($)	Total year to date ($)
Contributions made by you	0.00	0.00	0.00

SUMMARY OF YOUR FOREIGN CONTENT

Revenue Canada allows you to hold up to 30% of the total book value of your account in foreign investments, with no tax penalty.

	Book value ($)	% of total book value on Mar 30, 2001
Canadian investments	25,656.65	83.6
Foreign investments	5,047.13	16.4
Total book value	**30,703.78**	**100.0**

Page 1 of 2

Here are some points to note about the first page of the RRSP statement shown in Figure 18-1:

✔ It was not an especially good month for this RRSP investor, or for the market generally. The total value of her plan dropped by over $200. But she has a long way to go before retiring, and building her RRSP is not an unbroken straight line.

✔ Almost 90 percent of her RRSP is invested in fixed-income investments — in this case, government strip bonds. They're safe and secure, which helped avoid larger losses during this down-market period for equities. But at 42 years of age, she is much too young to have such a large portion in low-earning investments like these.

✔ No contributions were made to her RRSP during the first two months of 2001. She makes a lump-sum contribution near the end of each year. A series of 12 monthly contributions would be better, providing her with the advantages of dollar-cost averaging.

✔ The plan has just $5,047.13 in foreign content, representing 16.4 percent of the plan's total book value. With her next contribution, the RRSP owner should either sell some of her strip bonds or begin expanding her foreign portion closer to the 30-percent foreign-content limit, perhaps with a conservative global equity fund.

Figure 18-2 breaks down the plan contents in detail. A few things to note:

✔ The government strip bonds are laddered, maturing in 2006, 2008, and 2009, respectively.

✔ The bonds do not indicate their annual percentage yield. You have to figure that one out for yourself. The 2006 Government of Canada bond, for example, was purchased for $7,747.50 (book value); was worth $11,080.50 on March 30, 2001; and can be cashed for $15,000 on December 1, 2006 (face value). In the 5½ years until its maturity date, the bond will earn just under $4,000 — or about 6.4 percent annually, based on its current value.

✔ The Fidelity Focus Health Care Fund slipped almost $300 in value since it was purchased. It's a good long-term sector fund, not a core equity fund.

Remember, this is only a one-month snapshot of constantly changing asset values. In March 2001, Canadian equities generally were losing money, interest rates and inflation remained low, and the market was still reeling from the collapse of stock prices for Nortel and other tech-based companies. Assuming this RRSP owner was 15 to 20 years from retirement, what would you advise her to do?

ANYBANK CANADA, INC.

Registered Retirement Savings Plan
Statement of Account

March 2001

⊞ DETAILS OF YOUR INVESTMENTS — CANADIAN DOLLARS

We have identified foreign investments with the letter F.

Cash and cash equivalents	Book value ($)	Value on Mar 30, 2001 ($)
CASH	543.11	543.11

Fixed income	Face value segregated ■ custody ○ ($)	Book value ($)	Price per $100 on Mar 30, 2001 ($)	Value on Mar 30, 2001 ($)
CPN GOVERNMENT OF CANADA DUE DEC 01 2006	15,000 ■	7,747.50	73.870	11,080.50
CPN NEWFOUNDLAND & LABRADOR HYDRO DUE DEC 15 2008	11,860 ■	4,981.20	63.356	7,514.02
CPN NFLD LAB HYDRO DUE JAN 14 2009	29,707 ■	12,384.84	63.006	18,717.19
Total fixed income		25,113.54		37,311.71

Mutual funds	Number of shares or units segregated ■ custody ○	Book value ($)	Price per share or unit on Mar 30, 2001 ($)	Value on Mar 30, 2001 ($)
FFIDELITY FOCUS HEALTH CARE FUND DSC	261.197 ■	5,047.13	18.250	4,766.85
Total Canadian dollar investments		30,703.78		42,621.67

⊞ DETAILS OF YOUR ACCOUNT ACTIVITY — CANADIAN DOLLARS

Date	Activity	Description	Number of shares or units	Price per share or unit ($)	Added to (deducted from) your account ($)	Cash Balance ($)
Mar 1		Cash balance				542.03
Mar 16	Interest	INTEREST ON CREDIT BALANCE AT 2 3/4% 02/16 THRU 03/06			0.78	
Mar 16	Interest	INTEREST ON CREDIT BALANCE AT 2 1/4% 03/07 THRU 03/15			0.30	
Mar 30		Cash balance				543.11

Page 2 of 2

Figure 18-2: More specific account activity appears on page two of this RRSP statement.

✔ Sell the strip bonds and buy a broadly based Canadian equity mutual fund while stock prices are depressed?

✔ Sell the mutual fund at a loss and buy safer, more secure strip bonds?

✔ Sell some bonds and the mutual fund, and hold cash or T-bills until things settle down?

✔ Just grin and bear it?

Notice how it is always easier to make decisions about other people's money?

WARNING!

Embezzlement: The risk is low, but one never knows

From time to time, newspapers carry stories of some crooked financial consultant caught stealing money from his or her clients' investment portfolios. Can it happen to you and your RRSP? Where substantial amounts of money are involved, anything can happen. Stealing from an RRSP isn't easy, however, because any withdrawn funds are automatically reported to Canada Customs and Revenue Agency. As a result, withholding tax is applied and the RRSP owner usually learns about it by receiving an appropriate statement from the CCRA, or, if the withdrawn funds are not reported on the next income tax return, something much more direct and threatening, like a friendly "Pay up or go to jail, you creep!" letter from the CCRA.

But someone, somewhere, may even now be working out a plan to obtain and hide his or her clients' RRSP funds. So be aware. If you ever spot something on your RRSP statement that does not correspond with your directives, memory, or record, ask for an explanation immediately. If you do not receive a written confirmation that you had, in fact, approved any withdrawals or transfers, or an explanation that satisfies you 100 percent, send a letter (keep a copy for yourself) to the branch manager (you may have to call to get his or her name), who is required to alert the compliance officer. If you are still not satisfied, and the firm handling your RRSP is a member of the Investment Dealers Association (IDA), contact the IDA at Suite 1600, 121 King Street West, Toronto Ontario M5H 3T9, phone (416) 364-6133. Keep going until you are fully satisfied. It's your money, and it's your responsibility. And never, never agree to a withdrawal from your RRSP unless it's your idea and the money comes directly to you.

Heeding Warning Lights and Road Signs

It's a problem that faces every investor, especially a Canadian whose primary or even sole experience with investing is via his or her RRSP.

Everyone warns about the dangers of ignoring the progress of your investments. And everyone also warns about the folly of overreacting to the performance — or lack thereof — of those same investments. Where is the line of logic drawn between too little and too much involvement in managing your RRSP? Here's one way to look at it:

Imagine you are driving from St. John's to Vancouver. It's a long journey with various stops along the way. At the outset, you are content to simply head west. As you travel, you remain aware of highway signs to guide you. Some are of no importance at all, directing you to communities you don't plan to visit, or events unlikely to occur (such as encountering a sign, in the middle of July, reading "Bridge Freezes Before Roadway.") Others raise your alertness level ("Beware of Falling Rock" or "Dangerous Curve"). And still others, such as a flashing red light or a detour sign, demand that you take some unplanned action.

The closer you get to Vancouver, the more concerned you grow about information that seemed unimportant when you set out. You wonder if you have enough fuel in the tank to complete the journey without making another stop. Highway signs that once measured the distance in hundreds of kilometres are now more meaningful when they count down to just a few dozen or less.

Watching over your self-directed RRSP is a little like taking this long journey. At the outset, your statement needs to do little more than confirm you are heading in the right direction. The farther you travel, the more care you will take in the details.

Some data on your RRSP statement, however, are like flashing red lights and detour signs, to be heeded at all costs. If you see any of these, discuss them with your financial adviser and insist on a satisfactory explanation:

✔ Any unauthorized withdrawal or transfer

✔ Losses in the value of your RRSP that are not explained by changes in markets or interest rates

✔ A major imbalance in the foreign content of your RRSP

If your financial adviser or broker can provide no satisfactory explanation for the first two problems listed above, move up the ladder. Call or write to the branch manager, stating your concerns and asking for an explanation. If this gets you nowhere, ask for the name of the firm's *compliance officer*, who plays the role of a school principal, keeping people in line. If the compliance officer is unable or unwilling to explain things to your satisfaction, call a lawyer.

When Should You Lock in Your Profits?

Over time, assuming your RRSP portfolio is not populated exclusively with losers, you will find yourself with a profit in hand. Maybe even a substantial profit, especially from a volatile sector fund. You may be tempted at that point to *lock in* the profits by selling the mutual fund units and gloating over your new wealth, greedy little miser that you have become.

Locking in profits isn't the same as transferring from one fund that has performed well to another fund with even better opportunities. It's a matter of being satisfied with the return of one corner of your RRSP and salting it away, trading growth for security. Nobody, remember, ever went broke by taking profits.

Managing your own RRSP will, I trust, put you in the position of making this kind of decision at various times over the years. Before you take your profits, though, ask yourself some basic questions:

- Are the profits from mutual funds, bonds, or stocks?

- If they are from mutual funds, will you pay a back-load redemption fee to sell your units? How much of one? What makes you think the fund manager can't continue to deliver profits?

- If they are from bonds, will the profit you make from selling the bonds (on the assumption that interest rates have dropped, increasing the bond price to reflect the higher yield) earn just as much elsewhere? Where will you invest the profits? Are T-bills the only alternative?

- If they are from stocks, you probably will have no regrets taking a profit now. Unless, of course, the stock doubles in value a week or two after you sold it, but let's not think about that . . . .

- How will the profits change the growth/security mix of your portfolio? Are you happy with this?

- How close are you to retirement? The closer you get, the more it makes sense to lock in your profits now.

Should You Trade Stocks?

Eventually, the idea occurs to everyone who invests in equity-based mutual funds. With some people, it quickly fades. With others, it grips their ego and imagination with the same kind of latched-on fervour seen at certain bingo halls on Saturday night.

With MERs of 2.50 percent and higher becoming the norm for Canadian equity mutual funds, the temptation to manage your own portfolio begins to make sense. If you invest in a portfolio of stocks generating a 12.5-percent annual return, and a mutual fund achieves this before applying the MER, you pocket the entire 12.5 percent from the stocks while the mutual fund returns only 10 percent (12.5 percent – 2.5 percent MER).

Does it work? Surprisingly, it can. A study at York University revealed that a $60,000 portfolio of 40 stocks can deliver returns equal to a no-load, no-MER fund over five years, but only if the trades are made through a discount brokerage or via the Internet. If front-load mutual funds are compared with investing in your own stocks, the break-even amount drops.

Discount brokerages charge a small flat fee (typically $20 to $30 per transaction) for most stock trades, while full-service brokerages apply a hefty commission to all stocks bought and sold on your behalf. You must know what you are doing with a discount brokerage, however; they do not provide any observations or advice that could influence your decision. It's interesting to note that, while commissions and fees charged to trade stocks have fallen steeply and steadily in recent years, the median MER of Canadian mutual funds remains frozen at a relatively high level.

A U.S. study similar to the York research project suggested that sufficient diversification to minimize volatility would be obtained from 20 to 40 quality stocks, and trading one-quarter of all stocks in the portfolio would generate acceptable profits and new investment opportunities. Of course, index funds can provide similar opportunities at very low MERs. But if you are truly in control of your RRSP, shouldn't you be making these basic investment decisions instead of wimping out and leaving it all to some Jaguar-driving fund manager who collects a fee whether he makes money for you or not?

Before you answer, consider these facts as well:

- You need a substantial amount of money to make it worthwhile. A $60,000 portfolio of 40 stocks is minimal. If you want to outperform a professionally managed index fund, the U.S. study estimates you need a portfolio of more than $240,000 to break even using Internet trading.

- Discount and Internet trading does not provide you with professional guidance. The firms who do this kind of stock trading may send along financial reports on companies that may interest you, but most of the statistical digging and analysis are up to you.

- It doesn't really make sense to keep some stocks inside an RRSP, because you lose certain tax advantages. For example, as a shareholder in a Canadian corporation, you are paid dividends to share in the company's profits. Canada Customs and Revenue Agency likes that idea so much that they provide a dividend tax credit roughly equal to a deduction of about 14 percent off the tax you would normally pay for the dividend income. This can grow even fatter with lower provincial taxes, based on the federal calculations. And if you sell your shares at a profit, earning a capital gain, you pay only 50 percent of the taxes due; capital gains taxes are lower than those applied to earned income. Hold stocks inside your RRSP, however, and you lose these tax breaks. Money withdrawn from your plan is fully taxed as income, no matter what the source.

- Lawyers who defend themselves have fools for clients, and doctors who heal themselves have dunces for patients. Do you really want to be your own investment counsellor? Could you make cool, emotionless decisions to buy and sell? Are you sufficiently confident to assemble a portfolio of stocks to provide both growth and diversification? Will you have the time and inclination to trade 25 percent of your stocks annually? Can you decipher annual reports, balance sheets, and profit and loss statements to really understand the true value of a company's shares and its prospects for the future?

If you can honestly say "Yes!" to the above, perhaps you should hold some stocks in your RRSP. Otherwise, give in to your gambling instincts and attend bingo games. Things are safer that way.

A safer alternative is index funds, with MERs around 0.5 percent. Although they remove the "fun" from choosing your own stocks, they provide greater versatility, and are easy to track, if based on the TSE 300 or S&P 500 indexes.

It's not a stock or a mutual fund, it's an ETF!

The hottest RRSP-eligible investments these days are *exchange-traded funds*, or ETFs, crossbreeds of mutual funds and stock shares. Like mutual funds, they invest in stocks or bonds within a specific area. The i500R ETF, managed by Barclays Global Investors, mimics the Standard & Poor 500, an index that tracks 500 of the world's top companies. Sounds like those index funds we met back in Chapter 14, right? Except that shares in it and other ETFs are sold and traded on the stock market just like shares in IBM or Petro-Canada. You can, if you choose, buy your ETF shares in the morning and sell them the same day — at a profit, you expect.

That fast turnover is one appeal of exchange-traded funds. Another is their bargain price. The MER of the Barclays i500R ETF, for example, is a piddling 0.30 percent, very low even for an index fund. It costs less to acquire them too: If you use a discount broker, you can pick up 1,000 shares for $35 or less, total cost.

ETFs are breeding like rabbits in heat, and you can expect to hear more about them in the coming season. Do they live up to their billing? Yes —

any fund based on diversified quality investments, with an MER below 0.5 percent, bears serious consideration. Most are 100-percent RRSP eligible, including the Barclays i500R, providing you with exposure to the S&P 500 without eating into your foreign-investment limit.

But nobody's perfect. Unlike mutual funds, exchange-traded funds have no way of reinvesting dividends and capital gains in an ETF. Instead, you'll receive small amounts of cash each quarter, representing any earned dividends less an administration fee. Okay, getting some cash every quarter, even a few bucks, isn't a bad deal. It's just that things don't run as smoothly as with mutual funds.

Here's another concern: It's not practical to buy ETF shares in small monthly increments, the way you can purchase mutual fund units, because you'll pay a flat brokerage fee each month. (You'll also, of course, pay a brokerage fee when you sell.) Finally, you'll never beat the index in growth and returns — a potential drawback faced by every index-based investment.

In Case You Try This at Home

In spite of the concerns expressed in the preceding section, I suspect that you may at least consider including stocks in your RRSP anyway. The experience you gain from investing in mutual funds is certain to raise your interest in the TSE and other stock markets. When you read about investors making 30- and 40-percent profits on individual stocks, the 10- to 15-percent annual earnings from your equity-based mutual funds may seem very paltry indeed.

Well, as Oscar Wilde said, "The only way to get rid of a temptation is to yield to it." If, encouraged by your success at investing in your RRSP, you are overwhelmingly tempted to add individual stocks to your portfolio, at least stick to a few tried-and-true guidelines. The following observations have been cadged from various investment experts doing their usual thing for the usual range of business and investment publications. None are leading-edge strategies, but they may prevent you from committing a few investment-novice blunders.

Full-service or discount brokerage?

In case you didn't know, you can't phone the TSE and order a family-size box of common shares to go, hold the anchovies. To buy and sell stocks, you need a broker to fill the order for you.

Brokers operate in two styles: *full-service* and *discount* (or, if you prefer, self-serve).

Full-service brokers, such as Merrill Lynch Canada — formerly Midland Walwyn — and the bank brokerages (RBC Dominion Securities, TD Evergreen, ScotiaMcLeod, CIBC Wood Gundy, Bank of Montreal Nesbitt Burns, and National Bank First Financial), are like the gas stations that clean your windshield and check your oil while filling your tank. As a client, you will be assigned to a financial adviser/investment counsellor/account executive who is qualified not only to provide information on individual stocks and complete the buy/sell transactions, but also to offer advice and caution. You pay for this service through commissions charged as a percentage of your order to buy or sell shares.

Full-service brokerage commissions can be hefty, pulled as cash directly out of your RRSP nest egg. What's more, it's unlikely that any full-service brokerage will discuss its commission structure up front and unsolicited. Instead, the commission structure is treated like a heavily guarded state secret, and you are treated like you've suddenly broken some social taboo for even asking, which is ironic considering that the brokers exist (they tell you) only to help make you rich. Rummage through every secluded corner of a full-service brokerage Web site or wade through volumes of glitzy brochures, and you'll uncover more data about the brokerage's history, services, and corporate opinion of humanity than you'll ever need — but nary a whisper about their commissions policy.

The impact of full-service brokerage commissions is significant, yet you may not discover their effect until you receive a statement on your stock trade from the brokerage. Table 18-1 illustrates an actual purchase of Scotiabank stock purchased by ScotiaMcLeod within an RRSP:

Table 18-1	Full-Service Brokerage Commission
Number of shares:	900
Price per share:	$35.90
Gross amount:	$32,310.00
Commission charged:	$551.76
Total amount deducted from RRSP balance:	$32,861.76
Commission percentage (of purchase):	1.71%

As a percentage of the original trade, that's not an enormous amount. But remember that a similar commission will be charged when you sell the shares. If the share price doesn't move, the total commissions will add up to about 3.5 percent of the original investment. Or, to put it another way, the original price of the shares must climb by 3.5 percent just to break even.

The bare-bones service of a discount brokerage is a good place to save money, but only if you have the knowledge and confidence to make your own investment decisions. You can acquire this knowledge from various sources, including financial publications, company annual reports, columnists and commentators, and the Internet. Discount brokerage sales staff, by the way, are generally paid by salary, removing the conflict-of-interest risk associated with commissioned brokers ("If I close this sale, I'll make my BMW lease payment this month!"). Building confidence in your decision-making prowess is something you'll achieve (you hope) over time, with a series of successes.

While ScotiaMcLeod avoids getting its hands dirty by discussing commission rates on its Web site, its self-service cousin, Scotia Discount Brokerage Inc., can't wait to tell you how cheaply it can perform the same function, as shown in Table 18-2:

Table 18-2	Scotia Discount Brokerage Inc. Commission Schedule (Canadian Equities, June 2001)
Stock Price	*Commissions*
$0–$5.00	$35 + 4 cents per share
$5⅛–$10.00	$35 + 5 cents per share
$10⅛–$20.00	$35 + 6 cents per share
$20⅛–$30.00	$35 + 7 cents per share
$30⅛ and up	$35 + 8 cents per share

The same Scotiabank shares purchased through ScotiaMcLeod for a $551.76 commission would cost just $98.00 ($35 + 900 × $.07) to acquire through its discount arm. Was it worth $450.00 to have a full-service broker handle the transaction? Take your choice from two possible answers: No, if the original investment idea was your own; or Maybe, if purchasing the shares was the idea of the ScotiaMcLeod investment counsellor. But remember that the advice is not guaranteed. A professional adviser's suggestion may be better-qualified than your own, but if the stock nosedives in price you pay three ways no matter whose idea it was: You pay commission to buy it, you pay commission to sell it, and you absorb the loss as well. (Are you sure you want to do this?)

If you are confident enough in yourself to add individual stocks to your RRSP portfolio, give serious consideration to a discount brokerage. The Scotia Discount Brokerage, by the way, charges no annual administration fee for an RRSP of less than $15,000; over $15,000 the fee is a reasonable $75. Other discount brokerages include TD Waterhouse (formerly TD Greenline), Bank of Montreal InvestorLine, Royal Bank Action Direct, and CIBC Investor's Edge.

Covering your assets

Your RRSP is an investment, not a gamble. So if you still want to add individual stocks to your portfolio, reduce the speculative aspect as much as possible by following these basic guidelines:

✔ **Assume times will always be troubled.** There will always be worries about inflation, upheavals in the stock markets, and various despots around the world doing really dumb things to make you and every other investor nervous. This will not change, so consider investing in companies that tend to be immune to these upsets. The best Canadian stocks to ride out the constant shake, rattle, and roll are the chartered banks, utilities, and companies that service them (such as TransCanada PipeLines), solid retailers, such as Canadian Tire and The Bay, and integrated oil producers (they refine and sell the stuff they pump out of the ground), like Petro-Canada and Imperial Oil. These, by the way, are examples, not firm recommendations.

✔ **Plan to buy and hold.** Forget about trading back and forth between stocks, parlaying the profits from one trade to make more money on another. Assume that the stocks you're adding to your portfolio are there to stay, growing year by year through both an increase in their share price and dividends they pay you (you hope) as a valued shareholder.

✔ **Do basic homework.** Don't throw darts at the stock listings in your newspapers, don't follow hot tips on something your sister-in-law heard at the supermarket, and don't base any decision on emotions. Get the facts first. Start by looking at the company's earnings per share and its price to earnings ratio. This is the total amount the company made (or expects to make) this year, divided by the number of shares available. Then compare the figure with the current share price. Example: A company earning $100 million, with 10 million shares outstanding, rates $10 earnings-per-share. If the firm's shares are selling at $100 each, it has a ten-to-one price/earnings ratio, which is very good these days. Add it to your short list, but consider other facts as well.

✔ **Avoid "fashionable" or "hot" companies and industries.** In 2000, everyone jumped on the technology bandwagon, throwing their money at any company doing business on, near, under, or in the general vicinity of the Internet. Companies that had yet to make a profit, run by people who weren't sure how to define the word, were selling for a hundred times their original value. None of it made sense, but the bandwagon kept rolling, and many people could hardly wait to climb aboard. And then the wheels fell off. The darling of the hot tech stocks, Nortel, was selling at $124 per share in 2000. One year later, each share cost a piddling $14. Someday, tech stocks will rise again. Someday the Rockies will crumble, Gibraltar will tumble, and I'll learn to play piano like Jerry Lee Lewis. Patience is wonderful for investments, but you're investing for *your* retirement, not your grandchildren's.

✔ **Don't ignore companies that are out of favour.** This is the other side of the "fashionable" coin. If bank shares slip through the floor because everybody's worried about higher interest rates cutting into their profits, that could be the time to buy, since the market often overreacts to this kind of thing. Besides, the banks will always be there, and they will almost always be making money.

✔ **Concentrate on facts (not rumours or speculation) and their likely effects on companies.** Here are a few: The growth of economic liberalization due to fewer government regulations; the explosion in productivity gained from wider use of robotics and computerization; the influence of Baby Boomers moving from the workforce into their retirement years; and the impact of tax cuts in Canada and abroad. The industries most likely to benefit from these developments represent your best long-term investment opportunities.

Although they do not offer direct financial advice, discount brokerages provide a massive amount of information on earnings-per-share, earnings ratios, future prospects, and so on. Make use of this information to educate yourself before making any investment decision.

Chapter 19

Your Financial Adviser and You

In This Chapter

▶ Assigning your RRSP to a brokerage or an independent adviser

▶ Measuring performance

▶ Spotting problems with the way your portfolio is being managed

▶ Knowing when to change advisers

*I*n a self-directed RRSP, the administrator of your plan — the bank, trust company, or brokerage handling your transactions — will assign an adviser or investment counsellor to your account when it is sufficiently large. This varies from firm to firm, but you should certainly have someone handling your plan when its value reaches $100,000.

At that level, you should also consider assigning the plan to a brokerage firm. If your plan is with one of the chartered banks, they may make the suggestion for you, directing you to one of the firms owned and operated by them, such as Royal Bank's RBC Dominion, CIBC's Wood Gundy, TD Bank's TD Evergreen, Bank of Montreal's Nesbitt Burns, and Scotiabank's ScotiaMcLeod.

Here is where it gets sticky, and where you need to be armed . . . and beware.

In Your Best Interest

Brokers will tell you that their wisdom, research, connections, and dedication, plus the skills of their financial advisers (or "registered representatives," or "brokers," or, most accurate of all, "sales representatives"), will work magic in building your RRSP. This is the most outrageous promise you'll hear outside a singles bar.

First, nothing a broker will do for you is guaranteed. Accept it.

Next, brokers earn their money by charging hidden commissions on bonds and mutual funds, and from mutual fund *trailer fees*, which are annual kick-backs to whoever sold you the fund. For every year you hold on to the fund, it pays the brokerage between 0.25 and 1 percent of all the assets you hold in the fund. Where does the money come from? Why, from the MER, of course — the management fee taken from the fund, whether it earns a profit or not. Consider this: If I convince you to invest $100,000 in the Canadian Cat Fanciers' Specialty Fund and it loses 10 percent a year for five years, at least a portion of your dwindling assets are siphoned into my pocket. Neat idea, isn't it?

Finally, the most important factor for a commissioned financial adviser is not choosing the mutual fund or bond that will earn the most money for you, but *the one that will earn the most money for the adviser and the brokerage that employs him or her.*

That's a provocative statement, I know, and one that will set off howls among people in the investment industry. But it is true nevertheless. It doesn't mean, by the way, that commissioned salespeople in a full-service brokerage will knowingly push proven losers in your lap just to get their filthy hands on fat commissions. It means that they will ignore, for example, mutual funds that do not pay them commissions. In Canada, these include some of the best mutual fund performers.

In my 20 years of dealing with full-service brokerages, not one of them ever proposed that I invest in mutual funds from Phillips, Hager & North, Altamira, or Saxon Funds. Whenever I suggested any of these companies, or other highly regarded funds that failed to pay sales commissions, the broker wrinkled his/her nose, mumbled something nasty about one of the fund managers' relatives, and told me I would, of course, have to pay a special handling charge to acquire units in that particular fund.

So, know this going in: Brokers and their staff make their money from your money. When choosing between an investment that guarantees fat returns for them, and another that promises better returns for you, they will operate in their own self-interest.

The best alternative to a brokerage adviser or counsellor is an independent financial adviser, either on a fee or commission basis, to assist you in your decision-making. This will not cut either back-end loads or MERs on mutual funds (front-end loads are always negotiable), but you may be able to obtain better prices on bonds, resulting in higher interest earned, if you use a fee-only adviser. Even better: You can deal with a discount brokerage firm and save thousands of dollars.

Banks, credit unions, and trust companies do not provide personnel to make recommendations about investments. They can, of course, arrange for you to purchase GICs, mutual funds, and so on, but they are not permitted to make specific proposals. That's why they spin off full-service brokerages.

No fee doesn't mean no advice

Buying units of no-fee mutual funds such as Altamira, Phillips, Hager & North, or Saxon Funds doesn't mean you're on your own when it comes to advice. Both Altamira and PH&N provide access to qualified representatives who can advise you on the best funds for your needs. Will they be Altamira or PH&N funds? Probably — but you know that going in, don't you.

One note about no-fee mutual fund companies: they tend to demand larger initial investments. Phillips, Hager & North, for example, isn't interested unless you make a purchase of $25,000 or more. Saxon Funds asks for a $5,000 minimum investment. Most Altamira funds can be purchased with a minimum $1,000 investment (but note that Altamira's MERs tend to be higher than other no-fee funds).

Banks market no-fee mutual funds, but provide no direct investment advice. In place of this, Scotiabank, for example, offers a pre-packaged product called Scotia Partners Portfolios. You choose from one of four investment strategies: Income & Modest Growth, Balanced Income & Growth, Conservative Growth, or Aggressive Growth. The bank assembles a package of mutual funds from sources such as AGF, AIM/ Trimark, Fidelity, and others, according to the strategy you select. It's the mutual-fund equivalent of TV dinners.

Reviewing Your Portfolio

After you have established a relationship with either a brokerage-based investment counsellor or an independent financial adviser, don't totally abdicate responsibility. Plan on an annual review, by telephone if necessary, of your portfolio. Be prepared to question your adviser on his or her previous recommendations. What happened to that high-flying mutual fund he recommended two years ago — why is it under-performing the market? What can he do about boosting returns for your bonds this year? Why is the cash balance so high? Where can we go to top up the foreign exposure?

You should aim for a 10-percent average annual return from your RRSP portfolio, and don't settle for less than 8 percent. Yes, this puts pressure on your adviser. But the idea isn't to either stumble about on your own or pitch darts at the TSE stock listings. It's to benefit from the training, experience, resources, and skills of someone whose entire career is based on building assets.

Are You Still Compatible?

Don't forget that cash and chemistry are two measures of your adviser's performance.

Does your adviser justify the amounts being paid, either in fees or commissions? If you are making all or most of the investment decisions on your own, using your adviser as a (mostly positive) sounding board, one of you is redundant.

Does your adviser take your concerns seriously? Walking the narrow path between being under-involved and becoming a pest is not easy. Avoid calling your adviser at every market upheaval, but be sure to express any

Signs it may be time for a change

The vast majority of financial advisers and investment counsellors are bright, hardworking, and honest people. The vast majority of dogs are friendly, too, but that doesn't mean you won't ever find one attached to your leg by their teeth. Here are a few warning signs that an adviser or counsellor may be more interested in maximizing his or her income than in helping you build a giant-size RRSP nest egg:

✔ Pushing high-commission, unsuitable investments, such as limited partnerships or RRSP-eligible derivatives

✔ Failing to provide a prospectus or to reveal commissions earned from the sale of recommended investments

✔ Recommending active trading — selling one investment to purchase another — to generate commissions for themselves. (In the investment business, this is known as *churning*, and is more commonly found outside RRSP plans than inside them. But you never know. . . .)

✔ Failing to recommend an investment inside your employer's pension plan or group RRSP. These should be the first opportunities you explore, but they won't make money for your financial adviser or counsellor.

Some actions by a brokerage house or its representative are simply unacceptable and may be enough for you to take legal action. These include the following:

✔ **Misrepresentation:** If you were promised that a recommended investment would deliver 10-percent returns per year, guaranteed, and it lost money instead, you were misled.

✔ **Omission:** If you were not told that a substantial amount of your investment would be siphoned off as commissions or fees, this is another form of misleading.

✔ **Unsuitable investments:** If you need access to your funds and are talked into an investment with little or no liquidity, or if you are a cautious or unsophisticated investor and find your money in high-risk derivatives, you may have a case.

✔ **Churning:** If your broker or investment counsellor has been making excessive trades, buying and selling constantly to build up commissions, you are the victim of churning.

✔ **Unauthorized actions:** If sales and purchases for your RRSP investments are made without your knowledge or approval, you are the victim of discretionary trading, which is prohibited under most circumstances.

Should you suspect any of these actions are taking place, call the firm and ask to speak to the branch manager, who is required to report your concerns to the compliance officer. Or complain in writing to a superior at the firm, requesting a response within 15 days. If none arrives, or it is not to your satisfaction, call your lawyer.

legitimate complaint or serious investment question. If your adviser seems to be perpetually too busy to take your call, fails to return messages, or assigns your account to someone who gives you the impression that their last career involved delivering pizzas, consider looking elsewhere.

Changing Advisers

Each day, radio and newspaper advertisements tempt you to call or consult with representatives from independent financial counsellors, investment houses, banks, and trust companies promising you better service and new ways to build the value of your RRSP. The temptation is strong, especially if the pitch is made by some high-profile financial guru whose voice or face you recognize from radio phone-in shows or newspaper columns.

Ditching your financial adviser or investment firm isn't as traumatic as dropping your spouse or significant other, but try to follow a few rules of protocol.

- ✔ Don't be hasty. If the firm or individual administering your RRSP provided good service and assisted in growing your plan for a few years, don't punish them for one error (unless it's a serious one, such as misrepresentation, unsuitable investments, churning, or unauthorized trading) or one less-than-satisfactory investment proposal. Express your concern or dissatisfaction, preferably in writing, and ask that the problem be avoided in the future.

- ✔ Choose a new home for your RRSP with care. Look around and avoid jumping at the next advertisement or junk-mail plea you encounter. Ask friends with RRSPs similar to yours for recommendations. Talk to personnel at the two or three firms that seem appealing to you. Nail down things such as administration fees, frequency of statements, and so on. Remember the cash and chemistry factors.

- ✔ Once you choose the new home for your RRSP, ask them to provide you with an account application and asset transfer form for your RRSP. Use this form only. Never transfer funds directly into the hands of any financial adviser or brokerage representative.

- ✔ Complete and mail the forms back to the new firm. Do not, under any circumstances, withdraw the funds from your RRSP for transfer. No matter how good your intentions may be, Canada Customs and Revenue Agency will assume you're going to spend your RRSP assets on frivolous things like rent, food, and clothing — not to mention Ferraris and Rolexes. Only use official transfer forms.

- ✔ If it makes you feel better, and you have built up a relationship with the firm, or an individual in the firm, with whom you have kept your RRSP over time, write a letter. Explain your reasons for the transfer. This not only enables them to identify problems they may not have been aware of, but also keeps the door open for renewing things in the future. Don't get too personal or fret over it too much. This is still primarily a business relationship, and anyone who provides you with better service or greater wealth deserves your business.

Chapter 20

Resisting Temptation

· ·

In This Chapter
▶ Withdrawing money from your RRSP
▶ Using your RRSP for your child's education
▶ Using your RRSP for your education
▶ Using your RRSP to buy a house
▶ Retiring early

· ·

*I*t may burrow its way into your mind gradually, or it may spring full-blown when you open your RRSP statement someday and realize that you have more assets in your plan than you expected. The temptation may be to withdraw some funds now instead of waiting for retirement, or to borrow a few dollars — it's your money, after all — and arrange to pay it back later. You may even like the idea of using your RRSP assets as a mortgage on your home.

All of these options, and a few others as well, may present themselves. What do you do? The general answer is the same one you were told as a child: Resist temptation. If you've managed to do this without fail, you may not need this chapter. But if your hand slipped into the cookie jar from time to time, you should absorb the advice and guidelines carefully.

Your RRSP Is Not for a Rainy Day

The biggest risk as your RRSP builds is to think of it as an emergency stash, a lump of money you can use when there's not enough cash in the bank or room on your credit card. It's your money, after all, and no one will scold you for getting your hands on it years ahead of time. But if you do, you'll lose three ways.

Your first loss will be in withholding tax deducted even before you get your hands on the cash. This is just the beginning of Canada Customs and Revenue Agency's penalty for being impatient. The entire amount you withdraw will be added to your taxable income for the year, and, while the withholding tax will be credited, you will almost certainly pay even more according to your tax bracket (see Table 20-1).

Table 20-1	Withholding Tax Rates on RRSP Withdrawals	
	Canada (Excluding Quebec)	*Quebec*
Up to $5,000	10%	21%
$5,005 to $15,000	20%	30%
$15,000 and up	30%	35%

If you withdraw $10,000 from your RRSP, you'll actually receive only $8,000, because 20 percent, or $2,000, is sent to the CCRA to be credited on your income-tax return for the year. In Quebec you'll pocket just $7,000, even though your RRSP is now $10,000 poorer.

If you must withdraw funds (and only in dire circumstances, remember) make it in amounts of $5,000 or less, on consecutive days, to reduce the immediate tax impact. If you withdraw $5,000 today and $5,000 tomorrow, you'll receive a net amount of $9,000; withdraw the $10,000 all at once and you'll receive a net of $8,000.

Your second loss is the potential tax-sheltered growth you would have enjoyed inside your RRSP. This can be enormous and, in time, will dwarf the immediate funds you obtain (see Table 20-2).

Table 20-2	Future Cost of Early RRSP Withdrawals (Assuming 10-percent Annual Compound Returns)		
Amount	*In 10 Years*	*In 20 Years*	*In 30 Years*
$1,000	$2,600	$6,730	$17,450
$5,000	$12,970	$33,640	$87,250
$10,000	$25,940	$67,280	$174,550

If you're currently 30 years from retirement, the $5,000 you withdraw for today's needs will reduce your RRSP's value by almost $90,000 when you're ready to use it. That's a hefty price to pay on top of the income tax assessed.

The added risk of spousal RRSP withdrawals

Withdrawing funds from a spousal RRSP is fraught with even more risk. Only the planholder is permitted to take money from a spousal RRSP, and if no contributions have been made to the spousal plan within three years of the last contribution, the withdrawn funds will be taxed as the contributor's income, not the planholder's. Thus, if you contribute to your spouse's RRSP this year and he or she withdraws money from it any time during the next two years, Canada Customs and Revenue Agency taxes the money as though it went directly into your pocket. Exceptions to this rule:

✔ The parties are living apart due to a breakdown in the relationship

✔ The contributing spouse has died

✔ Either spouse is a non-resident

✔ The planholder transfers the money to purchase an annuity, which cannot be accessed for three years

✔ The money is transferred to a RRIF

✔ The money is transferred to a Registered Pension Plan and not withdrawn for three years

Finally, the third loss is contribution room in your RRSP. The $5,000 you withdraw today cannot be made up later. It was based on previous income levels, and no amount of future income or pleading to the CCRA will return it.

Financial emergencies arise, of course. But unless and until every other alternative has been explored, it simply does not make sense to take funds out of your RRSP to meet them.

Combining RRSPs and RESPs

RRSPs have siblings, including *RRIFs,* or *Registered Retirement Income Funds* — more about them in Part VI — and *RESPs,* or *Registered Education Savings Plans.* The objective of RESPs is to provide parents and grandparents with the opportunity to accumulate funds to cover the cost of higher education for their children and grandchildren. While RESP contributions cannot be deducted from taxable income the way RRSP contributions can, the money remains tax sheltered. As though to make up for the lack of tax benefits, the federal government adds an extra 20 percent of annual RESP contributions, to a maximum of $400 annually.

Here's where your RRSP comes in: If you open an RESP for your child and he or she decides not to pursue a higher education, you can transfer up to $40,000 from the RESP into your RRSP or a spousal RRSP. This can be done if

✔ The RESP has been in place for at least ten years

✔ The child has reached age 21

✔ Contribution room exists in the RRSP or spousal RRSP (if no contribution room exists, the RESP funds are returned to the contributor, subject to income tax plus a 20-percent penalty)

This makes an RESP a very attractive prospect. Your contributions build tax-free, helped along by government assistance, and if your pride and joy(s) decides to become a street vendor instead of a doctor or lawyer, you can soothe your disappointment by bumping up the value of your RRSP.

The Lifelong Learning Plan and Your RRSP

If your kids decide not to pursue their education past high school, this does not mean that you can't. In fact, the government's Lifelong Learning Plan enables you to finance an education for either you or your spouse with money from your RRSP without subjecting it to income tax or penalty. The maximum withdrawal permitted from each plan is $20,000 over a four-year period. Other rules include the following:

✔ You must be enrolled, on a full-time basis, in a qualifying educational program before March of the year following the withdrawal.

✔ A "qualifying educational program" is one at a university or college, or certain training programs of at least three months' duration and including at least ten hours of instruction or course work per week.

✔ The amounts withdrawn for this program are repayable to the RRSP in equal installments over a ten-year period.

✔ The first payment is due either during the last year you were enrolled in the program or during the sixth year after you made your first withdrawal under this program, whichever is earliest.

RESP rules

Keep these guidelines in mind as you merrily sock away dollars for your little one(s).

The maximum annual RESP contribution you can make is $4,000. Twenty percent of however much you contribute over a one-year period is matched by the federal government — to a maximum of $400. (This may not sound like much, but over time, it can really build up.)

A few more points to remember.

There is a cap on the RESP's value, at $42,000 per plan. And because the maximum life of the plan is 25 years, your pride and joy had better head off to school by then, or better yet, be back and graduated so they can start paying you back.

✔ Any missed required payments will be included in income for that year, and subject to tax.

✔ Just as with RRSP contributions, you have the first 60 days of a year — that is, until the end of February — to make a repayment and have it credited to the previous year.

The Home Buyers' Plan and Your RRSP

If you have built up funds in your RRSP and have yet to purchase your first home, here's another way to put the money to use before your retirement years. The *Home Buyers' Plan (HBP)* is a loan from your RRSP to you, free of tax and interest payments. To qualify, you or your spouse must not have owned a home and lived in it as your principal residence for five years prior to making the application.

Canada Customs and Revenue Agency counts "five years" this way, when it comes to the HBP: Take the four years preceding the year you withdraw the money, plus the period of the year you make your withdrawal, ending 31 days prior to the date you take the money out of your RRSP. Clear? Good.

The exception to the "five-year rule" applies where disabled family members are concerned. If you already own your own home, you can use the HBP to purchase a home that provides better accessibility for a disabled and dependent relative if he or she qualifies for the Disability Tax Credit.

You normally get one opportunity to use this plan. Here's how it works:

✔ The property you are purchasing must be in Canada and must not have been owned previously by you or your spouse.

✔ It must be occupied as your principal residence within one year of buying it.

✔ The home can be existing or brand-new.

✔ The home can be detached, semi-detached, a townhouse or condominium, a mobile home, an apartment, or a share in a co-op housing corporation where ownership is transferable.

✔ Both you and your spouse may borrow up to $20,000 each from your individual RRSPs.

✔ Funds contributed to your RRSP within 90 days of the loan cannot be withdrawn for this program. Thus, make a contribution to your RRSP on February 28 and it cannot be applied to the Home Buyers' Plan until June 1.

✔ Annual repayments to your RRSP must be made on or before December 31 of each year (but, as with RRSPs, any payment made within the first 60 days of the year can be credited to the previous year).

- Repayments begin in the second calendar year following the calendar year in which the withdrawal is made. (Repayments on loans made in the year 2002 must begin in 2004.)

- Annual repayments will be determined by dividing the amount borrowed by 15. Thus, a deduction of $20,000 from your RRSP under this plan will require annual repayments of $1,333.33.

- Repayments are kept separate from contributions and are not tax-deductible.

- Repayments are made to the financial institution administering your RRSP and must be accompanied by a special RRSP Repayment Form available from your bank, trust company, or whoever is holding your RRSP for you. This is to prevent the money from being credited as a regular, tax-deductible RRSP contribution.

- Repayments larger than the scheduled amount will reduce subsequent payments by a proportional amount.

- Miss an annual repayment and you're in deep doo-doo with the CCRA. The missed repayment will be declared as taxable income for that year. And, as a second slap on the wrist, the money will be deemed a permanent withdrawal, which means you can never put it back in your RRSP. Yikes!

Does this make the HBP worthwhile? It will for many people. From its inception in 1992 to the end of 2000, over half a million Canadians had taken advantage of it. Should you?

Buying your first home is as much an emotional decision as an economic one, and no one can put a price on another person's emotional satisfaction. Unless you can sweet-talk a relative or friend into providing an interest-free loan to help acquire your dream home, the Home Buyers' Plan is your only alternative. Just keep these serious drawbacks in mind before taking this step:

- Once the money is out of your RRSP, it is not building through compound interest. This inevitably reduces the value of your plan over time . . . by a significant amount.

- What happens if you find yourself unable to manage the repayments? You'll suffer that two-pronged penalty of both paying income tax on the missed repayment and not being allowed to return it to your RRSP. It probably means you won't be making any RRSP contributions either. Consider this: If you had difficulty raising money to purchase your home by other means, how will you be able to handle mortgage payments, maintenance, RRSP repayments, *and* RRSP contributions unless your income takes a major leap?

- Do not count on the value of your home increasing over time, making up for lost growth in your RRSP as a result of taking out this loan. Given recent decreases in property values, it's not likely to happen.

All in all, the program has more drawbacks than benefits. But if you still feel the way to your dream home is through your RRSP, applications for the Home Buyers' Plan can be obtained from a Canada Customs and Revenue Agency office.

Bowing Out Early

It may hit you while reviewing an especially rewarding RRSP statement or while sitting in traffic on your way to work, breathing the fumes of the car ahead of you. You may get the idea while on vacation, or upon hearing of the early demise of an old friend or school chum.

Wherever and whenever it occurs, at some point around 50 or beyond, you'll ask yourself: "Why am I still working? Why don't I turn my RRSP assets into something that will produce an income, and leave the rat race?"

It's a question only you can answer, along with assistance from your spouse, family, and financial adviser or investment counsellor. But before you go that far, here are some items to review:

- ✔ Take stock of your entire financial situation. Review your debts (including mortgage) as well as your RRSP assets.

- ✔ Do you have any other retirement income from private pensions? Will it enable you to retire early? Will there be a penalty (in reduced benefits) if you do?

- ✔ Will you be totally retired or do you plan to work part time? If so, how much will you earn? Is this realistic?

- ✔ Review the estimated percentage of current income you'll require. (See Chapter 3.)

- ✔ Consider carefully the benefits of holding off retirement for a year or more. At middle age, about half your RRSP assets should be in equities. If the stock market is currently at a low ebb, this could reduce your expected retirement income. It may turn around and boost your nest egg substantially by this time next year. If the markets are galloping along, the reward for delaying retirement could be substantial. For example, if your equities total $300,000 and the market returns 20 percent over the next year, that's a growth of $60,000 in this sector alone.

- ✔ Some investment counsellors suggest a fake "retirement trial" for a few weeks. You'll still be working, but try to live on only the amount of income you expect to have during retirement. (You can do this on paper, if you like.)

Retirement is no longer a 65-and-out proposition for most people. Careful long-term management of your RRSP provides you with options, and options create freedom.

Chapter 21

Death, Divorce, and Other Disasters

● ●

In This Chapter

▶ Getting a divorce

▶ Drafting a will

▶ Meeting financial emergencies

● ●

*L*ife has a way of bopping along on its own, dealing out sunshine and gloom at unpredictable times to unsuspecting people. Planning for the gloomy events is not much fun, but saying "It'll never happen to me!" is not realistic either. So in the midst of watching your RRSP assets rise, and before you reach for another golf-equipment catalogue or cruise-ship brochure, you might want to review the rules in case one of these distasteful events actually occurs.

Family Law and Your RRSP

Separation and divorce bring their own pain and heartache. If it happens to you and your partner, you don't need the complications of an RRSP division added to your woes. Actually, complex it won't be, under family law in Ontario and most other provinces. That's because all RRSP assets — yours, your spouse's, and any spousal plans you may have added — are simply lumped together and divided as though they were cash that had accumulated in a bank account during the relationship. Assets belonging to one party prior to the beginning of the relationship are usually set aside from the total before being divided, as shown in Table 21-1 in the case of Lou and Linda.

Table 21-1	Lou and Linda's Division of RRSP Assets	
	Lou	*Linda*
RRSP assets before marriage	$20,000	—
Personal RRSP assets accumulated	$60,000	$55,000
Spousal plan	—	$15,000
Total RRSP assets	$80,000	$70,000
Total RRSP assets divided	$60,000	$70,000
Total assets divided	$130,000 ($60,000 + $70,000)	
RRSP assets after divorce	$85,000 ($65,000 + $20,000)	$65,000

After several years of marriage, Lou and Linda called it quits. Lou had built up $20,000 in an RRSP before marrying Linda, and the plan had grown by $60,000 during the marriage. He also contributed to a spousal RRSP, which had $15,000 in assets when he and Linda split up. Linda opened her own RRSP during the marriage; it was worth $55,000 at the time of the separation.

According to the provincial family law applying to Lou and Linda, Lou's original $20,000 RRSP value is set aside before all three plans — Lou's, Linda's, and the spousal plan — are added together with assets evenly divided.

This is an RRSP book, not a primer on family law. While the preceding example usually applies, be sure to consult a lawyer to determine all the implications of separation and divorce on your RRSP.

Your Will and Your RRSP

If you're married and want to leave your RRSP assets to your spouse, be sure that he or she — *not* your estate — is named as the beneficiary of your plan. While it's common to add personal assets to an estate when a will is drafted, that's a serious error where an RRSP is concerned. In the event of your death, Canada Customs and Revenue Agency will consider your estate as a person, believe it or not. This "person," according to CCRA rulings, will be assumed to have cashed in your RRSP assets, making them instantly liable to one giant *whack!* of a tax bill, even if your will directs that your spouse is to inherit all of your estate. By naming your spouse as beneficiary, the CCRA permits him or her to transfer all your RRSP assets into their RRSP, free of tax. Or, as an alternative, your spouse can use the entire amount of the RRSP to purchase an *annuity,* which pays equal amounts of income at fixed periods for a defined length of time (see Chapter 22).

What are your options if your spouse predeceased you, or the relationship ended, or for any other reason you chose not to leave your RRSP to him or her? You could name a financially dependent child or grandchild under age 18 as beneficiary. *Financially dependent* means the child's total annual income is less than the CCRA's basic personal exemption, currently $7,231. Instead of claiming the entire amount of your RRSP in one lump sum, the funds can be used to purchase an annuity for a fixed number of years based on the child's age at the time of inheritance. The age is subtracted from 18, and the number of years remaining represents the maximum length of the annuity.

Under this rule, a ten-year-old child inheriting your RRSP assets could purchase an eight-year annuity. This doesn't avoid tax entirely. Let's face it, nothing does. But it divides the assets into smaller annual "chunks," each of them subject to lower income-tax levels.

For example, the ten-year-old child who receives your RRSP assets of $80,000 could purchase an annuity paying $12,000 per year for the prescribed eight-year period. Instead of being subjected to one massive tax bite on $80,000, the inheritance pays income tax eight times on $12,000, which is reduced by the child's personal exemption to less than half that amount.

If your child or grandchild is financially dependent as a result of a mental or physical disability, the tax folks bend a little. You can name this child as your beneficiary and he or she can use your RRSP assets to either boost their own plan (or open one, if none exists) or purchase an annuity. Either way, no tax is applied until money is withdrawn from the RRSP or paid out from the annuity.

Tax laws have a habit of changing, and they can also conceal little loopholes and *gotchas!* The advice provided above is current for mid-2001, but before making a final decision it's always wise to double-check with the CCRA, a chartered accountant, or a lawyer. Yes, double-check, and check often. These laws can change faster than you can cry "I've been scammed!" (Not to mention the fact that it keeps the aforementioned civil servants, chartered accountants, and lawyers steadily employed.)

A Financial Checklist

Once you have built a reasonable value in your RRSP it becomes a major part of your entire financial picture. Be sure to treat it that way, and be prepared in case a crisis situation occurs. This isn't much fun, and can cast a temporary cloud on a warm and sunny day, but clearly it's better to deal with these things when your emotions aren't either strung like a guitar string or as limp as leftover spaghetti.

✔ Make a list of all your assets, including the equity in your home, your life insurance policies, your RRSP (of course), and any investments outside your retirement plan.

✔ Identify the location of documents related to these assets. Where is the deed kept? Who administers the RRSP? How are the investments managed?

✔ Attach these documents to copies of your will.

✔ If you do not have a will, arrange to obtain one. It needn't be a complex document. If you have a will, review it now. Does it still represent your wishes? Have your assets changed enough to require a change in the will?

✔ Have you named the beneficiary of your RRSP or RRIF?

✔ Will your RRSP generate sufficient retirement funds to deal with inflation, if it rises to annual levels of 5 percent or more? If not, what can you do about it? How should your investments be altered to counter this risk?

✔ Who pays the bills and does the bookkeeping in your household? If one partner performs the lion's share of these chores, does the other partner know where to go for documents and records?

Part VI

Understanding RRIFs

The 5th Wave — By Rich Tennant

"I've been working over 80 hours a week for the past two years preparing for retirement, and it hasn't bothered me OR my wife, whats-her-name."

In this part . . .

You explore the options for cashing in your RRSP assets, including the ins and outs of annuities. The most appealing option for most people is a Registered Retirement Income Fund, or RRIF. RRIFs are introduced as rich cousins to deadbeat RRSPs — an RRSP borrows money from you, and a RRIF pays you back with interest. You discover how to apply knowledge gained from managing an RRSP to managing a RRIF, and set the potential earnings from a RRIF against your total retirement income needs.

Chapter 22

The Time Has Come to Cash In!

· ·

In This Chapter

▶ Facing the end of your employment career

▶ Winding down your RRSP

▶ Deciding whether to continue working

▶ Evaluating your options: Lump sum, annuity, or RRIF

· ·

*A*fter years of paying into your RRSP, you'll make a decision somewhere, sometime, to turn the tables on your plan so that it will begin paying you. These payments will form part of your retirement income.

Your decision to begin drawing benefits from your hard work and diligence will be based on economics and emotions. In all likelihood, the larger your RRSP balance, the smaller the emotional impact. Leaving your work career, after all, is a little like taking your first parachute jump. No matter how carefully you have planned, there is always the risk that something can go wrong.

Congratulations or Condolences?

Hey, you have lots of company . . . especially if you're retiring early. More than one-third of all Canadians are retiring before the age of 60. What's more, the odds are that you're healthier at 60 than your grandparents were at 50, which leaves more active years ahead of you. If you have sufficient RRSP assets to make those years comfortable, enjoyable, creating the same kind of excitement you felt as a kid during school recess, congratulations! But if you haven't quite reached your income goal . . . well, let's see what you can do about it.

The ideal way to launch your retirement is with enough capital in your RRSP to ensure 25 or more years of income that will allow you to maintain the lifestyle you want, including an allowance for inflation. If this can be achieved without depending on government or private sources of income, or using equity in your home, so much the better. Along with financial security, assets of this size also provide the freedom to choose the timing of your retirement. Or, to continue the parachute analogy, you can jump without being pushed.

Unfortunately, many Canadians discover their retirement decisions are being made by someone other than themselves. Corporate downsizing, once considered a rare periodic event, has become almost an ongoing policy, leaving many employees with a handshake, a lump-sum payment, and an anemic retirement plan. Aside from losing the luxury of deciding your own retirement date, this kind of career finale may require the potentially distasteful action of seeking part-time employment, cashing in the equity of your home, modifying your lifestyle, or all three at once.

Most of us can modify our lifestyle to a surprising degree, especially if it brings the unexpected reward of personal fulfillment. Even if the end of your working career comes out of the blue and leads to a sombre meeting with your boss or a human resources manager, your years of planning and regular review of your financial situation will make it easier to deal with the situation.

The End of Your RRSP as You Know It

You can begin drawing income from your RRSP assets at any stage of your life. Some people choose to do this in their 50s, expecting CPP (Canada Pension Plan) benefits to (they hope) kick in as early as age 60, supplemented (they hope again) with OAS (Old Age Security) benefits at age 65. Others enjoy the luxury — or bear the necessity — of continuing to contribute to their RRSP well beyond traditional retirement age.

The life of your RRSP winds up at the end of the calendar year in which you turn 69. This, by the way, is a brick-wall deadline. If you do not make some arrangement to convert your RRSP into an income-producing investment by that date, Canada Customs and Revenue Agency assumes you have deducted the entire amount as one lump sum and taxes you accordingly. If you think the income tax you pay on your annual salary is substantial, wait until you see the size of your tax bill on a lump-sum income that could total several hundred thousand dollars in one year. So ignore this date at your peril.

Until age 69, you can manage to be both semi-retired, drawing income from previous RRSP assets, and contributing to an RRSP — all at the same time. Income from a part-time job qualifies for RRSP contributions, which is one way to counter the risk of inflation.

Table 22-1	Earning and Saving Your RRSP Assets
Source	*Amount*
Old RRSP income	$20,000
CPP	$6,000
Private pension	$18,000
Part-time work	$15,000
Total	**$59,000**

Consider Brenda's situation. Brenda decided to retire at age 60 from her job with a large financial institution. She enjoyed her work but she enjoyed her garden and grandchildren more, and wanted to spend more time with both. Her RRSP assets were able to generate about $20,000 income annually. Added to the pension she was entitled to, and taking early CPP benefits, it provided about $44,000 in annual income (see Table 22-1).

A few months after Brenda retired, a small local advertising agency asked if she would be interested in handling some basic bookkeeping chores. She could perform most of them from a computer in her home by accessing the firm's financial records, requiring only an hour or two of her time each afternoon. The agency offered to pay $1,250 per month, or $15,000 annually. By accepting the job after the end of the calendar year in which she first began drawing CPP benefits, she did not affect her government pension income. (Had she done both in the same calendar year, Ottawa would have taxed back the CPP payments; Ottawa permits you to both earn an income and keep all your CPP benefits beginning the calendar year *after* your first CPP benefit.)

The part-time work, which Brenda found enjoyable and stress-free, not only provided extra income but also enabled her to open a new RRSP, contributing almost $3,000 annually to it and taking a tax benefit as a result. She will be able to do this, if she chooses, until she turns 69, which could provide her with an extra $40,000 or so in new RRSP assets.

Moving from RRSP to RRIF

Whenever you choose to begin cashing in on your RRSP assets, you must convert them to one or a combination of three alternatives: a lump-sum payment, an annuity, or a Registered Retirement Income Fund (RRIF).

For almost everyone, the choice will be either an annuity or a RRIF. Withdrawing your RRSP assets in a lump sum triggers income tax on the entire amount. There may be times when this makes sense to some people, but I can't think of any.

RRIFs

If you have been successful at managing your assets through a self-directed RRSP and still feel comfortable doing it, your best choice to produce retirement income will likely be a *Registered Retirement Income Fund*, or *RRIF*. A RRIF is similar in operation to an annuity and provides a better opportunity to generate more income. For example, you can build inflation protection into your RRIF through diversification and laddered GICs (guaranteed investment certificates).

Do you have private pension benefits or deferred profit-sharing plan assets from your working career? If they're not locked in, you can roll them into your RRSP assets when converting them to a RRIF, which gives you more investment clout with fewer administrative fees and headaches.

Two more pluses for RRIFs: They provide almost total flexibility, which will enable you to take advantage of certain economic conditions; and with careful management they can provide a lump-sum estate for your beneficiaries.

Annuities: Their Time May Have Passed

A generation or so ago, back when many Canadians considered life insurance almost a basic requirement, annuities were very popular. Promoted and managed by insurance companies, annuities could be purchased with the funds built up inside *whole-life insurance plans*. Whole-life insurance, thanks to higher premiums, provided both immediate life insurance coverage and a cash-value pot of gold on your 65th birthday. (The alternative to whole-life insurance, known as *term insurance*, provides only a lump-sum payment to your beneficiary and no cash value when you reach 65.)

Millions of Canadians chose whole-life insurance as a means of saving for the future, and in the process made the insurance companies very wealthy indeed. Part of the sales pitch used by insurance salespeople was that the money claimed by the policyholder at age 65 could be used to purchase an annuity from the same insurance company. An annuity is a contract that guarantees a series of payments in exchange for a lump-sum investment. The size of the payments depends on a number of factors, including the following:

✔ The amount of money used to purchase the investment

✔ The age of the person purchasing the annuity (the annuitant)

✔ The annuitant's gender

✔ The length of time the payments are guaranteed (anywhere from five years to the lifespan of the annuitant)

✔ Whether or not the annuitant chooses to continue the payments to his or her surviving spouse

In other words, you paid the insurance company while you worked, and the insurance company paid you after age 65. Or, to put it cynically: When you are paying insurance premiums, the insurance company is betting you will live; when you are collecting an annuity, the insurance company is betting you will die. Either way, money flows through the hands of the insurance company, providing it with many opportunities to make a profit.

Annuities began to fall out of favour around the same time that Canadians realized they could buy term insurance at a much lower premium price than whole-life insurance. They could invest the difference themselves and beat the insurance companies at their own game. Annuities continue to be popular with folks who prefer not to get their hands dirty and have their minds cluttered with investment decisions. They prefer to choose among various annuity options and settle down to a fixed income for the rest of their life. Market turbulence? Risk versus reward? Income versus growth? To an annuitant, those are all someone else's concern.

With an annuity, all your decisions are made up front; the most critical is choosing whom to purchase the annuity from. Annuity payments fluctuate not only according to the firm providing the annuity, but also according to the date you purchase the annuity. The $100,000 you invest in an annuity this month could purchase more or less of an income for you next month. Whether you choose to wait, hoping the rates will rise, or buy now, fearing the rates will fall, *you are locked in for life*. That's the minus side of annuities.

Annuities are calculated on the basis of the monthly income paid per $50,000 or $100,000 originally invested, and are influenced by various factors and options (see Table 22-2).

Table 22-2	Factors Influencing Annuity Payment Rates	
Factor	*Payments Increased*	*Payments Reduced*
Age	Older	Younger
Gender	Male	Female
Guaranteed term	5 years	10 years (or longer)
Surviving spouse	Excluded	Included

Why such a wide range in annuity payments?

Approach two different insurance companies for their annuity rates, and you'll discover different levels of payments — sometimes a substantial difference (see Tables 22-3 and 22-4). What accounts for such a wide range? Three things:

✔ **Tables of mortality:** Insurance companies employ actuaries who spend their entire careers estimating how long people will live. Each company's actuaries can arrive at different estimates, and the company who decides you will live longest will offer you the smallest annuity.

✔ **Interest rates:** The money you use to purchase your annuity is invested by the insurance company. Wise investments generate bigger returns, which enable the insurance company to pay you a bigger annuity.

✔ **Guarantees:** The cost of annuity options you choose, including guaranteed terms and surviving-spouse payments, are priced differently by each insurance company according to the expected risk.

As you can see, to earn the most income from an annuity it helps to be older (you won't be expected to live as long) and male (ditto), with a shorter guaranteed term and payments that cease upon your death. Payments due to you during the guaranteed term can be left to a beneficiary in the event of your death.

Table 22-3 provides some idea of the range of annuity payments provided by major Canadian insurance companies for a male in good health as of mid-May 2001. These rates change day to day, so don't expect them to be exactly on the mark when you read this. But if no major economic event has occurred between now and then, these rates may still be in the ballpark.

Table 22-3   Ten-Year Guaranteed Monthly Annuity Payments per $100,000 Invested, by Age of Annuitant (As of May 2001)

Male	Age 55	Age 60	Age 65	Age 70
Canada Life	$612.73	$656.81	$714.31	$784.24
Empire Life	$618.07	$673.00	$743.09	$814.57
Equitable Life	$626.85	$672.70	$732.40	$805.70
Imperial Life	$604.12	$648.06	$706.16	$778.13
Industrial Alliance	$620.37	$667.83	$729.62	$804.24
London Life	$607.74	$653.18	$720.41	$794.39

Male	Age 55	Age 60	Age 65	Age 70
Manulife Financial	$617.33	$663.16	$722.34	$789.05
Maritime Life	$619.39	$668.40	$730.86	$804.90
Royal & Sun Alliance	$624.84	$673.78	$736.39	$810.90
Standard Life	$603.96	$651.29	$711.74	$784.01
Sun Life of Canada	$584.86	$630.16	$690.19	$765.23
Transamerica Life	$610.11	$655.74	$716.42	$791.05

Source: Excite Canada & Quicken.ca, May 9, 2001

Using this payment schedule, a man aged 60 with RRSP assets of $400,000 could guarantee at least ten years of monthly income, before taxes, as low as $2,520.64 (if he chose Sun Life) or as high as $2,695.12 (if he chose Royal & Sun Alliance). Should he die before the guaranteed period expired, the payments would continue to his beneficiary to the end of the guaranteed period.

Based on the $400,000 original investment used to purchase the annuity, the Royal & Sun Alliance annuity would generate an annual income of $32,341.44, which equals an annual return of 8.1 percent. Five-year GIC rates at the time were hovering around 5.5 percent annually, so this sounds very attractive . . . until you remember that this form of annuity contains no protection against inflation, which could quickly erode the spending power. Annuities indexed to inflation are available, but they would generate substantially less income than the example shown here.

A couple of other points worth considering:

✔ That $32,341.44 annual income, guaranteed for ten years, means the insurance company is on the hook for only $323,414.40 if you croak before the ten-year guarantee is up. Even if the insurance company generates the current GIC rates of 5-percent annual return from your $400,000, it will earn $200,000 over the same ten years, for a total of $600,000. Is this a good deal for you? Perhaps, if peace of mind is your sole concern.

✔ Annuity payments aren't quite as volatile as the stock market, but they vary a surprising amount over relatively short periods of time. Transamerica Life, for example, paid 60-year-old males looking for a ten-year guarantee $607.32 per $100,000 per month in mid-1999. Less than two years later, 60-year-old males were collecting almost $50 per month more for the same amount under the same conditions from the same company.

▶ Waive the ten-year guarantee, which means payments cease when you die, and you don't increase your income all that much. Canada Life, for example, will pay you only another $20 per month per $100,000. Should you die after receiving just one payment, the insurance company cleans up and probably throws a party in your honour. Big deal. Take the guarantee.

For comparison's sake, Table 22-4 presents annuity rates for females from the same companies and for the same guaranteed term, posted on the same day. Notice that the rates are slightly lower, reflecting the longer life expectancy of females.

Table 22-4   Ten-Year Guaranteed Monthly Annuity Payments per $100,000 Invested, by Age of Annuitant (As of May 2001)

Female	Age 55	Age 60	Age 65	Age 70
Canada Life	$572.98	$607.25	$653.75	$715.78
Empire Life	$583.37	$627.35	$686.54	$754.04
Equitable Life	$592.31	$629.63	$679.50	$745.24
Imperial Life	$570.28	$605.87	$654.36	$719.35
Industrial Alliance	$580.77	$618.49	$669.37	$736.82
London Life	$570.78	$606.81	$662.97	$728.30
Manulife Financial	$582.76	$620.75	$670.91	$731.19
Maritime Life	$579.44	$620.18	$673.76	$743.00
Royal & Sun Alliance	$584.04	$624.26	$677.39	$746.40
Standard Life	$573.64	$613.49	$666.75	$737.08
Sun Life of Canada	$548.04	$585.20	$634.19	$697.47
Transamerica Life	$572.37	$608.53	$658.23	$725.01

Source: Excite Canada & Quicken.ca, May 9, 2001

Should You Choose an Annuity for Your Retirement Income?

Perhaps, if

▶ You have relatively small retirement savings that must generate an income for a very long time because you are relatively young, your family has a history of living to a ripe old age, or both of these factors.

✔ You want the peace of mind that comes from knowing you will have a fixed amount of income.

✔ You prefer to avoid making any decisions when it comes to investing your money.

But be aware of these drawbacks:

✔ You lose control of your savings and the returns they can generate for you.

✔ Lump-sum withdrawals — to deal with a financial emergency, for example — are not permitted.

✔ The rate of return will be lower than the rates available from quality mutual funds. If the stock market begins generating high annual returns, in the vicinity of 20 or 25 percent, and your annuity is returning only 6 or 7 percent, you'll just have to stand on the sidelines and watch.

✔ Unless you choose an indexed annuity, inflation could seriously erode your income over the years (but remember that indexed annuities also pay substantially less money to you each month).

✔ If you don't choose a guaranteed term or a surviving spouse option and you die shortly after the annuity begins (it happens more often than you may think), neither your beneficiaries nor your estate receive a penny.

✔ Choosing various options, such as guaranteed terms, payment to a surviving spouse, and so on, reduces your annuity income.

✔ Your annuity decision is locked in — literally for the rest of your life. So don't make it in haste, and be sure to discuss your decision with your spouse, your family, and your financial adviser before signing on the dotted line.

A final thought: You can purchase an annuity at any time. Some people who reject an annuity in their 60s find the idea more attractive at age 80. By that age, you have beaten the actuarial tables anyway and may want to remove the headache and concern of watching over your assets. That's when an annuity begins to make economic and emotional sense. And you can take a middle-of-the-road option by using just a portion of your RRSP assets to purchase an annuity and convert the rest into a RRIF.

Chapter 23

How a RRIF Works

In This Chapter

▶ Understanding RRIFs

▶ Withdrawing money from your RRIF

▶ Dealing with LIFs and L-RIFs

▶ Maintaining growth in your RRIF

▶ Choosing strategies for growth *and* income

▶ Ensuring you make objective decisions about your retirement and your RRIF

Self-directed RRSPs do more than provide you with the opportunity to maximize the value of your retirement assets. They also provide basic skills and experience in managing substantial amounts of money in pursuit of a logical strategy. That's one reason most RRSP owners choose a Registered Retirement Income Fund (RRIF) when they retire — all those years spent managing an RRSP have provided them with experience in making their own investment decisions. Because the RRIF can be administered by the same firm that handled the self-directed RRSP, it reduces some of the indecision or emotional trauma that can accompany this major turning point in life. Having the same financial adviser or investment counsellor at your elbow as you move from employment to retirement is some comfort, after all.

An RRSP in Reverse

The easiest way to grasp the concept of a RRIF is to consider it an RRSP in reverse. Over many years, you paid the RRSP. Now the RRSP pays you. You manage these two investment vehicles differently, but perhaps not as much so as you may expect. The biggest change is a shift in emphasis from growth to income, although you still need to pay attention to your plan's growth to counter the risk of inflation and avoid outliving your money.

If the biggest advantage of a RRIF over an annuity is flexibility, the biggest drawback to a RRIF is the fact that you have to pay as much attention to your assets as you did with your self-directed RRSP. This shouldn't be difficult with all those years of experience you've built up, plus the extra time you (may) have on your hands. But there are more benefits to RRIFs as well (see Table 23-1).

Table 23-1	RRIFs versus Annuities	
Feature	*RRIFs*	*Annuities*
You determine withdrawals	Yes*	No
Lump-sum withdrawals are permitted	Yes	No
Savings are tax-sheltered	Yes	N/A
You can react to economic conditions	Yes	No
You invest according to personal needs	Yes	No
Estate remains upon your death	Yes	No**

* *Minimum withdrawals required. See Rules for Withdrawals, next page.*

** *You can designate a beneficiary to receive any remaining payments during a guaranteed term, but this will reduce your annual income. If your death occurs after that term expires, your estate or beneficiaries receive nothing.*

Remember That Deadline

You may find yourself bopping along in your late sixties, healthy as a Queen's Plate winner and taking great delight in watching your RRSP grow by leaps and bounds. In fact, you could be having so much fun at your work that the *R*-word never enters your mind.

Well, it had better. Canada Customs and Revenue Agency makes no bones about it: By the end of the year in which you turn 69 (and it may even creep lower as Ottawa looks around for new sources of tax revenue), you must either purchase an annuity with your RRSP assets or convert them to a RRIF. Otherwise, the CCRA will assume you chose Door Number Three, behind which stands a smirking tax collector who will seize at least half of your RRSP assets in one fell swoop.

You avoid this menace by rolling your RRSP into a RRIF. No taxes are applied, nor are any gains made inside the RRIF subject to tax. Your retirement income from a RRIF is not a matter of withdrawing money from a lump sum; it's more like spinning off money from an asset that, under ideal conditions, earns about as much per year in fixed dollars as you take out as income.

Rules for RRIF Withdrawals

In case you may want to leave all your RRIF assets inside the plan, building to Everest heights of value . . . well, you can't. You must withdraw a minimum amount (sometimes called a *minimum annual payout*, or *MAP*) from your RRIF each year, measured as a percentage of the assets in your plan at the end of the previous year. The amount varies with your age, as shown in Table 23-2.

Table 23-2		Minimum Withdrawals from RRIF by Age (Percentage of Assets)			
Age	*Minimum*	*Age*	*Minimum*	*Age*	*Minimum*
69	4.76%	78	8.33%	87	11.33%
70	5.00%	79	8.53%	88	11.96%
71	7.38%	80	8.75%	89	12.71%
72	7.48%	81	8.99%	90	13.62%
73	7.59%	82	9.27%	91	14.73%
74	7.71%	83	9.58%	92	16.12%
75	7.85%	84	9.93%	93	17.92%
76	7.99%	85	10.33%	94	20.00%
77	8.15%	86	10.79%	95+	20.00%

Example: If your RRIF value was $400,000 at the end of the year in which you turned 69, you would have to withdraw at least 5 percent of that amount, or $20,000, the following year, when you are 70. The financial institution managing your RRIF can arrange to make payments to you during the year according to your direction. (You can always take out more than the minimum amount, of course.) At the end of each year, if you have not withdrawn the minimum amount, a cheque will be issued to you making up the difference.

If your spouse is younger than you, you can base the minimum withdrawal amount on your spouse's age, leaving more of your RRIF assets tax-sheltered to continue building in value.

No income tax is withheld when withdrawing the annual minimum from your RRIF. Taxes are withheld, however, on amounts exceeding the minimum. Using the example above, if you withdrew $25,000 instead of the minimum $20,000, income tax would be applied to the $5,000 above your minimum at source (that is, withdrawn by the financial institution managing your RRIF and paid to Canada Customs and Revenue Agency on your behalf). All RRIF income, of course, is subject to income tax, and a return must be filed.

LIFs and L-RIFs

If you are entitled to private pension benefits that are *locked in* (often referred to as a *locked-in retirement account,* or *LIRA*), you are faced with another decision. At one time, locked-in pensions accrued during your working years provided no withdrawals; the total amount of your pension was used to purchase an annuity, with all the drawbacks reviewed earlier in this chapter.

Various provinces, beginning with Quebec, saw the unfairness of this restriction years ago and introduced legislation permitting locked-in pension benefits to be converted into a *life income fund*, or *LIF*. Think of a LIF as a locked-in RRIF. You determine how to invest and manage your LIF in the same way you handle your RRIF, and you must be 55 years of age before you can make any withdrawals. The same minimum payouts apply for LIFs and RRIFs, but a LIF adds a restriction to the maximum amount you can withdraw. This is to ensure that assets remain in the LIF when you turn 80 and you are required to use money left in your LIF to purchase a life annuity.

This is where things get complicated.

Unlike the fairly simplified formula for determining minimum withdrawals from a RRIF, the calculations for maximum withdrawals from a LIF in most provinces may remind you of high-school algebra:

Maximum LIF withdrawal = B × M × F

B is the *balance* in your LIF account on January 1 of the year you withdraw the money.

M is the number of *months* remaining until you turn 90.

F stands for *factor*, based on a combination of current long-term Canadian bond rates and 6-percent annual returns.

Alberta, Saskatchewan, Manitoba, and Ontario tweak the LIF idea with a *locked-in retirement income fund,* or *L-RIF*, which does not require you to purchase a life annuity at age 80. Each province sets its own withdrawal formula for L-RIFs. In Ontario, for example, L-RIF owners can simply withdraw the previous year's investment return from their L-RIF. This ensures that some assets from their L-RIF will remain in their estate when they die.

If you have a LIRA, consult with your financial adviser, investment counsellor, or the pension fund administrator for maximum withdrawal guidelines in your province.

Look for Income, but Keep Your Eye on Growth

During your working years, you probably looked for ways to raise your salary level from time to time. Improving your education, adding new work skills, and changing employers are the most common techniques used in search of a bigger paycheque. Why not maintain the same approach with your RRIF? The tactics are different, of course, and since your basic expenses are likely fixed, you don't need a constantly growing amount of money each year. But some careful planning and periodic reviews can put several thousand dollars in your pocket each year from the same nest egg.

These current economic times present a challenge to RRIF owners looking for more income. Inflation remains low, which is a good sign. But low inflation also means low interest rates, which makes it difficult to obtain high returns from some RRIF assets. In mid-2001, five-year interest rates from GIC-based RRIF investments fluttered around the 5.5-percent mark, while one-year GIC rates hovered a full percentage lower. If you've managed to accumulate $200,000 in your RRIF, these interest-rate levels would produce an annual income of just $8,000 before eating into your principal. At that level, annuities begin to look pretty good, even with all their disadvantages.

Remember our old friends Risk and Reward? If we want to increase our earnings from the RRIF above a paltry 4 to 5 percent annually, we'll have to accept some risk. But this is not an easy time in your life to accept risk. You need both solid financial advice and an awareness of your own risk-tolerance level. Fortunately, by now you've spent many years getting to know both, so some of the following decisions may be a little easier to make than you think.

The Difference Down the Road

While you were building your RRSP assets, you could see the difference a few percentage points of annual returns made over time. When managing your RRIF, the impact can be just as dramatic and, best of all, more immediate. If you can manage to boost the average annual returns from your RRIF from 4½ percent to 8 percent, as shown in Table 23-3, both your retirement and your estate will be substantially more wealthy. The withdrawal levels are the minimum annual amounts set by Canada Customs and Revenue Agency.

Table 23-3		RRIF Returns by Age and Percentage Return			
		4½-Percent Return		8-Percent Return	
Age	Percentage	Fund	Withdrawal	Fund	Withdrawal
65	4.00%	$300,000	$12,000	$300,000	$12,000
66	4.17%	$301,209	$12,550	$311,486	$12,979
67	4.35%	$301,909	$13,126	$322,870	$14,038
68	4.55%	$302,051	$13,730	$334,061	$15,185
69	4.76%	$301,581	$14,361	$344,951	$16,426
70	5.00%	$300,443	$15,022	$355,417	$17,771
71	7.38%	$298,577	$22,035	$365,318	$26,960
72	7.48%	$289,444	$21,650	$366,429	$27,409
73	7.59%	$289,294	$21,274	$367,160	$27,867
74	7.71%	$271,117	$20,903	$367,472	$28,332
75	7.85%	$261,908	$20,560	$367,324	$28,835

Launch your RRIF with $300,000, accept 4½-percent returns, make minimum annual withdrawals, and at age 70 you'll be required to take just over $15,000 from a balance of $300,000. Get an 8-percent annual return — from income plus growth — and at age 70 your minimum withdrawal will be almost $3,000 higher, *plus your RRIF has increased in value by over $55,000.* If you can achieve this level of growth with a reasonable degree of risk, why not?

Where to Start When Adjusting Your RRIF Asset Mix

The changes needed to generate reasonable growth and returns from your RRIF may not be very substantial. While you may prefer a more conservative approach to investing than you took during your years of full-time employment, your risk threshold has probably not shifted far.

Begin by reviewing the current mix of investments in your RRSP before converting it to a RRIF. Consider moving a portion of your GIC and Canadian equity mutual funds to a Canadian dividend fund and/or a Canadian mortgage fund. (It goes without saying that you should maintain the same high percentage of foreign investments in your RRIF as in your RRSP.) Table 23-4 lists the top performers in Canadian dividend funds (which maintain at least 75 percent of their assets in shares of dividend-paying Canadian corporations) and recent return levels. As you can see, the returns in many cases are impressive, but the volatility can reach seasickness levels. Dividend funds are a good place to take your profits each year and move them to steadier ground.

Table 23-4 Canadian Dividend Funds: Annual Averaged Returns			
Fund	*1 Year*	*3 Years*	*5 Years*
AGF Dividend Fund	11.5%	2.7%	13.3%
Bissett Dividend Income Fund	20.8%	3.7%	12.8%
Industrial Dividend Growth Fund	27.7%	6.0%	15.6%
MAXXUM Dividend Fund	20.6%	7.4%	16.1%
PH&N Dividend Fund	32.3%	12.3%	24.1%
Royal Dividend Fund	22.0%	6.8%	18.6%
Scotia Canadian Dividend Fund	21.5%	6.5%	18.2%

Source: Globe & Mail Mutual Fund Report, April 17, 2001

Unitholders of the Phillips, Hager & North fund earned an average of 24 percent annually over five years. Even the conservative bank-operated funds generated almost 20 percent in annual income for the three years ending in mid-1999. During this time, GICs were returning an anemic 4 or 5 percent annually. Combining a well-managed dividend fund with laddered GICs should produce a combination of solid security and volatile growth, resulting in both fatter returns for your RRIF and lower stress levels for you.

Follow the Rule of Thirds

Start by making your RRIF an extension of your RRSP. Follow the rule of thirds by incorporating the familiar three components of cash, growth, and security, but this time think "income" in place of cash. Begin by dividing your total assets into thirds, according to the components shown in Table 23-5. Then decide where you stand regarding an aggressive or conservative investment policy, or something in between.

Table 23-5	RRIF Components Using the Rule of Thirds		
Component	**Suggested Investments**	**Proportion of Total**	
		Aggressive	**Conservative**
Cash/income	Canadian dividend fund(s)	25%	15%
	Canadian mortgage fund	10%	15%
	Money market fund	5%	10%
Growth	Canadian large-cap fund(s)	25%	15%
	Canadian sector fund	5%	—
	International equity fund	20%	20%
Security	Strip bonds	10%	10%
	Laddered GICs	—	15%
TOTALS		100%	100%

A Step-by-Step Approach to Making Decisions

Retirement is an emotional time, a mix of contrasting feelings that range from anticipation and achievement to uncertainty and regret. The feelings you experience, and the way you deal with them, are yours alone. You may want, however, to impose some sort of structure on the decision-making to assist your objectivity. Here are several things you should do:

✔ **Take your time.** Unless it's the end of the year in which you turn 69, there's no need to rush into converting your RRSP into a RRIF or annuity. So give yourself some time to think things over. What are the priorities of your retirement? Will you travel a lot? Buy toys such as a new car, a boat, or a home workshop? Spend more time in your garden or performing volunteer work? Are you concerned about leaving a fat inheritance to your children or grandchildren, or to charity? You had goals during your employment years, and you should set goals in retirement. It helps when making decisions about your RRSP assets.

✔ **If you don't need a RRIF income right away, don't use it.** You may take a part-time job or have some private pension income or assets outside your RRSP to live on for a while. If that's the case, and you are still under 69 years of age, don't be in a rush to convert your RRSP to a RRIF. If you can leave it alone for a year or two, it will continue to build value sheltered from tax.

Things to ask yourself before finalizing your RRIF investment mix

Are you planning any major changes to your lifestyle? Perhaps you're shopping for a vacation condominium, or you've come into a major inheritance. Or the change has been for the worse: You've lost your spouse, or your health has deteriorated substantially. How will any of these events affect your economic needs?

Have economic conditions changed? If inflation leaps out of the bushes and begins chewing up savings, or the stock market is riding either a severe bearish or wild bullish trend, this will influence your economic decisions.

Has your income-tax status changed significantly? This is likely to be the result of assets held outside your RRIF. For example, if you sell your home and invest the proceeds, these earnings will be added to your RRIF income and could bump your marginal income tax to a higher bracket.

Are you worrying more about your investments? During your working years it was easier to accept volatility and paper losses in your RRSP than it is after you retire. When those same dollars are put to work earning you a living, their ups and downs are a little harder to deal with. If that's the case, perhaps you should exchange some growth and income in your RRIF for a little more security.

Have you maintained a balance in your RRIF investments? Paying attention to the relative size of equities and bonds in your RRSP has probably maintained the balance that feels best for you. RRIF owners can become a little neglectful of this aspect, so check once a year to ensure the balance between secure investments — GICs, bonds, T-bills — and equity investments matches your strategy and comfort level.

Do you still need the same rate of return? You may be delighted when you discover a portion of your RRIF is churning out 15 or 20 percent in average annual returns, but remember that this kind of growth usually involves risk and volatility. Are the returns worth it? Should you shift more emphasis to security?

Have your goals changed? Sitting on your back porch each day may have been fun for the first several months, but if you have an urge to see more of the world or satisfy a craving for a sailboat, this puts new pressure on the performance of your RRIF investments. How badly do you want that new toy? How much pressure can you accept?

✔ **Consider splitting your C/QPP benefits.** This is an option available to couples where one spouse has a substantially larger income than the other. The spouse with the higher income can have up to 50 percent of his or her income transferred to the other spouse, reducing income-tax levels.

✔ **Set up a total review of your RRSP portfolio.** Do it sooner, rather than later. Call your financial adviser or investment counsellor and ask for a complete review of all your assets — RRSP, home equity, life insurance, private pension income, non-registered investments, the works. Give yourself at least an hour to discuss and evaluate them all. Include your spouse in the session. Then consider how each fits into your strategy.

✔ **Don't limit your investment horizon.** In your sixties and seventies, you could need a retirement income for another 20 years or more. That qualifies as a long-term investment horizon, which deserves the same kind of investment tactics you used when building your RRSP. So don't overlook equity investments, especially quality growth-oriented mutual funds, as a means of building your RRIF assets and a hedge against inflation.

✔ **You can still make investments — and should.** Past age 69, you can't enjoy the tax-sheltered advantages of an RRSP, but that's no reason to avoid investing with available income if you have it. With two incomes, these investments should be made by the spouse with the lower income, to reduce income-tax levels.

Chapter 24

Looking at the Whole Picture

● ●

In This Chapter

▶ Measuring other income sources

▶ Building your estate

▶ Winding down and out

● ●

*N*ot so long ago, retirement meant the three *R*s — reading glasses, relaxation, and a rocking chair . . . maybe with a round of golf thrown in. These days, retirement can mean almost anything you darn well please. This often means continuing to make decisions on your own. Some will be easier to make than others. But wouldn't you rather be making them yourself than have others making them for you?

Other Income Sources

Even after converting your RRSP assets into an income-producing plan, a number of other sources of money remain available to you. How you choose them and use them is up to you.

Your C/QPP benefits

When you turn 60, you are eligible for early C/QPP (Canada/Quebec Pension Plan) benefits. The formula sets full benefits at age 65, reducing them by one-half percent for each month under the threshold age. Thus, at age 60, you are entitled to 70 percent of full C/QPP benefits (5 years = 60 months × ½% = 30% subtracted from 100). Similarly, if you delay applying for C/QPP benefits past your 65th birthday, the benefits rise by one-half percent monthly.

Should you apply early? The consensus is a resounding "Yes!" for two reasons. First, if you wait until 65 to receive benefits, it takes a long time for the increased C/QPP payments to catch up with those lost five years. At current benefit rates, for example, you'll receive about $126,000 in total

The rule that doesn't mean much

When applying for C/QPP benefits, you will be asked to declare that you have ceased employment and have no earned income. Does this mean you cannot receive benefits if you are still employed, or you cannot choose to earn income after you begin receiving benefits before age 60? (Pension and other retirement-income sources are not included in eligibility rules.)

The answers are confusing, but in practical terms you can continue to work while receiving benefits. It's all a matter of some (nudge-nudge, wink-wink) skirting of the eligibility rules.

Your earned income, used to determine eligibility for C/QPP benefits, is measured by the calendar year. When you apply for benefits to begin at the end of the calendar year, your earned income for the same period you are receiving benefits is low enough to continue qualifying you for payments. You will have to "decide" to stop earning income when you apply for your benefits. Later, you will have to "change your mind" and return to employment on January 1 of the following year. No one, after all, wants to prevent you from choosing to return to the workforce. Another alternative is

to ask your employer for permission to resign from your job at the end of the month immediately prior to receiving C/QPP benefits, earn no income in the first month of benefits, and resume work after the benefits begin.

It's a silly little dance to get around the rules, and you may want to consult an accountant or someone totally familiar with the guidelines, who may identify a complication or two. But in practical terms, you can receive early C/QPP benefits while earning an income, if you choose to.

The second reason for applying early is the usual uncertainty about any government benefit. It may be withdrawn or seriously modified at any time. If you have been paying into it through all your working years, you are entitled to its benefits. Go get 'em. Just remember that your benefits won't begin appearing in your mailbox automatically when you turn 60 years of age. You must apply for them, preferably about six months in advance of your 60th birthday. Applications are available from your local office of Human Resources Development Canada, or call 1-800-277-9914. Information is also available on the federal government's Web site at www.canada.gc.ca.

payments over the 20 years between age 60 and age 80. Wait until you're 65 to receive them and you'll be paid $134,000 over the 15 years between age 65 and age 80. Few people believe it's worth waiting five years to obtain a paltry $8,000 more in total benefits.

Your home

Along with the money built up in your RRSP/RRIF, your house represents a substantial asset. For many people, its value is at least as high emotionally as it is economically. If you have raised your family, with all the attendant pain and pleasures, under the same roof for a few decades, selling your home can be a wrenching decision to make. Yet from a financial standpoint alone, your house, especially if it is mortgage-free, is both an underused asset and an ongoing expense. The equity in your home could be producing at least $5,000 annual income for each $100,000 of value, without depleting the principal by a penny.

Whether you choose to remain in the family home or another alternative is not a decision to be taken lightly, and it probably needn't be made right away either. So review all the options listed below, choose the one that you're most comfortable with at the moment, discuss it at length with your partner and family, and give it a good deal of thought.

✔ **Stay where you are.**

Pros: Comfort, security, no emotional stress, old friends and neighbours nearby.

Cons: Maintenance costs, physical labour needed for upkeep, no active use of equity.

✔ **Stay where you are and generate income from a reverse mortgage.**

Pros: Same as the preceding, plus active use of equity in home.

Cons: Maintenance costs and upkeep continue, possibility of little or no estate value remaining. (Be sure to review reverse mortgages, covered in Chapter 4.)

✔ **Sell current home, purchase smaller home or condominium, perhaps in less expensive neighbourhood or community.**

Pros: Reduce or eliminate maintenance and upkeep, opportunity for new friends and activities, some assets available for investment or income generation.

Cons: Moving expenses, perhaps some emotional stress, distance from friends and family, possible loss of rewarding activities such as a garden and workshop.

✔ **Sell current home and renting.**

Pros: Eliminate maintenance and upkeep, all home equity is available for investment or income generation.

Cons: Rental expense/drain on income.

✔ **Rent current home, move to apartment or other facility.**

Pros: Equity in home generates new source of income while maintaining asset value.

Cons: Maintenance, upkeep, tenant relationships, distance from family and friends.

Estate Planning

More than a few Canadians will discover their retirement years just happen to represent the wealthiest period of their lives. Their awareness and application of investment opportunities, primarily via RRSPs and RRIFs, plus accumulated equity in their home, can easily add up to several hundred thousand dollars. Add to this the expectation that Baby Boomers will inherit a few trillion dollars from their parents, and the need for a better understanding of estate planning becomes apparent.

At this point, the two biggest culprits to deal with are the familiar certainties of death and taxes. Both will eventually arrive almost simultaneously, and you might as well give some thought to reducing the impact of the latter. ("Simultaneously" is no joke. Canada Customs and Revenue Agency will assume that all of your assets are sold at precisely the same moment you pass away, making them taxable on their value at that time.)

It goes without saying that you should draft a will. Without one, your estate will be left in chaos, prey to the CCRA. You needn't have massive assets to justify a will, either. Anyone with a partner and an asset more valuable than a bicycle should make the effort to draft a will and keep a copy in a safe, accessible place.

Estate planning involves discussions with your spouse or partner and family; your financial adviser or investment counsellor; and your lawyer. All three should be aware of your goals and wishes to reduce conflict, misunderstandings, and taxes. Here are some basic guidelines and tools to use:

✔ **Spousal RRSP/RRIF rollovers.** This is an easy one. Simply designate your spouse as the beneficiary of your RRSP or RRIF assets. They will be transferred free of taxation. By the way, if you have a RRIF and your spouse or partner has an RRSP, your RRIF can be converted to an RRSP and transferred as such to your spouse's plan.

✔ **Spousal plan transfers.** Assets outside your RRIF or RRSP can be transferred into your spouse or partner's spousal RRSP if your spouse is under age 70 and contribution room exists. This transfer must be made in the year of your death or within the first 60 days of the following year.

✔ **Freezing your estate.** No, this has nothing to do with transferring your assets to Baffin Island. It means giving some of your assets to your beneficiaries well before your death. Note that any increase in value of the assets from the time you transfer them will be subject to capital-gains tax, payable by the beneficiaries. This also places control of the assets in the hands of the beneficiaries while you're still living, which may make you uncomfortable.

TIP

How to be both charitable and clever

One way to use the assets in your estate without taxation and get a good feeling at the same time is to name a qualified charity in your estate. This works equally well both inside and outside an RRSP or RRIF. If you name a charity or institution such as a college or university as beneficiary of all or a portion of your estate, and your estate as beneficiary of a fixed amount from your RRSP or RRIF, the charity bequest will arrive free of taxes. Technically, the amount is taxed when it leaves your plan, but the bequest generates a tax credit equal to the amount taxed. Isn't it neat the way lawyers and tax experts make an easy concept so complex? Here's an example:

✔ You name your estate as beneficiary of $50,000 in assets from your RRSP or RRIF.

✔ You leave your alma mater $50,000 as a bequest in your will.

✔ Your RRSP/RRIF funds are taxed at 48 percent = $24,000.

✔ Your estate receives a tax credit of $24,000, offsetting the tax.

You don't have to arrange a charitable donation in your will to benefit an organization you wish to support. If you're over 70 years of age, you can use a *charitable gift annuity* as a lump-sum bequest that pays you some income while you live. Here's how it works:

Make a contribution of $10,000 or more as an irrevocable gift annuity to a qualifying charity or institution (these are very popular with colleges and universities). A portion of the bequest will be used to purchase an annuity from an insurance company on your behalf, payable to you for life or for a guaranteed period. The remainder becomes an outright gift to the charity or institution. Your gift annuity payments may attract lower taxation than other forms of income, and you could even receive a tax-deductible receipt for your donation.

If these ideas appeal to you, discuss them with the charity or institution you wish to receive your bequest. They can answer most of your questions and arrange the necessary paperwork.

✔ **Setting up a trust.** You may be able to both reduce taxes to your beneficiaries and keep control of some assets through a trust arrangement. This can become very complex and filled with sharp corners, so obtain legal and financial advice from an expert in this field before choosing this alternative.

✔ **Investing in segregated mutual funds.** This is one way to control your assets and provide an estate for selected beneficiaries with minimum tax impact. Seg funds, converted in many cases directly from mutual funds you own, are treated like life insurance, which means they escape taxation in the hands of a beneficiary named by you. Be sure to check with your financial adviser to ensure eligibility and arrange the conversion. (For details on seg funds, see Chapter 16.)

✔ **Purchasing life insurance.** Most of us maintain life insurance for essentials, such as paying off a mortgage and covering debts. Beyond these functions, it can also be used to ensure that certain assets identified in your will won't have to be sold off to cover the taxes. At this point in your life, all you need is term insurance, guaranteeing a fixed period of specified coverage. Shop around for the lowest premium and reject the efforts of anyone who tries to sell you any other form of insurance, such as whole life, universal life, term to 100, and other stuff you don't need but will wind up paying for.

Stay-at-home, snowbird, or emigrant?

Faraway fields can look greener, even after you are retired. Escaping Canada's weather and tax burden can be a strong motivator for people with a steady income and few responsibilities, who seek happiness in other corners of the world.

Snowbirds take temporary leave during the winter to enjoy the sun of California, Arizona, Florida, Mexico, and other points south, between November and April. This is a fairly simple solution, if warm weather is your prime attraction. Some arrangements must be made for health care and other concerns. A good source of information and guidance is the Canadian Snowbird Association, which can be reached at 1-800-265-3200.

If weather, taxes, and other things motivate you to pull up stakes and abandon Canada entirely for your retirement years, give this option the degree of serious thought and extensive research it deserves. Here are a few down-to-earth concerns you'll be dealing with:

✔ You'll probably be leaving family and friends behind, a reality many people have difficulty accepting if the primary reason for emigrating Canada was just to save on taxes.

✔ Explore your new home country in great detail first. Ireland, for example, not only permits retired Canadians to live free of income tax, but the country also provides free electricity, a winter fuel allowance, and free transportation for everyone over age 66. Sounds good, except the cost of living in Dublin is sky-high and rural life in a thatched cottage can soon lose its romantic appeal.

✔ Immigration laws for many countries are complex and challenging. If you reside in the U.S. for more than 180 days in any calendar year without proper documents, you could be ruled an illegal alien and barred from the country for several years.

✔ Tax treaties between Canada and other countries vary widely. There is a serious danger of being taxed twice on your retirement income — once in Canada when the funds are released and again in the country of your residence.

✔ When you leave Canada to take up residence in another country, Canada Customs and Revenue Agency imposes taxes as though you sold all your property on the day you departed. While some assets remain tax-exempt, such as your principal residence and your RRSP/RRIF, others could attract capital-gains tax.

✔ Don't expect to find anything like the health care coverage you have used in Canada, unless you pay for it directly. This can create a major dent in anyone's budget, especially those in the post-65 age bracket.

A Long and Happy Life

By design, this book has focused almost entirely on the financial aspects of retirement planning. The basic principle is simple: The more money you can provide for your own retirement, the more freedom you'll have in choosing the kind of retirement you'll enjoy.

But by retirement age, you should have acquired sufficient wisdom to appreciate the limited amount of happiness that money alone can buy. Who deserves our envy more: The woman with a merely sufficient retirement income who is surrounded by friends and family, with plenty of time to enjoy her garden and hobbies? Or the man with a six-figure annual retirement income who lies awake at night worrying about his investments, gnashing his teeth because his neighbour's yacht is bigger than his, and plotting to keep his assets away from his ungrateful family?

Happiness is, after all, like a friendly cat who eludes your mad pursuit but, in quiet moments, settles himself in your lap and purrs contentedly.

Part VII
Where to Go from Here

The 5th Wave By Rich Tennant

"That reminds me – I have to figure out how to save for retirement _and_ send these two to college."

In this part . . .

You find a reference list of various information sources, including Canada Customs and Revenue Agency (formerly Revenue Canada, which was shorter and more descriptive), and other helpful leads. You can also use a personal RRSP and RRIF planner to determine the amount of money you will need in your plan, based on RRSP contributions, inflation levels, and so on. Consider it a cross between a parlour game and a graduation exam (neatness is up to you).

Chapter 25

Sources of Help and Information

· ·

In This Chapter

▶ Avoiding fraud and embezzlement

▶ Obtaining information and assistance

▶ Contacting Canada Customs and Revenue Agency

▶ Using bank and trust company resources

· ·

*A*ll the money invested in RRSPs by Canadians has spawned an entire industry to provide more products and services than you probably want or need. In the midst of appeals from individuals and companies who swear they are your best route to a millionaire's life in retirement — not to mention pundits and gurus popping up in newspapers and magazines and on radio phone-in shows — it's easy to become susceptible to promises of exceptional growth opportunities.

In a word: Don't. True, someone will always concoct an investment system or technique that flies in the face of traditional thinking, and its results will be impressive for a while. But concepts such as diversification and balancing growth with security are widely accepted because they work for most people in most circumstances most of the time.

Don't Be Conned

With so much RRSP money floating around, the competition for your RRSP funds can grow frantic, leading to one of two dangers from those who would love to seize your financial future in their grimy little paws.

The first is having a financial adviser or broker promise massive returns if you toss aside conventional thinking and accept his or her outrageous strategy. One mutual fund salesman posing as a financial adviser once told me I was a fool not to have every penny of my RRSP assets in equity-based mutual funds.

He sneered at my strip bonds, calling them "conventional thinking," claiming they acted like an anchor on the growth of my RRSP. When I asked what mutual funds he would recommend (he sold funds from several companies) and in what proportion, he replied, "Transfer your RRSP to me first, and then I'll let you know."

Apparently, this smug attitude actually worked with some people, because he appeared reasonably successful. How successful his clients were in building their RRSP balances is another story.

In mid-2000, another financial adviser associated with a firm specializing in equities and insurance practically ordered my wife and me to dump our bonds "because they're too risky" (they were all government-guaranteed strip bonds paying, on face value, almost twice as much as the current bond issues); sell our house; and purchase a few hundred thousand dollars in insurance on each of our lives. None of these actions would have profited us; all would have profited him and his company.

We held on to our bonds. One month later, the stock market slid into its bearish mood and the value of our equities declined at least 25 percent. The bonds held their value.

Before taking any advice from any financial adviser who does not work on a fee-only basis, ask yourself if the adviser stands to profit from what you do. This doesn't make it wrong on the surface. But it sure makes it questionable.

The second danger is more rare but potentially more disastrous, and involves the potential for investment fraud. Every few months, the news media carry reports of trusting investors, usually elderly people, who discover that their financial adviser, investment counsellor, or brokerage sales representative has bilked them of their assets. The people who commit these crimes are nothing more than greedy fraud artists and sociopaths. Invariably, they are described as smooth-talking individuals who appear totally trustworthy in their dealings and outstandingly successful in their profession — often projecting this apparent success with a flamboyant lifestyle.

There's no need to be paranoid about this risk. The danger of having your RRSP savings wiped out by an investment con artist is about equal to being mugged in your own town. In fact, some of the steps you can take to avoid RRSP losses involve the same good sense you would use to avoid being robbed on the street. They include the following:

> ✔ **Read each RRSP statement as soon as you receive it.** Check for errors. If you find any, ask for an explanation immediately. File all RRSP statements together for future reference if needed.

✔ **Be aware without being suspicious.** Sometimes things get fouled up by banks and investment firms. Your RRSP statement may be late, it may contain a mistake or two, or a transfer may not occur as quickly as it should. Ask for a correction, and for confirmation of the correction along with a revised statement.

✔ **Never step outside the organization with your RRSP.** If the financial adviser, investment counsellor, or account executive assigned to your account ever suggests making an investment directly with him or her, instead of within the structure of the firm they work for, refuse adamantly. Then call the firm and report this action. Any investments, contracts, or agreements made with a financial adviser or consultant not handled within his or her employer's firm may negate any opportunity you have of recouping your assets if fraud or embezzlement occurs.

✔ **Never permit your RRSP assets to be de-registered and placed in the hands of someone else.** Financial fraud artists have been known to promise clients that the growth in investment value will more than make up for tax losses resulting from pulling money out of an RRSP tax shelter. Fall for this one and your hard-earned RRSP assets will vanish faster than a snowball in a sauna.

✔ **Use your representative as your first source of information, not your sole source.** You owe the man or woman who assists you in managing your RRSP assets a reasonable degree of trust and loyalty. But you should not depend solely on him or her whenever you encounter a problem that could create a potential loss to you. If you are concerned about an error or do not fully understand a transaction in your account, call the individual you deal with immediately, express your concern, and ask for an explanation and correction, if necessary. If an error has occurred and a promise is made to correct it, remember to have the correction confirmed in writing on an appropriate official form. If the correction is not made within a reasonable time, or an acceptable explanation is not given, contact the compliance officer in the firm employing your adviser. If the firm cannot satisfy your concerns, and you have suffered or may have suffered a loss, call the Investment Dealers Association (see the following section), your lawyer, or the police.

✔ **Cut the risk by choosing a large bank-associated firm.** This may seem unfair to honest, hardworking independent financial counsellors, or even smaller brokerage and investment firms, but it's true nonetheless. If you place both your assets and trust in the hands of an individual or investment boutique with severely limited assets and your RRSP or RRIF money disappears through fraud, embezzlement, or mismanagement, your chances of recovering the money are zilch. Fraud artists have also been known to lurk among large bank-owned investment firms. But in the very few times that criminal actions resulting in the loss of a client's assets have occurred in these companies, the parent bank has usually done the right thing and replaced the money.

Information Sources

You are unlikely to suffer from a shortage of information on managing your RRSP. In fact, your biggest problem may be wading through all of the data, opinions, anecdotes, and statistics found in promotional material and in the print and broadcast media. Virtually all of it provides wisdom and guidance in some area or another of your RRSP/RRIF investment and management.

How much do you need? Probably less than you think, especially if you have absorbed all the information in the preceding pages. Still, everyone's retirement planning needs are unique in some aspect, so valuable sources of more specialized information are listed in the sections that follow.

Canada Customs and Revenue Agency

Contact the CCRA for any questions regarding tax-deductible or tax-sheltered aspects of your RRSP or RRIF by visiting one of the tax services offices listed below or calling a central toll-free number: 1-800-663-9033. They also maintain a fairly comprehensive Web site at www.ccra-adrc.gc.ca.

Newfoundland/Labrador
St. John's Tax Centre:
165 Duckworth St., P.O. Box 5968, St. John's NF   A1C 5X6

Prince Edward Island
Charlottetown Tax Services Office:
94 Euston St., P.O. Box 8500, Charlottetown PE   C1A 8L3

Nova Scotia
Halifax Tax Services Office:
1256 Barrington St., P.O. Box 638, Halifax NS   B3J 2T5

Sydney Tax Services Office:
47 Dorchester St., P.O. Box 1300, Sydney NS   B1P 6K3

New Brunswick
Bathurst Tax Services Office:
120 Harbourview Blvd., 4th Floor, P.O. Box 8888, Bathurst NB   E2A 4L8

Moncton Tax Services Office:
107–1600 Main St., P.O. Box 1070, Moncton NB   E1C 8P2

Saint John Tax Services Office:
126 Prince William St., Saint John NB   E2L 4H9

Quebec

Chicoutimi Tax Services Office:
211–100 Lafontaine St., Chicoutimi QC   G7H 6X2

Jonquière Tax Centre:
2251 de la Centrale Blvd., Jonquière QC   G7S 5J1

Laval Tax Services Office:
3131 St. Martin Blvd. W, Laval QC   H7T 2A7

Montérégie Rive-Sud Tax Services Office:
300–1000 de Sérigny St., Longueuil QC   J4K 5J7

Montreal Tax Services Office:
305 René Lévesque Blvd. W, Montreal QC   H2Z 1A6

Outaouais Tax Services Office:
15 Eddy St., 16th Floor, Hull QC   K1A 1L4

Quebec Tax Services Office:
165 de la Pointe-aux-Lièvres St. S, Quebec QC   G1K 7L3

Rimouski Tax Services Office:
320 St-Germain Rd. E, Rimouski QC   G5L 1C2

Rouyn-Noranda Tax Services Office:
44 du Lac Ave., Rouyn-Noranda QC   J9X 6Z9

Shawinigan-Sud Tax Centre:
4695–12th Ave., Shawinigan-Sud QC   G9N 7S6

Sherbrooke Tax Services Office:
50 Place de la Cité, P.O. Box 1300, Sherbrooke QC   J1H 5L8

Trois-Rivières Tax Services Office:
111–25 des Forges St., Trois-Rivières QC   G9A 2G4

Ontario

Barrie Tax Services Office:
99 Ferris Lane, Barrie ON   L4M 2Y2

Belleville Tax Services Office:
11 Station St., Belleville ON   K8N 2S3

Hamilton Tax Services Office:
120 King St. W, P.O. Box 2220, Hamilton ON   L8N 3E1

Kingston Tax Services Office:
993 Princess St., P.O. Box 2600, Kingston ON   K7L 5P3

Kitchener–Waterloo Tax Services Office:
166 Frederick St., P.O. Box 9015, Kitchener ON   N2G 4N1

London Tax Services Office:
451 Talbot St., London ON   N6A 5E5

Ottawa Tax Services Office:
1730 St-Laurent Blvd., 7th Floor, Ottawa ON   K1G 3H7

Peterborough Tax Services Office:
185 King St. W, 5th Floor, Peterborough ON   K9J 8M3

St. Catharines Tax Services Office:
32 Church St., P.O. Box 3038, St. Catharines ON   L2R 3B9

Sudbury Tax Services Office:
1050 Notre Dame Ave., Sudbury ON   P3A 5C1

Thunder Bay Tax Services Office:
130 South Syndicate Ave., Thunder Bay ON   P7E 1C7

Toronto Centre Tax Services Office:
36 Adelaide St. E, Toronto ON   M5C 1J7

Toronto East Tax Services Office:
200 Town Centre Ct., Scarborough ON   M1P 4Y3

Toronto North Tax Services Office:
1000–5001 Yonge St., North York ON   M2N 6R9

Toronto West Tax Services Office:
77 City Centre Dr., P.O. Box 6000, Mississauga ON   L5A 4E9

Windsor Tax Services Office:
185 Ouellette Ave., Windsor ON   N9A 5S8

Manitoba

Brandon Tax Services Office:
1039 Princess Ave., Brandon MB   R7A 4J5

Winnipeg Tax Services Office:
325 Broadway Ave., Winnipeg MB   R3C 4T4

Saskatchewan

Regina Tax Services Office:
1955 Smith St., Regina SK   S4P 2N9

Saskatoon Tax Services Office:
340–3rd Ave. N, Saskatoon SK   S7K 0A8

Alberta

Calgary Tax Services Office:
220 4th Ave. SE, Calgary AB   T2G 0L1

Edmonton Tax Services Office:
10–9700 Jasper Ave., Edmonton AB   T5J 4C8

Lethbridge Tax Services Office:
300–704 4th Ave. S, P.O. Box 3009, Lethbridge AB   T1J 4A9

Red Deer Tax Services Office:
4996–49th Ave., Red Deer AB   T4N 6X2

British Columbia

Kelowna Tax Services Office:
200–1835 Gordon Dr., Kelowna BC   V1Y 3H5

Northern B.C. and Yukon Tax Services Office:
1441 7th Ave., P.O. Box 7500, Prince George BC   V2L 5N8

Southern Interior B.C. Tax Services Office:
277 Winnipeg St., Penticton BC   V2A 1N6

Surrey–Burnaby–Fraser Tax Services Office:
9755 King George Highway, Surrey BC   V3T 5E1

Vancouver Tax Services Office:
1166 West Pender St., Vancouver BC   V6E 3H8

Vancouver Island Tax Services Office:
747 Fort St., P.O. Box 3400, Victoria BC   V8W 3R1

Northwest Territories

Yellowknife Tax Services Office:
5020–48th Street, P.O. Box 220, Yellowknife NT   X1A 2N2

Yukon Territory

Whitehorse Tax Services Office:
120–300 Main St., Whitehorse YK   Y1A 2B5

C/QPP and OAS

If you need more information on the C/QPP or Old Age Security program, call Human Resources Development Canada at 1-800-277-9914 for service in English. Persons with hearing/speech impairments using TDD/TTY devices should call 1-800-255-4786. The lines are busiest at the beginning and end of each month, so if your business can wait it's best to call at other times. Have your social insurance number handy.

Recorded information via touch-tone telephone is available 24 hours a day, 7 days a week. You can listen to news bulletins, monthly payment issue dates, and basic information on Old Age Security, the Guaranteed Income Supplement, and the Canada/Quebec Pension Plan, and even notify them of change of address 24 hours a day, 7 days a week by following the recorded instructions.

Banks, trust companies, and credit unions

Canada's banking industry in general has done a good job of providing products and services for RRSP owners. Their goal, of course, is to lasso all of your financial services under their roof. If they can attract your RRSP business, they may be able to sell you a mortgage, grant you a personal loan, issue you a credit card, and so on.

The banks won't admit this in public, but they offer multiple levels of service according to the size of your assets and the number of services you use. In this sense, it's a little like the airline industry. If you have enough bucks, you go first class, with comfortable seats and free champagne. If you're on a broom peddler's budget, you're back in economy class, drinking vile coffee out of plastic cups.

In the RRSP business, first class requires a six-figure self-directed RRSP as well as a mortgage in good standing, and perhaps a valid bank charge card. These are usually enough to produce a cordial welcome from the bank's brokerage arm, providing you with one of a personal financial adviser/ investment counsellor/account executive/securities salesperson — four different descriptions for the same kind of service. Which, by the way, will cost you both an annual administration fee plus commissions on each transaction within your RRSP.

If you are both confident and clever enough to make your investment decisions entirely on your own, you don't require the financial adviser/counsellor/etc.'s services, and you don't need to pay commissions either. Every bank and trust company provides a discount brokerage whose staff members are licensed to provide you with information on investment alternatives and complete the buy or sell transactions (but they cannot provide hard advice).

You get what you pay for

RRSP services from banks, trust companies, and credit unions are limited essentially to handing you literature and helping you complete forms. Certain staff members are trained and licensed for this role. Not everyone in a bank or trust company branch is permitted to deal in these securities.

Don't ask one of these staff members for advice or views on any investment alternative. They are not trained, licensed, or permitted to provide them. But then again, you don't pay commissions or (usually) mutual fund loads, either.

Financial institutions are a good source of basic and generic information about RRSPs, RRIFs, and retirement planning generally, if you stick to the various brochures and newsletters. Branch staff are not fully qualified in many areas and are usually too distracted by other chores to provide detailed answers and guidance. As your interest and needs grow more sophisticated, you should consider either the brokerage arm of the financial institution or an independent financial consultant.

Chapter 26

Your Personal RRSP Planner

• •

▶ Determining how much you need to retire comfortably

▶ Enjoying the relief when you realize the amount is reachable

• •

*T*he chartered banks are pleased to help you plan for your retirement in various ways, such as providing methods of calculating the assets needed to meet your anticipated income. This generic version of a widely used formula assumes a 3-percent annual inflation rate and an 8-percent annual return on your investments over a 20-year retirement period. Those are fairly conservative measurements, but hey — we Canadians have always been a little cautious when it comes to planning for the future.

STEP 1: How much annual income will you need? (Assume 70 percent of your current income): $_____

STEP 2: From Column A in Table 26-1, find the number of years until you plan to retire, choose the corresponding **Growth Factor for Income** from Column B, and write it here: _____

STEP 3: Multiply #1 by #2: _____

STEP 4: What is the current value of your RRSP? _____

STEP 5: From Column C choose the **Growth Factor for Investments** that matches the number of years until you retire and write it here:

_____

STEP 6: Multiply #4 by #5 and write it here: _____

STEP 7: Subtract #6 from #3 and write it here: _____

The last figure you calculate is the amount you'll need to contribute each year until you retire.

Table 26-1	Growth Factors	
A	B	C
Years to Retirement	**Growth Factor for Income**	**Growth Factor for Investments**
35	0.1440	0.0572
30	0.1947	0.0610
25	0.2697	0.0667
20	0.3875	0.0756
15	1.5912	0.0910
10	1.0100	0.1226
5	2.2901	0.2194

Once you're done, you'll likely realize that putting away the amount in STEP 7 on a yearly basis isn't going to be the monolithic task you at first thought. When you follow the process back to the somewhat intimidating amount in STEP 1, you can nevertheless breathe a little easier, as you realize, "Yes, I can do this."

At least, that's my hunch.

Part VIII
The Part of Tens

In this part . . .

You are reminded there is no *one big step* you can take to maximize the money in your RRSP without entailing nerve-shattering risk, but there are several ways — all right, ten to be precise — to take advantage of various opportunities. They're included here. Balancing these ten things to do are ten things to avoid doing, plus ten things to discover about your financial adviser (without getting too personal, of course).

Chapter 27

Ten Ways to Maximize Your RRSP Growth

● ●

▶ Reaping the benefits of time, money, and tax deferments

▶ Remembering the golden rule: Diversification

▶ Making use of a spousal RRSP

▶ Charting your growth yourself: Self-directed RRSPs

▶ Embracing the foreign-content factor

▶ Adopting a long-term approach

● ●

*G*rowing your RRSP assets is not really that different from growing anything else. You can do wonders by following healthy guidelines and applying common sense.

These ten suggestions will find no arguments with financial experts anywhere. Follow them faithfully and you can rest assured that you're taking charge of your financial future.

Contribute as much as you can afford to your RRSP, as early as possible

No matter how many times you break it down or how many ways you express it, the combination of time, money, and tax deferments is the most effective and easiest tool to use in building your retirement assets. Table 27-1 shows an example that illustrates the impact of time and money. It assumes that three RRSP contributors — a 20-year-old, a 30-year-old, and a 40-year-old — make monthly contributions to their RRSPs until age 65, and each manages to earn an average of 10 percent annual growth over the years. The younger person makes only a $100-per-month contribution. The 30-year-old doubles that amount, and the 40-year-old puts $300 monthly into the plan. So who will be wealthier at 65?

Table 27-1	The Impact of Time and Money		
Starting Age	*Monthly Amount*	*Total Investment*	*Value at 65*
20	$100	$54,000	$901,545
30	$200	$84,000	$679,758
40	$300	$90,000	$369,997

In spite of contributing almost twice as much in total as the 20-year-old, the 40-year-old winds up with barely a third of the younger person's assets. The impact on the retirement income of each will be similar. Time marches on. Time also makes money.

Keep your RRSP investments well balanced

You can't sit forever on a unicycle, and you can't build a nest egg over time on just one, or even two or three, investments. You need the stability of bonds and GICs, the growth potential of equity investments, the liquidity of cash and T-bills, the professional management of mutual funds, the greater potential of foreign investments, and as much sensible diversification as you can obtain. Concentrating on one option at the expense of all the others isn't investing. It's gambling.

Contribute to a spousal RRSP if it's to your advantage

Unless both you and your partner contribute equal amounts over the years to separate RRSPs, one is likely to generate substantially more RRSP assets than the other. This will produce a variance in retirement income, and the individual with the higher income will pay substantially more income tax. A spousal RRSP provides the opportunity to generate two lower incomes rather than one low and one high income, attracting lower taxes as a result. It may also prevent ineligibility for Old Age Security (OAS) benefits if the income of one spouse exceeds the maximum allowable.

A spousal RRSP generates the same tax deduction for the contributor, but does not affect the permitted contribution limit. Contributors should also be aware of withdrawal rules of spousal RRSPs, especially the one relating to tax implications if funds are withdrawn within three years of the contribution. Under these conditions the contributor, not the planholder, is deemed to have withdrawn the funds, and the amount will be added to his or her taxable income for the year.

Although the assets of a spousal RRSP belong to the planholder, if the relationship ends they are included in mutual asset calculations in almost every case. Both partners pool RRSP assets accumulated during the marriage and divide them equally.

Bottom line: Spousal RRSPs make sense because they ultimately reduce income-tax levels.

Take charge of your future with a self-directed RRSP

You can put your retirement assets on cruise control and assume they're heading in the right direction. Or you can take charge yourself with a self-directed RRSP, choosing the route and speed that suits you best.

A self-directed plan places certain responsibilities in your hands, but if you're capable of balancing your own chequing account each month, you can manage your RRSP with the same skills. Once the value of your RRSP hits $50,000, you should convert it to a self-directed plan. At its most basic, you simply need to do the following:

✔ Watch and correct the balance between growth and security, usually consisting of equity-based mutual funds and bonds/GICs

✔ Maximize foreign content where necessary

✔ Confirm contributions and transactions as reported on your RRSP account statement

✔ Measure growth from individual investments and make changes where necessary, discarding under-performers and expanding your investment in exceptional performers

✔ Make sure that you continue to follow your strategy, especially where your risk tolerance is concerned

Maximize your foreign content

You cannot achieve the maximum possible growth in your RRSP by keeping every penny of your assets in Canada. Foreign diversification is as vital to your RRSP as making regular contributions. At the very least, try to keep 30 percent of your assets in foreign investments, preferably widely diversified equities. Also, look for Canadian equity funds that maintain the maximum foreign content in *their* portfolios — which, in combination with your own foreign content, will bump the total as high as 50-percent-plus of your total assets. Finally, if your risk tolerance can take it, consider foreign indexed funds and notes, which qualify for RRSP content while providing exposure to markets outside Canada.

And don't feel the slightest bit unpatriotic for making these investments outside Canada or depriving the economy of your investments; there is no shortage of investment capital in Canada. Besides, charity begins at home. Your home.

Avoid having too many RRSPs and too many different funds

There's no limit to the number of RRSPs you can have, but there's not much benefit in having more than you need, either. Consolidating your assets into one RRSP makes them easier to manage and will reduce administration fees in self-directed plans as well.

You may be tempted to acquire units in several different mutual funds, but this rarely produces any benefits worth either the money or the effort. Two different mutual funds investing in Canadian equities according to identical philosophies, for example, provide little or no diversification. In reality, you probably need no more than three domestic equity funds, two foreign funds, and one money market fund, plus appropriate bonds or GICs.

Arrange to make regular monthly contributions via pre-authorized chequing

Besides making your contributions pain-free, 12 equal payments avoid the last-minute rush to beat the end-of-February RRSP deadline. If using your contributions to purchase mutual-fund units, you benefit from dollar-cost averaging; in turbulent or volatile markets, you'll purchase more units at a lower price and fewer units at a higher price, resulting in a lower average cost for each unit.

Call on professional advice but make your own decisions

Locate a qualified financial adviser you trust and who understands your investment goals. (Reject anyone whose advice is at odds with your instincts, who doesn't appear to listen to your concerns, or who seeks too much control over your investment decisions.)

If you're choosing an independent adviser, make it someone who charges a flat fee rather than working on a commission basis; the advice is likely to be more objective.

A good investment counsellor or financial adviser functions somewhat like a lawyer in a legal situation. The lawyer can advise you to plead either guilty or not guilty, but in the end the decision is yours to make. When making investment decisions in your RRSP, ask for all the facts and listen carefully to the adviser's suggestion before acting. Be wary of any adviser who bad-mouths or refuses to discuss a no-load mutual fund, for example, or who resents your efforts to obtain the best deal possible on a bond purchase or sale. One more time: *It's your money, doggone it!*

Keep your eye on the horizon

Unless you are exceptionally lucky, none of your investments will grow steadily at an above-average rate. Some will be up while others are down, and at times all will be up (*"Hooray!"*) or down (*"Gack!"*) together. These events can create waves of exhilaration or depression if you let them. Don't let them. If your strategy is sound, your investments are of good quality, and your investment horizon — the date when you stop paying your RRSP and your RRSP begins paying *you* — remains distant, you're probably doing fine. As the horizon draws closer, modify your strategy to lessen the impact of market changes.

Virtually every experienced investment counsellor or financial adviser agrees that more money is lost than earned by reacting to short-term market changes. In other words, do your homework up front, and the gyrations will eventually take care of themselves.

Remember that borrowing to save can really make sense

Among the easiest low-cost loans to obtain are those permitting you to make your basic RRSP contribution, top up an earlier contribution in that year, or use available contribution room. Interest rates for these loans tend to be among the lowest offered by banks, trust companies, and credit unions. You'll probably earn a tax refund that can be applied to the RRSP loan, and while the interest charged on your loan declines with the loan balance, the interest you earn on your RRSP keeps growing right up to your retirement date.

Best strategy: Try to pay the RRSP loan off in one year, if you can do it without crippling your cash flow.

Chapter 28

Ten Mistakes to Avoid at All Costs

• •

▶ Letting a little volatility get to you

▶ Dipping into your RRSP for a mid-winter getaway (or any other splurge)

▶ Over-contributing to your RRSP

▶ Eliminating the possibility of an RRSP loan

• •

*I*f Canada had a smugness index — a barometer measuring our collective level of feeling good about ourselves individually — it would probably peak on March 1 of every year. That's when a couple of million Canadians pat themselves on the back for making a contribution to their RRSP plan. Hey, there's money in the bank, Canada Customs and Revenue Agency owes me a tax refund, and spring is somewhere just beyond the hockey rink. Is this a great time of the year or what?

Well, being smug won't necessarily guarantee you a wealthy retirement. And if you make too many of these mistakes, you won't be feeling all that smug for long either.

Waiting until the last minute to make your RRSP contribution

This is the most common RRSP mistake Canadians make. Being lost among the RRSP crowds at the end of February is not the best environment in which to consider your options and make a wise investment decision. What's more, you have already lost out on the almost 14 months of compound interest you could have had if you'd made the same contribution in January of the previous year — and still qualified for a refund on the same income-tax return. Just to add insult to investment injury, you lose the advantages of dollar-cost averaging.

Thinking only of your tax refund instead of your RRSP growth

An RRSP is like a very long meal where dessert is served first. Dessert in this case is your income-tax refund. The main course is still several years down the road. It's the main course, with all its nutrition and goodness, that will sustain you, not the dessert.

Tax-free compound interest within your RRSP investment is quite simply the biggest monetary gift the federal government will ever give you. Take it, and make the most of it by paying attention to your RRSP investments. Eventually you'll be savouring the main course long after the pie and ice cream of a tax refund have been forgotten.

Choosing inappropriate investments

Your RRSP and your retirement needs are unique, but this doesn't mean your investment philosophy must be as offbeat and original as a Picasso portrait. Traditional investing philosophy follows a balance between security and risk, and this is neither the time nor the place to buck tradition. If you're too conservative, you'll be like the prodigal son who buried his talents, emerging with little more than he started with. If you go looking for excessive levels of growth with investments that are too risky, you're drifting out of investing and into gambling, which is not the point of the exercise.

Guidelines such as matching your secure deposits to your age and balancing growth and value equities may sound like clichés, but as a very wise man once said, "A cliché is a cliché because it is true."

Panicking at market volatility

It will snow in Edmonton in January. There will be lobster dinners in P.E.I. in June. And investment markets will experience various levels of volatility, when prices move up and down as though being jerked by some invisible puppeteer. All of these events are predictable. None should send you into either whirlwinds of panic or depths of depression.

In early 2000, many Canadians followed the herd, and their financial advisers' advice, and invested some of their RRSP assets in tech stocks and Internet-based companies. A year later, these investments had shrunk by half. Was this fun, boys and girls? Is it a joy to watch your shiny new bicycle being flattened by a Mack truck?

Unlike crushed bicycles, quality investments tend to recover over time. Technology continues to advance and growth stocks belong in the RRSP portfolio of anybody who is more than ten years from retirement. Some Canadians, so disgusted with the drop in growth-stock values, sold out at half price and took their losses. This, in the investment trade, is called "crystallizing" — which means, like the flattened bicycle, you'll never ride it again.

RRSP investing demands long-term thinking, planning at least five years ahead. Do you recall what the stock markets were doing five years ago today? Precisely. Do your homework. Set a strategy. Choose quality over trendiness. And stay cool.

Withdrawing money from your RRSP

Oh, the temptation of it all. There you are, eating hamburger on a cold day in January while your friends are slurping margaritas in Mexico. Why not pull a couple of grand from that fat RRSP balance you've accumulated and join them? Don't you dare.

Your RRSP assets are not and should never be a source of mad money. Withdraw funds from your RRSP and the CCRA immediately holds back at least 10 percent in taxes, and probably dings you for even more when you file your income-tax return.

Retirement funds should be a very last resort for cash. You will almost certainly be further ahead borrowing money than withdrawing cash from your plan. In fact, the interest you pay on the loan will likely not be as high as the income tax payable on your withdrawals and the lost compound interest.

Making excessive RRSP contributions

This is almost always the result of miscalculations, but whatever the cause, the CCRA slaps a penalty of 1 percent per month on all contributions beyond your RRSP limit. So one more time:

You are entitled to contribute up to 18 percent of earned income, less any pension adjustment, to a maximum of $13,500 per person, with a one-time over-contribution of $2,000.

Ignoring the benefits of an RRSP loan

It's not a habit you should get into, but it can make sense to borrow money either for your annual RRSP contribution or to make up available contribution room created by contributing less than the amount you were entitled to in past years.

If you maintain a good relationship with your bank, trust company, or credit union, and especially if the same financial institution or one of its divisions administers your RRSP, you can expect the most favourable interest rate available.

Failing to file an income-tax return while still a student

This comes too late for most of us, but it's a lesson you can pass on to your kids. Students who earn perhaps $5,000 each year may not bother to file an income tax return because their basic personal exemption exceeds their earned income. Why file an income-tax return if there is no tax either payable or refundable?

This is why: By filing a tax return, the student establishes RRSP contribution room that can be used in the future if he or she chooses. The $5,000 annual income creates a potential $900 RRSP contribution to be used any time in later life.

Believing you can do it all on your own

You don't need financial advice to successfully manage an RRSP, and you don't need to invest in an equity-based mutual fund to enjoy potential growth from the stock market. But ignoring either is like driving across the country without a map.

Along with experience and access to information, financial advisers bring the value of objectivity to your RRSP plan. If their skills are good, their fees are fair, and the chemistry between you is positive, the benefits of a financial adviser can be the single most powerful influence on your RRSP's growth. As for choosing stocks on your own instead of relying on a well-managed mutual fund investing in equities: Don't.

Misunderstanding the rules of risk and reward

Risk exists everywhere in life, and your RRSP is no exception. Slap every cent in long-term GICs and you risk losing the value of your investment to inflation. Slide too much of your money into this year's hot new exotic mutual fund, and you may be staring at negative returns (translation: you have lost money) for years to come.

There is no reward without risk, and there is no such thing as a sure thing. Accept these realities, make the most of them, and find a way to sleep well at night.

Chapter 29

Ten Things to Know about Your Financial Adviser

● ●

▶ Knowing how he or she gets paid

▶ Knowing how qualified he or she is to handle your money

▶ Knowing someone else at the firm you can talk to

● ●

*I*n the long run, you are your own best financial adviser. No one knows or understands your goals, fears, and abilities better than you. As long as you're managing a self-directed RRSP or RRIF of reasonable size — between, perhaps, $50,000 and $500,000 in total assets — the more hands-on approach you take, the better.

But you have a life to lead beyond your investments, and it probably doesn't involve mastering market statistics, following developments in mutual funds, or tracking bond prices. Establishing a relationship with someone who has both access to, and an understanding of, these types of data will make management of your retirement funds easier and more profitable.

Let's call anyone capable and licensed to actively assist in managing your RRSP/RRIF a *financial adviser* and assume that his or her primary duties are to provide you with professional guidance and counsel in establishing your investment strategy and following it efficiently to reach your goals. They may or may not execute trades — that is, purchase and sell bonds, mutual funds, and other investments — on your behalf. They may be either independent advisers or associated with an investment firm such as Bank of Montreal's Nesbitt Burns, Royal Bank's RBC Dominion Securities, CIBC's Wood Gundy, TD Bank's Evergreen, Scotiabank's ScotiaMcLeod, or an unaffiliated firm such as Merrill Lynch Canada.

That's who they are. Here's what to know about them before awarding them your business.

Is he or she paid by commission, by salary, or by direct fees from you?

The best answer is direct fees, assuming the fees themselves are reasonable. Their advice will be objective, because whether you buy and sell constantly or simply do nothing has no impact on their remuneration. Investment-firm representatives are usually paid through a combination of salary and commissions earned from buying and selling investments for you. You still pay a management fee to the firm administering your RRSP, no matter who provides the advice.

I wish I could say that every commissioned financial adviser makes his or her investment recommendations according to what is best for you, as opposed to the commissions they will make for the adviser.

But I can't.

What is his or her hourly rate, if on a fee basis?

Independent financial advisers function like lawyers and accountants, charging an hourly fee that reflects their status and reputation as well as the relative affluence of their clients. Be suspicious of any hourly fees below $50 and above $200. If you can obtain a couple of hours per year of specific financial advice at $100 to $150 per hour and see the results in good returns, it's a reasonable investment to make.

What formal qualifications does he or she have as a financial adviser?

Generally speaking, the more experience and education your adviser has, the better. Degrees such as an MBA (Master of Business Administration) and CFA (Chartered Financial Analyst) carry a good deal of weight, and it's best to avoid someone who shows up at your door still wearing their graduation cap and gown.

But financial advisers deal as much with people as they do with markets and figures. If a financial adviser you are considering cannot explain things in plain language or you simply don't connect in terms of trust and confidence, no number of degrees after his or her name will be sufficient.

How much effort does he or she put into discovering things about you?

No, not about your no-good brother-in-law or that time you danced naked on a bar table in Antigonish. An adviser should ask about your financial situation, your investment goals, your familiarity with investment options, your comfort with various levels of risk, and your realistic expectations. If they're not interested in these concerns, you shouldn't be interested in giving them your business.

Can you obtain references from clients with needs and assets similar to your own?

Don't avoid this one, but don't swallow it whole, either. By all means ask for references and contact at least one of the people whose names are provided. But recognize that no one, including yourself, will refer a potential client to someone who was not satisfied with past service or performance.

Expect to hear good things about the adviser from any references he or she provides. Then go beyond that and ask about style, attitude, and availability, and see if these meet your expectations.

Will he or she provide a brief opinion of your current RRSP plan components?

This isn't a way of obtaining free financial advice on a speculative basis, but a test of the adviser's ability to explain concepts and ideas in terms you can easily grasp. Count on him or her to find some area of improvement (otherwise, your portfolio is ideal and you don't need any assistance) while congratulating you on one aspect or another (to avoid being too critical of your past decisions).

Listen carefully not just to the opinions of the adviser but also to how well they are being explained. Can you grasp the ideas? Is the adviser talking neither up nor down to you, but using language you can understand without reaching for a dictionary? If not, don't expect things to become more comprehensible when you're a client.

If the financial adviser will be handling trades, has he or she explained the "Know Your Client" form?

Also known as a KYC, a Know Your Client form must be completed by you and anyone handling securities trades on your behalf. It acknowledges both your broad investment strategies and the level of your investment sophistication. If you are an unsophisticated investor with a five-year investment horizon, for example, you should clearly not be investing in specialty funds or other complex, high-risk areas. Both you and your adviser sign the KYC form. You retain a copy, and another is filed with the compliance officer of the investment firm employing your adviser.

This document offers some degree of protection against fraudulent or inappropriate activity by your adviser. You should have it carefully explained to you and discuss its implications before signing. And never, ever sign a blank form, with the promise that the broker will "fill in all the details later."

Who else can you call on at the adviser's firm, if necessary?

Play this one by ear. You have a right to be concerned about a "lone wolf" adviser, especially if he or she proposes doing trades on your behalf. The higher the reputation and assets of a firm assisting you with financial decisions, the less likely you will lose money due to embezzlement, fraud, or mismanagement of your account. It's wise, for example, to ask the name of the adviser's assistant and superior, in case you are unable to reach the individual handling your account, or if some difficulty is not resolved to your satisfaction.

What can you tell from his or her lifestyle?

This is your call, and it's probably a gut response. Successful financial advisers are well paid and deserve to be. But if their emphasis seems to be on creating a display of ostentatious wealth, should your alarm bells go off.

When a financial swindle or embezzlement occurs involving a financial adviser or investment counsellor dealing with retirement savings, you will often discover that the accused lived a lavish lifestyle. Fleets of expensive cars, several large homes, a fashionable and expensive wardrobe, and boats and other playthings all create an aura of wealth and success among these people.

Instead of raising concerns, such lavish splendour creates enthusiasm among many clients. "If he/she can become so rich from their investment skills, maybe I can too!" is the usual refrain. Later, of course, the bilked clientele discovers that *their* hard-earned bucks were paying for all the toys and glamour.

The fact that your financial adviser drives a Mercedes and dresses like a window mannequin in Holt Renfrew shouldn't make you suspicious. Just don't let yourself be overly impressed by an expensive lifestyle. And if these toys and flamboyance represent a major portion of the adviser's values, how much is left over for you?

How often will you receive statements of your account?

If dealing with an investment firm appointing a counsellor or adviser to your account, check on the frequency of account statements. Some are issued monthly, others quarterly. For most people, quarterly is sufficient. But if your RRSP is substantial — with assets of $250,000 or more — you may want to see monthly statements.

Also, ask to look at a sample statement. Each firm follows its own design, and some are more understandable than others. If you can't easily follow changes in your RRSP as they occur, how much value is the statement to you?

Glossary

Accrued interest: Interest earned but not received.

Annual report: A financial report sent yearly to the shareholders of a publicly held firm. Figures in the report provide information on sales, expenses, assets, liabilities, and profits, and are confirmed by independent auditors.

Annuitant: Someone who purchases an annuity and receives payments from it.

Annuity: A contract that guarantees a series of payments in exchange for a lump-sum investment.

Asset value: The current worth of all the assets in an investment portfolio. This value will fluctuate to some degree day by day.

Assets: What a firm or individual owns.

Back-end load: A sales charge levied when mutual fund units are redeemed. It is measured as a percentage either of the original investment or of the redeemed value, and usually declines for each year the units are held. Mutual funds with back-end loads are sometimes called *back-load funds*.

Balanced fund: A mutual fund that uses an investment policy of "balancing" its portfolio between bonds and shares. The proportion of each varies according to the fund's investment strategy.

Bear market: A financial market that declines over a long period of time. A bear market in stocks is usually brought on by the anticipation of declining economic activity, and a bear market in bonds is caused by rising interest rates.

Bellwether index: The performance of a group of investments selected to identify trends in a specific industry or market area before their impact is felt by a benchmark index. The NASDAQ 100, for example, tracks leading technical stocks and serves as a bellwether for that industry sector.

Benchmark index: The performance of a group of investments whose performance represents a broad spectrum of securities. The TSE 300 and the S&P 500 are considered benchmark indices.

Blue-chip: A descriptive term used to identify high-grade equity securities.

Bond: A long-term debt, secured by property and including a schedule for regular interest payments at a fixed amount of interest. The principal amount is to be paid on a specified maturity date.

Bond fund: A mutual fund whose portfolio consists primarily of bonds.

Book value: The value of net assets belonging to an individual or corporation. For individuals, book value is considered the original purchase price or the most recent evaluation price.

Broker: An agent who handles orders to buy and sell securities, commodities, or other property.

Bull market: A financial market whose prices continue to rise for an extended period of time. Bull markets may last from a few months to several years, and are characterized by high trading volume.

Canada/Quebec Pension Plan (C/QPP): Either a government-managed retirement income program or an authorized scam, depending on your point of view. The C/QPP collects money through payroll deductions from Canadians during their working years, and pays them a monthly income from age 60 on. Many doubt that enough funds will be available in the future to meet the demands of a population with more geezers than workers.

Canada Savings Bond (CSB): Bonds issued each year by the federal government of Canada. They can be cashed at any time for their full face value.

Capital: Money or property used in a business. It also applies to cash in reserve, savings, or other property of value.

Capital gain/loss: The difference between the price you pay for an investment when you purchase it and the price you receive when you sell it. If you buy low and sell high, you make a *capital gain*, which will be taxed more gently than other ways of making money. Buy high and sell low, and you achieve a *capital loss*, which can be used to reduce your income tax.

Capitalization: The total value of all securities issued by a company.

Collateral: Assets that can be pledged as security against a loan. Your pledged collateral can be seized to settle an unpaid debt. Using your RRSP as collateral is difficult, risky, ill-advised, and usually just plain dumb.

Clone fund: Fancy footwork used by mutual fund managers to exceed the 30-percent foreign investment limit. Clone funds keep 70 percent of their assets in Canadian bonds, using the remaining 30 percent to trade in derivatives. The *derivatives* (see below) are assembled in the same proportion as a "parent" mutual fund comprising 100-percent foreign investments. In an ideal situation, the clone fund will match the performance of the parent fund whose investments it mirrors.

Closed-end fund: A mutual fund with a fixed number of units that are not redeemable but are bought and sold on stock exchanges or "over the counter."

Common stock: A security representing ownership of a corporation's assets and normally including voting rights at shareholders' meetings.

Compounding: The process of earning income on income previously earned.

Corporation: A legal business entity created under federal or provincial statutes, which operates as a separate entity from its owners. Thus, shareholders have no legal liability for its debts.

Coupon rate: The annual interest rate of a bond.

Custodian: A financial institution, usually a bank or trust company, contracted to hold a mutual fund's securities and cash in safekeeping.

Day trading: The practice of purchasing securities such as stocks, bonds, and derivatives in order to sell them for a profit within a short period of time — often that same day.

Debenture: A bond not secured by property but supported by the general credit of the issuing corporation.

Debt: An obligation to repay a sum of principal plus interest. In corporate terms, this often refers to bonds or similar securities.

Deferred profit-sharing plan (DPSP): A plan that allows an employer to set aside a portion of company profits for the future benefit of employees.

Defined benefit pension plan: A pension plan that guarantees a fixed amount of retirement income for participating employees, based on earnings level and years of employment.

Defined contribution pension plan: A pension plan that provides retirement benefits according to the performance of investments made with contributions to the plan.

Deposit insurance: Protection of certain types of assets (including cash, GICs, and so on) against loss. Bank and trust company deposits are covered by the Canada Deposit Insurance Corporation (CDIC) to a maximum of $60,000 per account. Mutual funds are not covered by deposit insurance.

Derivatives: Investments that derive their value from underlying assets such as currencies, treasury bills, and bonds, or that are linked to indices such as a stock market index. Derivatives can be used to speculate on market movements or to protect investments against major swings in market prices.

Discretionary power: The granting to a financial adviser or broker of the right to trade a client's investments without prior approval or acknowledgement from the client. This is not a wise move under almost any circumstance — sort of like putting yourself at the mercy of a pit viper.

Distributions: Payments to investors of a mutual fund from income or profit realized from the fund's investments and transactions.

Diversification: Investment in a number of different securities to reduce risk. Diversification may be among types of securities, companies, industries, or geographic locations.

Dividend: A payment to shareholders, designated by a company's board of directors. Preferred shareholders generally receive a fixed amount. Dividends to holders of common shares vary with the fortunes of the company and the amount of cash on hand. Dividends may be omitted if business is poor or if the directors choose to withhold earnings for investing in plants or equipment.

Dividend fund: A mutual fund investing in common shares of senior Canadian corporations with a history of regular dividend payments.

Dollar-cost averaging: An investment strategy using equal amounts of money to purchase securities at regular intervals. Dollar-cost averaging can reduce average share cost by acquiring more shares in periods of lower securities prices and fewer shares in periods of higher prices.

Earned income: For tax purposes, it is considered money made by an individual from employment, plus some taxable benefits.

Equity: The net worth of a company, representing the ownership by shareholders (both common and preferred) of a company. Shares are often known as *equities*.

Equity fund: A mutual fund whose portfolio consists primarily of common stocks.

Exchange-traded fund (ETF): A portfolio of stocks designed to track one specific index. ETFs can be bought and sold exactly like stock in an individual company. Some ETFs allow you to invest by industry sector, size, region, or investment style. A commission is charged whenever an ETF is bought or sold. While an ETF will distribute any dividends paid by companies in which it is invested, these cannot automatically be reinvested into the ETF.

Face value: The principal amount, or value at maturity, of a debt obligation such as a bond or debenture. Also known as the par value or denomination.

Fixed assets: Land, buildings, and other assets that are not easily liquidable.

Fixed-income investments: Investments that generate income that does not vary over the life of the investment.

Front-end load: A sales charge levied at the time of purchase of mutual fund units. Mutual funds with front-end loads are sometimes called *front-load funds*.

Global mutual fund: A mutual fund that invests in several countries, including its home nation.

Growth stocks: Shares of companies with earnings that are expected to increase over time.

Guaranteed investment certificate (GIC): A deposit instrument sold by banks, trust companies, and other financial institutions that pays a predetermined rate of interest

for a specified term. Some GICs may link the interest paid to a market index such as the TSE 300, but with restrictions. See *Market participation rate*.

In kind: A form of RRSP contribution, other than cash. If you own an eligible bond, shares in a Canadian corporation, or units in a qualifying mutual fund, and hold these securities outside your RRSP, they can be placed within your RRSP instead of cash. Their market value on the day you transfer them to your plan must not exceed your current contribution limit. Thus, $5,000 in shares of Royal Bank, for example, can be transferred to your RRSP in place of a $5,000 cash contribution.

Income fund: A mutual fund investing primarily in fixed-income securities such as bonds, mortgages, and preferred shares to produce income while preserving capital.

Index: In investment circles, the statistical tracking of a particular group of securities such as stocks and bonds. The TSE 300 index, for example, tracks the value of 300 companies chosen from those listed on the Toronto Stock Exchange as being representative of the market as a whole. The index value is set at 100 at a given point in time and tracked up or down from there.

Index fund: A mutual fund that matches its portfolio to a specific financial market index to duplicate the general performance of the market in which it invests.

Inflation: A condition of widely based and steadily increasing prices.

International fund: A mutual fund investing in securities from a number of countries, often with the exception of its home nation.

Investment fund: Generally interchangeable with "mutual fund."

Leverage: The financial advantage of controlling a property or asset of greater value than the cash invested.

Life annuity: Payments are guaranteed for the life of the annuitant.

Life income fund (LIF): The RRIF version of a locked-in retirement account (LIRA). A LIF is more restrictive than a RRIF; maximum withdrawal limits are set, and you must use any money remaining in your LIF by age 80 to purchase an annuity.

Limited partnership (LP): Business agreements that enable partners to grow wealthy by using other people's money. They are unsuitable for RRSPs.

Liquidity: The ease with which an investment may be converted to cash at a reasonable price.

Load: Commissions charged to holders of mutual fund units.

Locked-in retirement account (LIRA): A company pension that prevents you from withdrawing any funds until you reach age 65.

Locked-in retirement income fund (L-RIF): An exception to the demand that you must purchase an annuity at age 80, available to residents of Alberta, Manitoba, Saskatchewan, and Ontario.

Management expense ratio (MER): The total cost of operating a mutual fund expressed as a percentage of average total assets.

Management fee: The amount paid to the investment company's adviser or manager for supervising its portfolio and administering its operations.

Marginal tax rate: The rate of tax applied against the last dollar of taxable income.

Market correction: Broker-speak to describe a sudden and usually drastic drop in stock market prices, attributed to a sudden epiphany on the part of investors that stocks were overpriced.

Market index: A vehicle used to measure trends in securities markets. The most popular in Canada is the Toronto Stock Exchange 300 Composite Index (TSE 300).

Market participation rate (MPR): A predetermined limit applied to index-linked GICs. An MPR of 85 percent, for example, means the GIC holder benefits from only 85 percent of the index growth when calculating the interest to be paid.

Maturity: The date a loan or bond or debenture must be redeemed or paid off.

Money market: Where short-term debt obligations such as T-bills, commercial paper, and bankers' acceptances are bought and sold.

Money market fund: A mutual fund investing in T-bills and other low-risk, short-term debt instruments.

Mortgage fund: A mutual fund that invests in mortgages. Portfolios usually consist of first mortgages on Canadian residential property, plus some commercial mortgages.

Mutual fund: An investment operation that pools money from shareholders or unitholders to invest in various securities. The units or shares are redeemable by the fund on demand by the investor, and their value is determined by the current price of the fund's underlying assets.

Net asset value: The value of all the holdings of a mutual fund, less the fund's liabilities.

Net asset value per share: The assets of a mutual fund (less liabilities) divided by the number of shares or units outstanding. Commonly abbreviated to NAVPS.

No-load fund: A mutual fund that does not charge a fee for buying or selling its shares.

Old Age Security (OAS): A pittance (just over $400 per month) paid to everyone over age 65 who failed to invest wisely for their retirement. Those who, through perspicacity and determination during their working years, manage to generate an annual income of $54,000 or more will watch their OAS benefits being clawed back by Ottawa.

Open-end fund: A mutual fund that continuously issues and redeems units, so the number of units outstanding varies from day to day.

Option: The right to buy or sell a specific quantity of a security at a fixed price within a determined period of time.

Over-the-counter market: A market for securities that are not listed on stock exchanges.

Pension adjustment: The amount by which the RRSP contribution limit is reduced based on the benefits earned from the employee's pension plan or deferred profit-sharing plan.

Pension plan: An arrangement in which an employer and its employees contribute to a fund to provide the employee with a lifetime income after retirement.

Portfolio: All the securities owned by an investment company or individual.

Preferred share: Shares of a corporation, with preferred claim on assets in case of liquidation and that receive a specified annual dividend.

Premium: The amount by which a bond's selling price exceeds its face value.

Price/earnings ratio: The market price of a common share divided by its earnings per share over a 12-month period.

Prospectus: A document issued by a corporation offering a new issue of securities to the public.

Real estate fund: A mutual fund investing primarily in residential and/or commercial real estate to produce income and capital gains.

Redemption: The right of a shareholder to sell, at any time, some or all of his or her shares back to the investment fund for cash.

Registered Education Savings Plan (RESP): A tax-deferral plan for contributors, usually parents or grandparents, to accumulate assets to pay for a beneficiary's post-secondary education.

Registered Retirement Income Fund (RRIF): An option available for RRSP owners to provide a stream of income at retirement. Growth of assets inside the RRIF remain tax-sheltered until withdrawn.

Registered Retirement Savings Plan (RRSP): A tax-deferred retirement plan that allows individuals under age 69 to set aside sums of money within certain limits. Contributions are deductible from taxable income and can grow on a tax-free basis.

Risk: The measurable possibility of losing or not gaining value. Risk is differentiated from uncertainty, which is not measurable.

Risk threshold: The degree of risk that prevents you from sleeping soundly at night in fear of spending your retired years living off roadkill.

Sector fund: See *specialty fund*.

Securities Act: Provincial legislation regulating the underwriting, distribution, and sale of securities.

Share: A document signifying part owner-ship in a company. The terms *share* and *stock* are often used interchangeably.

Shareholders' equity: The amount of a corporation's assets belonging to its common and preferred shareholders.

Simplified prospectus: An abbreviated prospectus distributed to potential pur-chasers of units or shares in mutual funds.

Small-cap fund: A mutual fund investing in companies whose *capitalization* is less than $500 million. These companies tend to be more flexible and often demonstrate greater growth potential than larger firms. Sometimes they are neither, which makes small-cap funds rather volatile.

Socially responsible fund (SRF): A mutual fund that restricts its investments to companies behaving within the fund manager's criteria. These often relate to tobacco or alcohol production, nuclear generation, weapons, armaments, and other military paraphernalia; environmental policies, and so on. These funds are designed to generate warm and fuzzy feelings in the hearts of their unitholders (which they do); and higher-than-average returns (which they don't necessarily do).

Specialty fund: A mutual fund concentrating its investments on a specific industry, economic sector, or geographical area. Also known as a *sector fund*.

Strip bonds: Portions of a bond from which the coupons have been stripped and sold individually as coupons (the interest paid on certain dates) or the residual (the bond's original face value).

Term insurance: Life insurance that covers the policyholder for a specific period of time.

Trailer fee: An annual service commission paid by mutual fund companies to sales representatives according to the value of all units sold by the representatives to his or her clients. These fees generally range between 0.25 percent and 1 percent of customers' assets and are paid out of the fund's management expenses.

Transfer fee: The price charged to transfer mutual fund assets to another fund.

Treasury bill (T-bill): Short-term government debt. Treasury bills bear no interest, but are sold at a discount; the difference between the discount price and the cash value represents the return earned by the investor.

Universal life insurance: A life insurance term policy renewed each year and containing both insurance coverage and an investment component. Sometimes called *whole-life insurance*.

Vesting: In pension terms, the right of an employee to all or part of the employer's contributions, in the form of cash or as a deferred pension.

Volatility: A measure of price variation applied to investments. A volatile mutual fund will vary widely in its average annual returns, achieving high returns one year and substantial losses the next. A volatile stock market index will swing back and forth, showing an increase today and a decrease tomorrow. Volatile mutual funds are to be avoided or minimized as you approach retirement, when preservation of capital becomes important.

Yield: The annual rate of return earned on investments, usually expressed as a percentage of the market price of the security.

Index

• A •

A-rated bonds, 120
AA-rated bonds, 120
AAA-rated bonds, 120
academic degrees, financial
 advisers, 79, 336
account executives, self-
 directed RRSPs, 67
account summary statement,
 progress measurement
 tool, 86, 246
account valuation statement,
 progress measurement
 tool, 87
accreditation, financial
 advisers, 79
active fund management,
 bonds, 198. *See also*
 aggressive fund
 management
active trading recommendation, financial adviser
 dismissal, 262
actively managed funds, 187
Acuity Pooled Canadian Equity
 Fund, 184, 185
administration fees
 closing mutual fund, 151
 financial adviser types, 316
 mutual fund distribution, 150
 mutual fund types, 150–151
 self-directed RRSP issues,
 68–69, 77
 transferring funds, 70
after-tax dollar, 15, 17, 82
age
 and annuity payment, 283,
 284–286
 and LIFs, 292
 and minimum withdrawals,
 RRIF, 290, 291
 and C/QPP, 54, 299–300
 and diversification, 133
 =GIC percent guidelines, 64
 investment/goal matching,
 94–96, 297
 non-participation excuse
 debunked, 25
 retirement, 17, 18, 45, 280
 and risk threshold, 103, 157,
 189, 233, 297

 and RRIF returns, 294
 RRSP contribution variable, 45
AGF America Growth Class
 Fund, 192, 193, 224
AGF Canadian Bond Fund, 234
AGF Canadian Stock Fund, 234
AGF Fund family, 135, 234
AGF Dividend Fund, 295
AGF International Value Fund,
 140
AGF Management Limited, 135,
 148, 149
AGF Global Bond Fund, 225
aggressive fund management,
 198, 296
aggressive mix, 141
AIC American Advantage Fund,
 189
AIC Diversified Canada Fund,
 180, 224
AIC Value Fund (U.S.), 224
AIM Canadian First Class Fund,
 184, 185
AIM Global Bond Fund, 225
AIM Global Health Sciences
 Fund, 225
AIM Global Theme Class Fund,
 182, 183
AIM/Trimark Fund, 114, 135,
 148, 149, 224, 261
AIM/Trimark Select Canadian
 Growth Fund, 156, 168, 221
AIM/Trimark Select Canadian
 Fund, 167, 168
Alberta
 CCRA, 314–315
 vested pension plans, 56
Altamira Bond Fund, 224
Altamira Capital Growth Fund,
 167, 168
Altamira Equity Fund, 179
Altamira Funds, 178, 260, 261
Altamira Investment, 149
alternative minimum tax
 (AMT), 33
Amazon.com, 175
Anderson Exploration Ltd., 163
annuities
 beneficiary uses RRSP to
 purchase, 275
 converting RRSP to, 50,
 282–287

 described, 282
 drawbacks, 94, 287
 indexed, 287
 interest rates, payment
 factor, 284
 and LIFs, 292
 payment ranges, 283–295
 payment size factors, 283
 RRIFs versus, 290
 when to use for retirement
 income, 286–287
antiques, non-qualifying
 investment, 21, 93
artwork, non-qualifying investment, 93
Asia-Pacific region, invest
 ments in, 140, 143,
 173, 189
asset allocation funds, 208, 210
asset-size diversification, 134
assets
 managed, 98
 mutual fund companies,
 149–150
 percentage of, fee type, 81
 pledged, 49–50
Atlas, 180
Australia, traditional market,
 214
average, 236
average annual return, 104, 105

• B •

Baby Boomers, 238, 257, 302
back-end load funds, 147–148
back-end load penalty, 148,
 234, 251
balance, maintaining in
 investments, 65, 324
balanced diet strategy, 64–65
balanced funds, 139. *See also*
 income balanced funds;
 names of specific funds
balanced mutual funds
 benefits of, 208, 209
 described, 207–208
 drawbacks, 209
 exceptional, 210
 MERs, 208, 209, 210
 objective issues, 210

reasons to include in RRSP, 209–210
recommendations, 225
versus asset allocation funds, 208, 210
Bank Act, 133
bank funds, 135, 159–161
bank-owned brokerages, 124, 254, 311, 316, 317, 335
Bank of Montreal
    funds performance, 150
    holdings comparisons, 163
    load/no load policies, 149
    top-performing funds, 157
Bank of Montreal Equity Index, 219
Bank of Montreal InvestorLine, 256
Bank of Montreal Money Market Fund, 202
Bank of Nova Scotia. See Scotiabank
banks
    bond source, 121, 124
    information, 316–317
    mutual funds source, 159–61, 261
    principal risk avoidance, 71
    RRSP source, 24, 316
    self-directed RRSP source, 67, 68, 78
Barclays Global Investors, 253
BB-rated bonds, 120
BBB-rated bonds, 120
BCE Inc (Bell Canada Enterprises), 163
bear market, 89, 201
before-tax dollar, 15, 57, 82
Bell Canada, 121, 163
beneficiary
    charity, 303
    estate planning, 50
    financially dependent child/grandchild, 275
    RESP, 38
    RRIF, 302
    RRSPs, 274–275, 302
    segregated funds, 222
    spouse, 274–275, 302
Berkshire Hathaway Fund, 180
Beutel Goodman Money Market Fund, 202, 225
Bissett Canadian Equity Fund, 154, 155, 224
Bissett Canadian Equity Class F Fund, 237
Bissett Dividend Income Fund, 295

Bissett Income Class Fund, 177, 178
Bissett Money Market Fund, 202
Bissett Small Cap Fund, 224
blue-chip companies, 112, 121, 185, 186, 240
Bombardier Inc., 121, 163, 177, 185
bond funds
    debentures, 196
    described, 139, 196–197
    diversification, 195, 196
    foreign, sample portfolio, 192–193
    global, 199–200, 225
    interest rates, 197
    long-term, 197–198
    management styles, 198
    medium-term, 197–198
    MER, 200
    quality, 196
    recommendations, 224–225
    risk issues, 135
    short-term, 197–198
    units, 197
    versus money market funds, 201–202
bond mutual funds, 139
bonds
    callable, 125
    Canada RRSP (Canada Premium), 121
    CDS (Central Depository System), 122
    commissions on, 125–126
    contribution in kind, 99
    corporate, 119, 120
    coupons, 122
    described, 96, 117–119
    extendable, 125
    extra features, 125
    final decision to purchase yours, 126–127
    gilt-edged, 121
    government-guaranteed, 119–120
    high-yield, 121–122
    interest calculations, 118–119
    interest rates, 72, 197
    inverted yield curve, 124
    issuer, 118
    junk, 120, 121–122
    long-term, 123
    maturity, 118, 125, 197
    mutual funds investment type, 133
    normal yield curve, 124

par value of, 122
purchasing guidelines, 124–125
ratings, 119–120
reverse yield curve, 124
risk issues, 72, 120
RRSP qualifying investment type, 21
selling on secondary market, 124–125
short-term, 123
steep yield curve, 124
strip, 111, 122–124
trading services, 120
versus bond fund units, 197
U.S., 73
zero-coupon, 122
bonuses, 14, 86
book-based coupons, 122
book value, 34–35, 190
bottom-up management style, 168, 178
Brazil, 190
British Columbia
    CCRA, 315
    vested pension plans, 56
broker, 259–260. See also financial advisers
brokerage houses
    bond source, 124
    dismissal reasons, 262
    full-service versus discount, 254–256
    legal action against, 262
    and risk avoidance, 72
    self-directed RRSP fee advantages, 77
    self-directed RRSP source, 67
Buffett, Warren, 180
bull market, 89, 201
buy and hold strategy, 167, 180, 257
buy low/sell high, 179, 197
buying and selling stocks. See stock trading

• C •

caisses populaires
    bond source, 124
    RRSP source, 24
calculations
    assets needed to meet anticipated income, 319–320
    bond interest rates, 118–119
    C/QPP monthly payment, 53
    foreign assets, 190

growth rate, RRSP, 231
interest earned, strip bonds, 122
maximum LIF withdrawals, 292
maximum RRSP contributions, 29–34
mutual fund returns, 142
retiring allowance contributions, 33
RRSP investment program, 60
share/unit price, mutual funds, 138
stock value, 174
calendar-year returns, 167, 168
call options, non-qualifying investment type, 21
callable bonds, 125
Cambridge Growth Fund, 156
Canada Customs and Revenue Agency (CCRA), 14
contribution limits, 30–32
deductions, claiming techniques, 39–40
deemed disposition, 50, 99
definition of spouse, 48
information sources, 312–315
Notice of Assessment, 30
pledged assets, 49
Canada Deposit Insurance Corp. (CDIC), 71–72, 123
Canada/Quebec Pension Plan. *See* C/QPP
Canada RRSP Bonds, 121
Canada Premium Bonds, 121
Canada Savings Bonds (CSBs)
contribution in kind, 99
growth expectations, 42
liquid investment type, 65, 66
and risk avoidance, 72, 121
RRSP qualifying investment type, 21
Canada/U.S. tax treaty, 51
Canadian Bond Fund, 159
Canadian dividend funds, top performers, 295. *See also* dividends
Canadian dollar, 35, 73, 105, 188, 200
Canadian Investment Protection Fund, 72
Canadian Medical Discoveries (fund), 218
Canadian Pacific Limited, 163
Canadian Securities Course, 79
Canadian Securities Institute, 79
Canadian Snowbird Association, 304

Canadian Stock Fund, 159
Capital Alliance Ventures, 218
capital gains, 19, 57
capital growth, 105
capital loss, 19
capital reserves, 103
capitalization, 134
capped, 113
career-average formula, 12
carry-forward option, 34, 86
cash balance statement, progress measurement tool, 87
cash deposits, RRSP qualifying investment type, 21
cash, foreign, non-qualifying invesment, 193
cashable GICs, 111
CCFA (Chartered Financial Analyst), 336
CCRA. *See* Canada Customs and Revenue Agency
Central Depository System (CDS), 122
Centrefire Growth Fund Ltd., 218
CFP (Certified Financial Planner), 79
charities, estate planning, 303
chartered banks
money market funds performance, 202
mutual funds performance, 160–161
self-directed RRSP source, 67
Chartered Financial Analyst (CCFA), 336
children
and C/QPP benefits, 54
estate planning guidelines, 50
financially dependent, 275
infirm, 50, 275
opening own RRSP, 26
and overcontribution, 32
and RESPs, 38
China, emerging markets, 214
churning, financial adviser dismissal reason, 262
CI Emerging Markets Fund, 225
CI Funds, 148, 149
CI Global, 140
CI Global Bond Fund, 225
CI Global Boomernomics RSP Fund, 238
CI Global Consumer Products, 225
CI Harbour Fund, 237

CI Signature High Income Fund, 177, 178
CIBC
balanced funds, 209
bank funds performance, 160
holdings comparisons, 163
load/no load policy, 149
CIBC Core Canadian Equity, 160
CIBC Index Funds, 136
CIBC Investor's Edge, 256
CIBC Money Market Fund, 202
CIBC Premium T-bill Money Market Fund, 202, 225
CIBC U.S. Index RSP Fund, 238
Clarica Premier Blue Chip Fund, 167, 168
Clarington Funds, 158
Clarington Canadian Equity Fund, 237
clawback
OAS, avoidance techniques, 48
retirement income effects, 55
Clean Environment Equity Fund, 216
clone funds, 238–240
closed funds, 140–141
closing fees, 151
coins, non-qualifying invest-ment, 93
collateral, 49–50
collectibles
non-qualifying investment, 93
RRSP non-qualifying investment type, 21
commercial paper, 201
commissions. *See also* fees; MERs
bonds, 125
buying/selling investments in RRSP, 67
and conflict-of-interest issues, 255, 260
discount brokerage, 67, 256
fee plus, 81
full-service brokerage, 254–255
limited partnerships, 94
mutual funds, 146–152. *See also* MERs
and principles, RRSP, 14
stock trades, 252, 255
commodities
non-qualifying investment, 93
and risk issue, 72
common shares, 97
common stock, 97
companies

blue-chip, 112, 121, 185, 186, 240
creditworthiness, 125
employer's, investing in, 88
foreign, contributions in kind, 99
mid-sized, 186
pension plans, 55–56
resource-based, 35, 188
small-cap, 156, 185–186
small, investments in, non-qualifying, 94
and mutual funds, 134, 181
and special equity funds, 211–212
compliance officer, 250, 262, 311
compound interest, tax-sheltered, 15, 17
compounded returns, historical rates of, 167
Confederation Life, 135
conflict-of-interest, commis-sioned brokers, 255, 260
confusion, non-participation excuse debunked, 25, 27
conservative investment mix, 141. *See also* overly conservative approach
contribution receipt, 39
contributions
borrowing to save, advantages, 37–38
carry-forward option, 34, 86
calculating, 29–34
deductions at source, 27
and dollar-cost averaging, effects of, 230
early, 30
excessive, 331
and foreign employment effects, 51
growth level effect, 319–320
last-minute, 36, 329–330
limit, RESP, 267
limit, RRSP, 331
maximum, RESP, 258
monthly versus lump-sum payments, 36–30
monthly via pre-authorized chequing, 326
Notice of Assessment, 30
over-contribution effects, 32–33, 85–86
PA (pension adjustment) factor, 30–31
results of 1 percent boost, 232
retiring allowance formulas, 33

RRSP variable types, 45
self-directed RRSP strategy planning, 83–91
share purchase plan, 88
statement. *See* RRSP statement
summary, progress measurement tool, 86
time and money, impact of, 323–324
undercontributing, 86
unused contribution room, 34, 86
versus paying down mortgage, 58
versus savings accounts, 56–57
contributions in kind
described, 70, 99–100
unused contribution money source, 86
contributors
estate planning guidelines, 50–51
retiring earlier/living longer, 17–18
RRSP averages, 25
controlled-risk investment, growth differentials, 104–105
convertible GICs, 114
corporate downsizing, 280
corporate bonds, 119, 120
corporate takeovers, 121
cost of living, C/QPP inflation indexing, 49
cottage, retirement investment issue, 57
coupons, 122
C/QPP (Canada/Quebec Pension Plan)
average married couple benefit level, 16
delaying payments, 54
described, 53–55
disability payments, 14
early, 54, 299–300
eligibility rules, 300
formula, 299
future health issues, 13
inflation indexing, 53
information sources, 315
maximizing payout, 18, 45, 53
"pay as you go" concept, 54
receiving benefits while working, 281, 300

splitting beneftis, 297
credit cards, paying down balance, 34, 40, 57
credit unions
bond source, 124
information, 316–317
mutual funds source, 160, 217
principal risk avoidance, 71–72
RRSP source, 24, 316
self-directed RRSP source, 67, 78
creditworthiness, lender, 125
Crocus Investment Fund, 218
CSBs. *See* Canada Savings Bonds
currency risk, 73
currency values, 35, 105
custodian, mutual funds, 125

• *D* •

daily interest savings account (DISA), 110
death. *See* estate planning
debentures. *See also* commercial paper
described, 196
RRSP qualifying investment type, 21
debt instruments, 82, 203. *See also* bonds; GICs; T-bills
debt obligations, RRSP qualify-ing investment type, 21
deduction room, unused, 34, 86
deductions at source, 27, 36–37
deductions (tax), claiming, 39–40
deemed disposition, 50, 99
deferred profit-sharing plan (DDSP), 30, 31
deferred sales charge fund (DSC), 114
deferred taxation, 13
defined benefit pension plan
career-average formula, 12
described, 12
final-average formula, 12
flat-benefit formula, 12
and PA factor, 31
defined contribution pension plan
described, 12–13
money purchase plans, 31
dependents, children (minor), estate planning guideline, 50. *See also* children

derivative-based index funds, 238

derivatives, 188, 223

Desjardins Environment Fund, 216

devaluation, currency, 73

disability benefits
C/QPP, 54
and principles, RRSPs, 14

discount brokerages
information, 258, 316
self-directed RRSP source, 67
trading investments, 77, 252
versus full-service brokerages, 254–256

discretionary power, 69

discretionary trading, financial adviser dismissal reason, 262

distribution fees, mutual funds, 150

distributions
mutual fund payments, 138, 142
versus dividends, 142

diversification
asset size, 134
balanced mutual fund advantage, 208, 209
bond fund versus equity fund, 196–197
described, 133
and determining risk threshold, 74
equity funds, 172–173
foreign, 199–200, 325–326
formula, by RRSP assets, 225–225
geographical, 134, 182–184
goals, 84
management-style, 135
mutual funds, 133–135, 223
recommended mutual funds by category, 224–225
RRSP principle, 23
sector, 134
value and growth funds, 180

dividend funds
described, 211
top performing, 295

dividend mutual funds, 140

dividend tax credit, 252

dividend yield, 174

dividends
defined, 105
preferred versus common shares, 97, 105

divorce, effects on RRSP, 26, 273–274, 325

documents and records, keeping track of, 276

dollar, Canadian, changes in value of, 35, 73, 105, 188, 200

dollar-cost averaging
and monthly contributions, advantage, 36
described, 229–230
effects of, 230–231
and late contributions, 329

dollars. *See also* dollar, Canadian; U.S. dollar
before- versus after-tax, 15
currency risk, 73

donations, estate planning, 303

Dow Jones Average, 187

downward trends, measuring performance, 232–233

Dynamic Americas Fund, 189

Dynamic Focus and Canadian Fund, 184, 185

Dynamic Mutual Funds, 148, 149

● **E** ●

early retirement, 17, 271, 279

earned income
C/QPP efects, 54
described, 13–14
earnings, comparing investment alternatives, 106

economic downturns, 89–90, 232–233

economy, Canadian, 35

education, financing. *See* Lifelong Learning Plan; RESPs

effective yield, money market funds, 202

Elliott & Page Cabot Cdn. Equity Fund, 237

Elliott & Page Monthly High Income Fund, 177

embezzlement, 133, 239, 311, 338–339

emerging markets, 140, 143, 162–163, 213–215

employers
C/QPP contributions, 53, 54
group RRSPs, 21–22
locked-in RRSP, 56
monthly deduction advantage, 36
pension plan issues, 55–56

self-directed RRSP investment guidelines, 88
and source deductions, 27, 36–37

employment, foreign, effect on RRSPs, 51

equities
mutual fund investment type, 133, 134
versus securities, 234–235

equity, 57

equity-fund manager
management styles, 173–180
role of, 172

equity funds
advantages of, 172–173
bottom-up fund managers, 178
costs/expenses, 165
described, 139, 172–173
dividend yield, 174
emerging market, 189
foreign fund types, 189–191
global, 189
growth fund managers, 175–178
holding types, 180
index funds, 186–188
international, 189, 190
large versus small-cap companies, 180–181, 185–186
management styles, 173–180
market timing fund managers, 178–180
P/E ratio (price-to-earnings ratio), 174
performance, 160
price-to-book ratio, 174
prospectus information, 182
top-down fund manager, 178
recommendations, 224
regional, 189
returns, 233, 237
risk issues, 135
sample portfolio, 241
U.S., 189, 190
value fund managers, 173–175
versus bond funds, 196–197
versus labour-sponsored venture funds, 219

equity investments, comparing investment alternatives, 106. *See also* mutual funds; real estate

escalating-rate GIC, 114

estate planning
freezing your estate, 302

infirm children, 50, 275
purchasing life insurance, 304
RRSP guidelines, 50–51
segregated mutual funds,
    222, 303
setting up a trust, 303
spousal RRSP/RRIF rollovers,
    302
spousal plan transfers, 302
using charities, 303
wills, 51, 274–275, 302
Ethical Global Bond Fund, 200
Ethical Growth Fund, 158, 160,
    161, 216–217
ethical investing, 215–217
Europe, traditional market, 214
exchange-traded funds (ETFs),
    253
excuses, non-participation,
    debunked, 25–26
executors, 51
exotic funds
    dividend funds, 211
    precious metals, 212
    real estate funds, 213
    resource funds, 212–213
    special equity funds, 211–212
extendable bonds, 125

● *F* ●

family law, RRSP effects,
    273–274
FCSI (Fellow of the Canadian
    Securities Institute), 79
fee plus commission, 81
fees. *See also* administration
    fees; commissions; MERs
    discount brokerage, 17
    financial advisers, 336
    fund transfers, 70, 234
    professional advice, 80
    on savings accounts, 109
    self-directed RRSPs, 67, 68, 77
    stock trades, 252
    trailer, 260
Fellow of the Canadian
    Securities Institute
    (FCSI), 79
females, annuity rates, 286
Fidelity Canadian Growth
    Company Fund, 224
Fidelity International Portfolio
    Fund, 224
Fidelity Investments, 135, 148,
    149, 261
final-average formula, 12

financial advisers. *See also*
    financial consultants;
    financial planners;
    independent financial
    advisers; investment
    advisers
advantages of using, 332, 335
alternatives to, 260
bond source, 124
changing, 263–264
commissioned, 81, 255, 260,
    309–310, 336
described, 79
dismissal procedure, 263
dismissal reasons, 262–263
drawbacks of using, 259–260
duties of, 335
embezzlement, 338–33
failure to use, 332
fee types, 80–81
first not sole source info., 311
hourly rate, 336
Know Your Client form, 338
knowing when to change, 262
legal action against, 262
lifestyle evaluation, 338
"lone wolf," avoiding, 338
performance, measuring,
    261–263
qualifications, 79, 336
rapport with, 69, 77, 261–262,
    263, 326–327
references, 337
reporting inappropriate
    actions, 262
salary, 81
selection guidelines, 79–80,
    327, 337
financial checklist, 275–276
Financial Concept Group, 124
financial consultants, 79. *See
    also* financial advisers
financial planners
    bond source, 124
    paying, 80–81
    qualifications, 79
Financial Planning Group, 124
financial seminars, 78
financial situation, RRSP
    variable type, 45
financially dependent, 275
First Canadian Growth Fund,
    224
First Canadian Equity Index
    Fund, 154, 155, 188
First Canadian Mortgage Fund,
    203

First Ontario Labour
    Sponsored Investment
    Fund Ltd., 218
5-Year Protected Balanced
    Index Fund, 209
five-year rule, qualifying Home
    Buyers' Plan, 269
fixed-income investments
    comparing alternatives, 106
    described, 139
    GICs, 96
flat-benefit formula, 12
flexibility, 64, 73
forced savings GICs, 114
foreign cash
    non-qualifying investment, 93
    RRSP non-qualifying
        investment type, 21
foreign companies, contribu-
    tions in kind, 99
foreign content goals, 66, 84,
    169, 188, 191
foreign content limits, 190–191
foreign content statement,
    progress measurement
    tool, 87
foreign derivatives/Canadian
    securities combination,
    238
foreign diversification,
    199–200, 325–326
foreign employment, effects on
    RRSPs, 51
foreign equity funds
    described, 189
    exceeding 30 percent limit,
        191
    types of, 189–191
    Morgan Stanley indexes, 236
foreign exchange rates, 35
foreign exchange risk, 188
foreign exchange shares, RRSP,
    qualifying investment
    type, 21
foreign funds, performance,
    239–240
foreign government bonds,
    RRSP, qualifying invest-
    ment type, 21
foreign index funds, 236,
    325–326
foreign investment
    book value limitation, 34–35
    currency risks, 73
    derivative based index funds,
        238
foreign investment

30 percent limit, 112, 139, 188, 189
50 percent, 239, 325
100 percent opportunity, 199–200
raising limit beyond 30 percent, 191, 238
foreign stocks, RRSP non-qualifying investment type, 21
formulas
assets needed to meet anticipated income, 319–320
balancing equities and securities, 234
career average, 12
C/QPP benefits, 299
final average, 12
flat benefit, 12
maximum withdrawals, LIFs, 292
retiring allowance contribution, 33
fraud, investment, 310–311, 338
freezing estate, 302
Friedburg Currency Fund, 212
front-end load, 146–147
full-service brokerage
financial information, 67
self-interest, 81
versus discount brokerage, 254–256
fund families
described, 135
back-end load redemption charges, 148
funds within, 159
switching fees, 234
top performers, 157–158
fund managers
background, 136
bond fund management styles, 136–137
described, 132, 133
desirable qualities, 136–137
embezzlement avoidance, 133
embezzlement risk, 249
equity fund management styles, 171–180
investment path differences, 134–135
investment resources, 137–138
MER (management expense ratio), 144–146
personality of, 134, 135

futures
non-qualifying investment, 93
risk issue, 72
RRSP non-qualifying investment type, 21

• *G* •

gender, and annuity payment rate, 283
females, 284–285
males, 286
geographic diversificaton, 134, 182–184
GICs (Guaranteed Investment Certificates)
age= GIC percent guidelines, 64
cashable, 111
compared with strip bonds, 123
convertible, 114
described, 96
escalating rate, 114
financial institutions' preference for, 109
forced-savings, 114
index-linked, 112–113
interest payments on, 111
interest rate risk, 72
laddered versus savings accounts, 57
laddering, 72–73, 91, 111
liquidity issues, 64, 110, 113
long-term risk issues, 64
market participation rate, 112
maturity date, 110
money market, 97, 113
needs matching, 110–114
purchasing guidelines, 111
reasons for avoiding, 110–111, 113
redeemable versus non-redeemable rates, 111
risk and reward concept, 20, 71, 72–73
rolling strategy, 72–73
RRSP qualifying investment type, 21
shopping around for, 111
short-term, liquidity, 23
specialty, 113–114
tiered rates, 111
transfers before maturity, 70, 71
weaknesses, 63–64
withdrawals from, 110–111
gift annuity payments, 303

gilt-edged bonds, 121
global bond funds, 199–200, 225
global equity funds
described, 189
MERs, 190
global mutual funds, 140
Global Strategy Europe Plus RSP, 239
Global Strategy Funds, 148, 150
global-trading capitalization, 213, 238
goals
being realistic about, 158
foreign content, 66, 84, 169, 188, 191
investment matching, 94–96, 168–169, 297
gold, 21, 212
government-guaranteed bonds, 119–120
Green Line Canadian Equity Fund, 154, 144, 224
Green Line Canadian Index Fund, 188
Green Line Focus Self-directed RRSP, 68
Green Line Mutual Funds, 113
Green Line RRSP, 68
group RRSPs, 21–22
growth
contribution level, 320
inflation effects, 43–44
mutual funds, 105
paying attention to, 46–47
reasonable expectation by investment type, 42–43
RRSP investment principle, 13
versus income, 23–24, 82
versus value, 173, 176
growth differential, overly conservative approach, 104–105
growth fund managers, 175–178
growth investments, 65, 93. *See also* mutual funds; stocks
growth-oriented industries, 176, 177
growth stocks versus value stocks, 176
Guaranteed Income Supplement, 315
guaranteed investments, 103–127. *See also* GICs; savings accounts; T-bills
guarantees, annuity payment factor, 284
Guardian fund family, 148

• H •

handling fees, mutual funds, 151
high-yield bonds. *See* junk
bonds
historical rates, compounded
returns, 167
Home Buyers' Plan, 27, 269–271
home equity, investment
issue, 57
Hongkong Bank of Canada,
160. *See also* HSBC Bank
Canada
house
keep or sell, 300–301
non-participation excuse
debunked, 26
HSBC Bank Canada, 158
HSBC Canadian Balanced Fund,
210, 225
HSBC Equity, 160

• I •

IBM Canada, 121
icons, used in book, 6
i500R ETF, 253
immigration, pros and cons,
304
impulsive behaviour, avoiding,
107–108
income
contribution limit table, 31
earned, 13–14
measuring all sources,
299–301
selling home, 300–301
income balanced funds
described, 177
top performing, 177–178
income investment type, 65,
93. *See also* bonds; GICs;
mortgages
income splitting, 47–48, 49,
297, 298
income units, 177
income tax return, students
failing to file, 332
independence, power of, and
RRSP, 22
independent financial advisers,
260, 317, 327
index funds
Canadian equities, 191
cost/expenses, 165
foreign, 325–326

investment guidelines,
187–188
and MER, 186, 187–188, 253
passively managed, 187
index-linked GICs, 112–113
index-linked notes, 112–113
indexed annuity, 287
India, 140
Individual Retirement Account
(IRA), 51
Indonesia, 190, 214
Industrial Dividend Growth
Fund, 295
industries, growth-oriented,
176, 177
infirm children, estate planning,
50, 275
inflation
C/QPP indexing, 49
effects on investment growth,
43–44
GIC long-term risk issues, 64
postage stamp price as
benchmark, 44
self-directed RRSP concern,
90–91
information
banks, 316
CCRA, 312–315
C/QPP and OAS, 315
credit unions, 316
discount brokerages, 258
obtaining, 236, 255
trust companies, 316
inheritance. *See* beneficiaries;
estate planning; wills
insurance
annuities, 282–287
CDIC (Canada Deposit
Insurance Corporation),
71–72, 123
term, 282, 283, 304
whole-life plans, 282, 283
insurance companies
RRSP source, 24
segregated funds, 141, 221
interest
on balance, RRSP loan, 38
and bond rating, 121
on bonds, calculations,
118–119
effects of early withdrawal, 15
tax-free compounded, 15, 17
interest-rate risk, 72–73
interest rates
annuity payment factor, 284
bond prices, 118–119
fluctuating levels, 197

junk bonds, 122
long-term versus short-term
bond funds, 197
predicting, 198, 199
RRIF income, 293
RRSP loans, 327
RRSP mortgage, 98
international equity funds,
189, 190
international mutual funds, 42,
140, 182–184
international stock indexes, 214
Internet stocks, trading, 105,
135, 175, 177, 252, 257
Interprovincial Pipeline, 121
inverted (reverse) yield
curve, 124
investment advisers. *See also*
financial advisers
discretionary power given
to, 69
and self-directed RRSP
administration, 66, 68–69,
78–81
investment brokers, bond
source, 124
Investment Dealers
Association (IDA), 249
investment fraud, 310–311, 338
investment houses, self-
directed RRSP source, 67
investment management
courses, 79
investment objectives, mutual
fund prospectus, 161–164
investment professionals, self-
directed RRSP advisers,
68–69. *See also* financial
advisers
investment risk, 71–72
investment styles, 107–108
investments. *See also* specific
types of investments
average fund return by
category, 143
balanced, 65, 324
buy and hold strategy, 167
CDIC coverage limits, 72
common mistakes, 80,
329–333
comparing alternatives,
105–106
contributions in kind, 80,
99–100
and currency devaluation, 73
debt instruments, 82, 203
equity, 35, 42, 65, 82
fixed-income, 96, 103, 106, 139

flexibility, importance of, 73
foreign investments book
    value limitations, 34–35
fund manager resource
    activities, 137–138
goal-matching techniques,
    94–99, 297
growth, 65
growth expectations, 42–43
guaranteed, 103–127
impact of world events on,
    179, 245
inappropriate, 262, 330
income, 65
liquidable type,, 23, 65, 66, 93
mix, 141
mutual funds types, 139–141
non-qualifying types, 21,
    93–94
past age 69, 298
progress measurement tools,
    86–87
rental income property, 57, 59
RRSP principles, 23–25
RRSP qualifying types, 21
sheltered, 14–15
stocks, 88–89, 251–253
time to quit a fund, 236–237
transferring, 70–71
unsheltered, 15
in U.S. market, 140
Investors Group, 150
IRA (Individual Retirement
    Account), 51
issuer, bond, 118
Ivy Canadian Fund, 166, 193,
    224, 232, 233
Ivy Foreign Equity Fund,
    182, 183

● J ●

Japan, 140, 175, 189, 214
junk bonds, 120, 121–122

● K ●

Kenya, 214
Know Your Client form, 338

● L ●

labour funds, 217–220
labour mutual funds, 141
labour-sponsored venture
    capital corporation
    shares, RRSP investment
    type, 21

labour-sponsored venture
    funds, 217–219
Labrador, CCRA, 312
laddering, 72–73, 91, 111
Latin America, 140, 162–163,
    173, 189
life insurance, estate planning,
    304
life insurance companies,
    annuity payment rates,
    284–286
Lifelong Learning Plan (LLP),
    268–269
lifespan, RRSP contribution
    variable, 17–18, 45
lifestyle
    financial adviser, 338
    RRSP contribution variable, 45
LIFs (Life Income Fund), 292
limited partnership units,
    RRSP qualifying invest-
    ment type, 21
limited partnerships (LP) RRSP
    drawbacks, 94
liquidable investment type, 65,
    66, 93
liquidity
    comparing investment
        alternatives, 106
    GIC weakness, 64, 110, 113
    risk, 73
    RRSP investment principle, 23
LIRA (Locked-in Retirement
    Account), 292, 293
loans
    benefit RRSPs, 332
    borrowing to save RRSP
        contribution advantages,
        37–38, 86, 327, 332
    pledged asset, 49–50
    prime rate, 39
    to start RRSP, 24
unusued contribution money
    source, 86
Loblaw Companies Limited, 185
    gift-edged bonds, 121
    funds source, 136
Locked-in Retirement Income
    Fund. See L-RIF
Locked-in RRIF. See LIFs
locked-in RRSP, 56
locking in profits, 250–251
long bonds, 123
long-term bond funds, 197
long-term goals, 84
long-term risk, GIC weaknesses,
    64

lotteries, versus sound RRSP
    contributions, 18
loyalty, where to leave a fund,
    236–237
L-RIF (Locked-in Retirement
    Income Fund), 56, 292
luck, versus tax-sheltered
    savings, 18
lump-sum payments, versus
    monthly contributions,
    36–39
lump-sum withdrawals,
    annuities, 287

● M ●

Mackenzie Cundill Value Fund,
    190
Mackenzie Financial, 135,
    148, 150. See also under
    Ivy funds
Mackenzie/Ivy RSP Foreign
    Equity Fund, 238
Mackenzie Universal Future
    Fund, 180, 219
Mackenzie Universal RSP
    Select Managers, 239
McLean Budden, 158
males, annuity payment rates,
    284–285
managed assets, 98
management-style
    diversification, 135
management styles
    bond funds, 198
    equity funds, 173–180,
        184–185
Manitoba
    CCRA, 314
    vested pension plans, 56
Manulife Financial, 163
marital status, non-participation
    excuse debunked, 26
market correction, 89
market indexes
    described, 187
    emerging markets, 214
market participation rate
    (MPR), 112
market-timing fund managers,
    178–180
market volatility, panic cause,
    330–331
Masters of Business Admin-
    istration (MBA), 336
maturity, bonds, 118, 125, 197
maturity dates, staggered. See
    laddering

maturity, GIC transfers before, 70

maturity, money market funds, 201

MAXXUM Dividend Fund, 295

MD Management Ltd., 150

median, 236

medium-term bond funds, 197

MER (management expense ratio)
  balanced funds, 208, 209, 210
  boosted, 237
  clone funds, 238
  described, 144–146
  equity mutual funds, 251
  ETF shares, 253
  funds with low, 165–166
  global bonds, 200
  global equity funds, 182
  index funds, 186, 187–188, 253
  labour-sponsored venture funds, 218
  money market funds, 202
  prospectus cost explanations, 164–166
  segregated funds, 212–213
  specialty equity funds, 212
  U.S. versus Canadian, 145

Merrill Lynch Canada, 66, 81, 124, 254, 335

Mersch, Frank, 178, 179

Microsoft, 177

Midland Walwyn. *See* Merrill Lynch Canada

minimum annual payout (MAP), RRIFs, 291

minor dependents, estate planning guidelines, 50

misrepresentation, financial adviser dismissal reason, 262

mistakes
  common investment, 80
  failing to file income tax return, 332
  ignoring loan benefits, 332
  making excessive contributions, 331
  making late contributions, 329–330
  misunderstanding rules of risk and reward, 333
  not using financial adviser, 332
  overcontributing, 32–33
  panicking at market volatility, 330–331
  in RRSP statement, 310–311

selecting inappropriate investments, 330

thinking of tax refund, 330

withdrawing money, 331

Money Concepts, 124

money market funds
  costs/expenses, 165
  mutual funds investment type, 133, 134
  performance, 202
  recommendations, 225
  versus bond funds, 201
  versus savings accounts, 57

money market GICs, 97, 113

money markets
  described, 139
  mutual fund investment type, 133, 134

money purchase plans. *See* defined contribution pension plan

Morgan Stanley indexes, 236

mortgage funds, 203

mortgage rates, 98, 203

mortgages. *See also* reverse mortgages
  contributions in kind, 99
  described, 98
  investment risks, 98
  mutual fund investment type, 133, 134
  non-participation excuse debunked, 26
  paying down versus maximizing contribution, 58
  risk issues, 72
  RRSP qualifying investment type, 21

multiple RRSPs
  avoiding, 24, 326
  cost, complications, 70
  and foreign content, 190–191
  and self-directed RRSPs, 66

mutual fund companies
  GIC source, 114
  load/no load policies of, 149–150
  name changes, 240
  no fee, 260, 261
  RRSP source, 24

mutual funds. *See also* names of specific funds
  annual returns record, 167–168
  average annual return, 104, 105
  average fund return by category, 143

back-end load, 147–148

balanced, 139, 207–210

bank funds, 159–161

bank-managed, 135

bigger versus smaller, 167, 180–181

bond, 139

closed, 140

closing fees, 151

commissions, 146–152

comparing investment alternatives, 106

compounded returns, 167–168, 181

contributions in kind, 99

custodian, 133

deferred sales charge fund (DSC), 114

described, 97–98. 131–135

distribution fees, 150

distribution payments, 142, 145

distributions, 138

diversification, 133–135, 159

dividend, 140

emerging markets, 213–215

equity, 139

expenses, 164–166

families, 135

fees, 150–152,164–166, 260

financial performance, 166–167

financial statements, 137

fixed-income, 139

formula, 223–226

front-end load, 146–147

global, 140

growth expectations, 42

handling fees, 151

historical rates of compounded return, 167–168

initial minimum investment, no fee, 261

international, 140

Internet-based stocks, 105, 135, 175

invest in investments, 132

investment objectives, 161–164

kinds of, 139–41

labour venture funds, 141

liquidity, 23, 106

low performers, 158

managers. *See* fund managers

matching objectives to own, 168–169

MER (management expense ratio), 144–146, 165–166

money market, 139, 201–202
mortgage-based, 99, 203
name changes, 240
NAV (net asset value), 138, 142, 166
NAVPS (net asset value per share), 166
net assets, 166
no fee, 260, 261
no-load, 148–150
non-qualifying investment types, 93
objective matching, 161–164
open, 140, 181
performance, 142, 143, 144, 153–169
pooled, 141
professional management, 132–133
prospectus content, 161–168
recommendations by category, 224–225
redemption fees, 150
return, 142
risk issues, 135
royalty trusts, 141, 177
RRSP qualifying investment type, 21
sector, 139–140
sector diversification, 134
segregated, 141
set-up fees, 151
shares (units), 138
size, 166–167, 180–181
small-cap, 134, 185–186
socially responsible, 215–217
special equity, 139–140, 211–212
switching fees, 151, 234
T-bills, 139
top performers, 157–158
total assets, 166
transfer fees, 70, 234
transferring, 70–71
trustee, 133
types of investment , 133–135
underperforming, 236–237
value of, 105
volatility, 233
when to leave, 236–237

• N •

name changes, 240
NASDAQ composite index, 175
National Bank Canadian Equity Fund, 160, 161

National Bank First Financial, 254
NAV (net asset value), 138
NAVPS (net asset value per share), 166, 142
Nesbitt Burns,124, 254, 335
net assets, 166
New Brunswick
CCRA, 312
vested pension plans, 56
Newfoundland
CCRA, 312
vestd pension plans, 56
Nexen Inc., 163
no fee mutual funds, 260, 261
no-load funds, 148–150
non-participation excuses debunked, 26–27
non-qualifying investment types, 93–94
normal yield curve, 124
Nortel, 163, 176, 186, 257
Northwest Territories, CCRA, 315
notes, index-linked, 113
Notice of Assessment, 30, 86
Nova Scotia
CCRA, 312
vested pension plans, 56

• O •

OAS (Old Age Security)
benefit levels, 55
clawback avoidance, 48
clawback effects, 48
described, 55
development history, 11
information source, 315
omission, financial adviser dismissal reason, 262
Ontario
CCRA, 313–314
vested pension plan, 56
Ontario Hydro, 120, 121
open funds, 140, 181
Optima Canadian Equity Value Pool, 232, 233
options
non-qualifying investment, 93
risk issues, 72
outperformers, 157
over-contributions, 32–33, 85–86
overly conservative approach, investing, 104–105, 296

• P •

PA factor, 30–31
par, 122
passive fund management, bond funds, 198
passively managed funds, 187
pavilions, mutual fund sales, 136
penalties
back-end, 234
over-contributions, 32
early withdrawals, 266
failing to make RRSP repayments, 270
GIC transfers before maturity, 70
pension adjustment, PA factor, 30
pension income tax credit, 48
pension plans
described, 55–56
defined benefits versus defined contributions, 12
development history, 11–12
vested, 56
perceived value, 141
percentage of assets, fee type, 81
performance
bank funds, 160
benchmarks, 236
Canadian equity funds, 237
clone funds, 239–240
downtrends, measuring, 233–234
index funds, 188
labour-sponsored venture funds, 218, 219
money market funds, 202
mutual funds, 142, 144, 147, 153–158, 224
past not indicative of future earnings, 153–154, 156, 158, 167, 168, 237
prospectus statements, 166–168
segregated funds, 220–221
selected SRFs, 216–217
Trans-Canada Value Fund, 154–156
personal savings
described, 56
retirement planning guidelines, 56–57
Petro-Canada, 177

Phillips, Hager & North, 150, 166, 260, 261
Phillips, Hager & North Balanced Pension Trust Fund, 210
Phillips, Hager & North Bond Fund, 224
Phillips, Hager & North Canadian Equity Fund, 154, 155, 193, 219, 224
Phillips, Hager & North Canadian Growth Fund, 232, 233
Phillips, Hager & North Dividend Fund, 295
Phillips, Hager & North Canadian Money Market Fund, 202, 203, 225
pledged assets, 49–50
pooled funds, 141
portfolio
  average annual return goal, 261
  calculating growth rate, 231–233
  changing needs, 233
  dollar-cost averaging, 229–31
  downward trends, 232–233
  embezzlement risk, 249
  excess volatility, 233
  managing, 229–242
  moving among funds, 233–234
  out-of-balance equities and securities, 234–236
  reading statements, 231–233
  reviewing annually, 261, 297
  samples, 192–194, 203–205, 226–227, 240–242
  turnover rate, 167
  when to leave a fund, 236–237
postage stamps, inflation benchmark, 44
pre-authorized chequing, contribution via, 326
precious metal funds, 212
preferred shares
  described, 97, 105
  dividend funds, 211
pre-retirement income, level needed at retirement, 18–19
preservation of capital, 103–104
President's Choice Financial Services, 136
price-to-book ratio, 174
price-to-earnings ratio (P/E) ratio, 174

prime rate, 39
Prince Edward Island
  CCRA, 312
  vested pension plans, 56
principal, 111
principal residence, 57
principal risk, 71–72
profits
  locking in, 250–251
  versus social responsibility, 215–217
prospectus
  annual returns record, 167–168
  cost explanations, 164–155
  described, 161
  equity funds, 182–184
  financial performance statements, 166–167
  investment objectives, 161–164
  portfolio turnover rate, 167
PRS Income RSP Portfolio, 209
public service employees, pensions, 56
put options, RRSP non-qualifying investment type, 21

• *Q* •

qualifications, financial advisers, 79, 336
qualifying educational program, 268
qualifying investment types, 21, 65, 93
quality bond funds, 196
Quebec
  CCRA, 313
  vested pension plans, 56
Quebec Pension Plan. *See* C/QPP
Quebecor World Inc., 163, 185

• *R* •

ratings, bonds, 120–121
RBC Dominion Securities, 67, 254, 335
real estate
  liquidity risk, 73
  non-participation excuse debunked, 26
  non-qualifying investment types, 94
  principal residence, 57
  retirement planning guidelines, 57–58

reverse mortgage guidelines, 58–59
real estate funds, 213
real estate mortgages, RRSP qualifying investment type, 21
redemption fees, mutual funds, 150
references, financial advisers, 337
regional equity funds, 189
Registered Financial Planner (RFP), 79
registered savings, 13
rental investments, 14, 57, 59
representatives. *See* financial advisers
residual, 122
resource-based companies, 35, 188
resource funds, 212–213
RESPs (Registered Education Savings Plan), 38, 267–268
retirement
  desire to leave Canada, 304
  early, 17, 271, 279
  income sources, 299–301
  modern view of, 17
  when to begin drawing income from RRSP, 271, 279–281
  while still working, 280–281
retirement age, 17–18, 45, 280
  retiring earlier/living longer, 17–18
  RRSP contribution variable, 45
retirement income
  guidelines, estimating, 45–46
  variable types, 45
retirement planner, 319–320
retirement planning
  C/QPP benefits, 53–55
  company pension plans, 55–56
  four-step strategy, 60
  real estate, 57–59
  reverse mortgage, 58–59, 301
  RRSP contribution variable, 45–46
  strategy, 83–91
retirement trial, 271
retiring allowance, 33
Revenue Canada. *See* Canada Customs and Revenue Agency
reverse mortgages, 58–59, 301
reverse yield curve, 124
RFP (Registered Financial Planner), 79

rights, RRSP qualifying
     investment type, 21
risk minimization
  investment alternative
     comparisons, 105–106
  overly conservative risk
     effect, 105–106
  secure foundation, 103–104
risk and reward concept
  currency risk, 73
  described, 20, 71–72
  interest rate risk, 72–73
  importance of under-
     standing, 330
  liquidity risk, 71–72
  misunderstanding rules
     of, 333
  risk threshold, 73–74
  risk types, 71–73
risk threshold, 73–75
rolling GIC strategy, 72–73
Royal Bank, 67
  funds performance, 160
  holdings comparisons, 163
  load/no load policy, 150
Royal Bank Action Direct, 256
Royal Canadian Equity, 160
Royal Canadian Money Market
     Fund, 202
royalty trusts, 14, 177
RRIF (Registered Retirement
     Income Fund)
  advantages of, 282, 289
  age deadlines, 290
  asset mix, adjustment
     guidelines, 294–295, 297
  converting from RRSP to,
     281–282, 290
  decision-making guidelines,
     296–298
  described, 282, 289–290
  drawback, 290
  growth/income, 289, 293
  locked-in. See LIFs
  maximizing average annual
     returns, 293–294
  minimum annual payout, 291
  returns by age and
     percentage return, 294
  rule of thirds, 295–296
  spousal plan transfers, 302
  spousal, rollover, 302
  versus annuities, 290
  withdrawals, rules, 291–292
RRSP-eligible invest-ments,
     assessment comparisons,
     105–106
RRSP loans, 37–38, 86

RRSP statement, 86–87,
     231–233, 245–248, 310, 339
RRSPs (Registered Retire-ment
     Savings Plans)
  age for contribution, 15–16
  average annual return goal,
     261
  avoiding cons, 309–311
  balanced diet strategy, 64–65
  balancing equities and
     securities formula, 234
  basic principles of, 23–25
  benefits of, 11, 13, 22
  borrowing from, 100
  calendar period limitatoins,
     29–30
  and capital gains, 19
  carry-forward option, 34
  cashing in while in U.S., 51
  and children, 26
  comparing investments,
     105–106
  consolidation, 190–191
  contributing too little, 34
  contribution statistics, 25
  converting, alternatives, 281
  converting to annuity,
     282–287
  converting to RRIF, 281–282,
     290
  deductions, claiming, 39–40
  de-registering, warning
     against, 311
  described, 13
  DISA (daily interest savings
     account), 109–110
  diversifying investments
     in, 74
  and divorce/separation, 26,
     273–274
  early withdrawals, 265–266
  excessive contributions, 331
  exchange-traded funds
     (ETFs), 253
  family law effects, 273–273
  foreign asset calculations, 183
  and foreign content, 34–35,
     190–191
  and foreign employment,
     effects, 51
  fund transfer fees/methods, 70
  goals, 84
  group, 21–22
  growth expectations, 42–43
  growth rates, calculating,
     231–233
  holding stocks in, 252–254

Home Buyers' Plan, 27,
     269–271
impact of time and money,
     323–324
investments mix, 141
last-minute contributions,
     36, 329
Lifelong Learning Plan,
     268–269
loans, 24, 327, 332
locked-in, 56
managing your own. See
     self-directed RRSPs
maximizing contributions,
     calculations, 29–34
maximizing growth of,
     guidelines, 323–327
mistakes to avoid, 329–333
mortgage, 98
multiple, 24, 66, 70, 190–191,
     326
non-participation excuses,
     25–27
non-qualifying investments,
     21, 93–94
overcontribution to, 32–33
pledging as collateral, 49–50
power of independence, 22
qualifying investment types,
     21, 65, 93
retiring allowance
     contribution types, 33
risk and reward concept, 20
self-directed, 65–71
social responsibility versus
     profit, 215–217
source deduction, 27
source type, 24
spousal, 26, 47–49, 302
starting late, 24
tax-deferred versus
     tax-free, 20
tax-sheltered savings, 14–22
transferring funds, 70–71, 263
transferring RESP to, 267–268
transferring to self-directed
     plan, 68
unauthorized withdrawals,
     249, 250
unused deduction room,
     34, 86
variable types, 45
versus C/QPP benefit
     levels, 16
versus luck/lotteries, 18
versus savings accounts, 56
when to begin drawing
     income from, 271, 279–281

when to begin saving, 15–16
will guidelines, 274–275
withdrawals from, 19,
    265–266, 267, 331
withdrawal transfer forms, 263
rule of thirds, 295–296

• S •

Sagit Management, 154
salary, financial adviser
    payment type, 81
Salomon Brothers, 200
Saskatchewan
    CCRA, 314
    vested pension plans, 56
savings accounts
    described, 56–57, 96
    DISA (daily interest savings
        account), 110
    liquidity, 23
    reasons for avoiding, 25–27,
        109–110
    retirement planning
        guidelines, 56–57
    tax-sheltered, 14–22
    versus money market
        funds, 201
    versus RRSP contributions, 56
Saxon Balanced Fund, 210, 225
Saxon Canadian Stock Fund,
    184, 185
Saxon Funds, 158, 260, 261
Saxon Small Cap Fund, 219, 224
Scotia Canadian Balanced
    Fund, 210, 225
Scotia Canadian Blue Chip
    Fund, 163–164
Scotia Canadian Dividend
    Fund, 295
Scotia Canadian Growth, 160,
    162, 163–164, 219
Scotia CanGlobal Income
    Fund, 164
Scotia Discount Brokerage Inc.,
    255–256
Scotia Latin American Growth
    Fund, 162
Scotia McLeod, 67, 81, 254,
    255–256, 335
Scotia Partners Portfolio, 261
Scotiabank, 67, 261
    funds performance, 160
    load/no load policy, 149
    stock-indexed GICs, 113
Scotiabank Money Market
    Fund, 202
sector, 134, 139

sector diversification, 134
sector funds, 139, 225
securities courses, 79
segregated, 133
segregated estate planning, 303
segregated funds, 141, 220–222
security
    debentures versus bond
        funds, 196
    and GICs, 64
    RRSP component, 196
self-directed RRSPs
    administrative fee issues, 67,
        68–69
    advantages of, 66, 289
    choosing where to place,
        guidelines, 67–68
    cost of, 77
    described, 65–66
    discretionary power, 69
    economic downturn survival
        techniques, 89–90
    foreign content goals, 66
    fund transfer fees/methods,
        70–71
    goals, 84
    inflation concerns, 90–91
    investments, mixing, 141
    market correction effect, 89
    multiple, 66
    non-qualifying investments,
        93–94
    planholder's responsibilities,
        325
    professional advise/advisers,
        66, 68–69, 78–81
    professional assistance
        selection guidelines, 79–80
    qualifying investments, 65, 93
    startup issues, 78–82
    statement, interpretation,
        245–250
    unused contribution makeup
        sources, 86
    versus managed RRSPs, 66
    when to make adjustments,
        74–75, 88
self-employment
    C/QPP contributions, 53
    and principles, RRSP, 14
self-interest, brokers, 259–260.
    See also conflict of interest
selling home, 300–301
seminars, financial, 78
separation (marital), efects on
    RRSPs, 26, 48, 273–274, 325
set-up fees, mutual funds, 151
share purchase plan, 88

shares
    common, 97
    contributions in kind, 99
    investing in employer's
        firm, 88
    mutual fund holdings, 138,
        140–141
    mutual funds investment
        type, 133
    preferred, 97, 105
    risk issues, 72
    RRSP qualifying investment
        type, 21
sheltered, 14, 15
short-term bond funds, 84,
    123, 197
short-term goals, 84
short-term bond funds, 198
silver, RRSP non-qualifying
    investment type, 21
SIGICS. *See* Stock-Indexed GICs
small business shares, RRSP
    qualifying investment
    type, 21
small-cap companies, 134, 156,
    185–186
smart money, 91
snowbirds, 304
socially responsible funds
    (SRFs), 215–217
source deduction, 27
South Korea, 190
S&P/TSE 60, 165
S&P500, 187, 237, 253
special equity funds, 139–140,
    211–212. *See also under*
    names of specific funds
Spectrum Global Growth, 140
Spectrum Investments, 148, 150
Spectrum United American
    Growth Fund, 189
Spectrum United Canadian
    Investment Fund, 224
spousal RRSP
    advantages of, 324–325
    described, 47
    early withdrawals, 267
    family law effects, 273–274,
        325
    income splitting, 47–48, 49
    non-participation excuse
        debunked, 26
    OAS clawback avoidance,
        48, 55
    rollovers, 302
    RRIF/RRSP transfers, 302
    withdrawal rules, 324

spouse
CCRA definition, 48
with higher income. *See*
income splitting
named as beneficiary, 50
non-participation excuse
debunked, 26
surviving, annuity payments,
284
younger, minimum
withdrawal, RRIF, 291
stamps, non-qualifying investment, 93
Standard Life equity Mutual
Fund, 224
standard of living, pre-retirement income vs.
retirement income, 18–19
Standard & Poor 500
Composite index. *See*
S&P500
statements
frequency provided by
financial adviser, 339
mutual funds, 137
reading, to avoid cons, 310
RRSP, 86–87, 231–233.
245–248, 249
sample, 339
self-directed RRSPs, 67, 74, 86
stock trade, 255
warning signs, 249–250
steep yield curve, 124
stock brokerage houses, RRSP
source, 24
stock funds. *See* equity funds
stock-indexed GICs, 113
stock indexes, 112, 165, 214
stock market indexes. *See*
market indexes
stock markets
bull versus bear market, 89,
201
Canadian versus foreign, 35
fluctuations, 87, 89–90,
115–116
stocks
asset coverage techniques,
256–257
avoiding fashionable or hot
companies/industries, 257
buy and hold planning, 167,
180, 257
common, 97
comparing alternatives, 106
concentrate on facts, 257
described, 97

foreign, RRSP non-qualifying
investment type, 21
full-service versus discount
brokerage, 254–256
growth investment type,
175–178
Internet, 105, 135, 175,
177, 257
investigating before
purchasing, 257
investing in U.S., 73
oil and gas, 212, 213
revisiting ignored companies,
257
technical, 175
trading issues, 251–253
value, 173–175
strip bonds
described, 122
interest earned calculation,
122
purchasing, source, 124
reasons for investing, 123
versus GICs, 111, 123
students, income tax return,
332
supplemental unemployment
insurance, principles,
RRSP, 14
surviving-spouse payments,
annuities, 284, 287
survivor benefits payments,
C/QPP, 54
Synergy Mutual Funds, 158, 180
switching fees, 151, 234

● *T* ●

tables of mortality, 284
Talvest (funds), 180
Talvest Global RRSP Fund,
192, 193
tax credit
dividend, 252
labour funds, 218–219
pension income, 48
tax deferred, 13, 20, 189
tax-free compound interest, 15
tax laws, changing, 275
tax refund, 14, 27, 86
tax services, provincial/
territorial, 312–315
tax-sheltered savings
before- versus after-tax
dollars, 15
described, 14–15
risk and reward concept, 20
tax-deferred vs. tax-free, 20

versus luck/lottery jackpots,
18
when to begin saving, 15–17
tax treaties, 51, 304
T-bills
described, 96–97, 114–115
earnings, 115
liquid investment type, 65
mutual fund investment fund,
133, 139
RRSP qualifying type, 21
TD AmeriGrowth RSP, 239
TD Bank, 68
funds performance, 160
holdings comparisons, 163
index-linked GICs, 112–113
strip bonds, source, 124
TD Canadian Bond Index
Fund, 224
TD Canadian Equity Fund, 160
TD Canadian Money Market
Fund, 202
TD Evergreen, full-service
brokerage, 254, 335
TD Greenline. *See* TD
Waterhouse
TD Green Line Global RSP
Bond Fund, 192, 193
TD Market Growth GICs, 112
TD Waterhouse, 256
technical stocks, 175
Templeton Canadian Bond
Fund, 234
Templeton Funds, 135, 148,
150, 158
Templeton Growth Fund, Ltd.,
159, 182, 183, 224, 234, 240
Templeton International Stock
Fund, 190, 224
Templeton, Sir John, 182
term deposits, income
investment type, 21
term insurance, 282, 283, 304
top-down management style,
178
Toronto Stock Exchange (TSE),
90, 97, 112, 186, 187
total assets, 166
trading stocks, 251–253
trailer fees, 260
transactions statement,
progress measurement
tool, 87
transfer forms, 263
Transamerica Growsafe Japan
Fund, 239
Trans-Canada Value Fund,
154–156, 232–233

transfer fees, 234
transferring funds, 70–71, 263
Triax Growth Fund, 218
Trimark Fund, 149
Trimark Select Growth Fund,
149, 237
trust companies
bond source, 124
information, 316–317
principal risk avoidance,
71–72
RRSP source, 24, 316
self-directed RRSP source, 24,
67, 78
trust, setting up (estate planning), 303
trustee, mutual funds, 133
TSE 35, 112, 165, 186
TSE 100, 112, 165, 186, 187
TSE 300, 165, 186, 188, 232, 233,
236, 253, 300

• U •

uncovered call options, RRSP
non-qualifying investment
type, 21
unauthorized actions, financial
adviser dismissal reason,
262
undercontributing, 86
units
bond funds, 197
mutual fund holdings, 138,
140–141
unsheltered investment, 15
unsuitable investments,
financial adviser dismissal
reason, 262
unused deduction room
described, 34
RRSP loan advantages, 37–38
U.S./Canada tax treaty, 51
U.S. dollar, 73, 105
U.S. equity market, 189, 190,
236. *See also* S&P500
U.S. MERs versus Canadian, 145
U.S., moving to, 304
U.S. mutual funds, RRSP
non-qualifying investment
type, 21
U.S., RRSP non-qualifying
investment type, 21

• V •

value fund managers, 173–175
value versus growth, 173
variable annuity contracts. *See*
segregated funds
VenGrowth Investment, 218
vested pensions, 56
volatile market, 110
volatility, 110, 133, 155, 156, 158

• W •

warrants, RRSP qualifying
investment type, 21
whole-life insurance plans,
282, 283
wills, 51, 274–275, 276, 302
withdrawal tax, Home Buyers'
Plan, 27
withdrawals
early, drawbacks, 265–266
LIFs, 292
RRIF, rules, 291–292
RRSP, 19, 331
spousal RRSP, 324
transfer forms, 263
unauthorized, 249, 250
withholding tax, 51, 249,
266, 331
Wood Gundy, 81, 254, 335
Working Ventures Canadian,
218, 219
world events, impact on
investments, 179, 245

• X •

Xerox, 176

• Y •

year-end bonuses, unused
contribution money
source, 86
Yukon Territory, CCRA, 315

• Z •

zero-coupon bonds. *See*
strip bonds